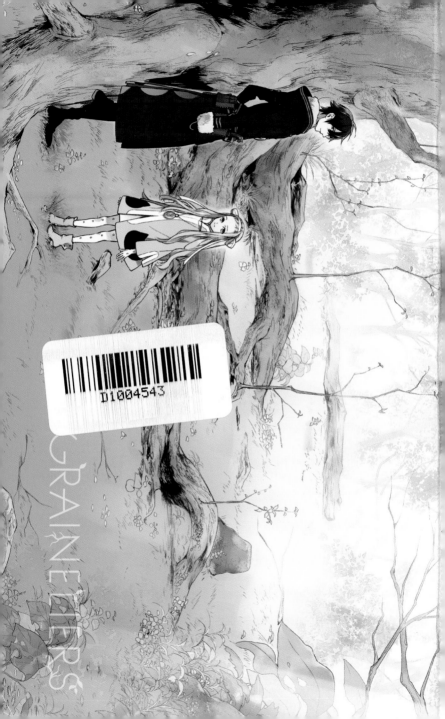

GRAINELIERS

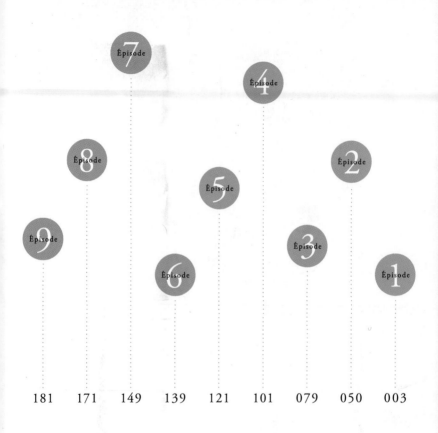

GRAINELIERS 1

Épisode 《1》——《9》

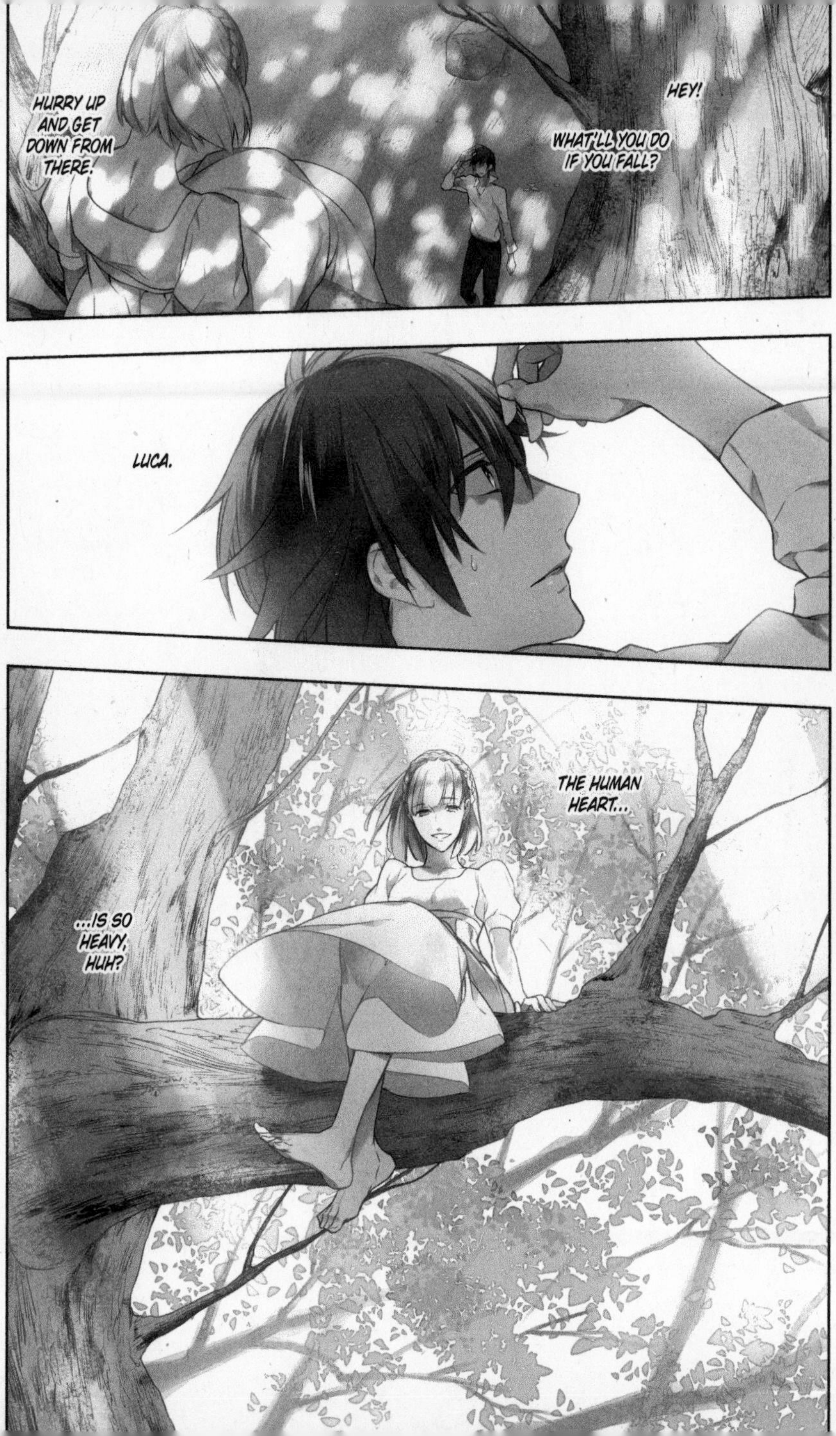
HEY!
WHAT'LL YOU DO IF YOU FALL?
HURRY UP AND GET DOWN FROM THERE.
LUCA.
THE HUMAN HEART...
...IS SO HEAVY, HUH?

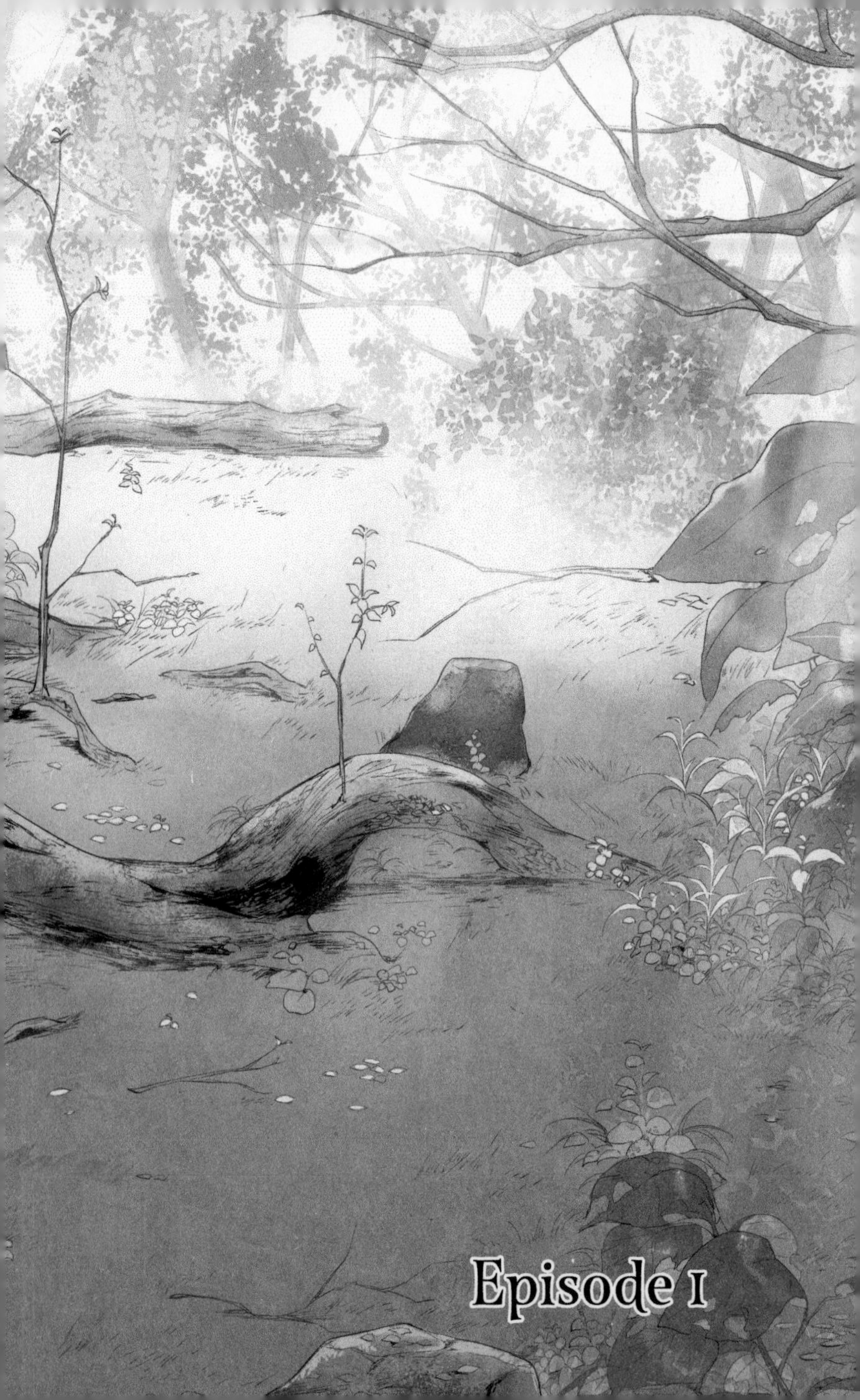
Episode 1

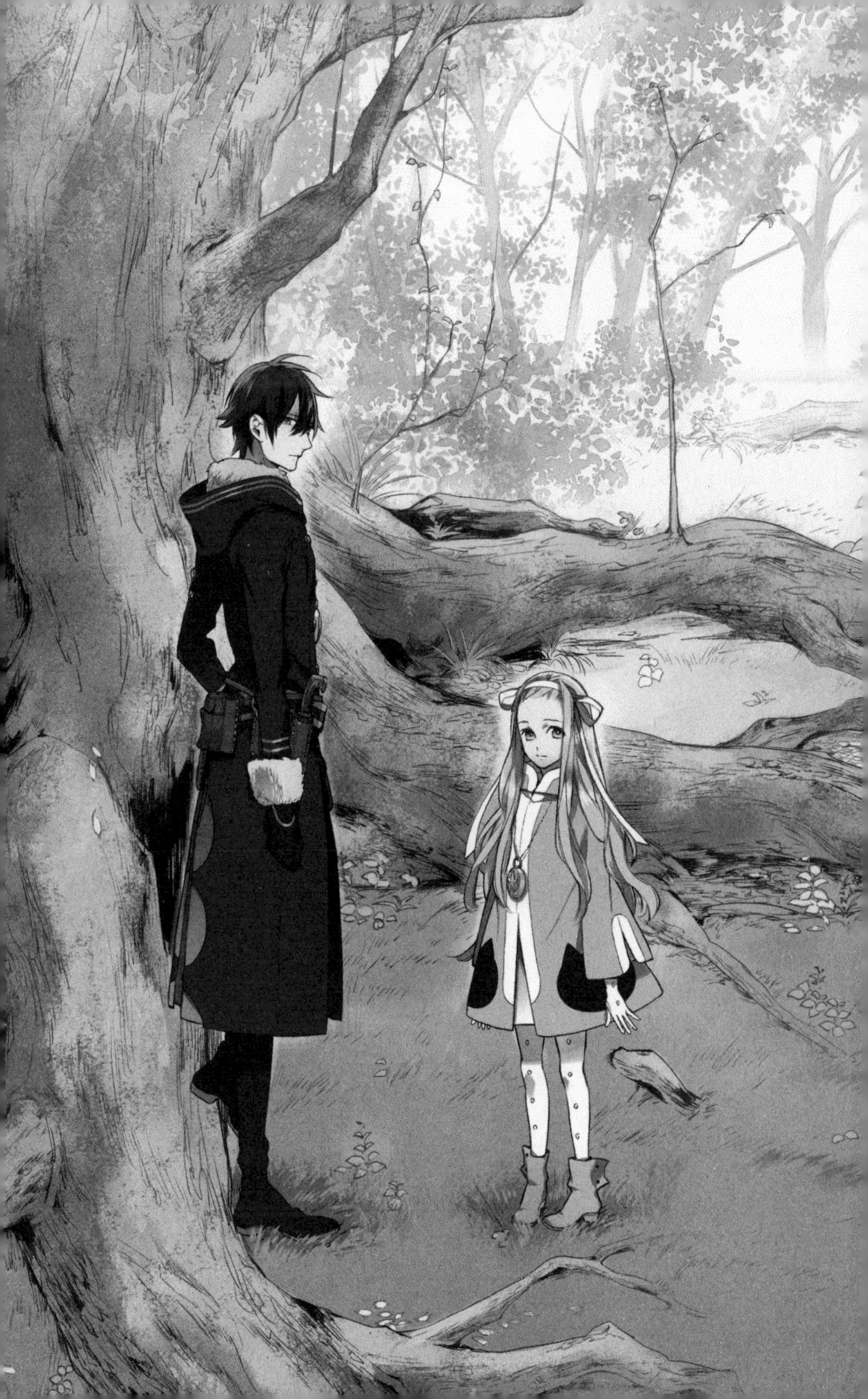

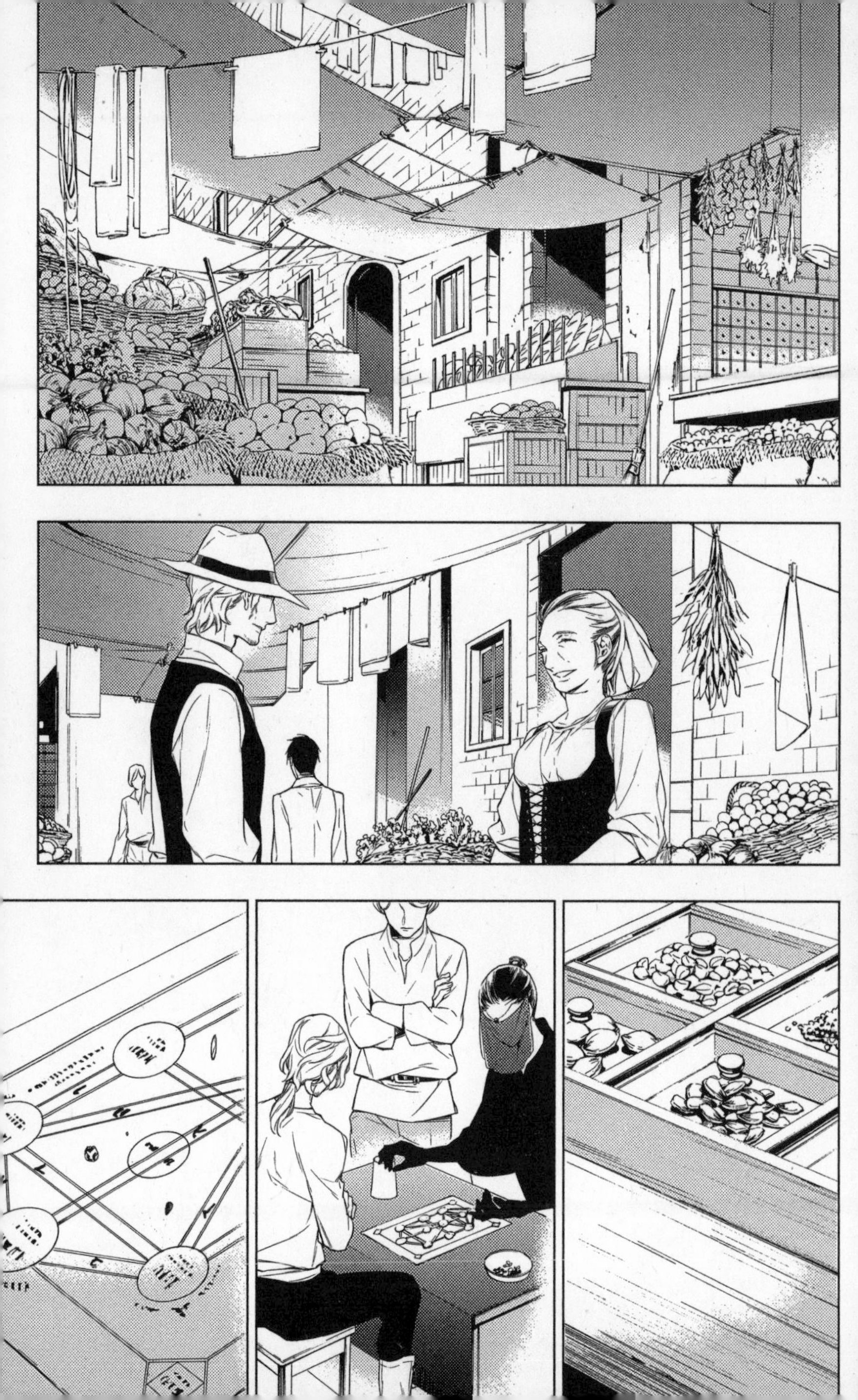

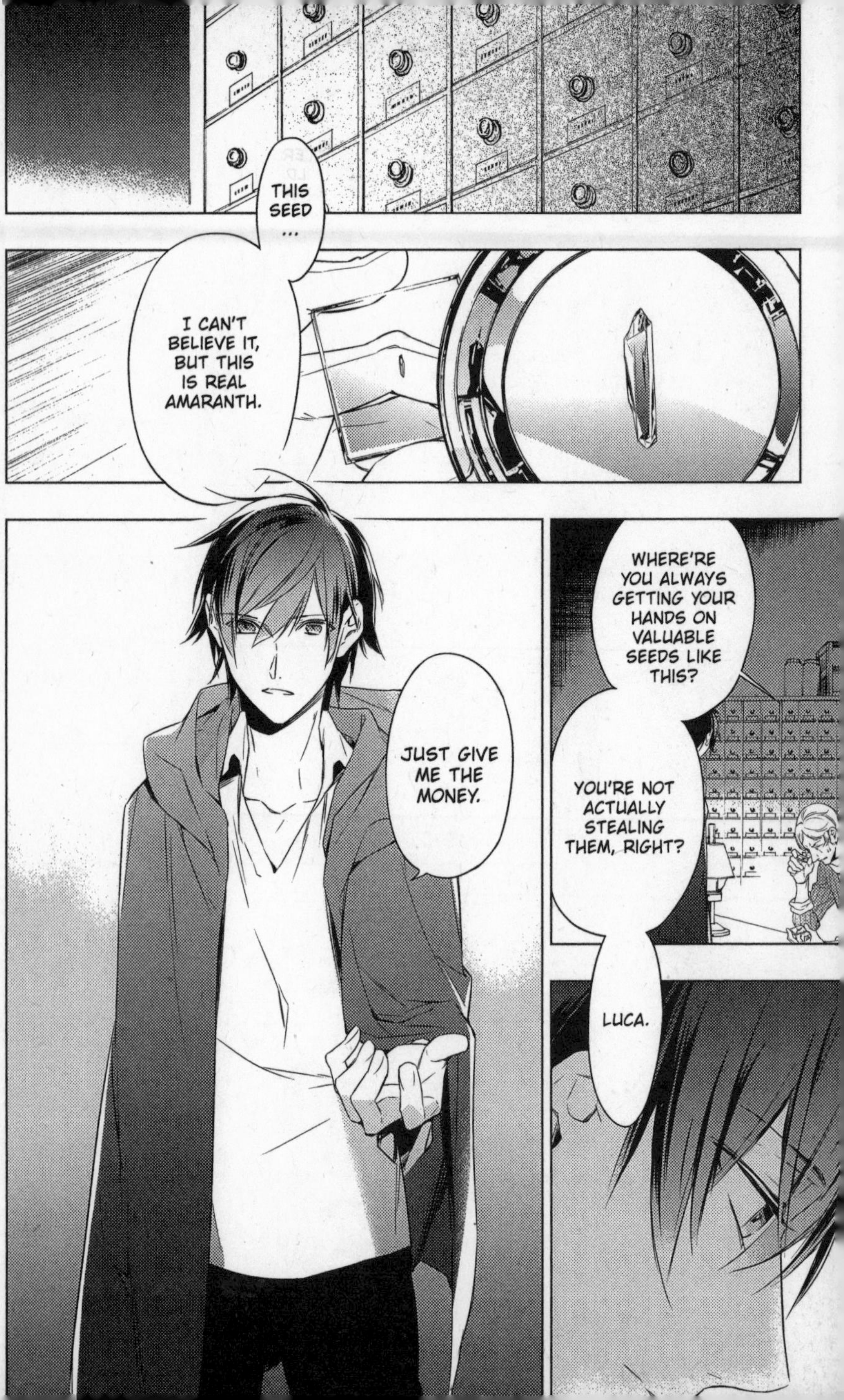
THIS SEED ...
I CAN'T BELIEVE IT, BUT THIS IS REAL AMARANTH.
WHERE'RE YOU ALWAYS GETTING YOUR HANDS ON VALUABLE SEEDS LIKE THIS?
YOU'RE NOT ACTUALLY STEALING THEM, RIGHT?
LUCA.
JUST GIVE ME THE MONEY.

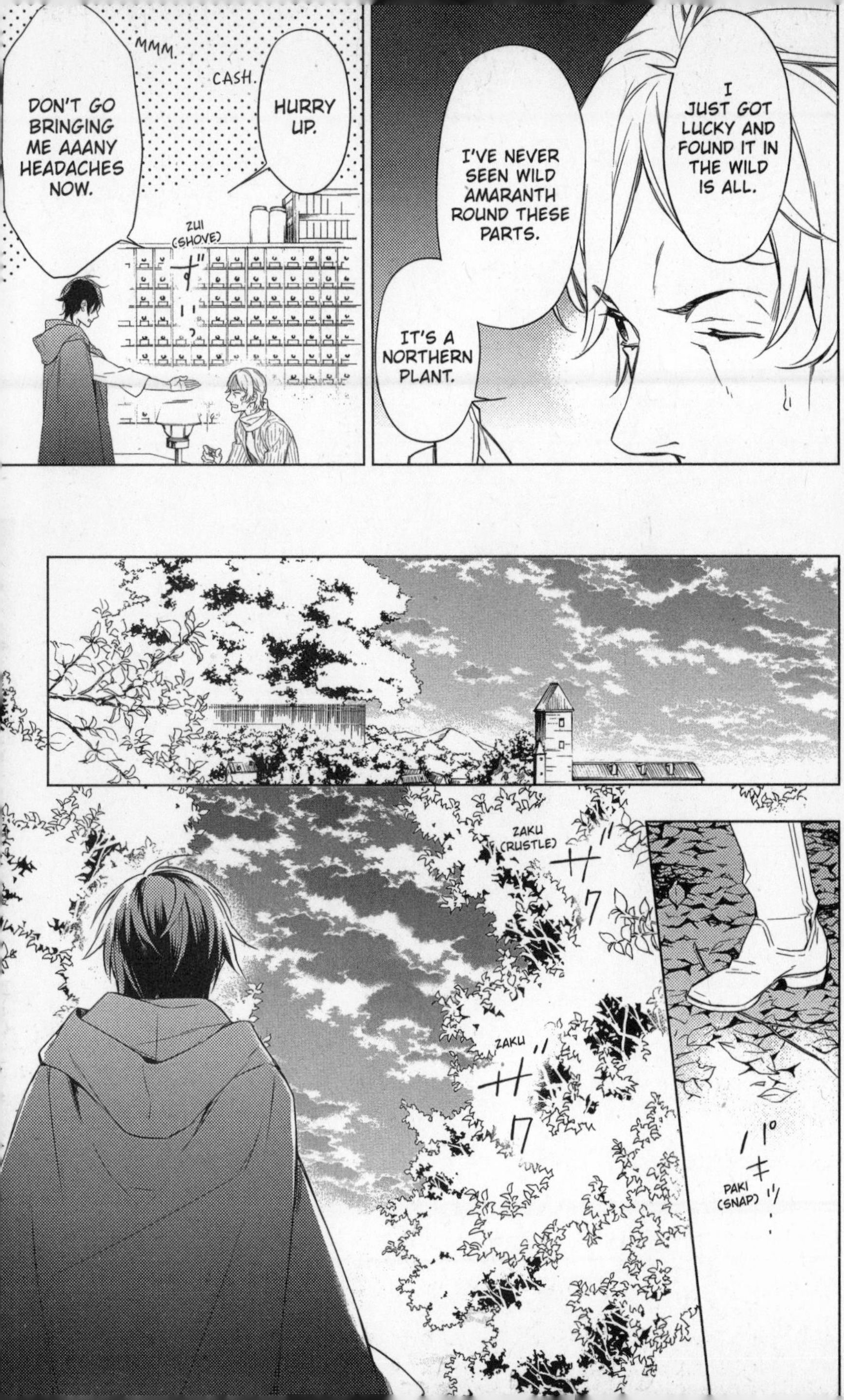
I JUST GOT LUCKY AND FOUND IT IN THE WILD IS ALL.
I'VE NEVER SEEN WILD AMARANTH ROUND THESE PARTS.
IT'S A NORTHERN PLANT.
HURRY UP.
CASH.
MMM.
DON'T GO BRINGING ME AAANY HEADACHES NOW.
ZUI (SHOVE)
PAKI (SNAP)
ZAKU (RUSTLE)
ZAKU

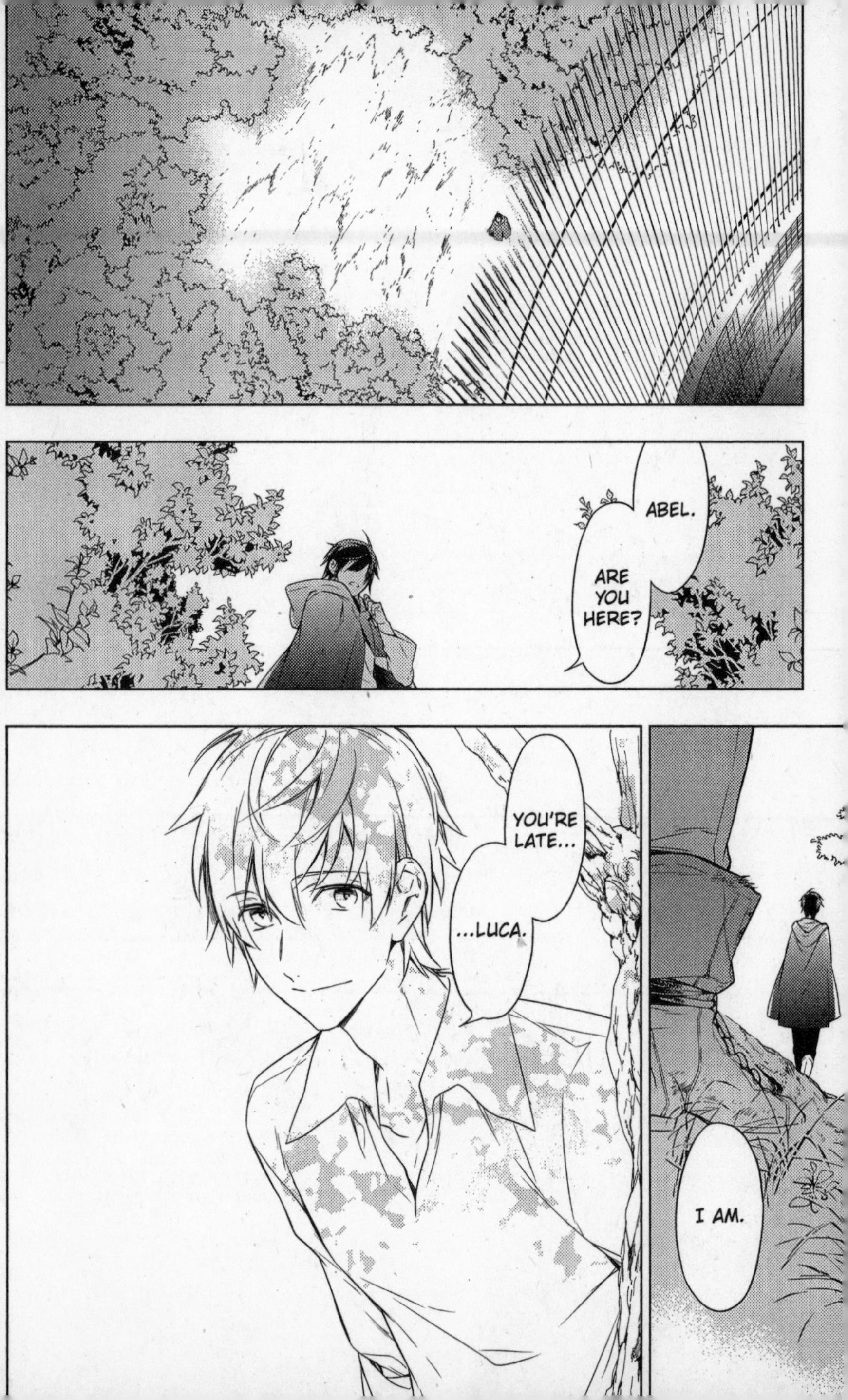
ABEL.
ARE YOU HERE?
I AM.
YOU'RE LATE...
...LUCA.

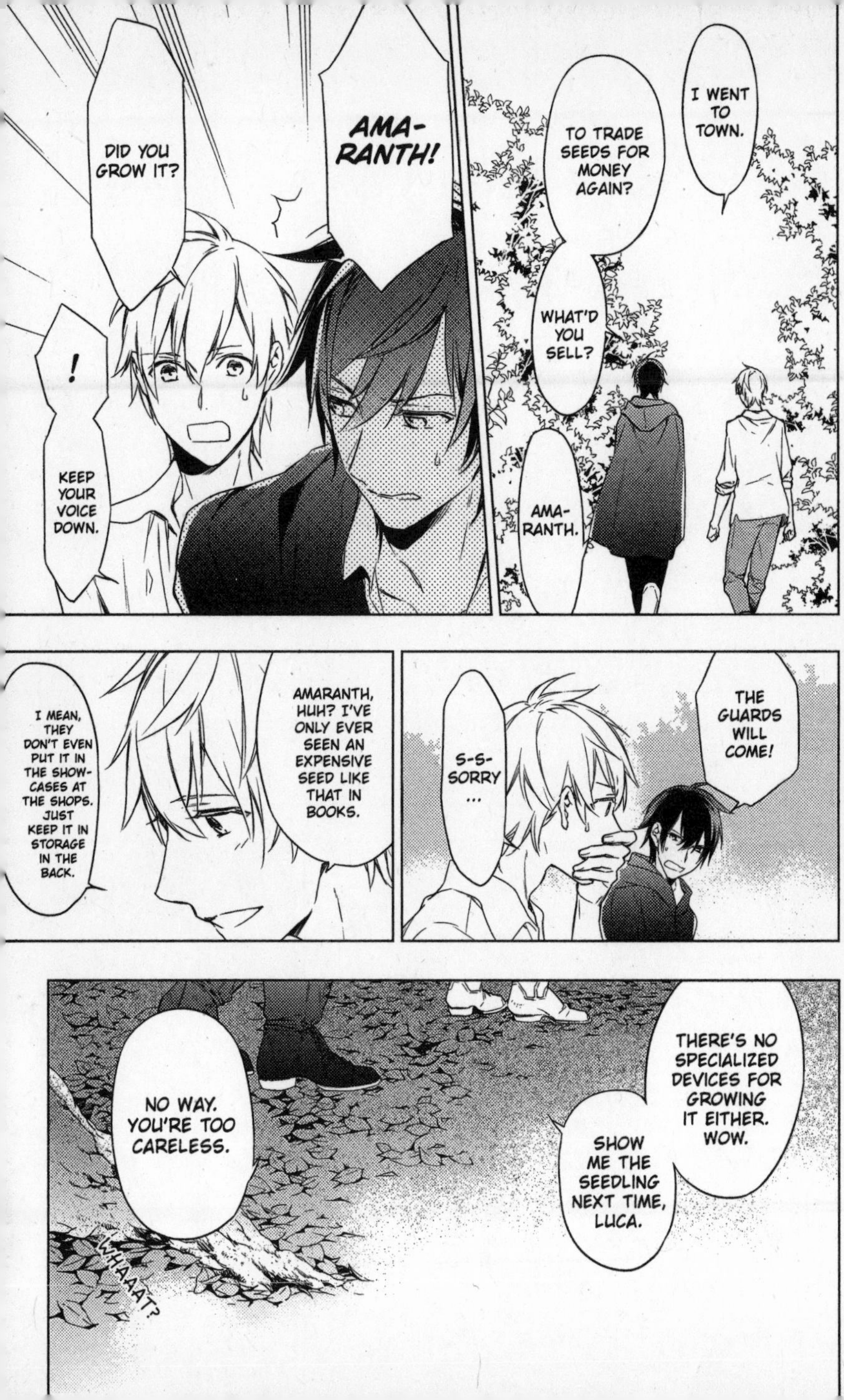
I WENT TO TOWN.
TO TRADE SEEDS FOR MONEY AGAIN?
WHAT'D YOU SELL?
AMA-RANTH.
AMA-RANTH!
DID YOU GROW IT?
!
KEEP YOUR VOICE DOWN.
THE GUARDS WILL COME!
S-S-SORRY...
AMARANTH, HUH? I'VE ONLY EVER SEEN AN EXPENSIVE SEED LIKE THAT IN BOOKS.
I MEAN, THEY DON'T EVEN PUT IT IN THE SHOW-CASES AT THE SHOPS. JUST KEEP IT IN STORAGE IN THE BACK.
THERE'S NO SPECIALIZED DEVICES FOR GROWING IT EITHER. WOW.
SHOW ME THE SEEDLING NEXT TIME, LUCA.
NO WAY. YOU'RE TOO CARELESS.
WHAAAT?

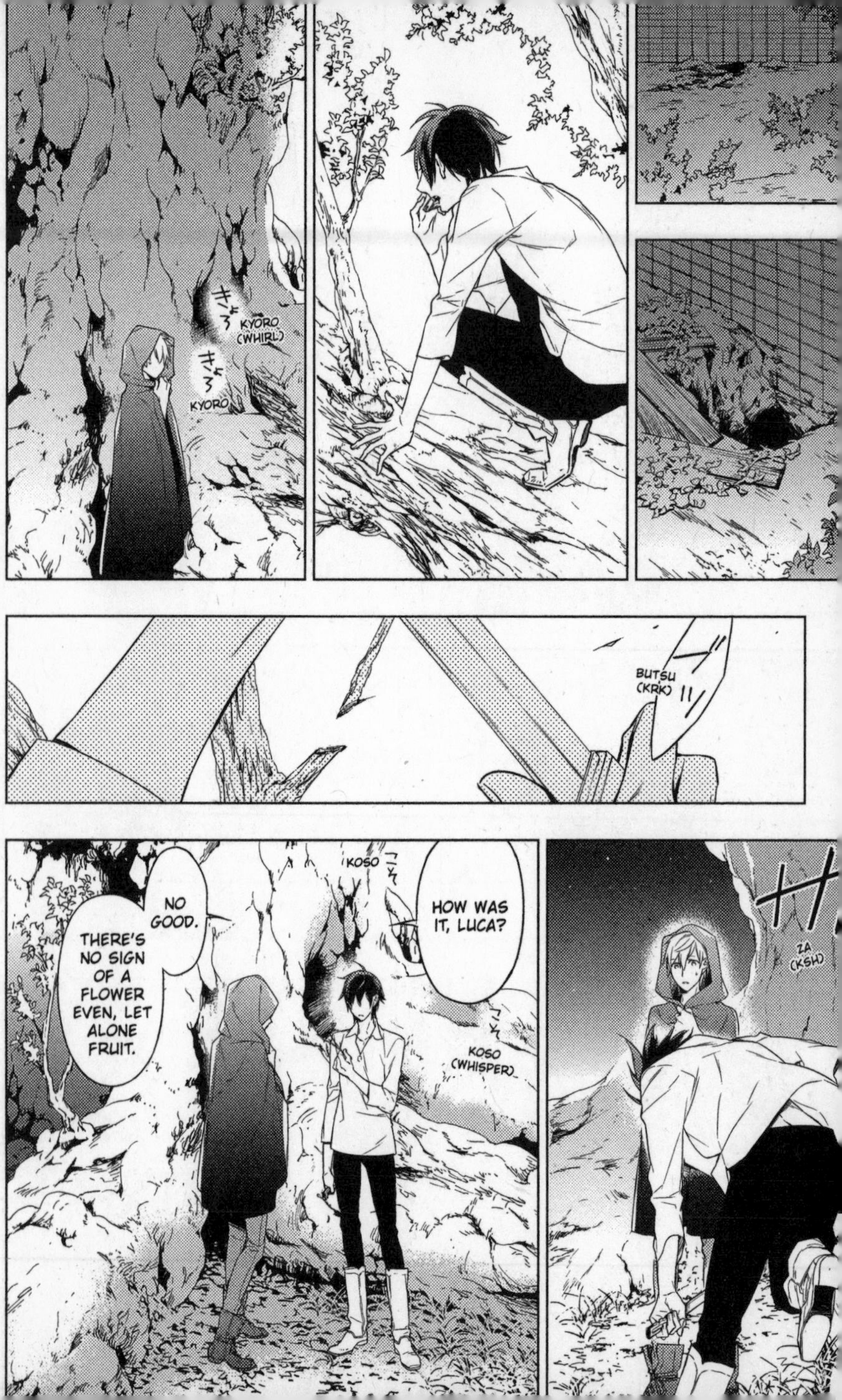

きょろ
KYORO (WHIRL)
きょろ
KYORO
BUTSU (KRK)
ZA (KSH)
コソ
KOSO
HOW WAS IT, LUCA?
コソ
KOSO (WHISPER)
NO GOOD.
THERE'S NO SIGN OF A FLOWER EVEN, LET ALONE FRUIT.

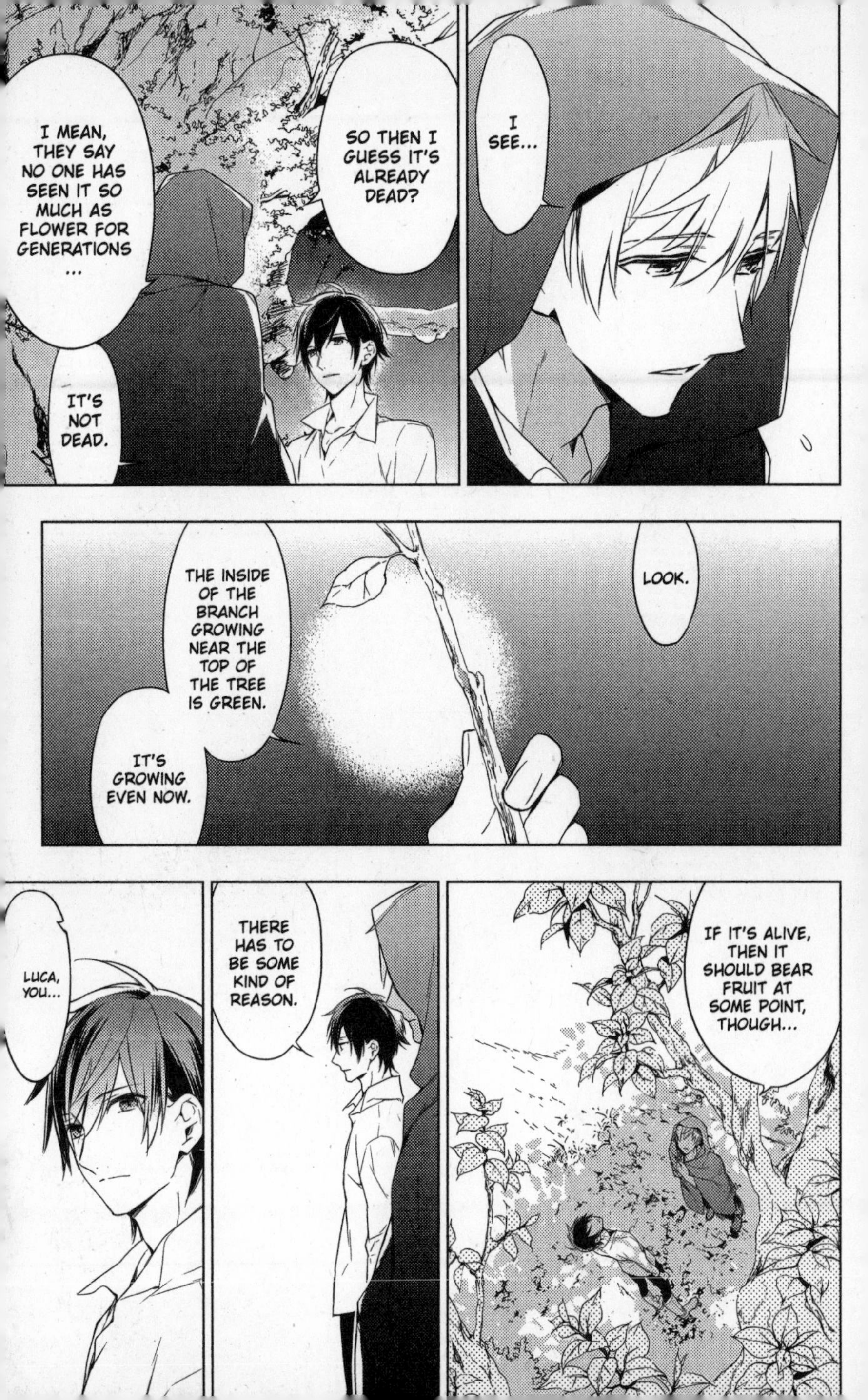
I SEE...
SO THEN I GUESS IT'S ALREADY DEAD?
I MEAN, THEY SAY NO ONE HAS SEEN IT SO MUCH AS FLOWER FOR GENERATIONS...
IT'S NOT DEAD.
LOOK.
THE INSIDE OF THE BRANCH GROWING NEAR THE TOP OF THE TREE IS GREEN.
IT'S GROWING EVEN NOW.
IF IT'S ALIVE, THEN IT SHOULD BEAR FRUIT AT SOME POINT, THOUGH...
THERE HAS TO BE SOME KIND OF REASON.
LUCA, YOU...

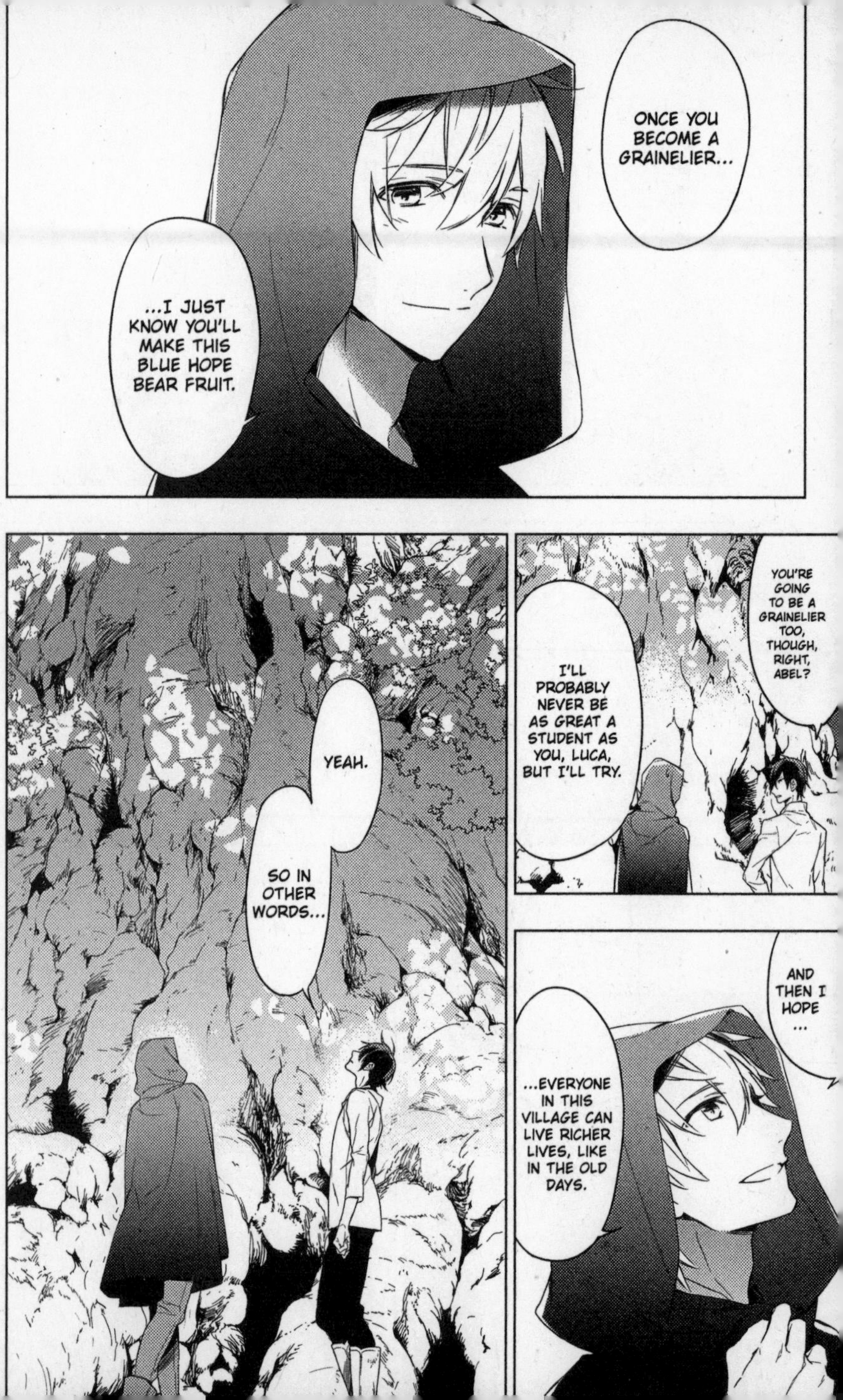
ONCE YOU BECOME A GRAINELIER...
...I JUST KNOW YOU'LL MAKE THIS BLUE HOPE BEAR FRUIT.
YOU'RE GOING TO BE A GRAINELIER TOO, THOUGH, RIGHT, ABEL?
I'LL PROBABLY NEVER BE AS GREAT A STUDENT AS YOU, LUCA, BUT I'LL TRY.
AND THEN I HOPE ...
...EVERYONE IN THIS VILLAGE CAN LIVE RICHER LIVES, LIKE IN THE OLD DAYS.
YEAH.
SO IN OTHER WORDS...

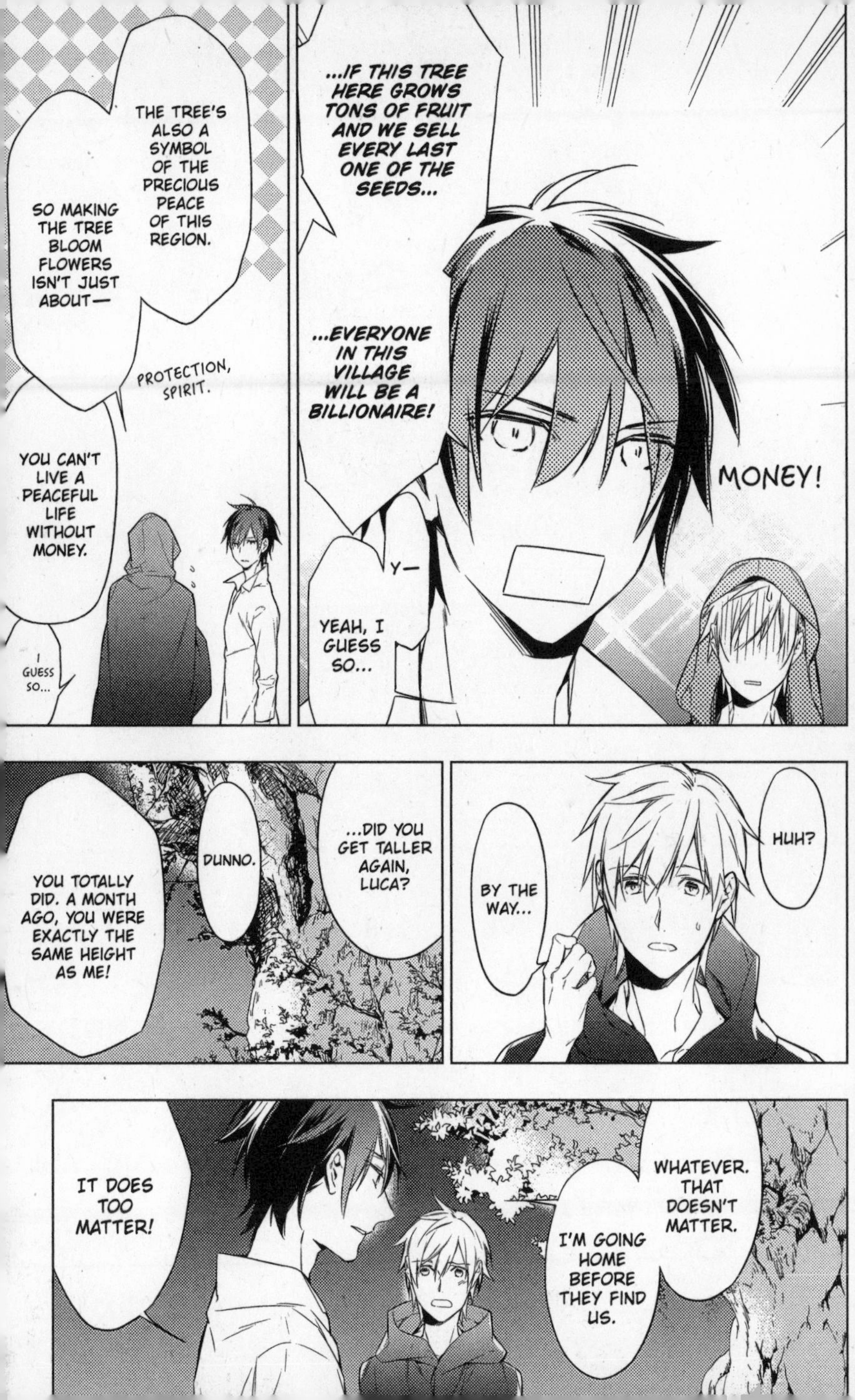
...IF THIS TREE HERE GROWS TONS OF FRUIT AND WE SELL EVERY LAST ONE OF THE SEEDS...
...EVERYONE IN THIS VILLAGE WILL BE A BILLIONAIRE!
MONEY!
Y—
YEAH, I GUESS SO...
THE TREE'S ALSO A SYMBOL OF THE PRECIOUS PEACE OF THIS REGION.
SO MAKING THE TREE BLOOM FLOWERS ISN'T JUST ABOUT—
PROTECTION, SPIRIT.
YOU CAN'T LIVE A PEACEFUL LIFE WITHOUT MONEY.
I GUESS SO...
HUH?
BY THE WAY...
...DID YOU GET TALLER AGAIN, LUCA?
DUNNO.
YOU TOTALLY DID. A MONTH AGO, YOU WERE EXACTLY THE SAME HEIGHT AS ME!
WHATEVER. THAT DOESN'T MATTER.
I'M GOING HOME BEFORE THEY FIND US.
IT DOES TOO MATTER!

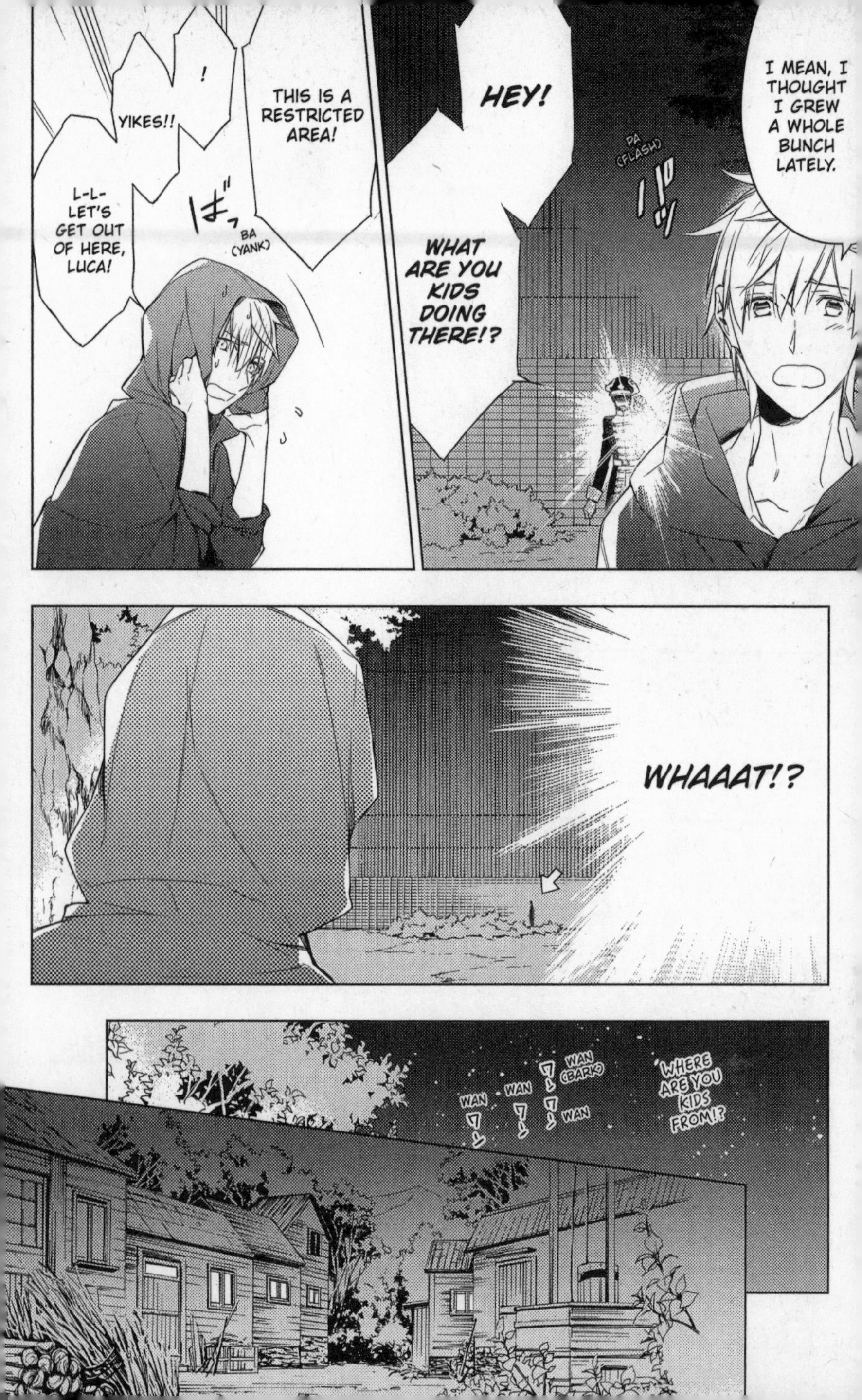
I MEAN, I THOUGHT I GREW A WHOLE BUNCH LATELY.
PA (FLASH)
HEY!
WHAT ARE YOU KIDS DOING THERE!?
THIS IS A RESTRICTED AREA!
!
YIKES!!
BA (YANK)
L-L-LET'S GET OUT OF HERE, LUCA!
WHAAAT!?
WHERE ARE YOU KIDS FROM!?
WAN (BARK)
WAN
WAN
WAN

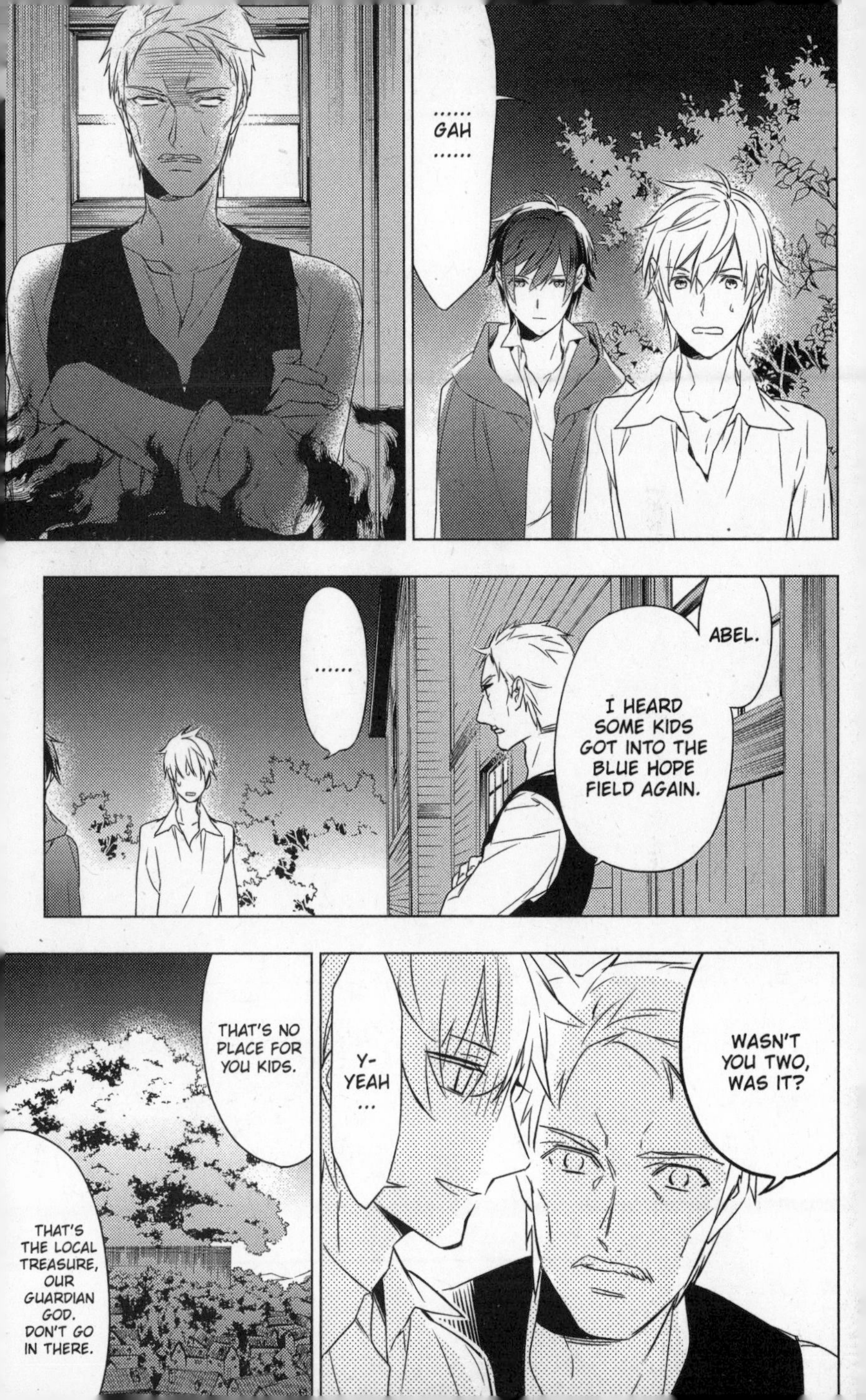
...... GAH ......
ABEL.
I HEARD SOME KIDS GOT INTO THE BLUE HOPE FIELD AGAIN.
......
WASN'T YOU TWO, WAS IT?
Y-YEAH ...
THAT'S NO PLACE FOR YOU KIDS.
THAT'S THE LOCAL TREASURE, OUR GUARDIAN GOD. DON'T GO IN THERE.

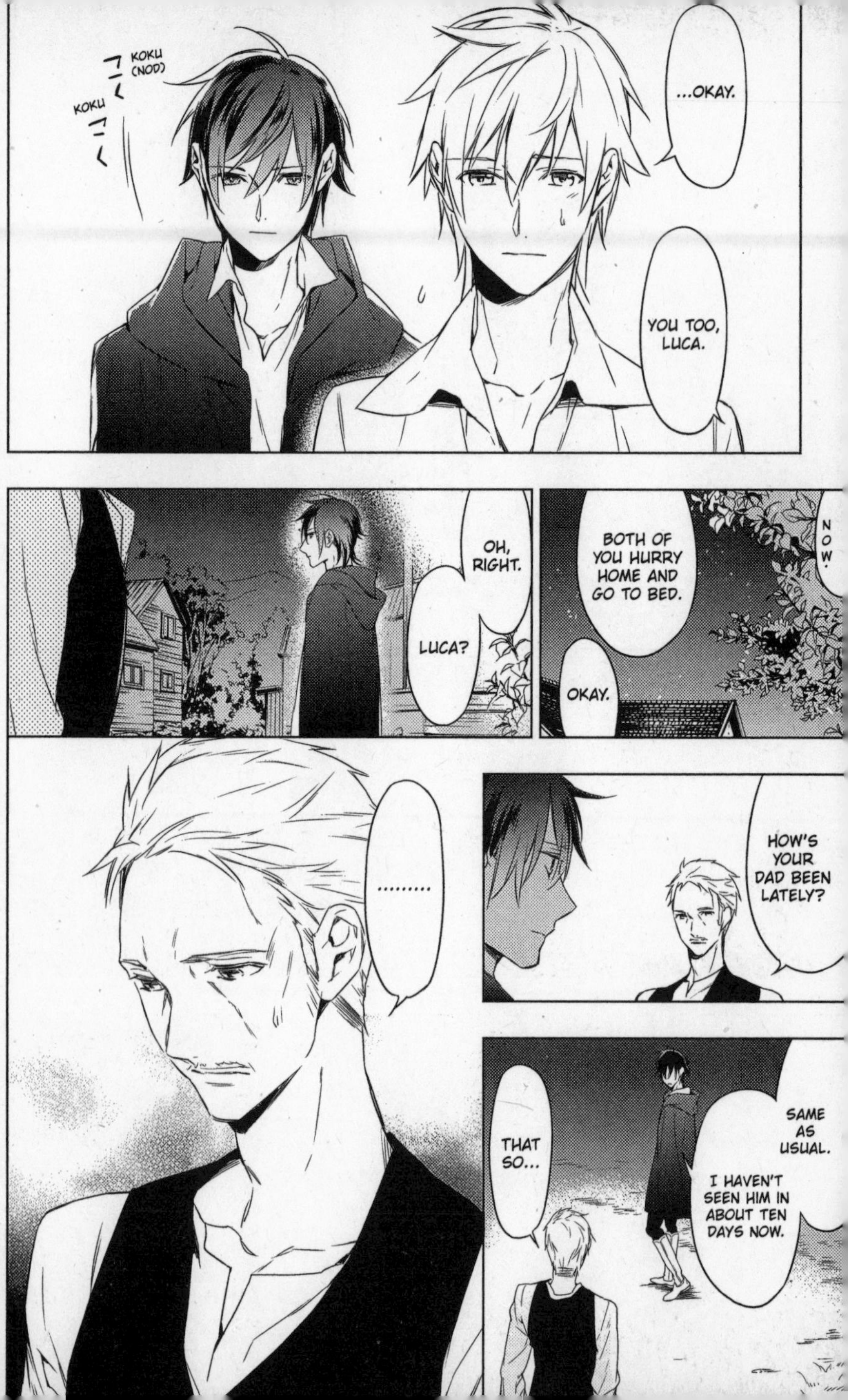
...OKAY.
YOU TOO, LUCA.
KOKU (NOD)
KOKU
NOW.
BOTH OF YOU HURRY HOME AND GO TO BED.
OKAY.
OH, RIGHT.
LUCA?
HOW'S YOUR DAD BEEN LATELY?
SAME AS USUAL.
I HAVEN'T SEEN HIM IN ABOUT TEN DAYS NOW.
THAT SO...
....

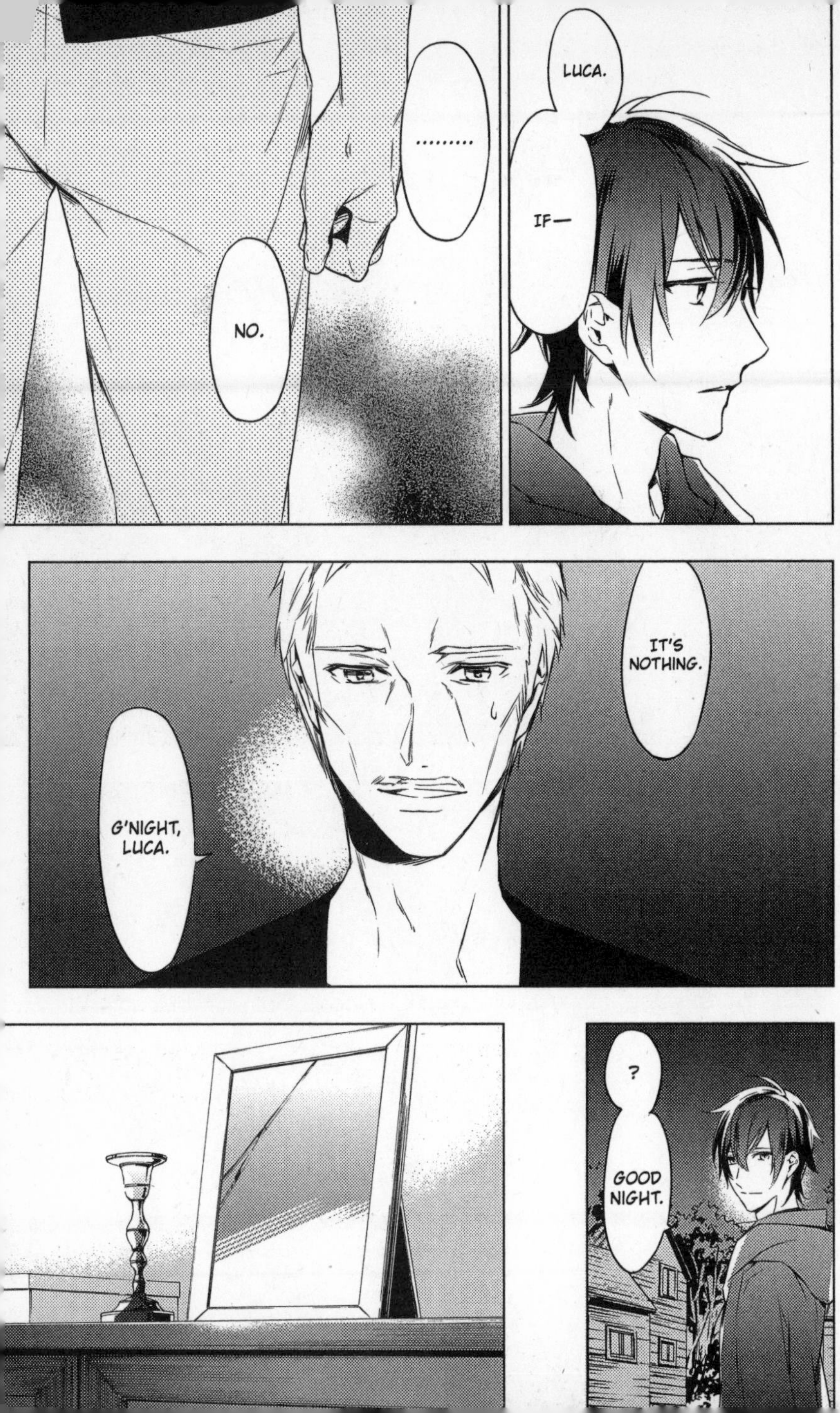
LUCA.
IF—
....
NO.
IT'S NOTHING.
G'NIGHT, LUCA.
?
GOOD NIGHT.

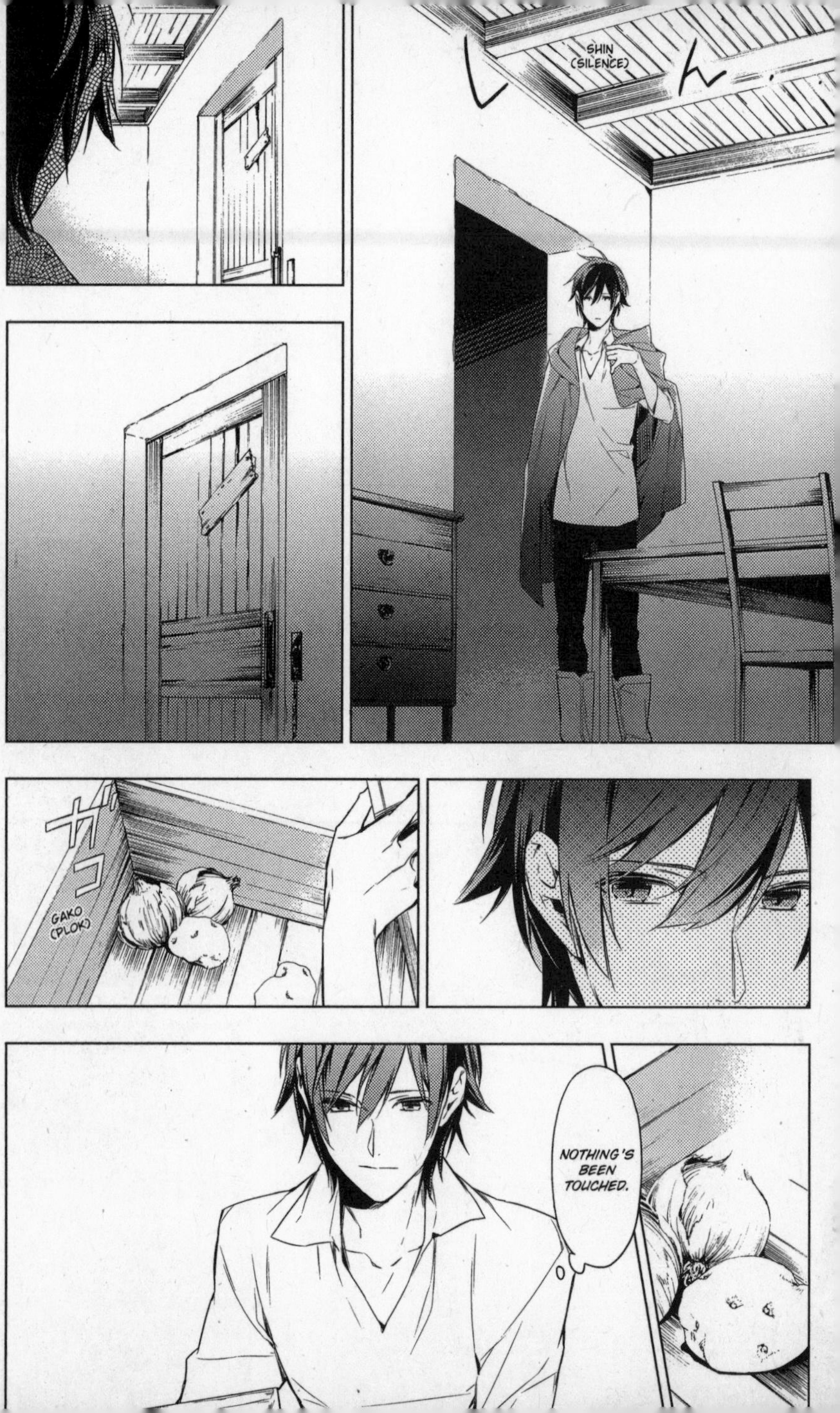
SHIN (SILENCE)
GAKO (PLOK)
NOTHING'S BEEN TOUCHED.

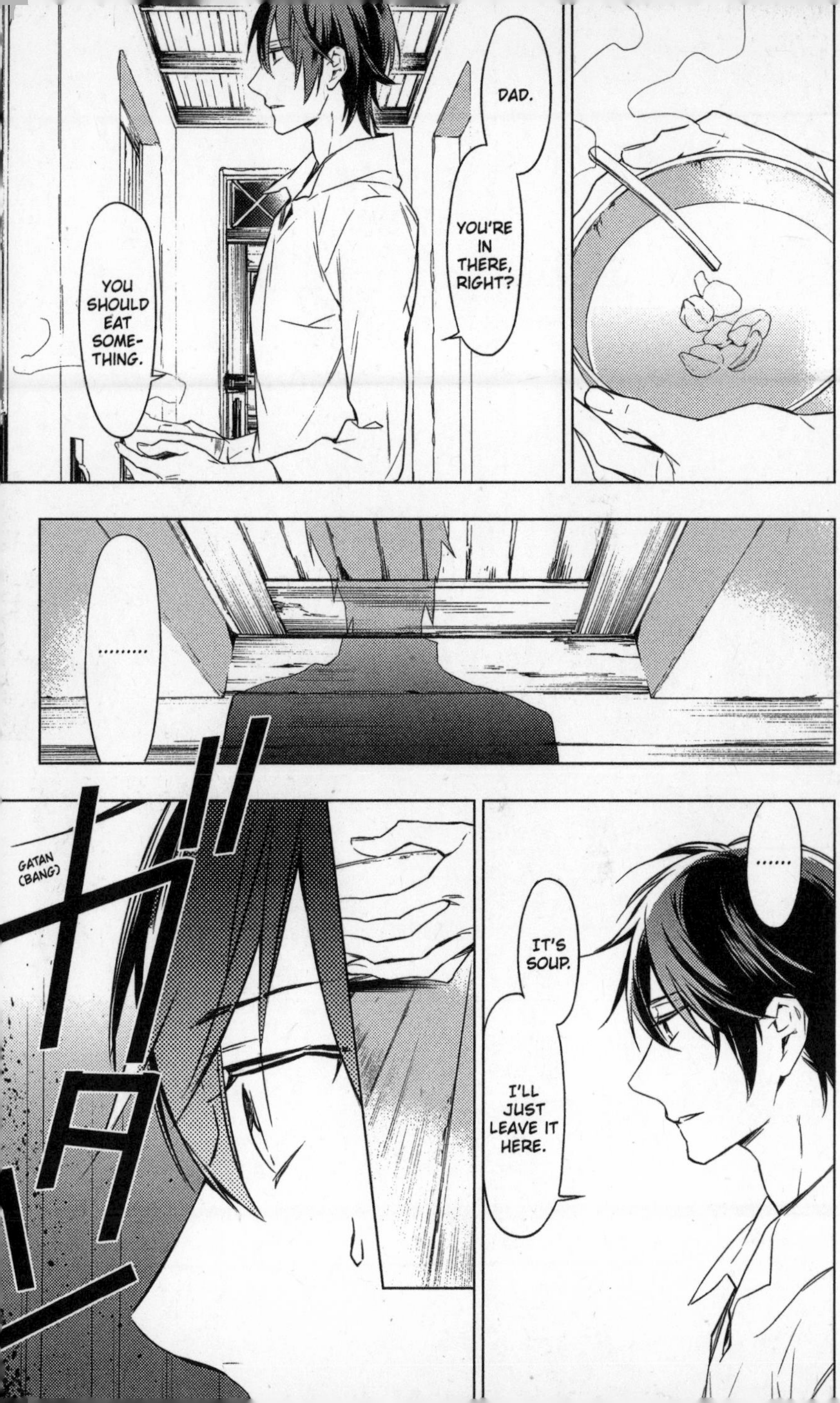
DAD.
YOU'RE IN THERE, RIGHT?
YOU SHOULD EAT SOME-THING.
....
......
IT'S SOUP.
I'LL JUST LEAVE IT HERE.
GATAN (BANG)

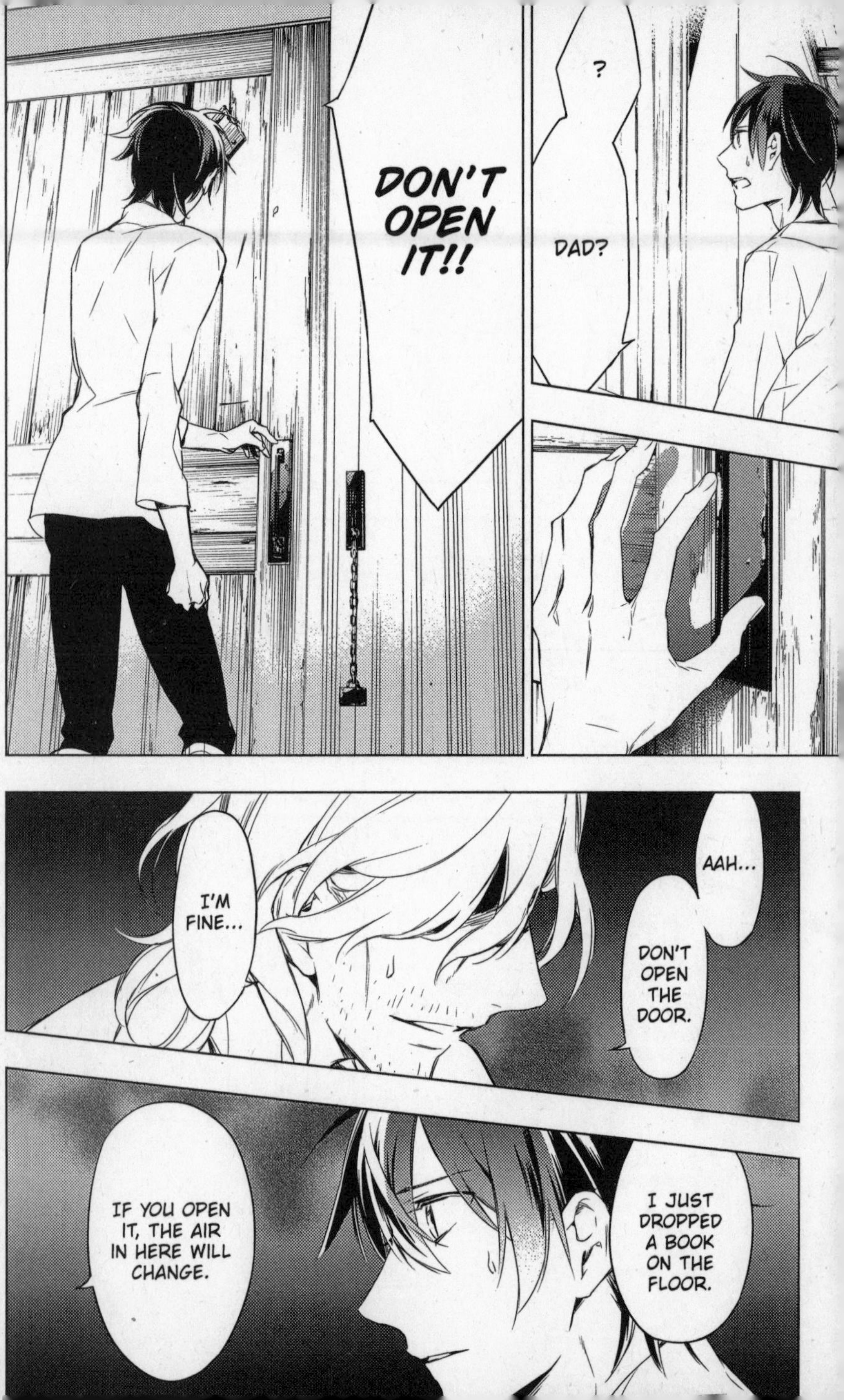
?
DAD?
DON'T OPEN IT!!
AAH...
DON'T OPEN THE DOOR.
I'M FINE...
I JUST DROPPED A BOOK ON THE FLOOR.
IF YOU OPEN IT, THE AIR IN HERE WILL CHANGE.

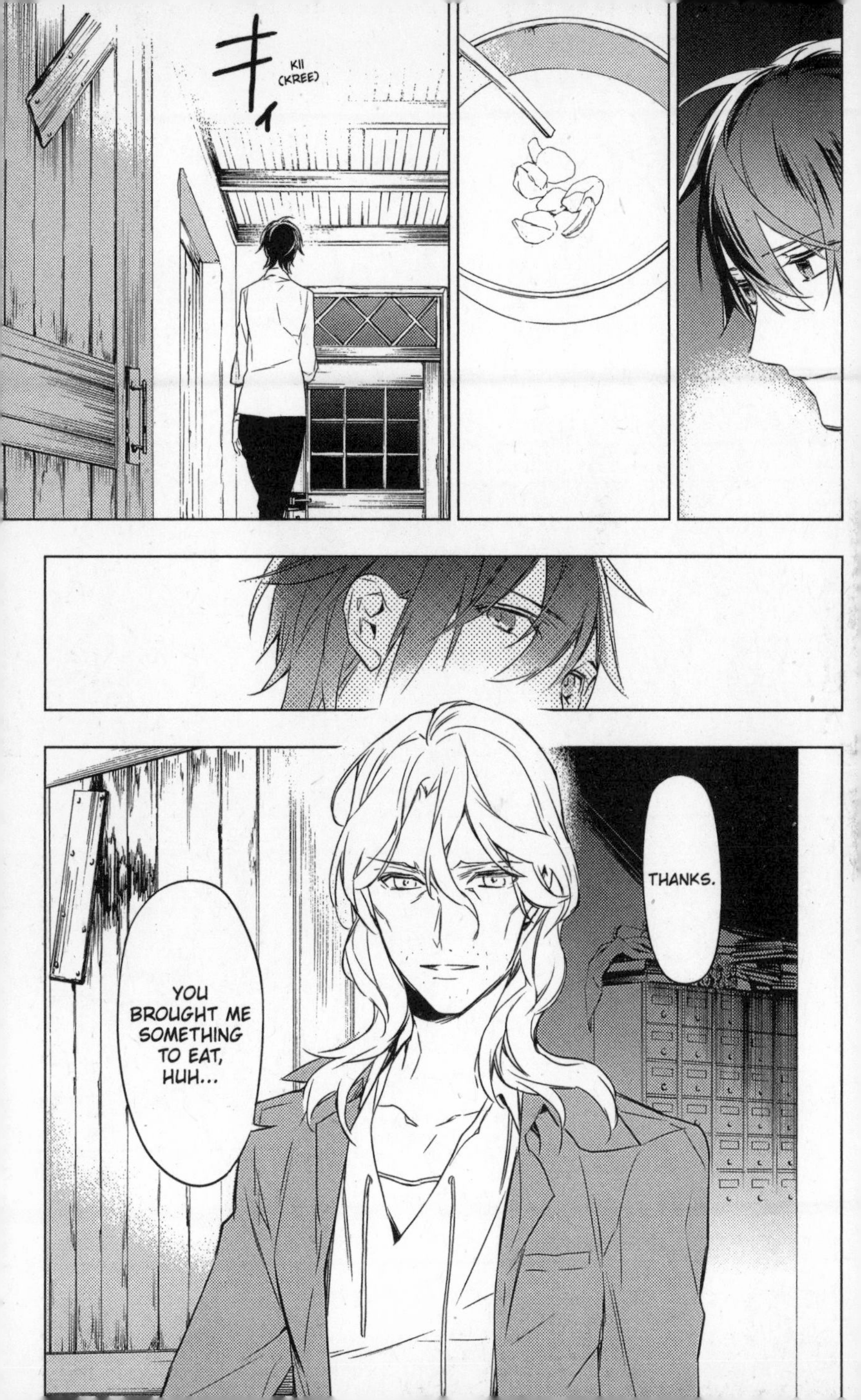

キィ
KII (KREE)
THANKS.
YOU BROUGHT ME SOMETHING TO EAT, HUH...

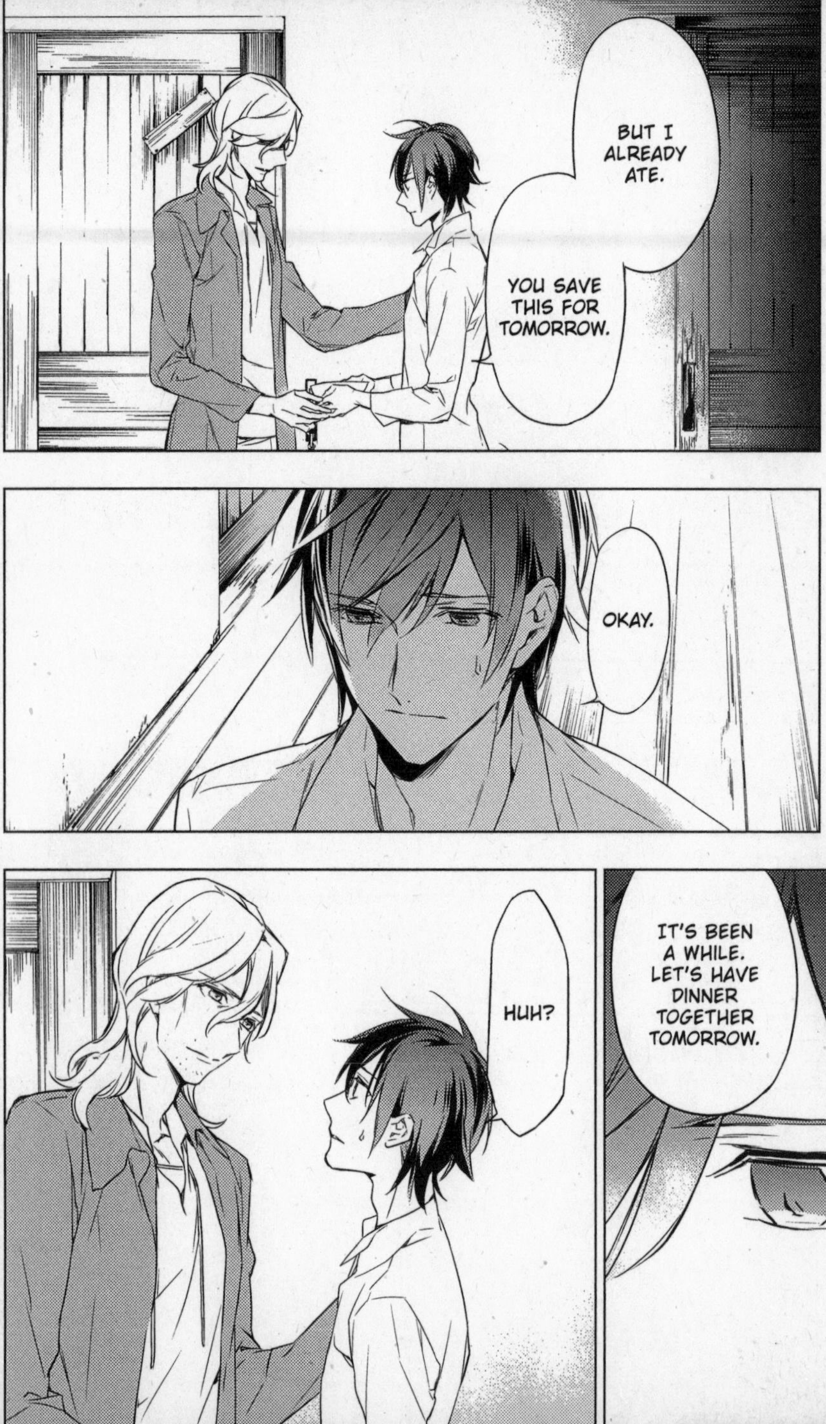
BUT I ALREADY ATE.
YOU SAVE THIS FOR TOMORROW.
OKAY.
IT'S BEEN A WHILE. LET'S HAVE DINNER TOGETHER TOMORROW.
HUH?

JUST A LITTLE LONGER.

IT'LL BE JUST A LITTLE LONGER...

...LUCA.

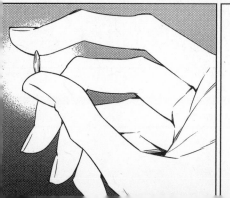

ZARA (KLAK)

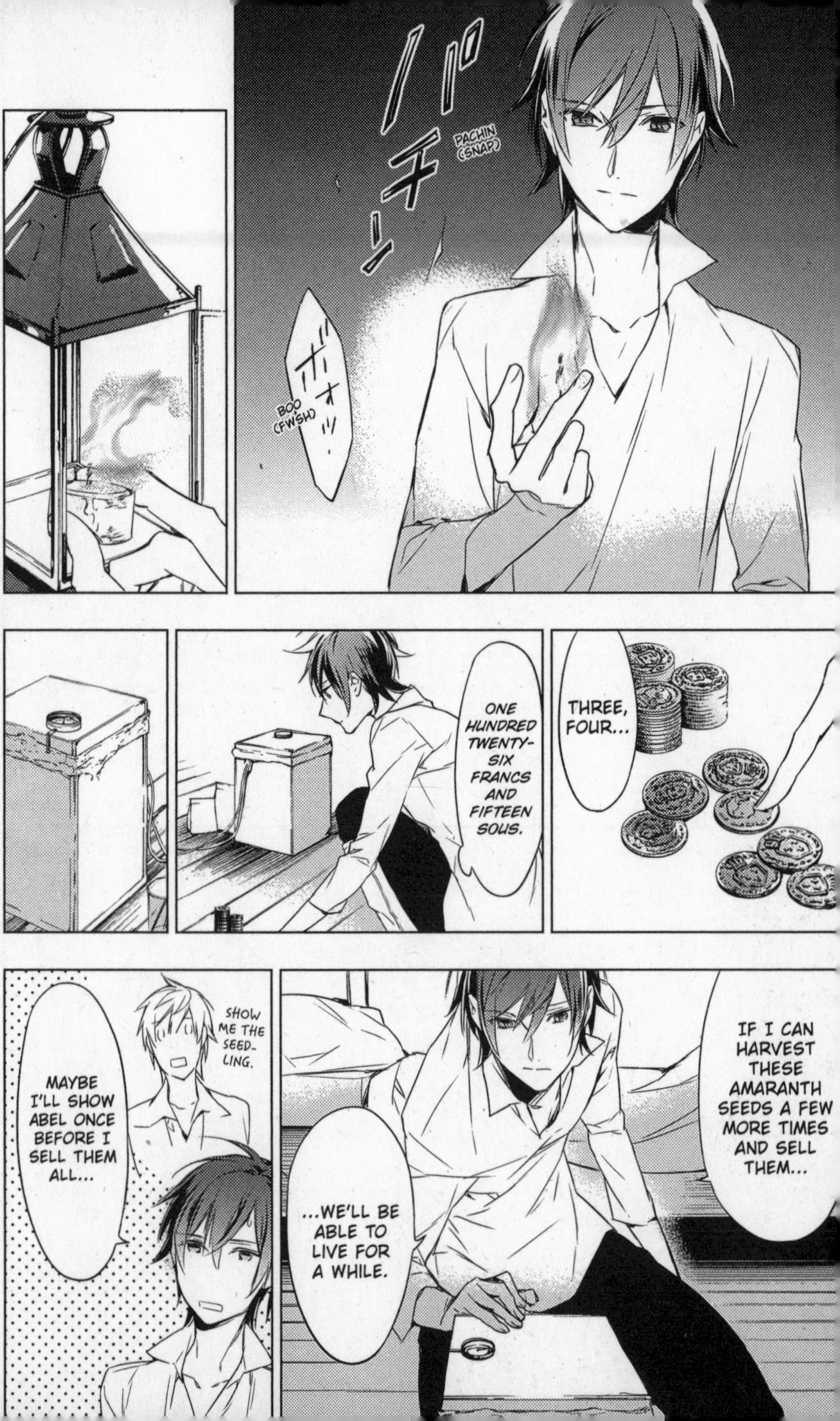
PACHIN (SNAP)
BOO (FWSH)
THREE, FOUR...
ONE HUNDRED TWENTY-SIX FRANCS AND FIFTEEN SOUS.
IF I CAN HARVEST THESE AMARANTH SEEDS A FEW MORE TIMES AND SELL THEM...
...WE'LL BE ABLE TO LIVE FOR A WHILE.
SHOW ME THE SEED-LING.
MAYBE I'LL SHOW ABEL ONCE BEFORE I SELL THEM ALL...

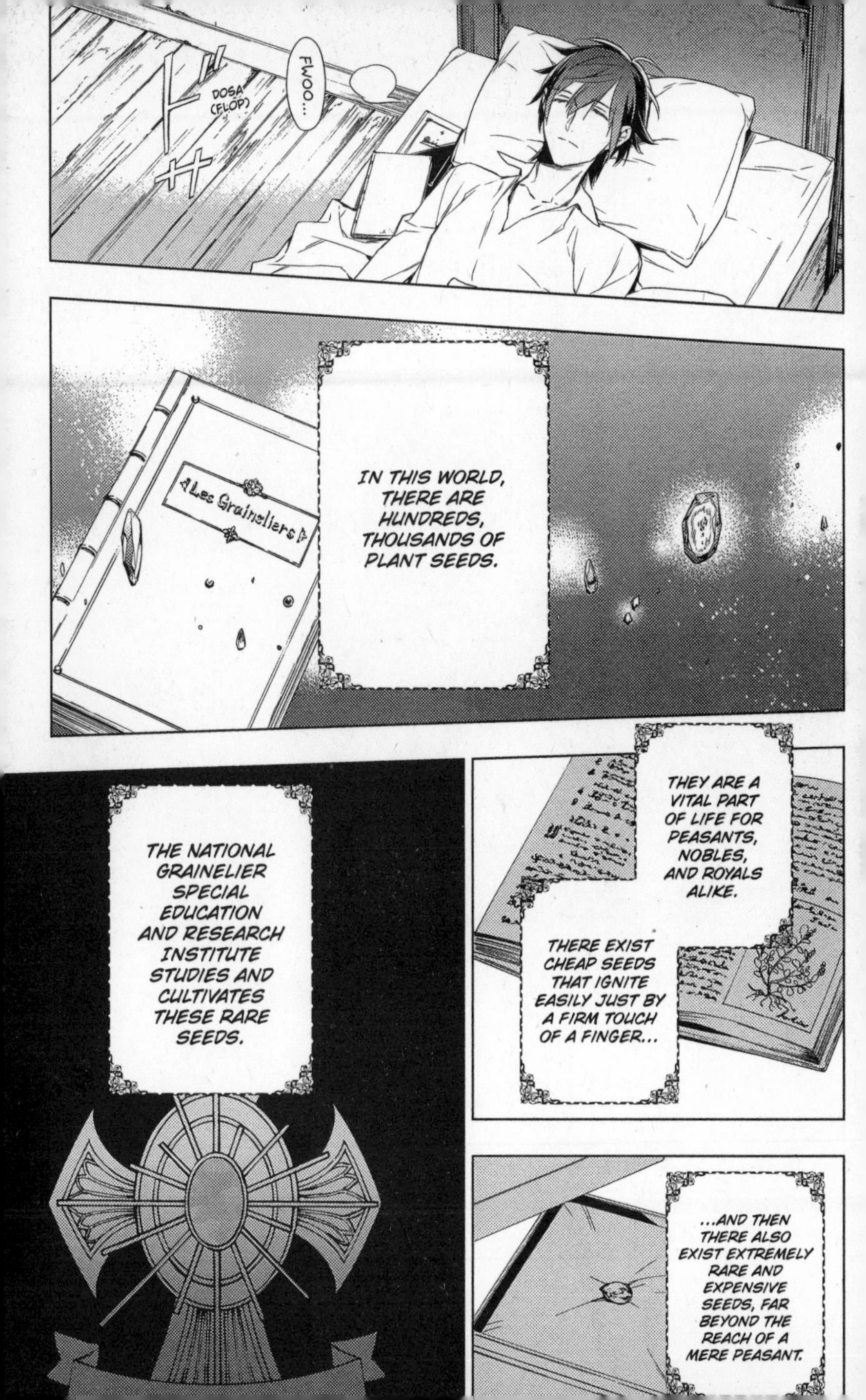
FWOO...
DOSA (FLOP)
IN THIS WORLD, THERE ARE HUNDREDS, THOUSANDS OF PLANT SEEDS.
Les Graineliers
THEY ARE A VITAL PART OF LIFE FOR PEASANTS, NOBLES, AND ROYALS ALIKE.
THERE EXIST CHEAP SEEDS THAT IGNITE EASILY JUST BY A FIRM TOUCH OF A FINGER...
...AND THEN THERE ALSO EXIST EXTREMELY RARE AND EXPENSIVE SEEDS, FAR BEYOND THE REACH OF A MERE PEASANT.
THE NATIONAL GRAINELIER SPECIAL EDUCATION AND RESEARCH INSTITUTE STUDIES AND CULTIVATES THESE RARE SEEDS.

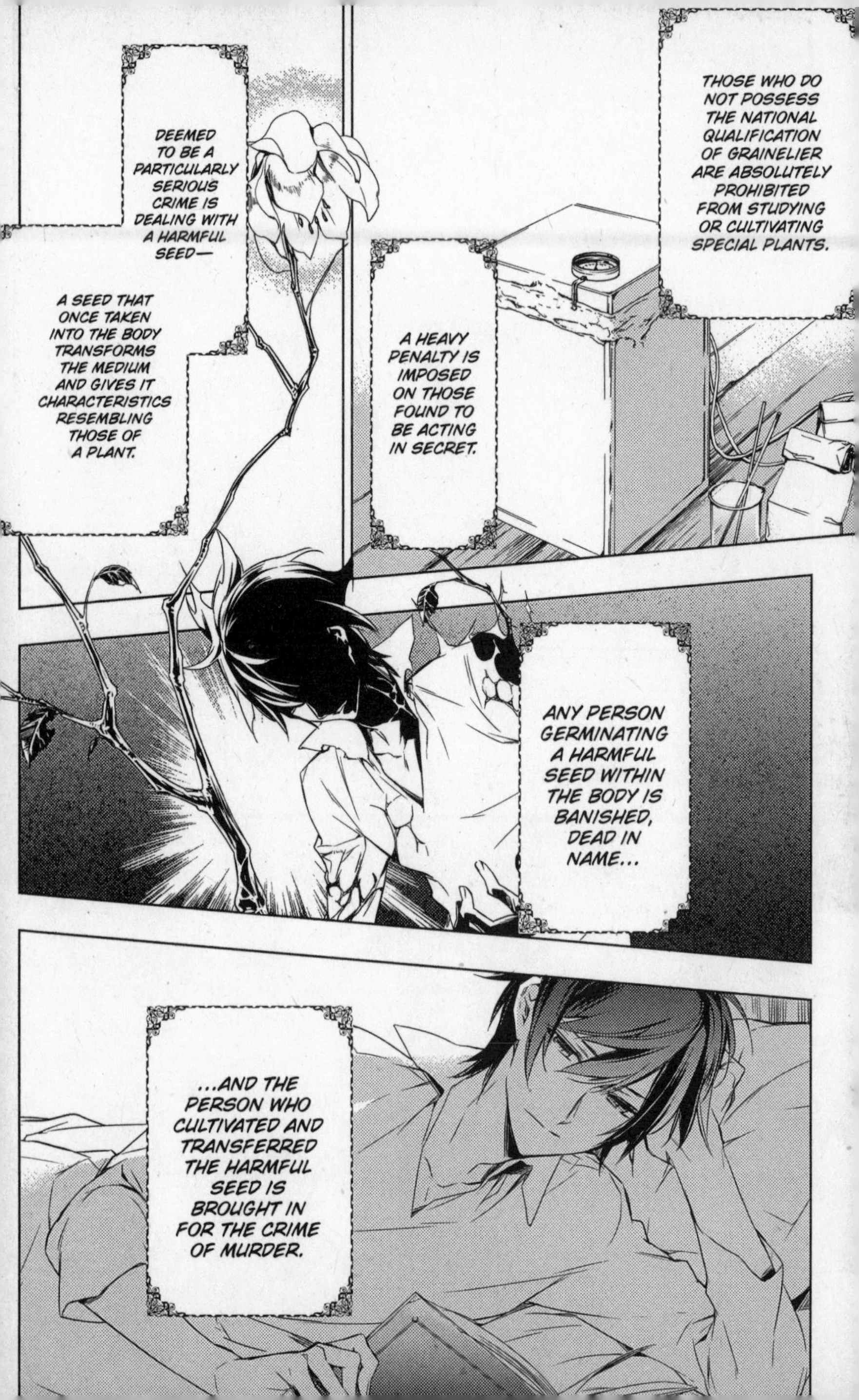
THOSE WHO DO NOT POSSESS THE NATIONAL QUALIFICATION OF GRAINELIER ARE ABSOLUTELY PROHIBITED FROM STUDYING OR CULTIVATING SPECIAL PLANTS.
A HEAVY PENALTY IS IMPOSED ON THOSE FOUND TO BE ACTING IN SECRET.
DEEMED TO BE A PARTICULARLY SERIOUS CRIME IS DEALING WITH A HARMFUL SEED—
A SEED THAT ONCE TAKEN INTO THE BODY TRANSFORMS THE MEDIUM AND GIVES IT CHARACTERISTICS RESEMBLING THOSE OF A PLANT.
ANY PERSON GERMINATING A HARMFUL SEED WITHIN THE BODY IS BANISHED, DEAD IN NAME...
...AND THE PERSON WHO CULTIVATED AND TRANSFERRED THE HARMFUL SEED IS BROUGHT IN FOR THE CRIME OF MURDER.

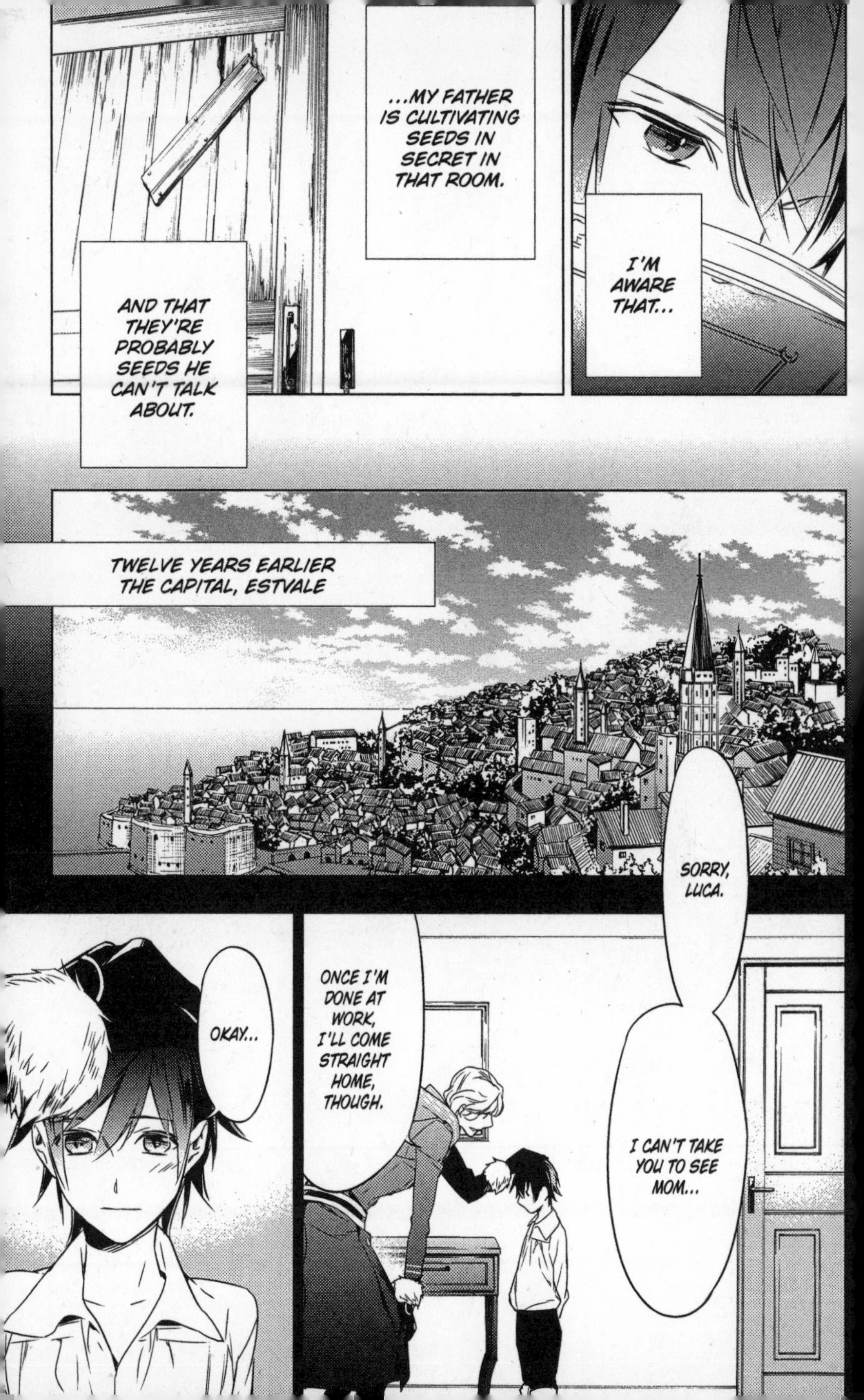
I'M AWARE THAT...
...MY FATHER IS CULTIVATING SEEDS IN SECRET IN THAT ROOM.
AND THAT THEY'RE PROBABLY SEEDS HE CAN'T TALK ABOUT.
TWELVE YEARS EARLIER THE CAPITAL, ESTVALE
SORRY, LUCA.
I CAN'T TAKE YOU TO SEE MOM...
ONCE I'M DONE AT WORK, I'LL COME STRAIGHT HOME, THOUGH.
OKAY...

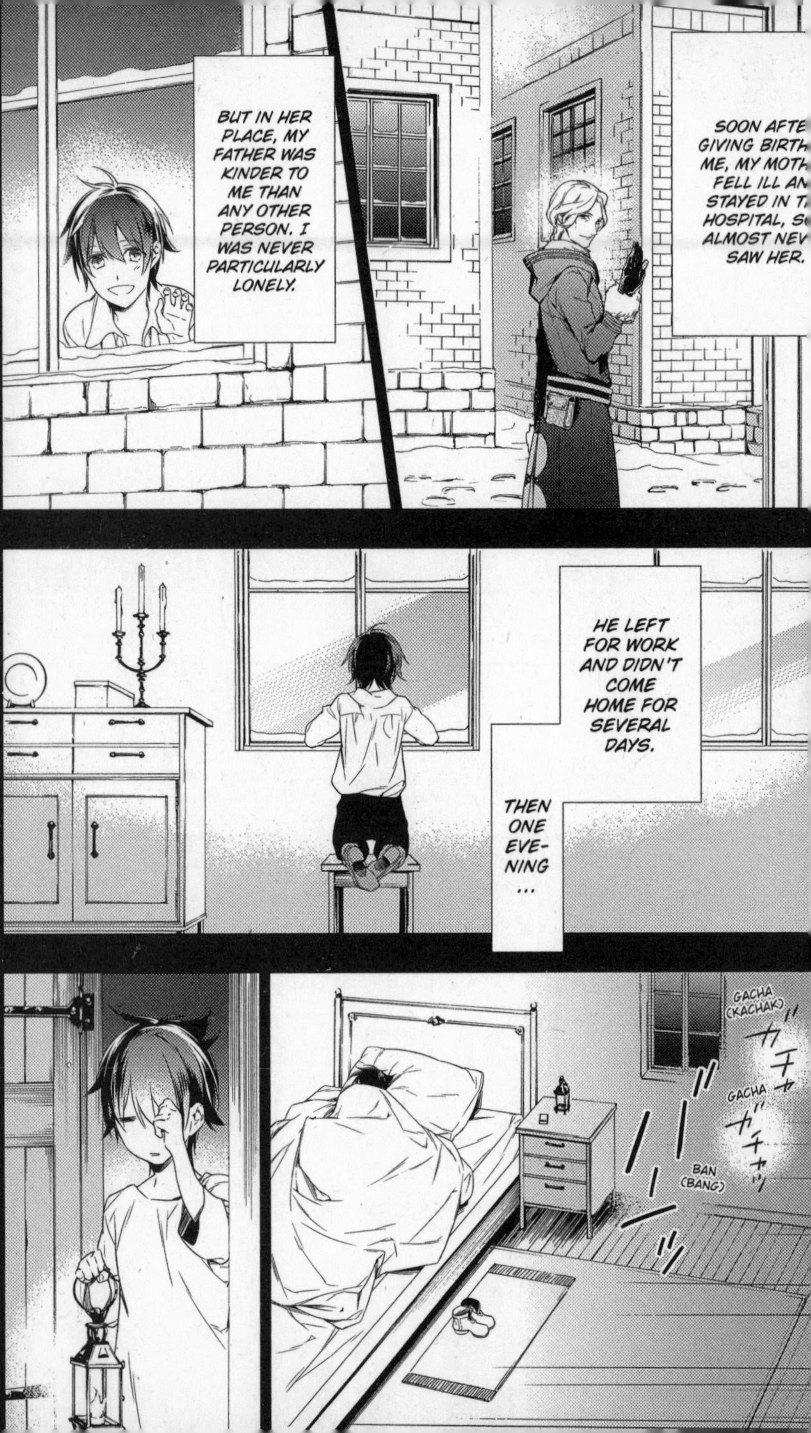
SOON AFTE
GIVING BIRTH
ME, MY MOTH
FELL ILL AN
STAYED IN T
HOSPITAL, S
ALMOST NEV
SAW HER.
BUT IN HER PLACE, MY FATHER WAS KINDER TO ME THAN ANY OTHER PERSON. I WAS NEVER PARTICULARLY LONELY.
HE LEFT FOR WORK AND DIDN'T COME HOME FOR SEVERAL DAYS.
THEN ONE EVE-NING...
GACHA (KACHAK)
GACHA
BAN (BANG)

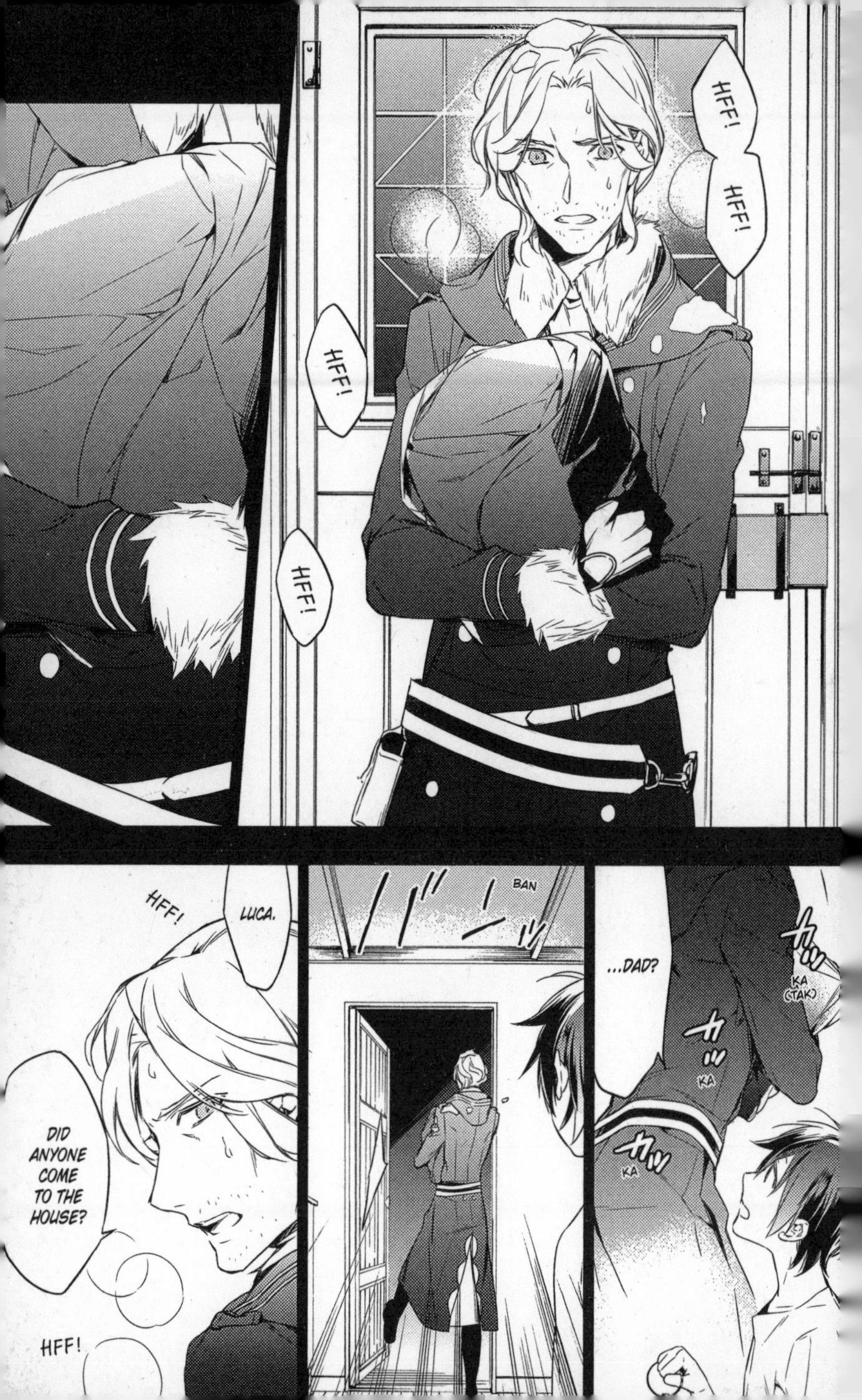
HFF!
HFF!
HFF!
HFF!
KA (TAK)
...DAD?
KA
KA
BAN
LUCA.
HFF!
DID ANYONE COME TO THE HOUSE?
HFF!

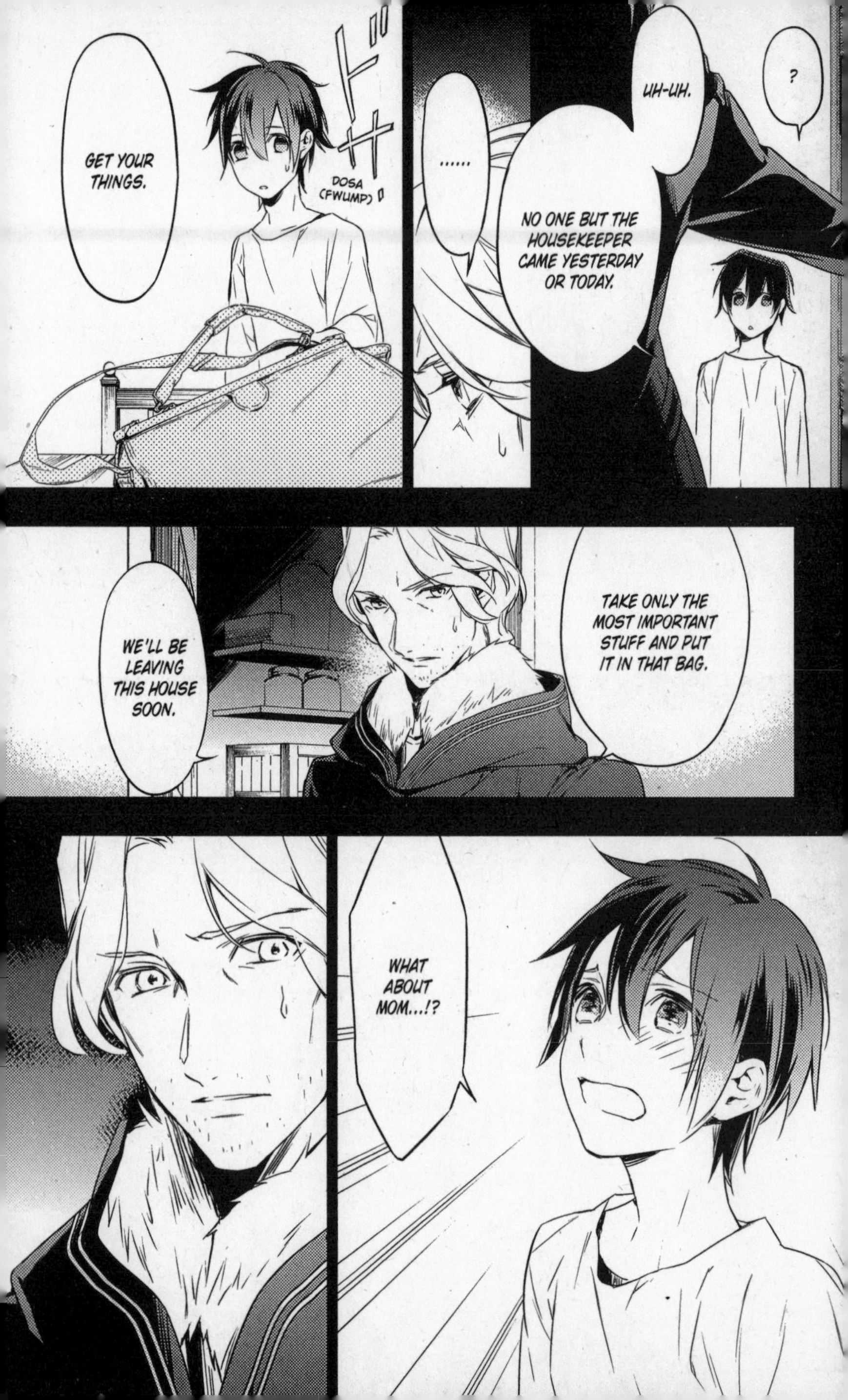
?
UH-UH.
NO ONE BUT THE HOUSEKEEPER CAME YESTERDAY OR TODAY.
......
ドサ
DOSA (FWUMP)
GET YOUR THINGS.
TAKE ONLY THE MOST IMPORTANT STUFF AND PUT IT IN THAT BAG.
WE'LL BE LEAVING THIS HOUSE SOON.
WHAT ABOUT MOM...!?

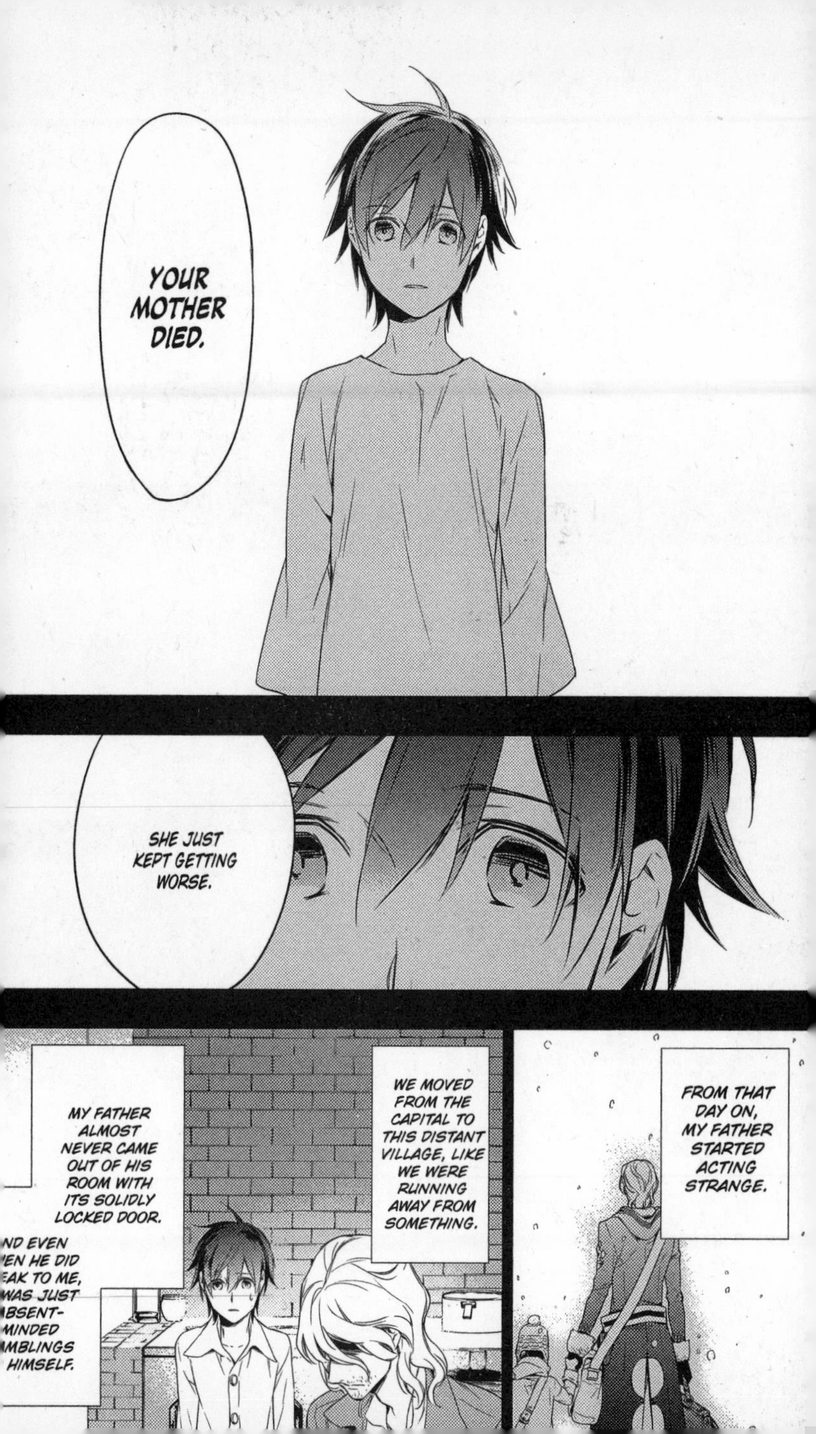
YOUR MOTHER DIED.
SHE JUST KEPT GETTING WORSE.
FROM THAT DAY ON, MY FATHER STARTED ACTING STRANGE.
WE MOVED FROM THE CAPITAL TO THIS DISTANT VILLAGE, LIKE WE WERE RUNNING AWAY FROM SOMETHING.
MY FATHER ALMOST NEVER CAME OUT OF HIS ROOM WITH ITS SOLIDLY LOCKED DOOR.
ND EVEN EN HE DID EAK TO ME, WAS JUST BSENT-MINDED MBLINGS HIMSELF.

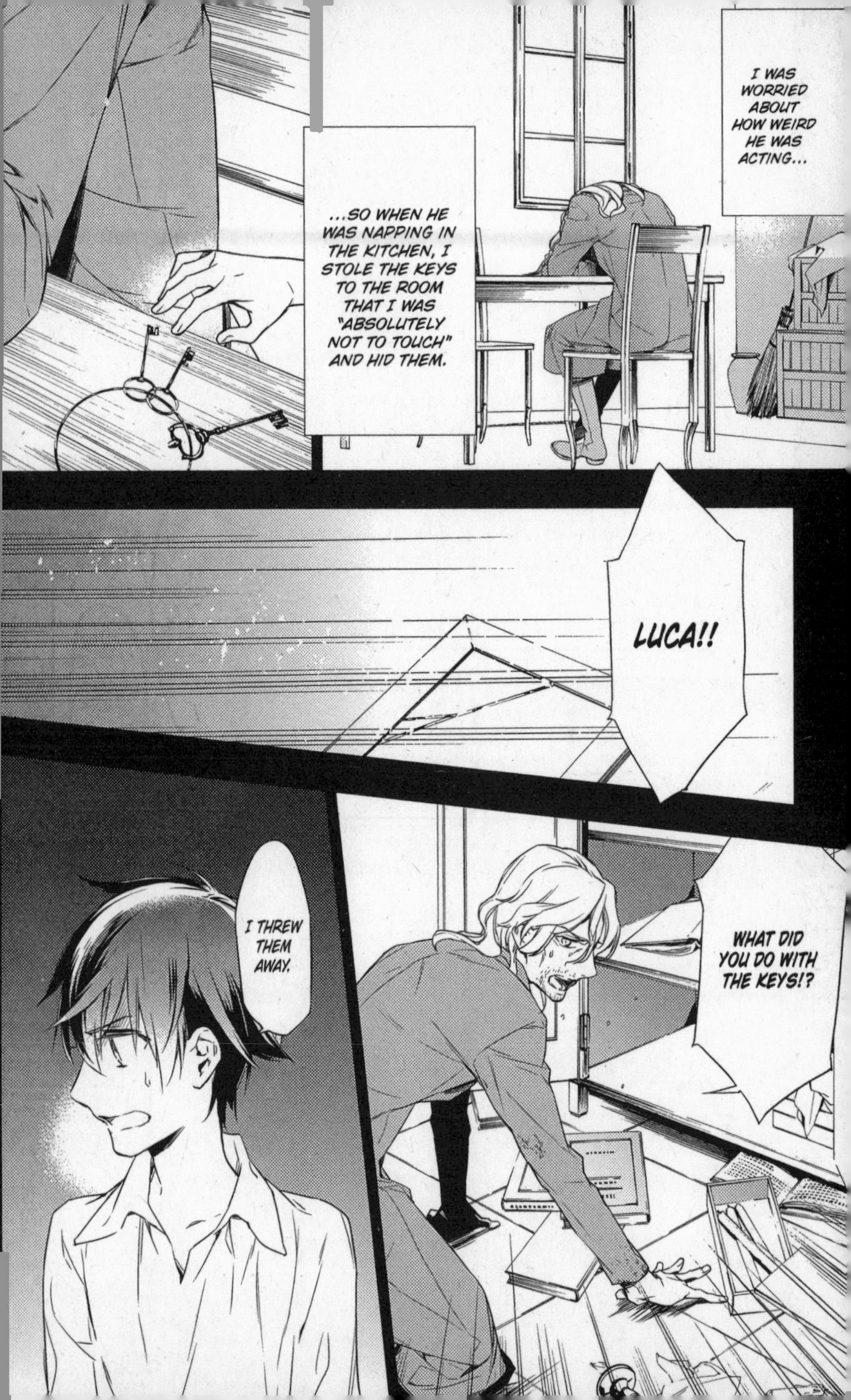
I WAS WORRIED ABOUT HOW WEIRD HE WAS ACTING...
...SO WHEN HE WAS NAPPING IN THE KITCHEN, I STOLE THE KEYS TO THE ROOM THAT I WAS "ABSOLUTELY NOT TO TOUCH" AND HID THEM.
LUCA!!
WHAT DID YOU DO WITH THE KEYS!?
I THREW THEM AWAY.

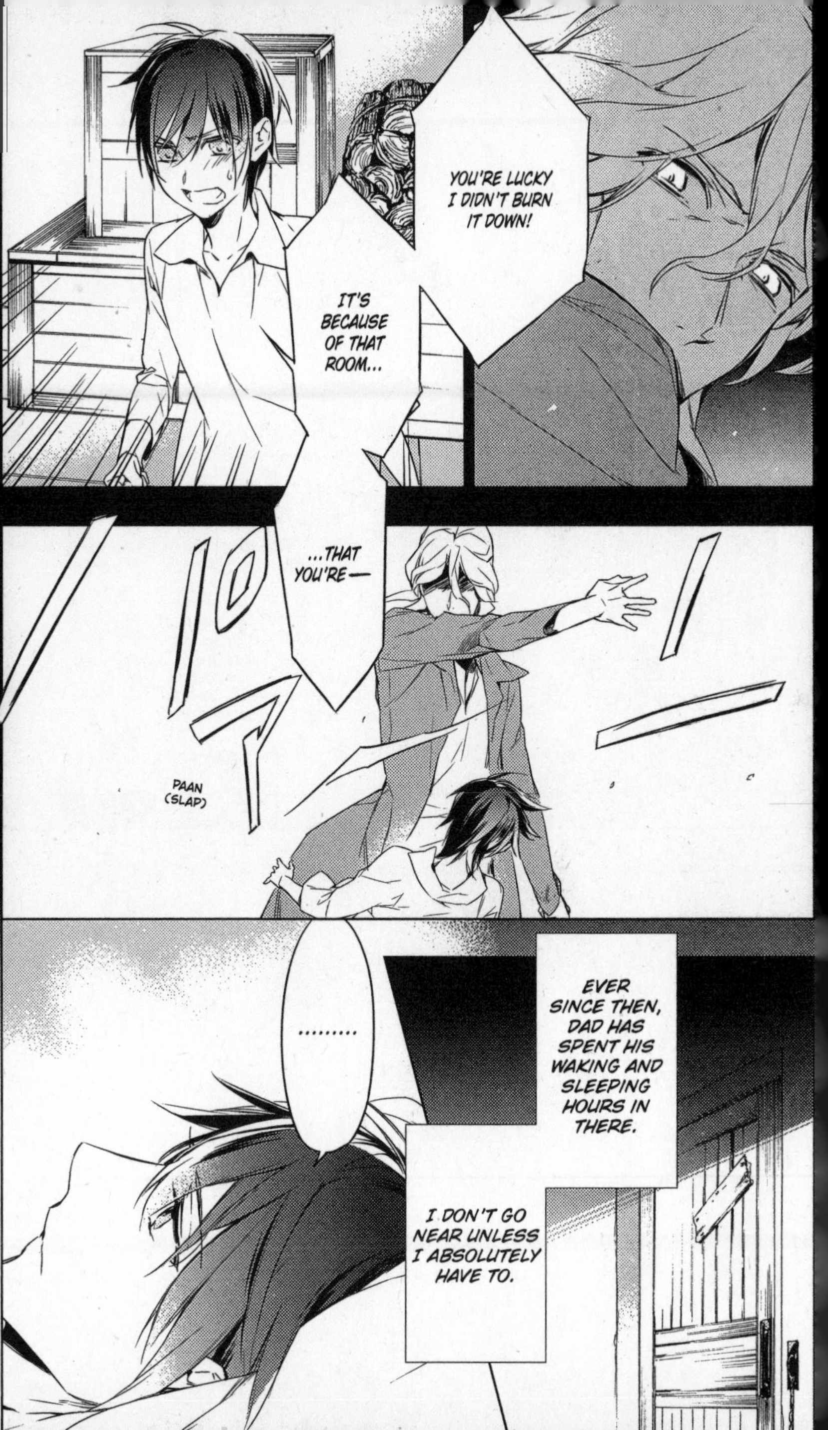
YOU'RE LUCKY I DIDN'T BURN IT DOWN!
IT'S BECAUSE OF THAT ROOM...
...THAT YOU'RE—
PAAN (SLAP)
EVER SINCE THEN, DAD HAS SPENT HIS WAKING AND SLEEPING HOURS IN THERE.
....
I DON'T GO NEAR UNLESS I ABSOLUTELY HAVE TO.

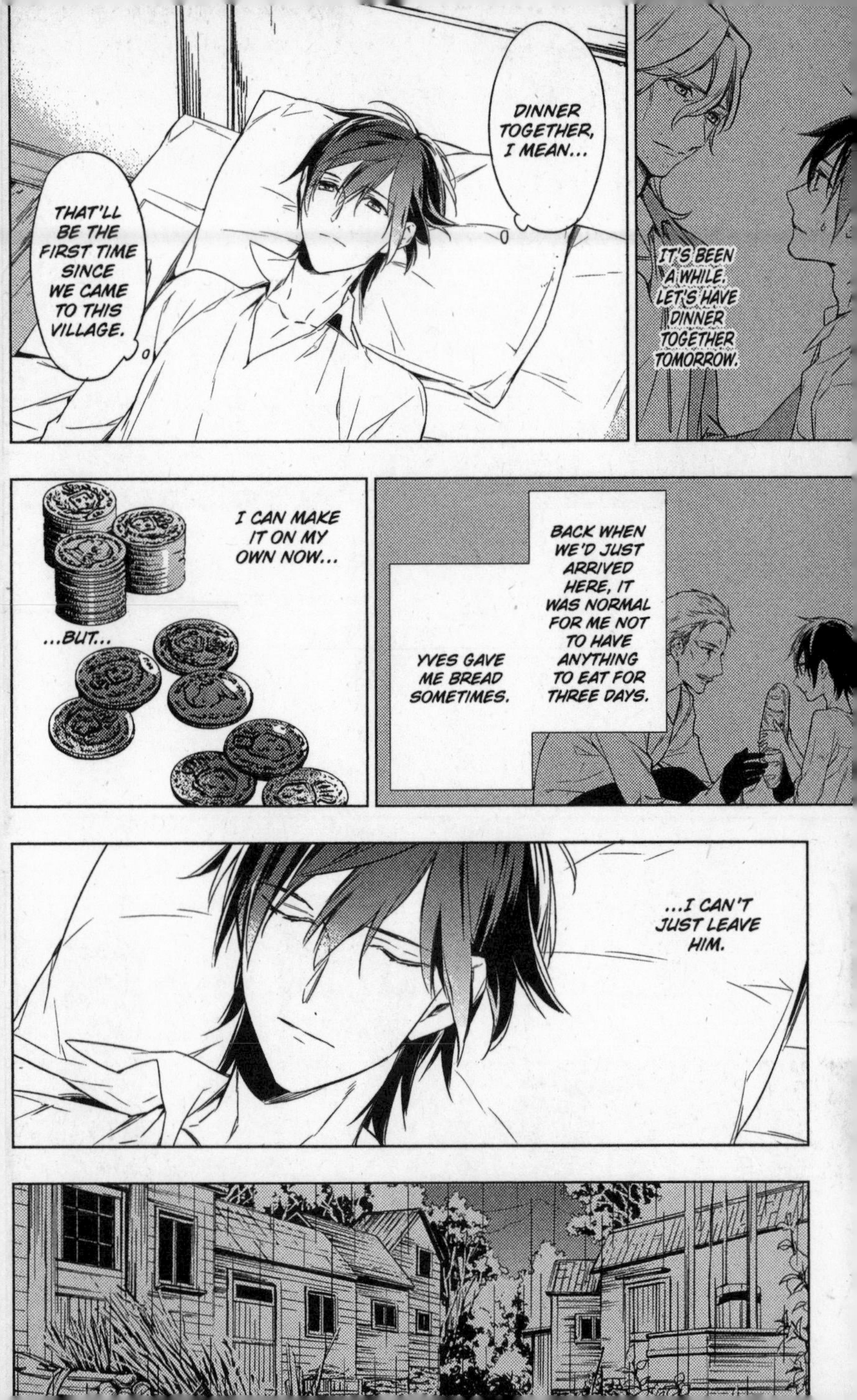
IT'S BEEN A WHILE. LET'S HAVE DINNER TOGETHER TOMORROW.
THAT'LL BE THE FIRST TIME SINCE WE CAME TO THIS VILLAGE.
DINNER TOGETHER, I MEAN...
BACK WHEN WE'D JUST ARRIVED HERE, IT WAS NORMAL FOR ME NOT TO HAVE ANYTHING TO EAT FOR THREE DAYS.
YVES GAVE ME BREAD SOMETIMES.
I CAN MAKE IT ON MY OWN NOW...
...BUT...
...I CAN'T JUST LEAVE HIM.

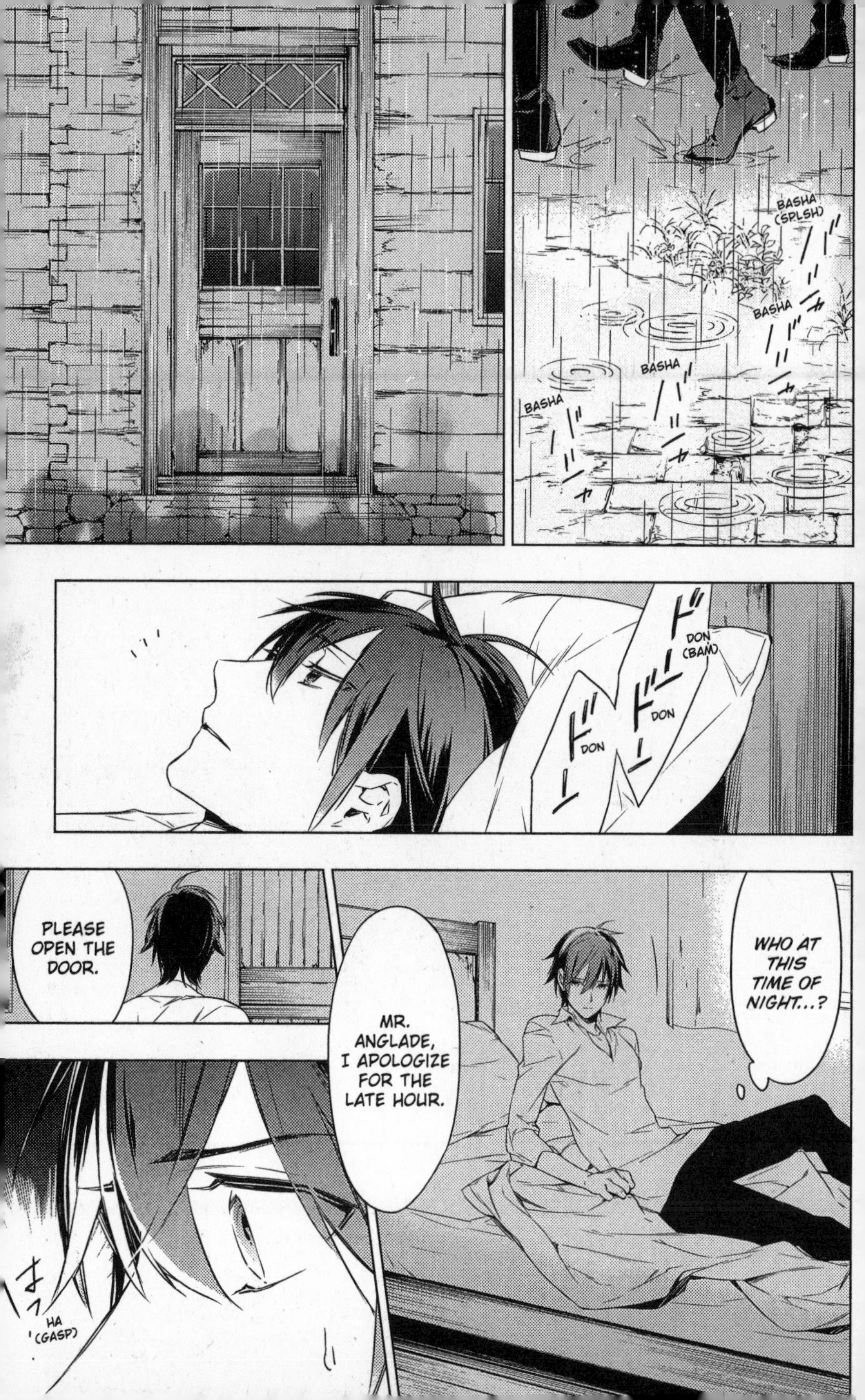
BASHA (SPLSH)
BASHA
BASHA
BASHA
DON (BAM)
DON
DON
WHO AT THIS TIME OF NIGHT...?
MR. ANGLADE, I APOLOGIZE FOR THE LATE HOUR.
PLEASE OPEN THE DOOR.
HA (GASP)

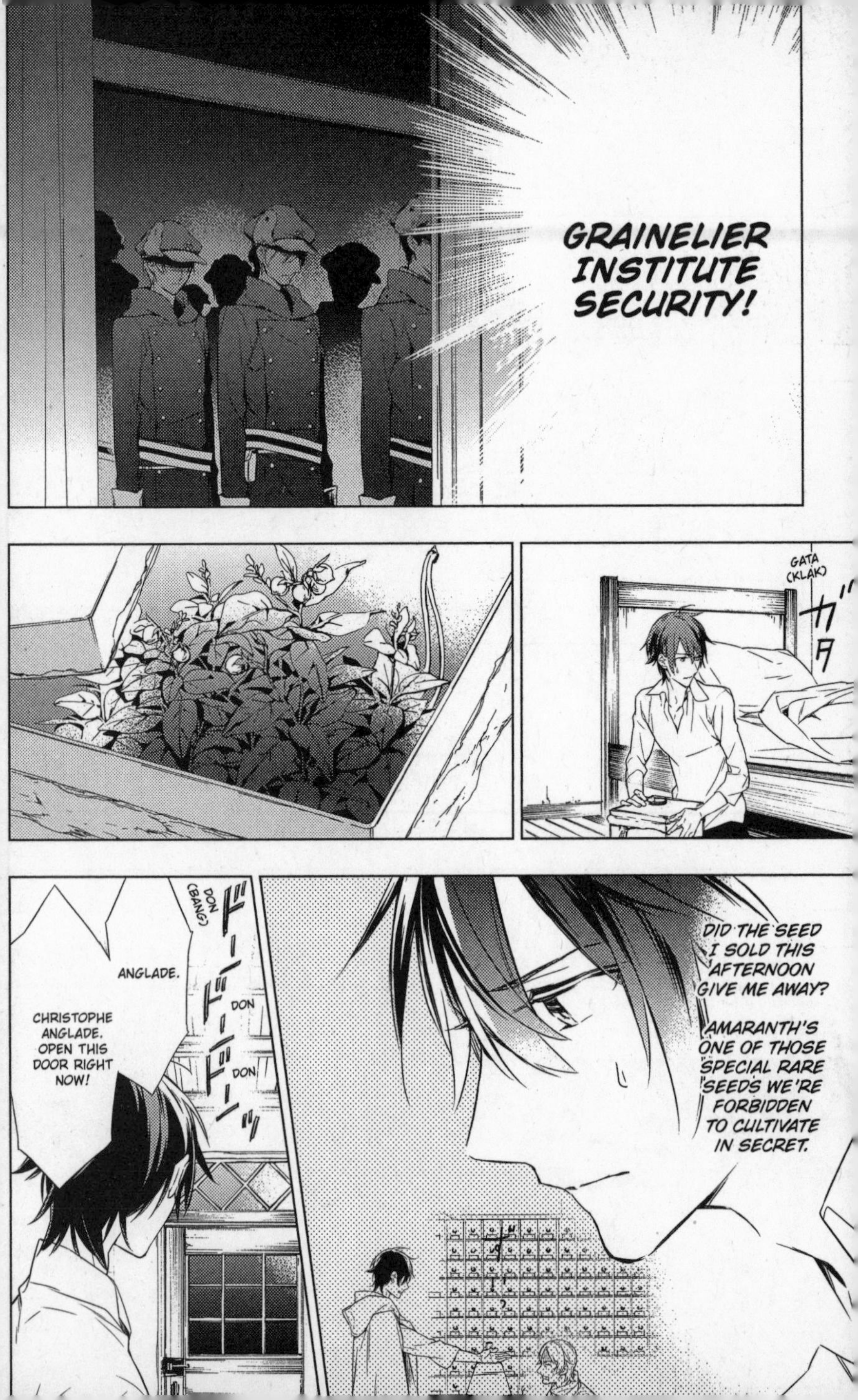
GRAINELIER INSTITUTE SECURITY!
GATA (KLAK)
DID THE SEED I SOLD THIS AFTERNOON GIVE ME AWAY?
AMARANTH'S ONE OF THOSE SPECIAL RARE SEEDS WE'RE FORBIDDEN TO CULTIVATE IN SECRET.
DON (BANG)
ANGLADE.
CHRISTOPHE ANGLADE. OPEN THIS DOOR RIGHT NOW!
DON
DON

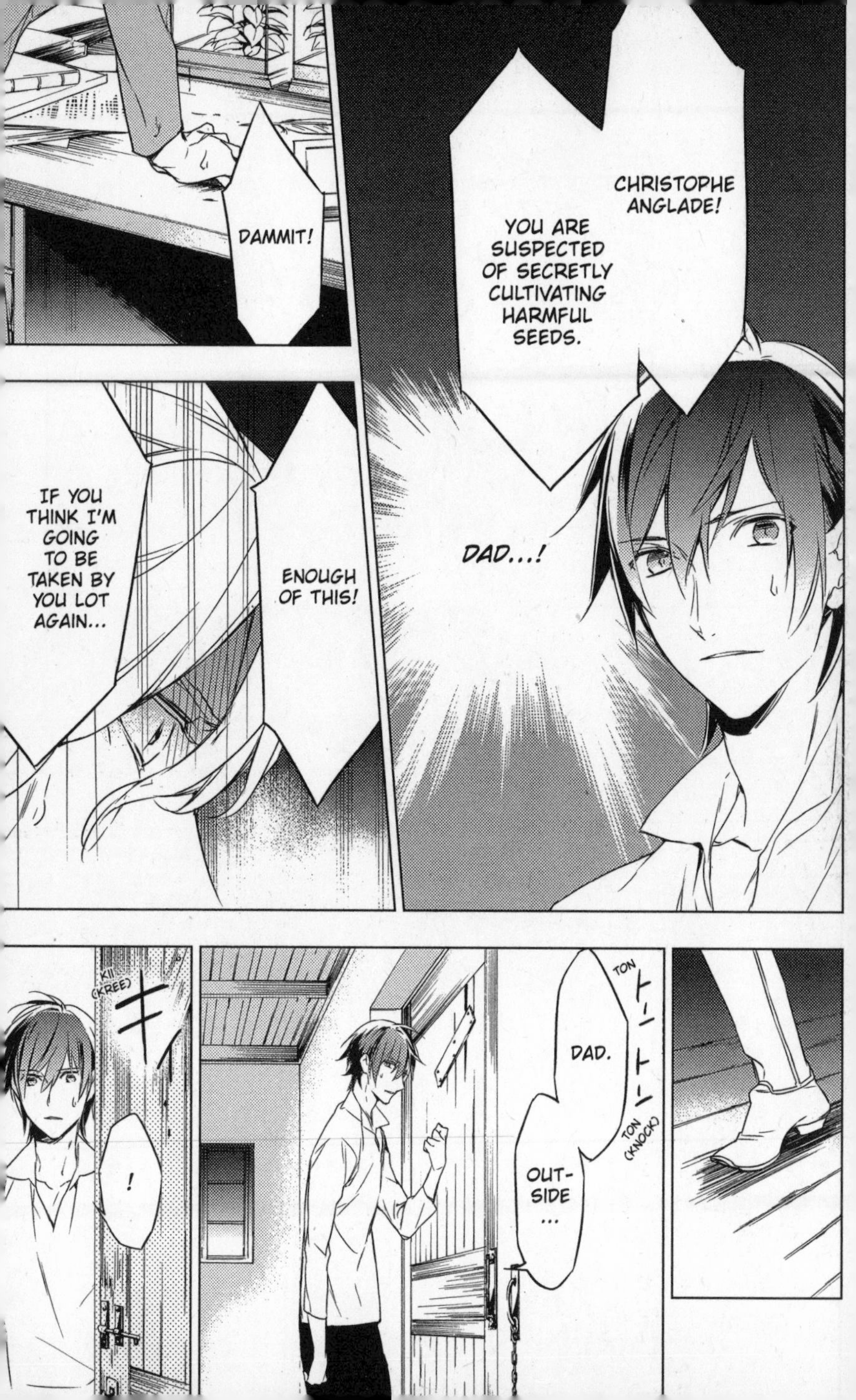
CHRISTOPHE ANGLADE!
YOU ARE SUSPECTED OF SECRETLY CULTIVATING HARMFUL SEEDS.
DAD...!
DAMMIT!
ENOUGH OF THIS!
IF YOU THINK I'M GOING TO BE TAKEN BY YOU LOT AGAIN...
TON
DAD.
TON (KNOCK)
OUT-SIDE
...
KII (KREE)
!

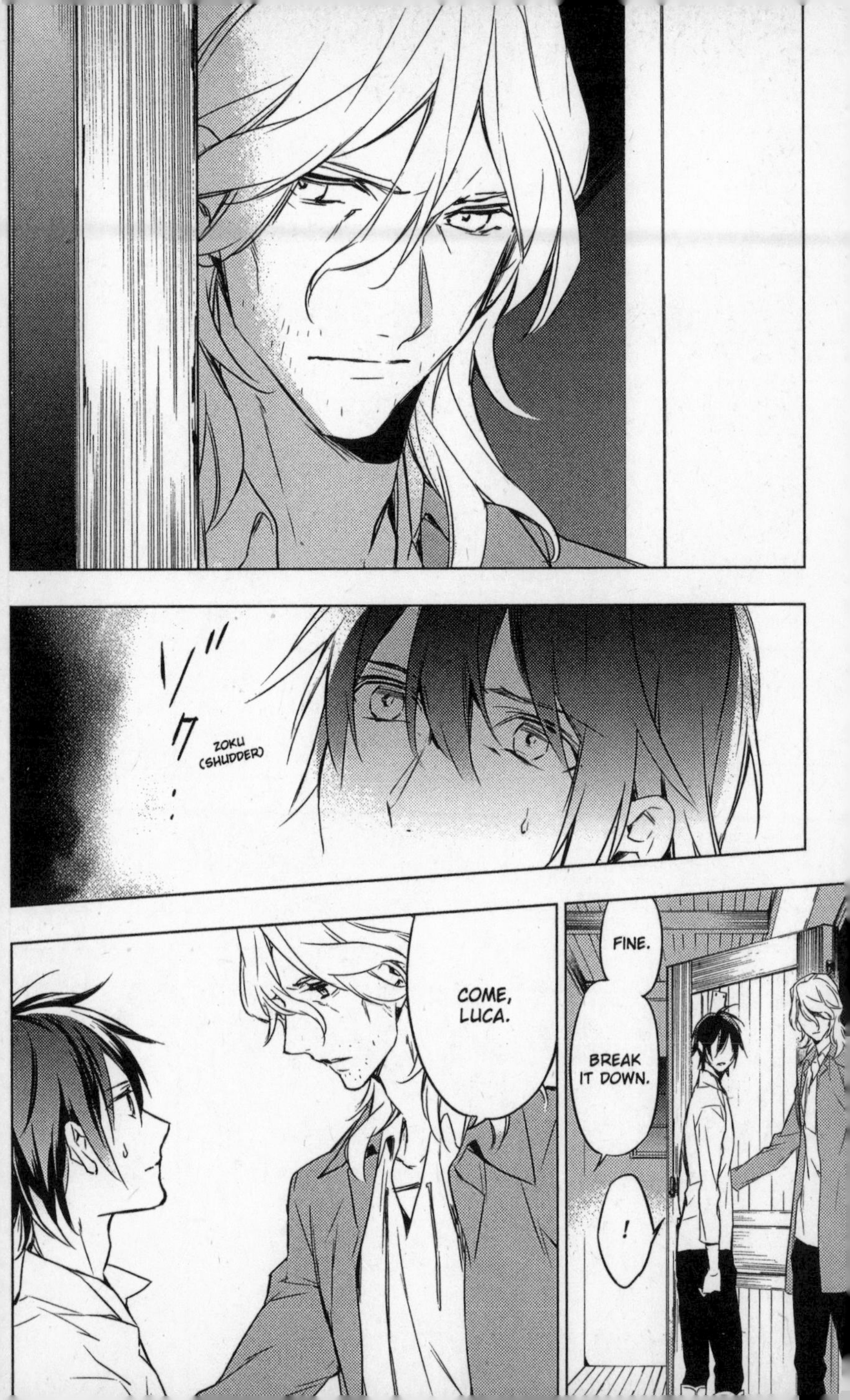
ゾク
ZOKU (SHUDDER)
FINE.
BREAK IT DOWN.
!
COME, LUCA.

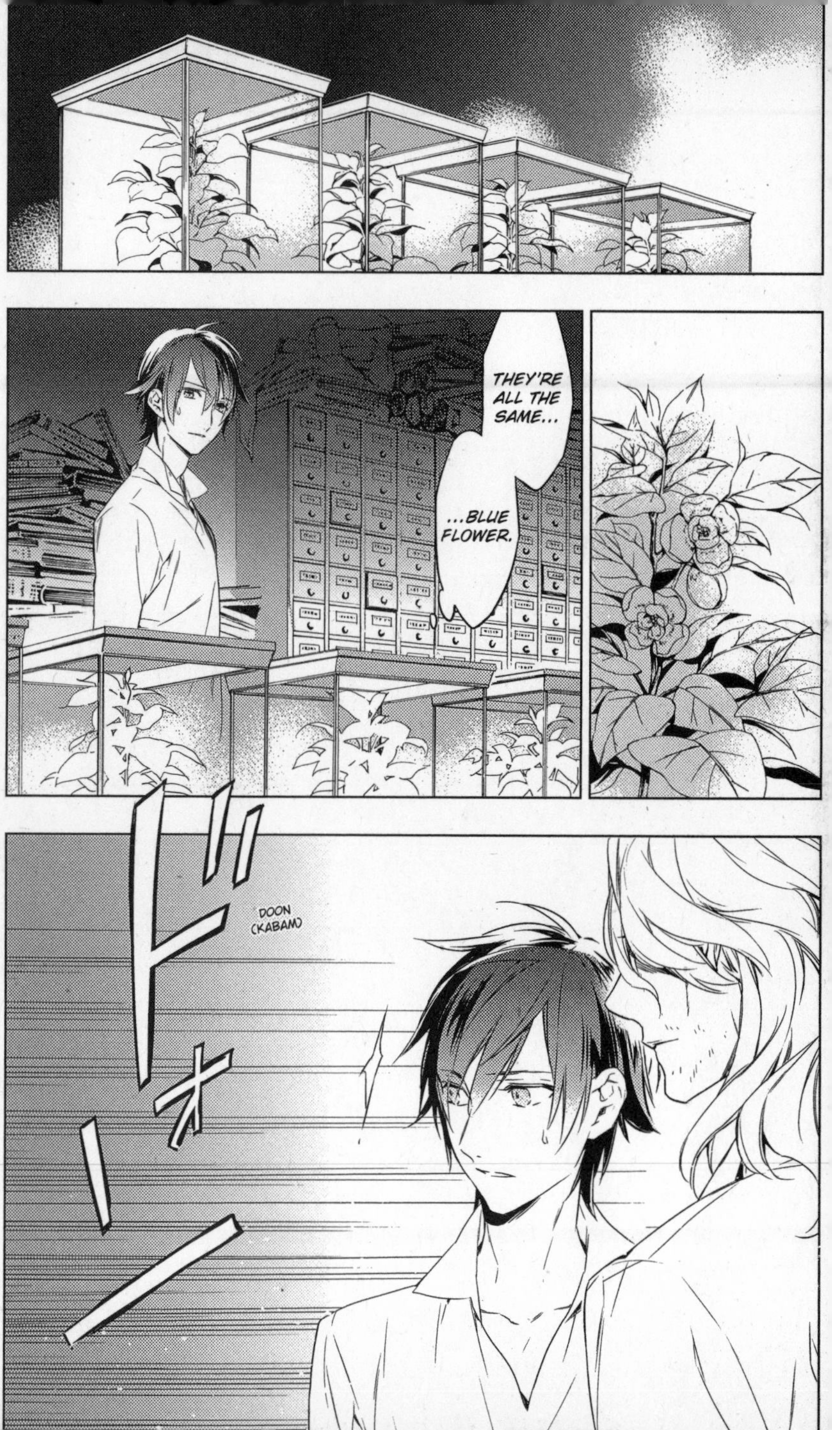
THEY'RE ALL THE SAME...
...BLUE FLOWER.
DOON (KABAM)

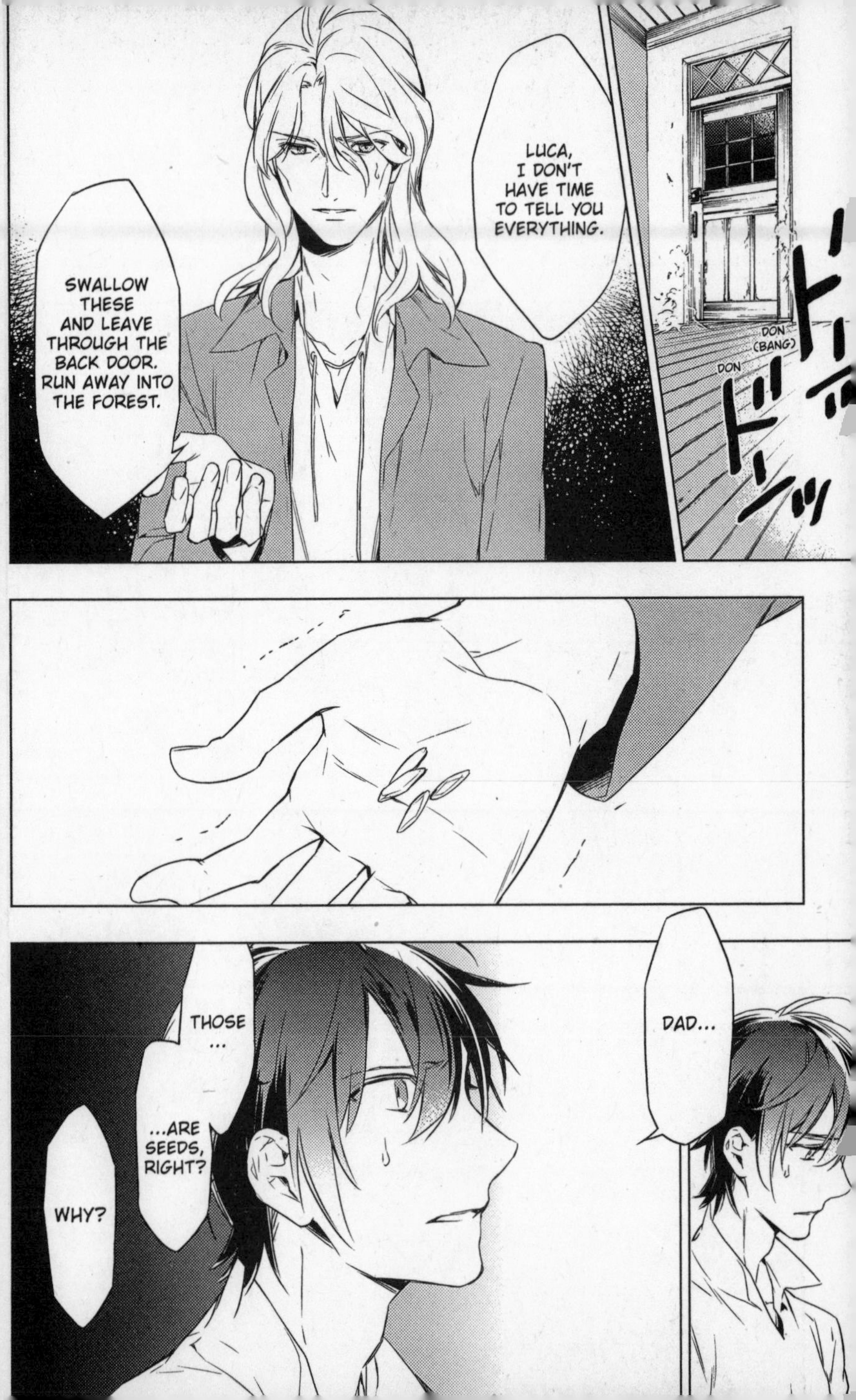
DON
(BANG)
DON
LUCA, I DON'T HAVE TIME TO TELL YOU EVERYTHING.
SWALLOW THESE AND LEAVE THROUGH THE BACK DOOR. RUN AWAY INTO THE FOREST.
DAD...
THOSE ...
...ARE SEEDS, RIGHT?
WHY?

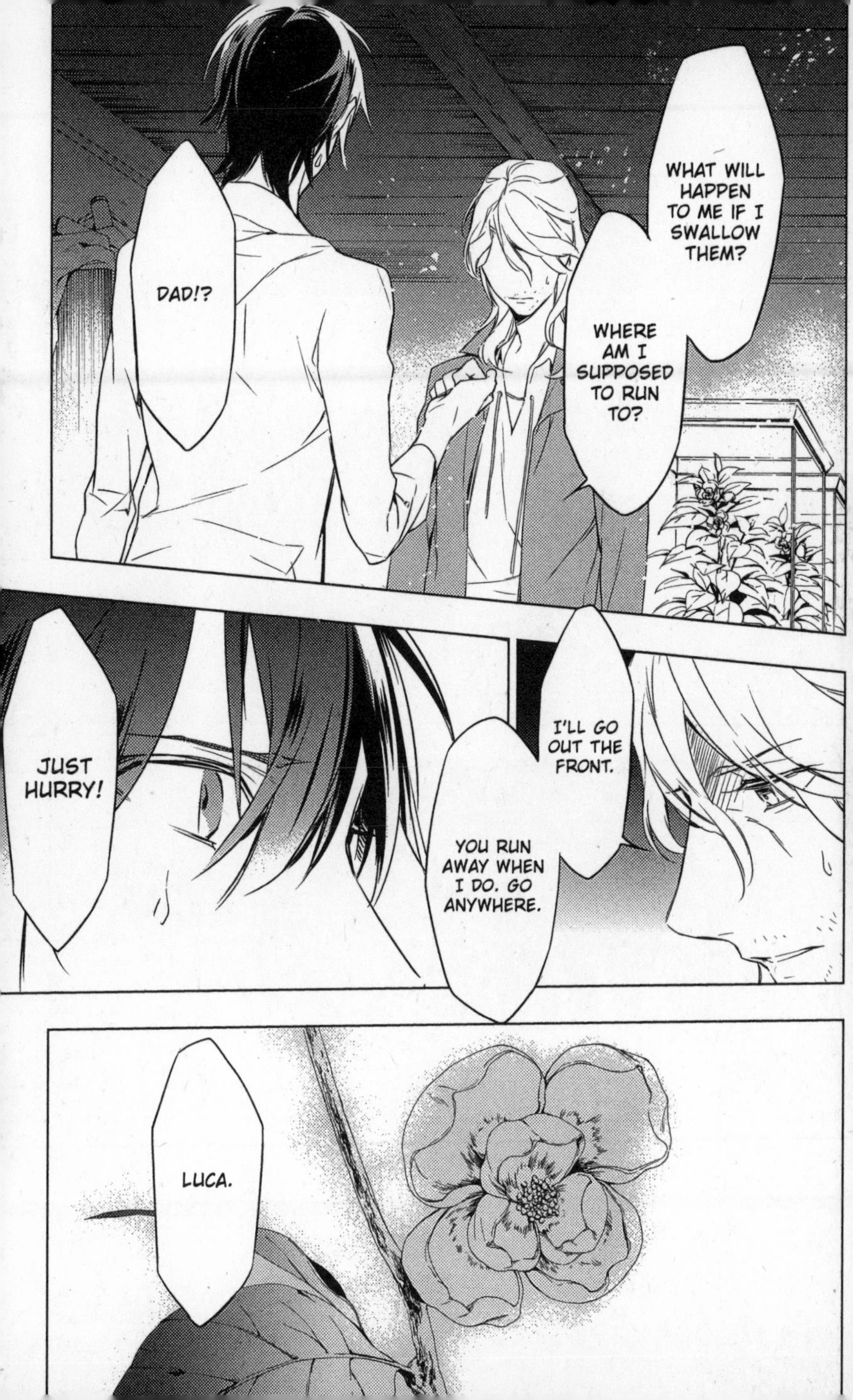
WHAT WILL HAPPEN TO ME IF I SWALLOW THEM?
WHERE AM I SUPPOSED TO RUN TO?
DAD!?
I'LL GO OUT THE FRONT.
YOU RUN AWAY WHEN I DO. GO ANYWHERE.
JUST HURRY!
LUCA.

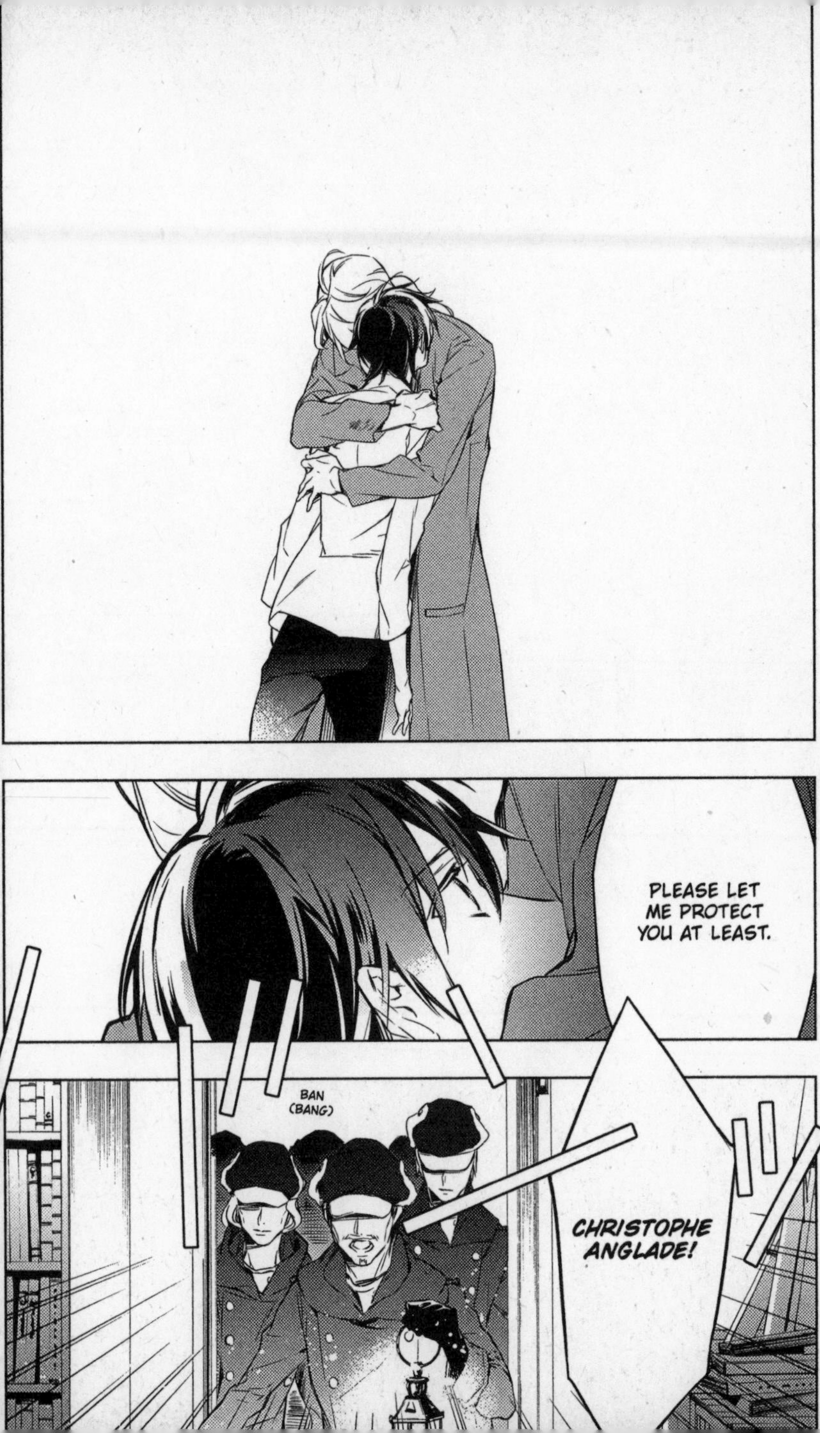
PLEASE LET ME PROTECT YOU AT LEAST.
BAN (BANG)
CHRISTOPHE ANGLADE!

ZAAAA
(PSSSH)

WHY DO I HAVE TO RUN AWAY?

HFF!

HFF!

HFF!

BASHA (SPLSH)

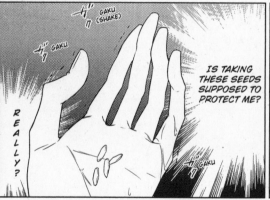

GAKU (SHAKE)

GAKU

IS TAKING THESE SEEDS SUPPOSED TO PROTECT ME?

REALLY?

GAKU

WHY?

HFF!

HFF!

...IS THIS THE LONE HOPE MY FATHER HAS LEFT ME?

IN THE END...

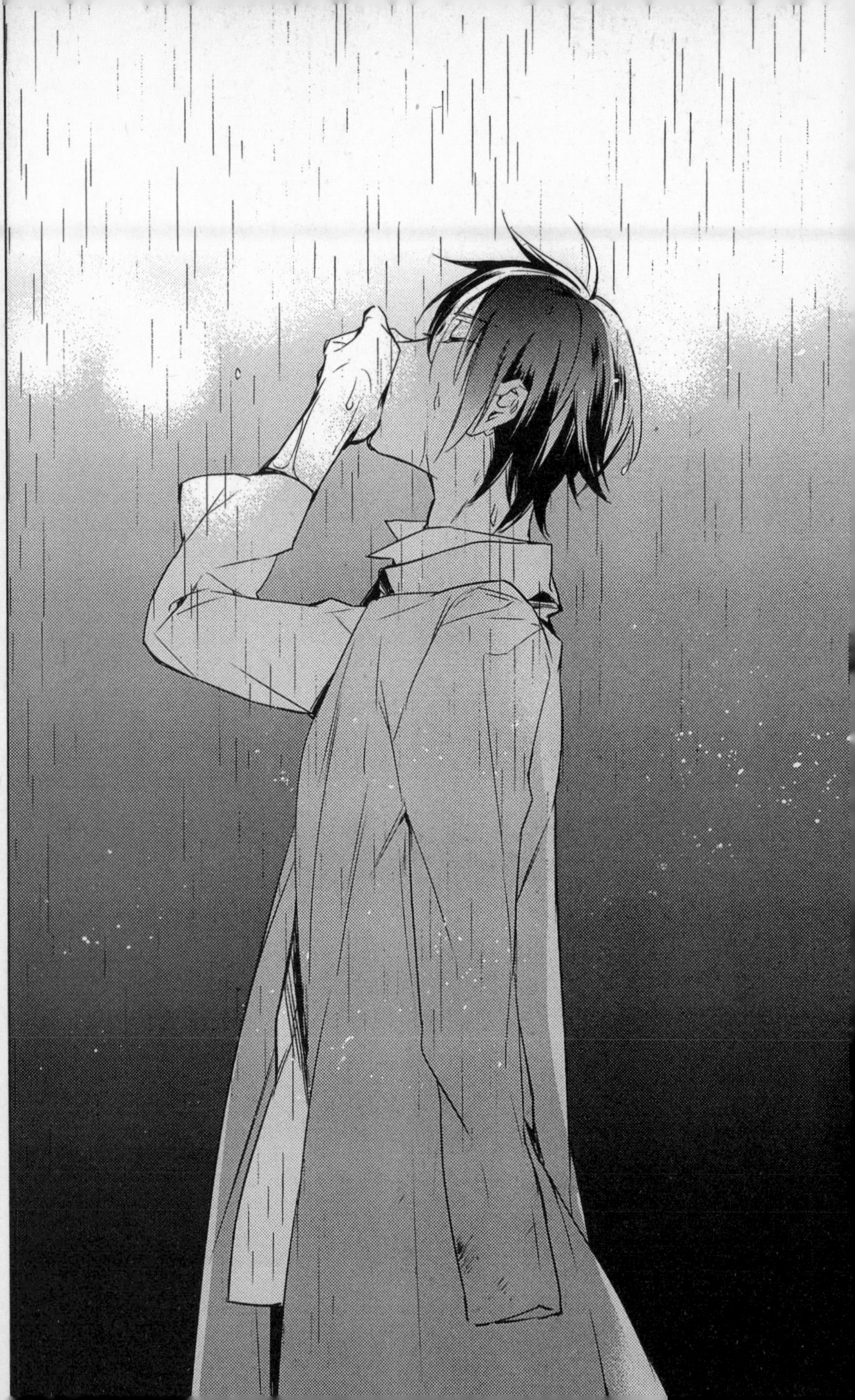

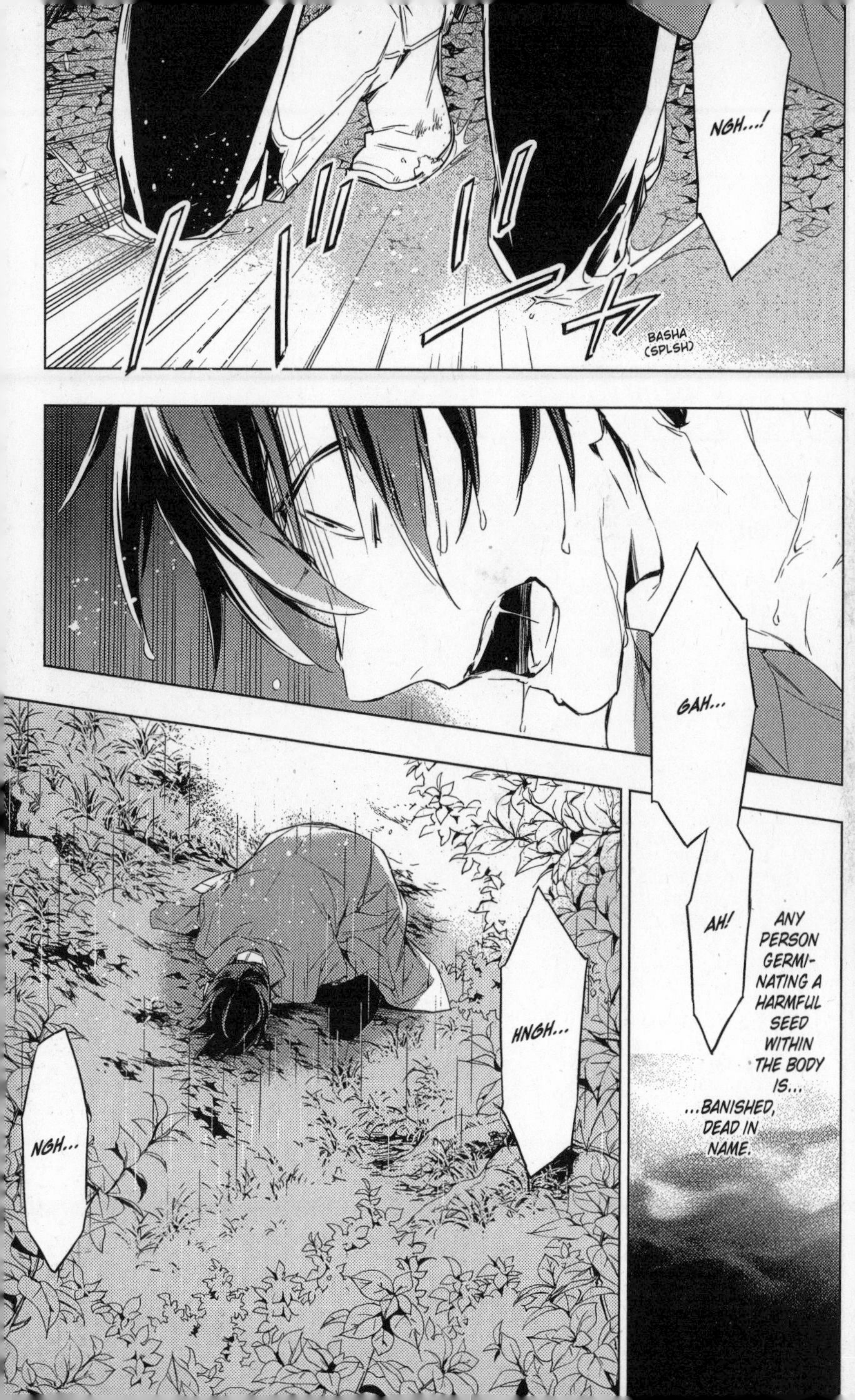
NGH...!
BASHA (SPLSH)
GAH...
AH!
ANY PERSON GERMINATING A HARMFUL SEED WITHIN THE BODY IS...
...BANISHED, DEAD IN NAME.
HNGH...
NGH...

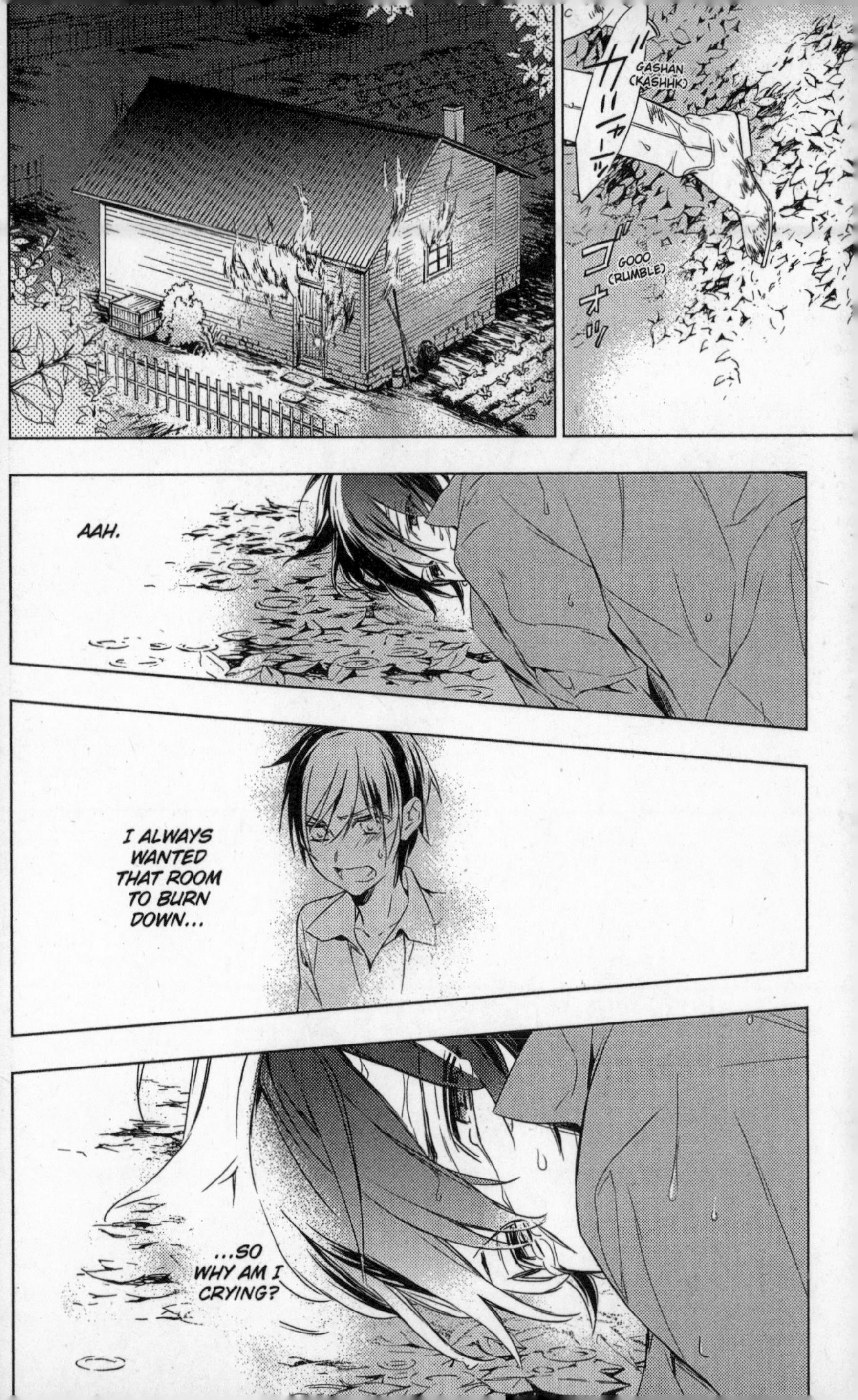
GASHAN (KASHHK)
GOOO (RUMBLE)
AAH.
I ALWAYS WANTED THAT ROOM TO BURN DOWN...
...SO WHY AM I CRYING?

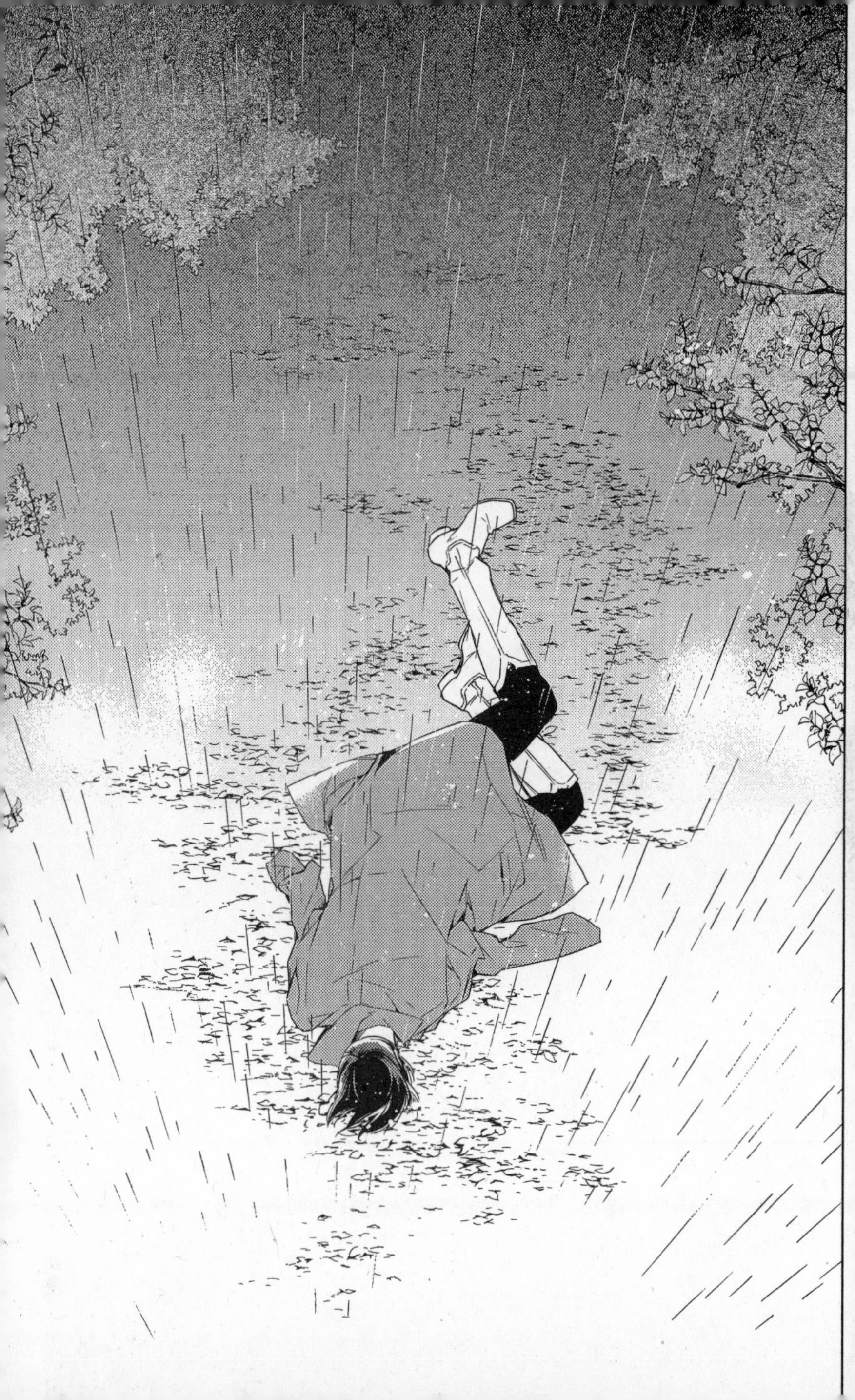

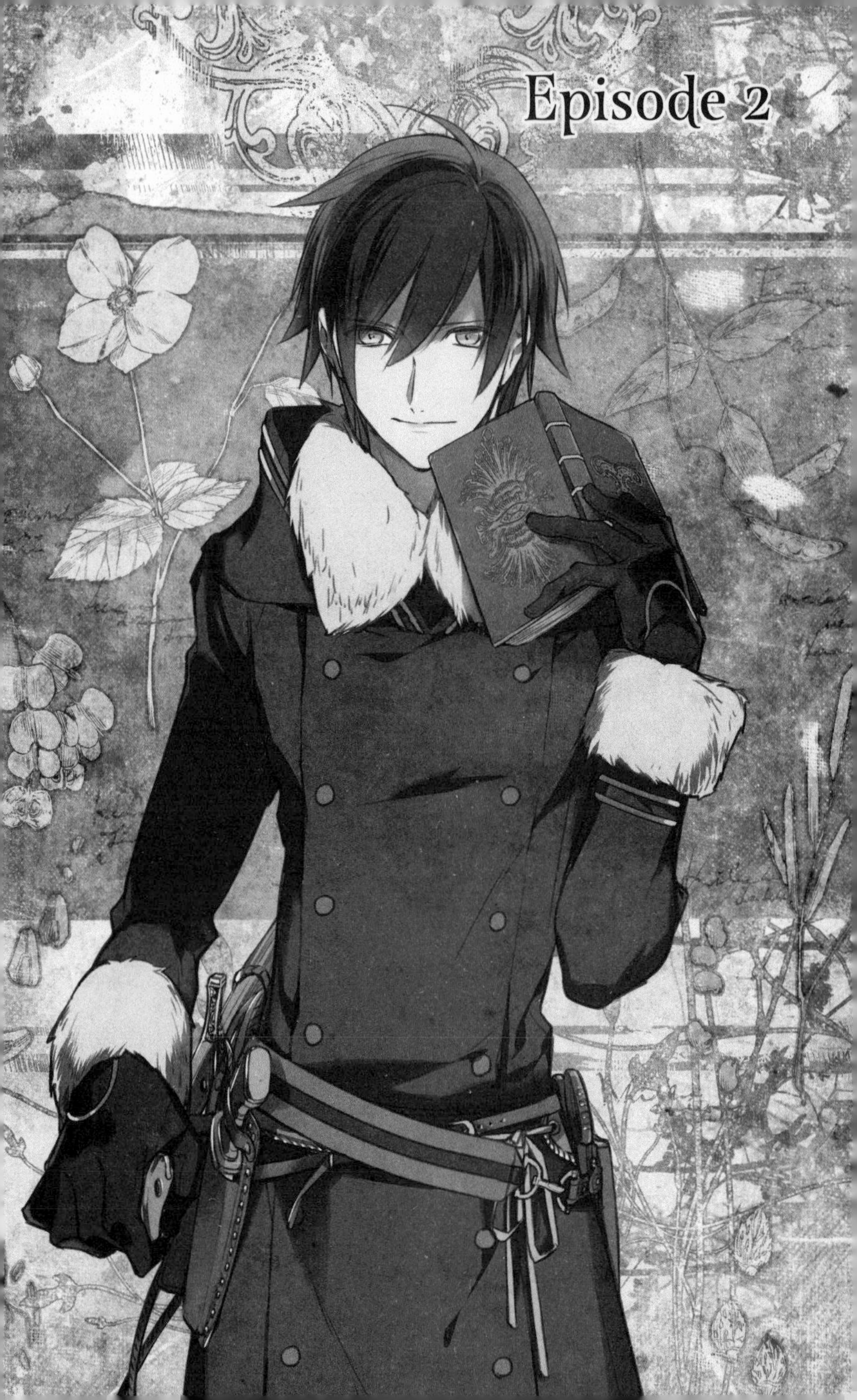
Episode 2

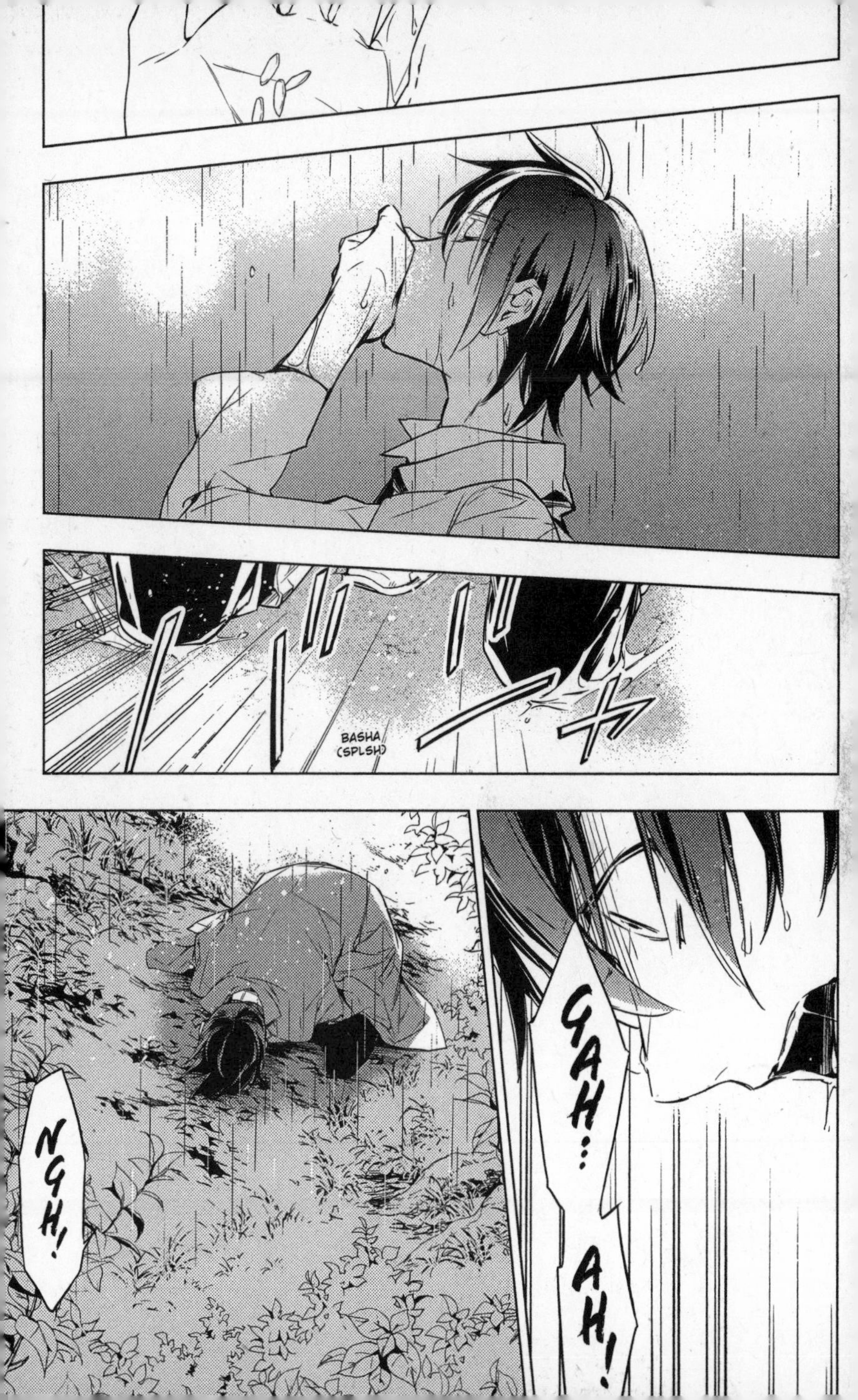
BASHA
(SPLSH)
GAH... AH!
NGH!

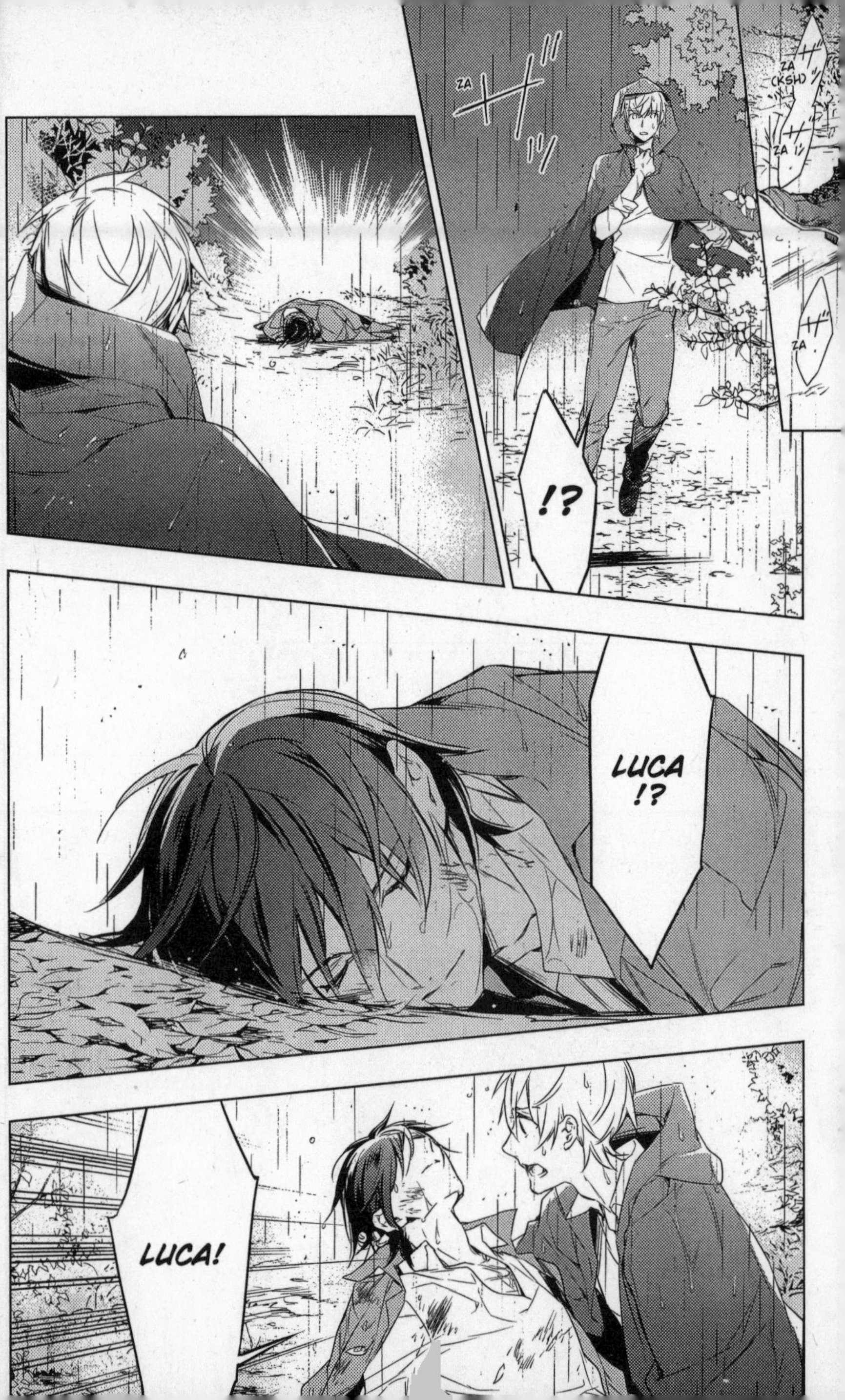
ZA (KSH)
ZA
ZA
ZA
!?
LUCA !?
LUCA!

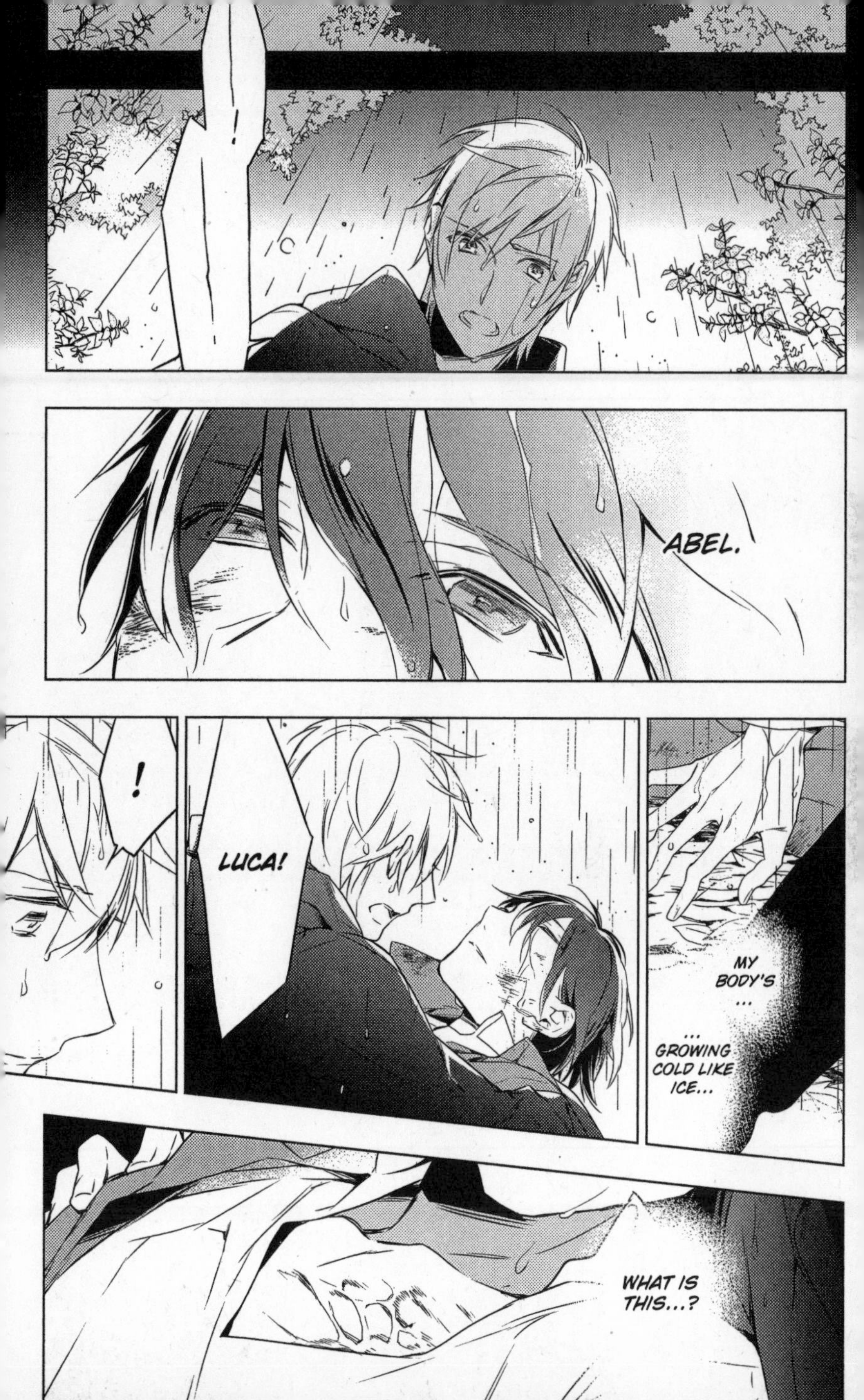
ABEL.
MY BODY'S ...
... GROWING COLD LIKE ICE...
LUCA!
!
WHAT IS THIS...?

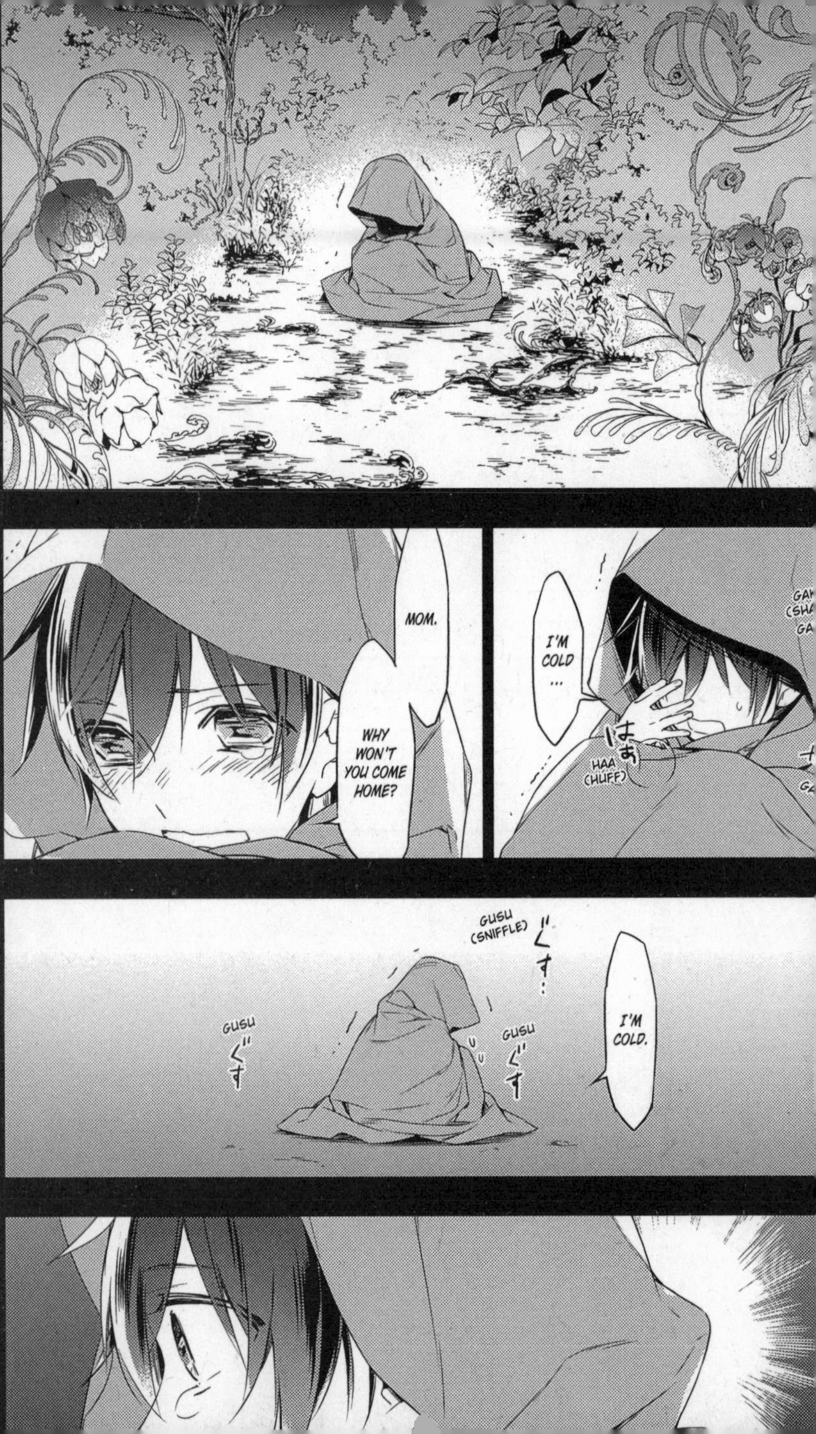
I'M COLD ...
はぁ
HAA (HUFF)
MOM.
WHY WON'T YOU COME HOME?
I'M COLD.
ぐす…
GUSU (SNIFFLE)
ぐす
GUSU
ぐす
GUSU

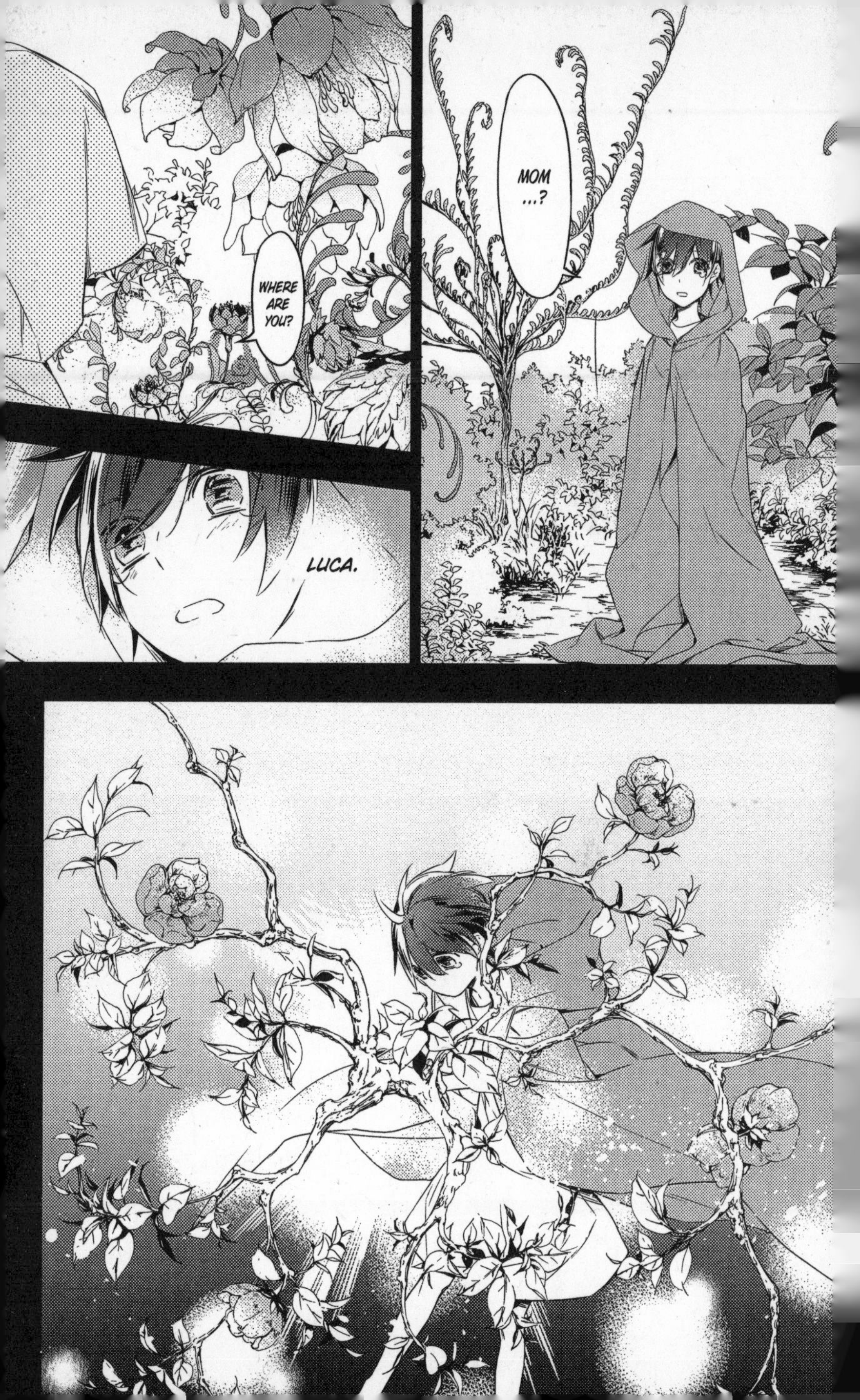
MOM ...?
WHERE ARE YOU?
LUCA.

WAS I...

...DREAMING OF
SOMETHING—?

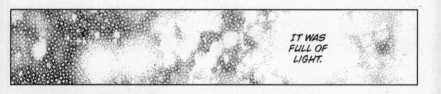

IT WAS
FULL OF
LIGHT.

AN
AUTOMATIC
WATERING
BOTTLE
FOR
PLANTS.

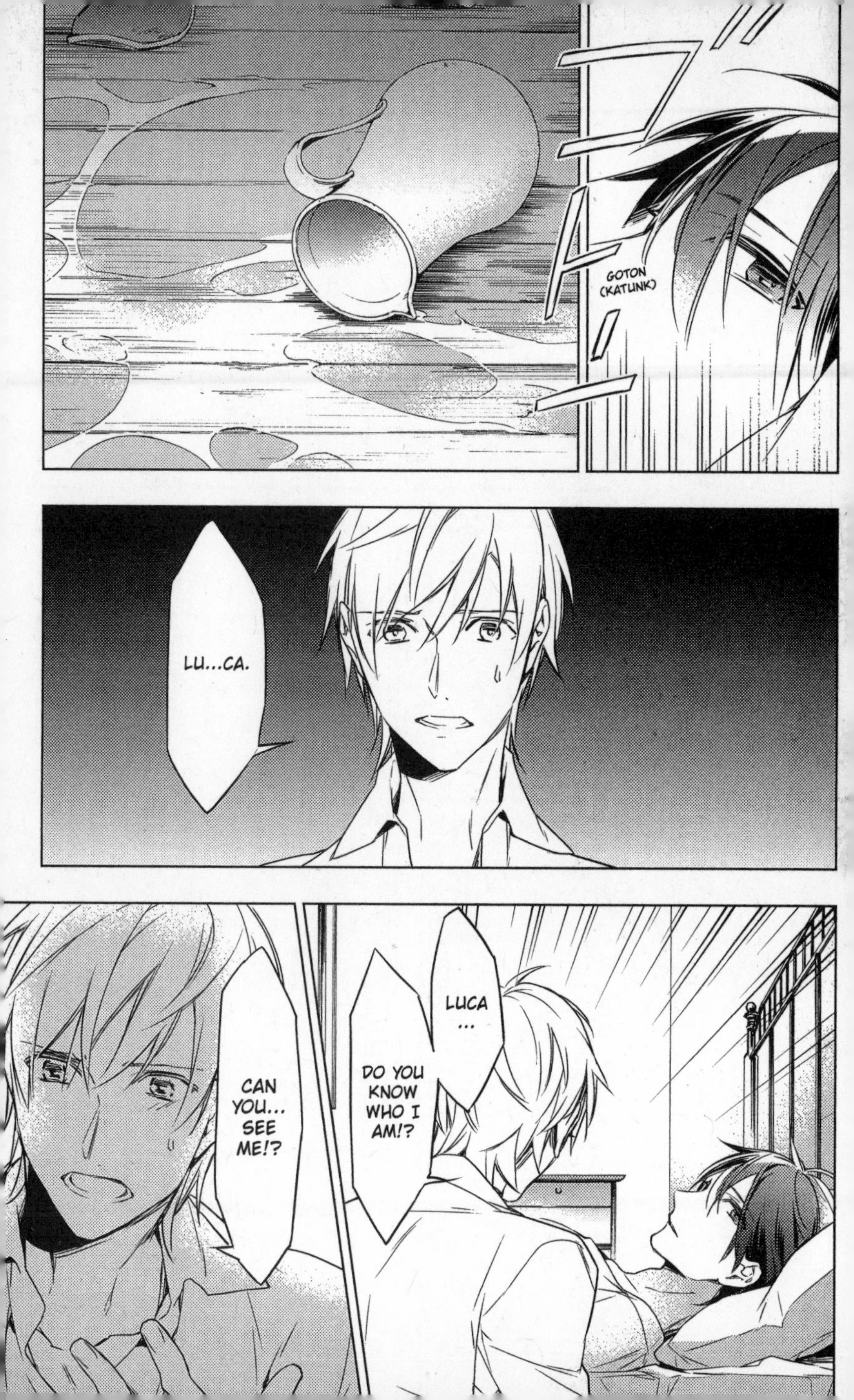

GOTON (KATUNK)
LU...CA.
LUCA
...
DO YOU KNOW WHO I AM!?
CAN YOU... SEE ME!?

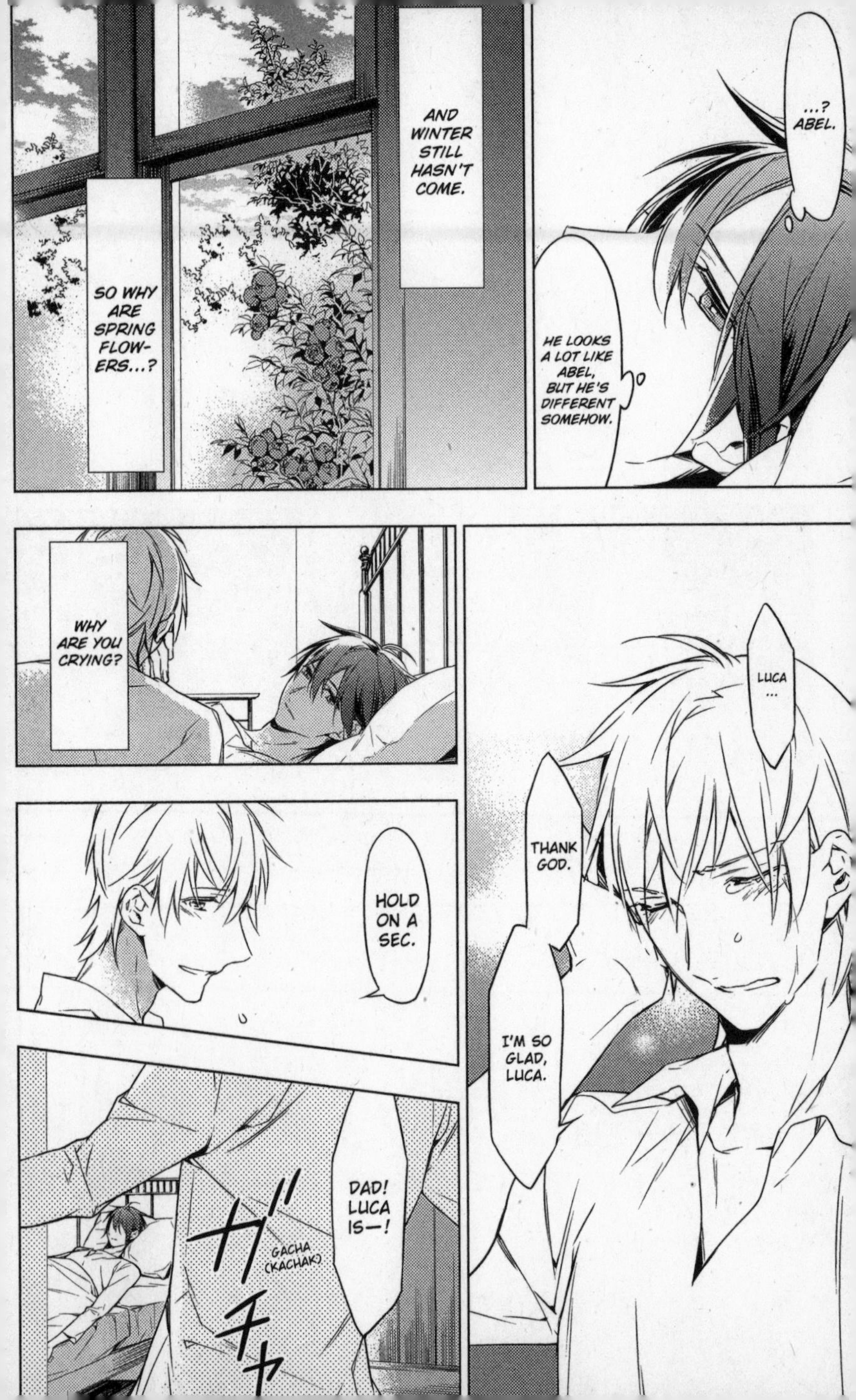
...? ABEL.
HE LOOKS A LOT LIKE ABEL, BUT HE'S DIFFERENT SOMEHOW.
AND WINTER STILL HASN'T COME.
SO WHY ARE SPRING FLOWERS...?
LUCA...
THANK GOD.
I'M SO GLAD, LUCA.
WHY ARE YOU CRYING?
HOLD ON A SEC.
DAD! LUCA IS—!
GACHA (KACHAK)

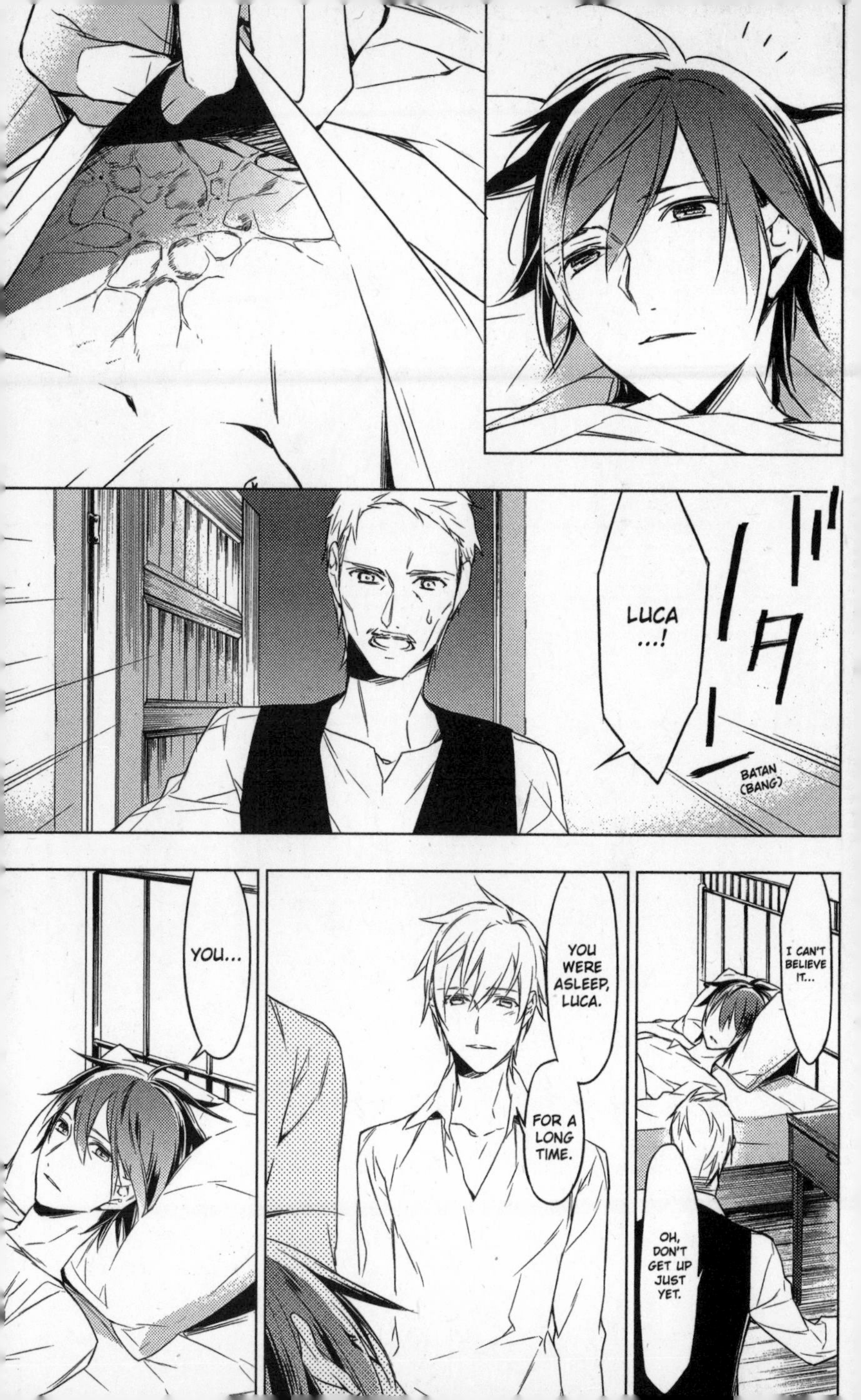
LUCA ...!
BATAN (BANG)
I CAN'T BELIEVE IT...
OH, DON'T GET UP JUST YET.
YOU WERE ASLEEP, LUCA.
FOR A LONG TIME.
YOU...

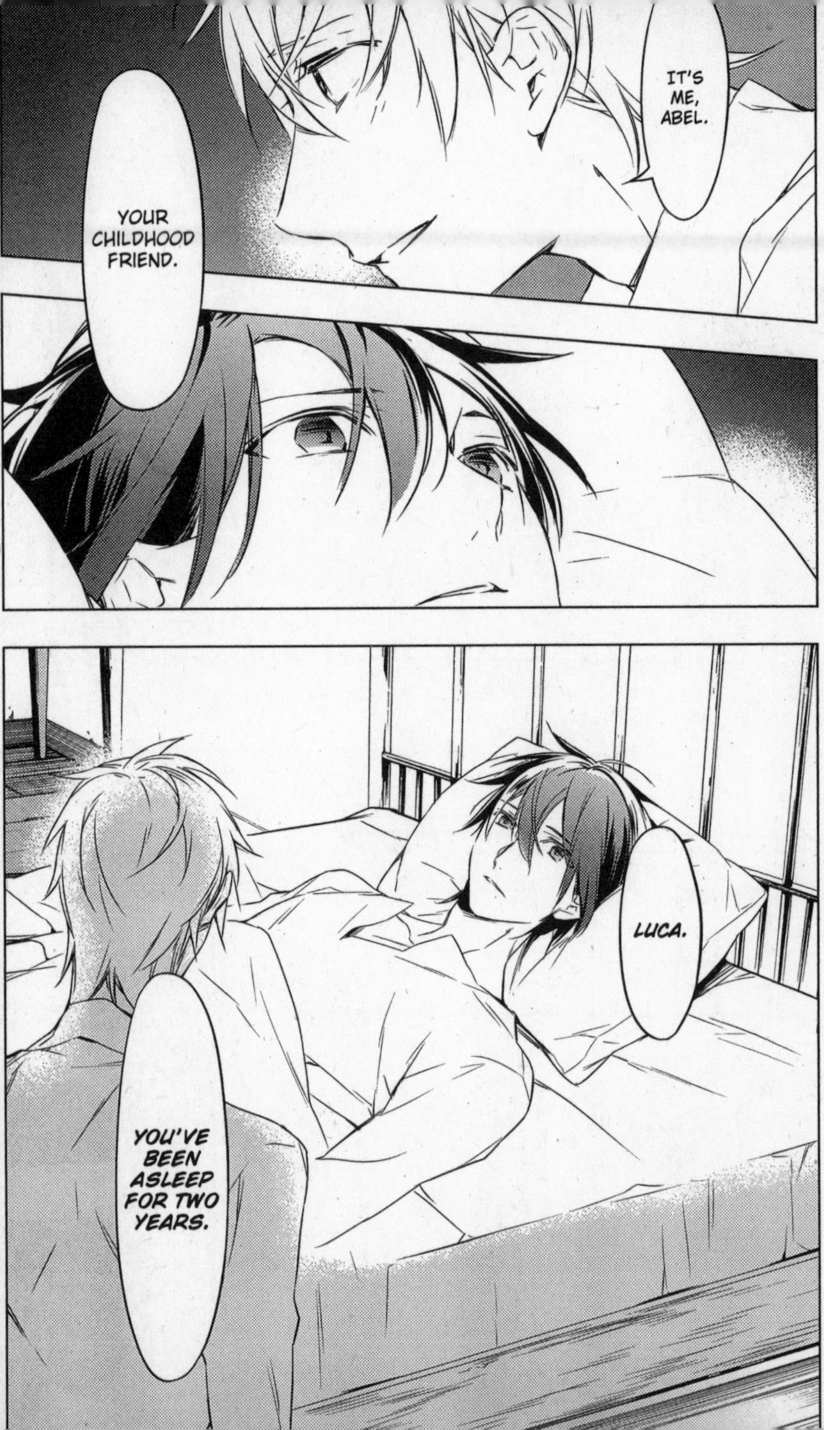
IT'S ME, ABEL.
YOUR CHILDHOOD FRIEND.
LUCA.
YOU'VE BEEN ASLEEP FOR TWO YEARS.

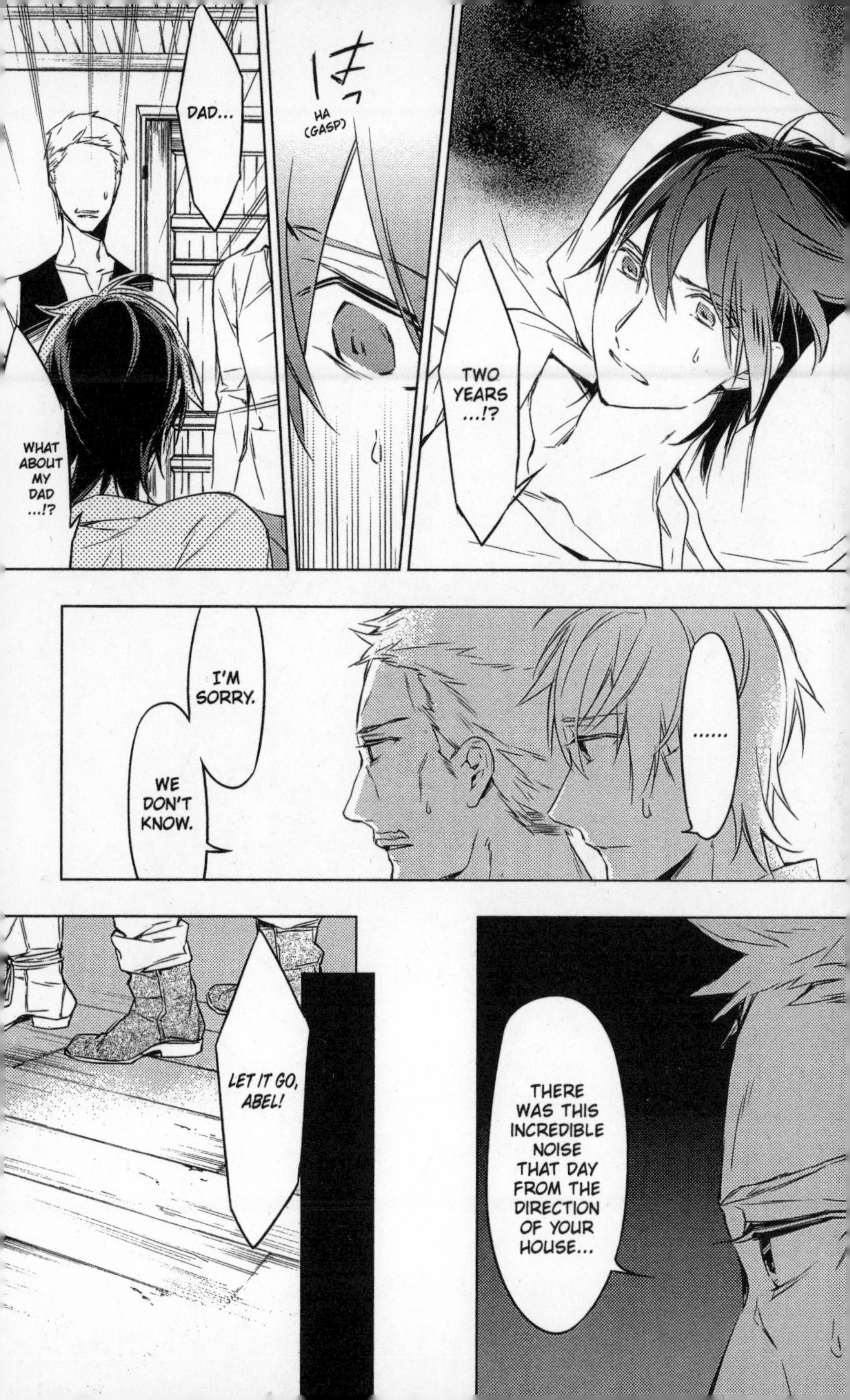
TWO YEARS ...!?
はっ
HA (GASP)
DAD...
WHAT ABOUT MY DAD ...!?
......
I'M SORRY.
WE DON'T KNOW.
THERE WAS THIS INCREDIBLE NOISE THAT DAY FROM THE DIRECTION OF YOUR HOUSE...
LET IT GO, ABEL!

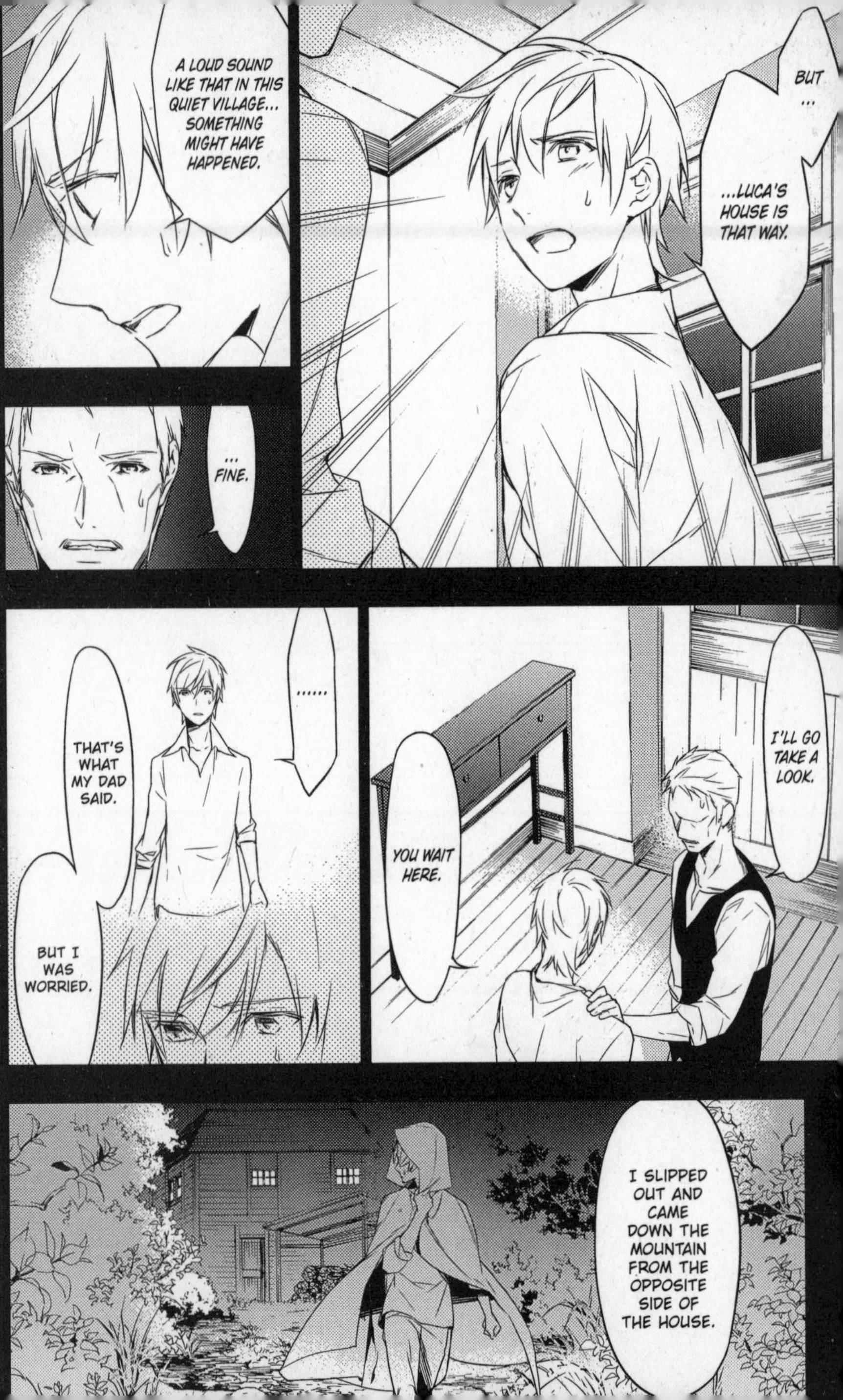

BUT ...
...LUCA'S HOUSE IS THAT WAY.
A LOUD SOUND LIKE THAT IN THIS QUIET VILLAGE... SOMETHING MIGHT HAVE HAPPENED.
... FINE.
I'LL GO TAKE A LOOK.
YOU WAIT HERE.
......
THAT'S WHAT MY DAD SAID.
BUT I WAS WORRIED.
I SLIPPED OUT AND CAME DOWN THE MOUNTAIN FROM THE OPPOSITE SIDE OF THE HOUSE.

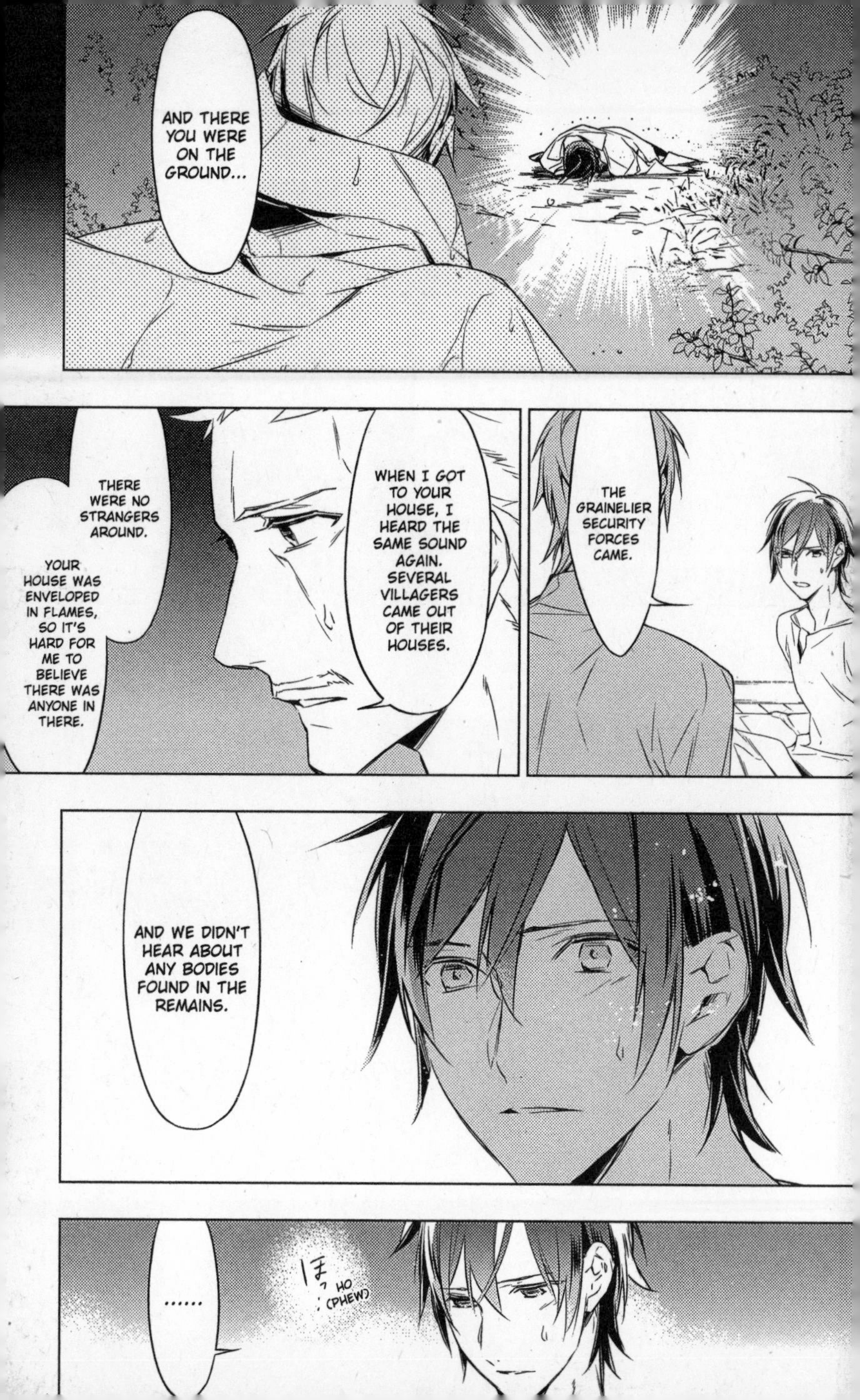
AND THERE YOU WERE ON THE GROUND...
THE GRAINELIER SECURITY FORCES CAME.
WHEN I GOT TO YOUR HOUSE, I HEARD THE SAME SOUND AGAIN. SEVERAL VILLAGERS CAME OUT OF THEIR HOUSES.
THERE WERE NO STRANGERS AROUND.
YOUR HOUSE WAS ENVELOPED IN FLAMES, SO IT'S HARD FOR ME TO BELIEVE THERE WAS ANYONE IN THERE.
AND WE DIDN'T HEAR ABOUT ANY BODIES FOUND IN THE REMAINS.
ほっ
HO (PHEW)
......

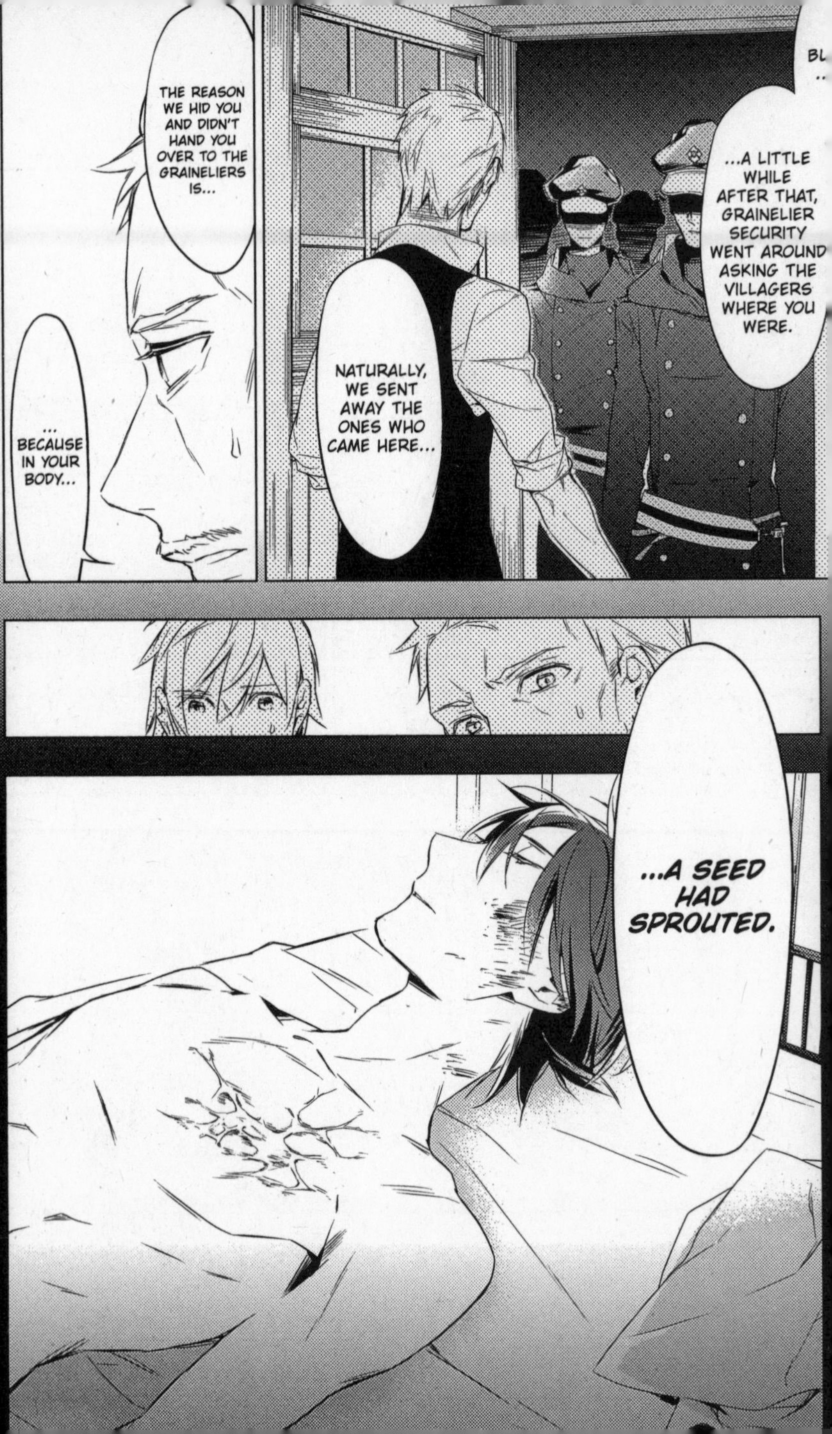
...A LITTLE WHILE AFTER THAT, GRAINELIER SECURITY WENT AROUND ASKING THE VILLAGERS WHERE YOU WERE.
NATURALLY, WE SENT AWAY THE ONES WHO CAME HERE...
THE REASON WE HID YOU AND DIDN'T HAND YOU OVER TO THE GRAINELIERS IS...
...BECAUSE IN YOUR BODY...
...A SEED HAD SPROUTED.

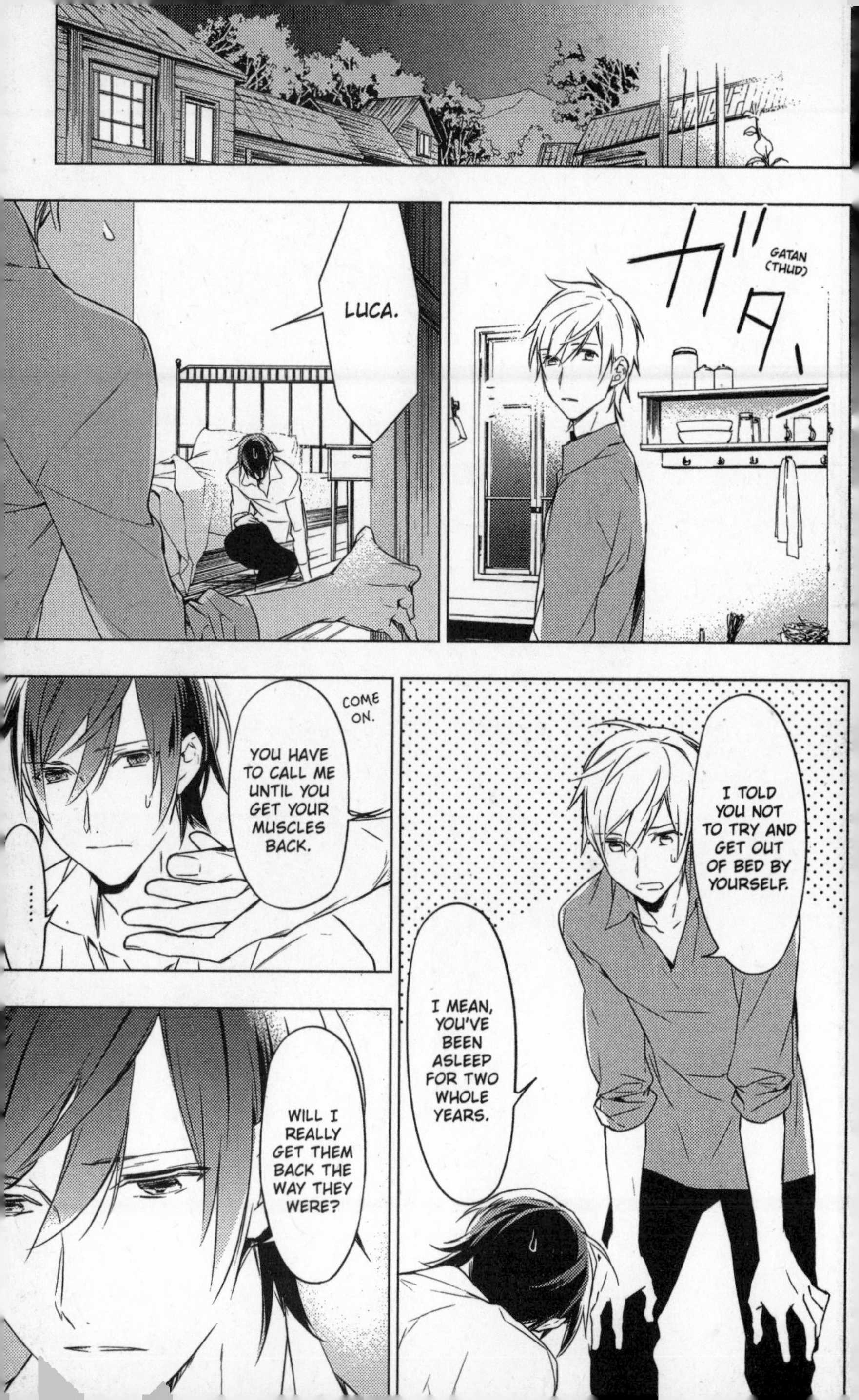
ガタ、
GATAN (THUD)
LUCA.
I TOLD YOU NOT TO TRY AND GET OUT OF BED BY YOURSELF.
I MEAN, YOU'VE BEEN ASLEEP FOR TWO WHOLE YEARS.
COME ON.
YOU HAVE TO CALL ME UNTIL YOU GET YOUR MUSCLES BACK.
......
WILL I REALLY GET THEM BACK THE WAY THEY WERE?

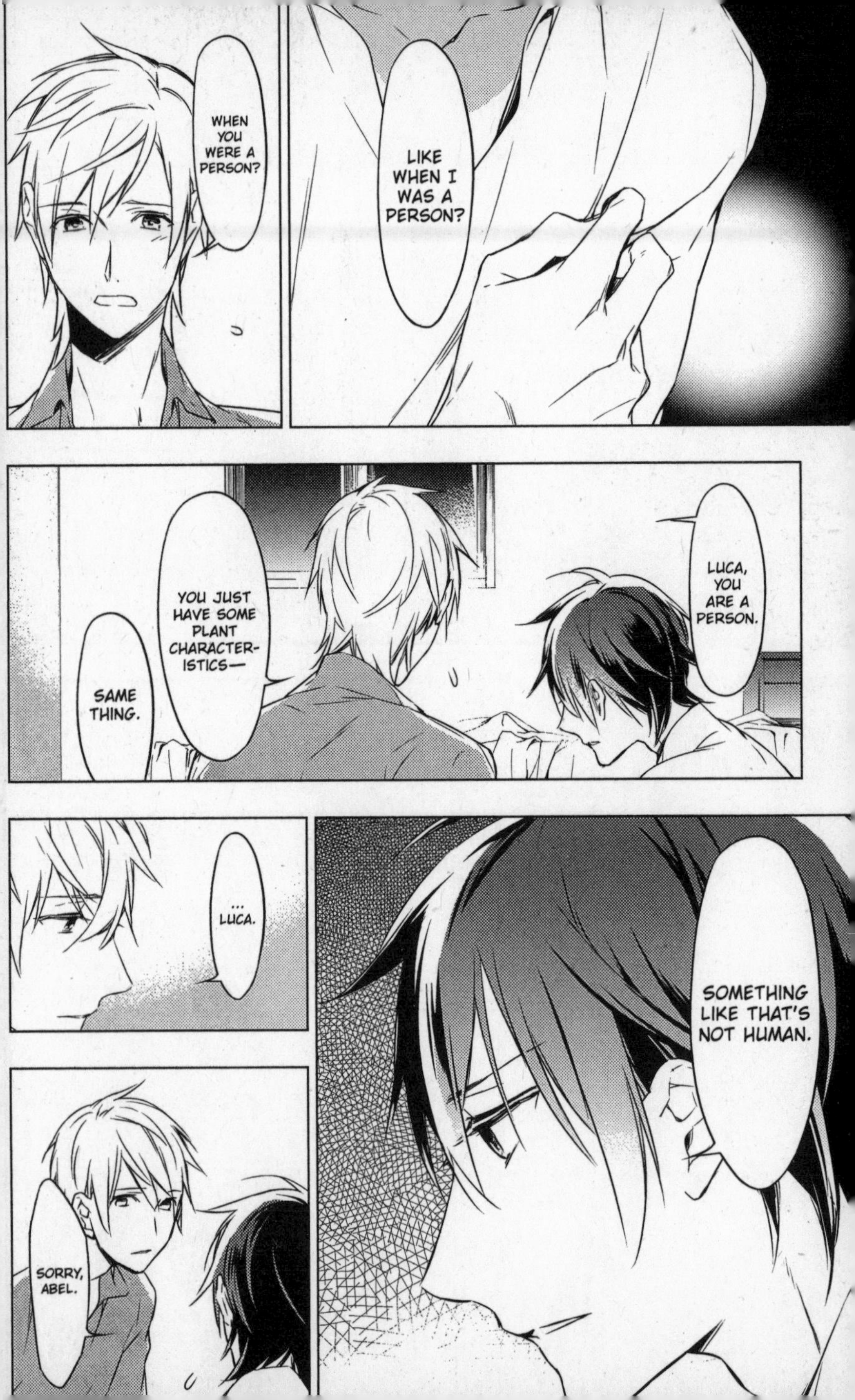
LIKE WHEN I WAS A PERSON?
WHEN YOU WERE A PERSON?
LUCA, YOU ARE A PERSON.
YOU JUST HAVE SOME PLANT CHARACTER-ISTICS—
SAME THING.
SOMETHING LIKE THAT'S NOT HUMAN.
... LUCA.
SORRY, ABEL.

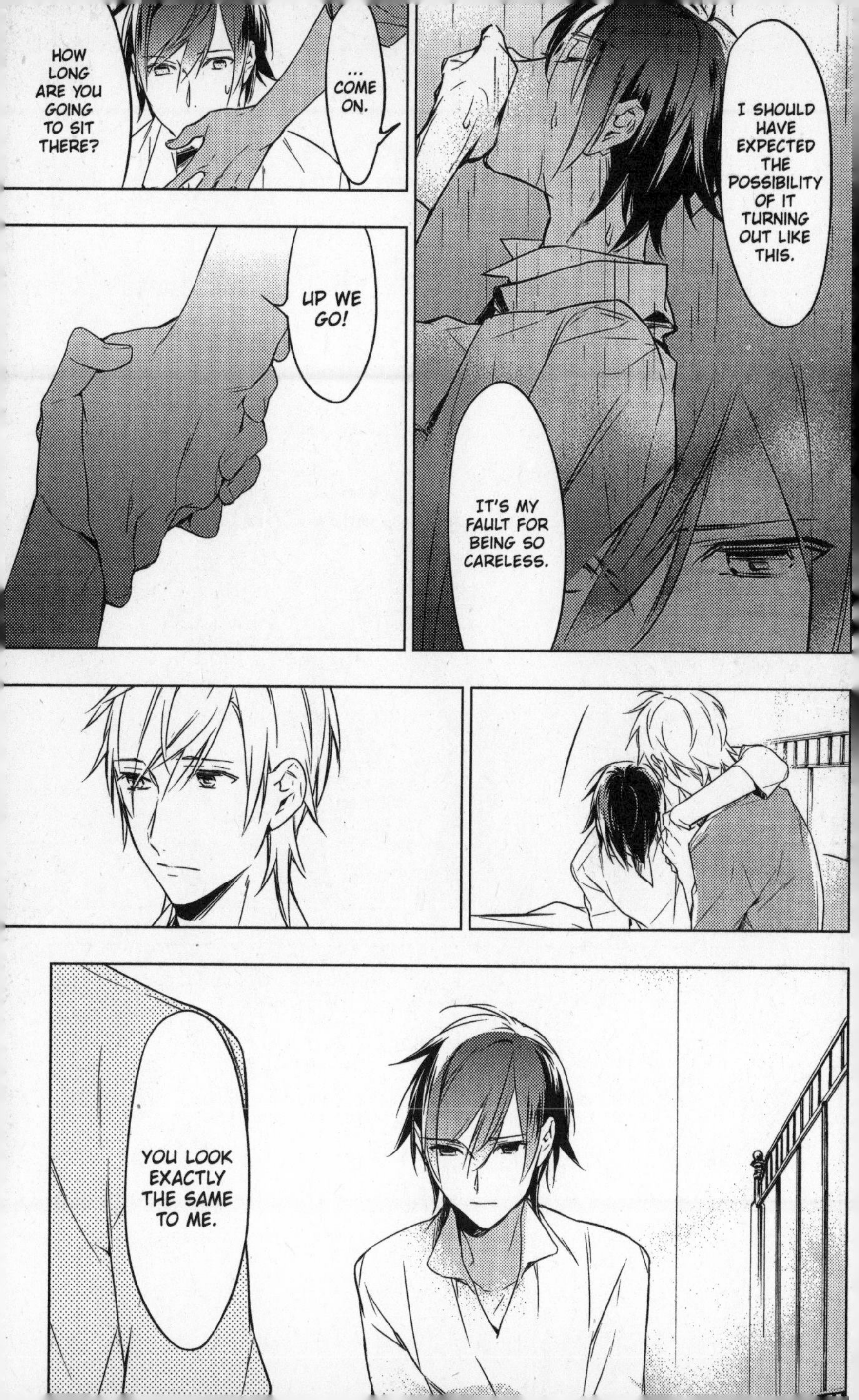
I SHOULD HAVE EXPECTED THE POSSIBILITY OF IT TURNING OUT LIKE THIS.
IT'S MY FAULT FOR BEING SO CARELESS.
... COME ON.
HOW LONG ARE YOU GOING TO SIT THERE?
UP WE GO!
YOU LOOK EXACTLY THE SAME TO ME.

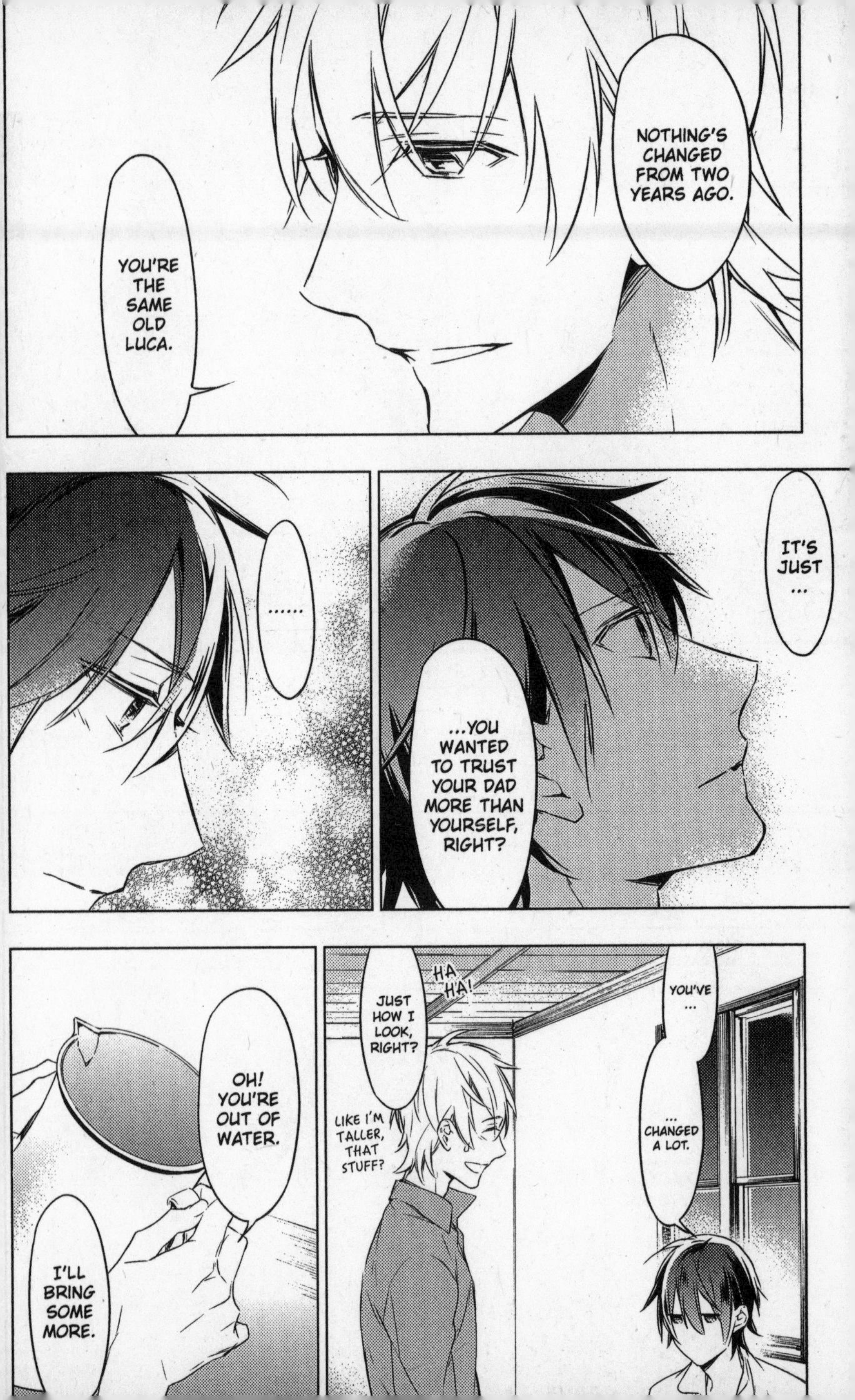
NOTHING'S CHANGED FROM TWO YEARS AGO.
YOU'RE THE SAME OLD LUCA.
IT'S JUST ...
...YOU WANTED TO TRUST YOUR DAD MORE THAN YOURSELF, RIGHT?
......
YOU'VE ...
... CHANGED A LOT.
HA HA!
JUST HOW I LOOK, RIGHT?
LIKE I'M TALLER, THAT STUFF?
OH! YOU'RE OUT OF WATER.
I'LL BRING SOME MORE.

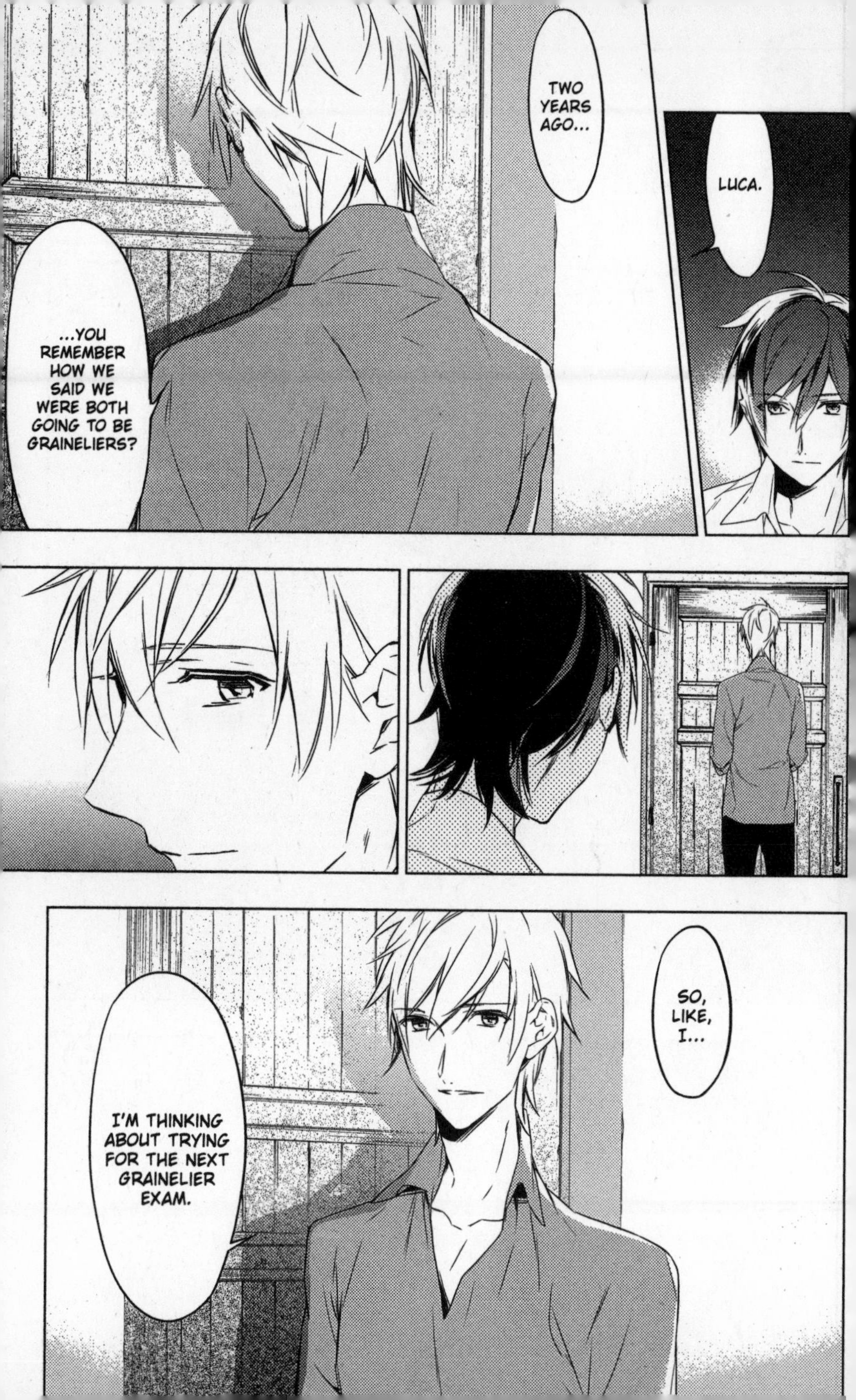
LUCA.
TWO YEARS AGO...
...YOU REMEMBER HOW WE SAID WE WERE BOTH GOING TO BE GRAINELIERS?
SO, LIKE, I...
I'M THINKING ABOUT TRYING FOR THE NEXT GRAINELIER EXAM.

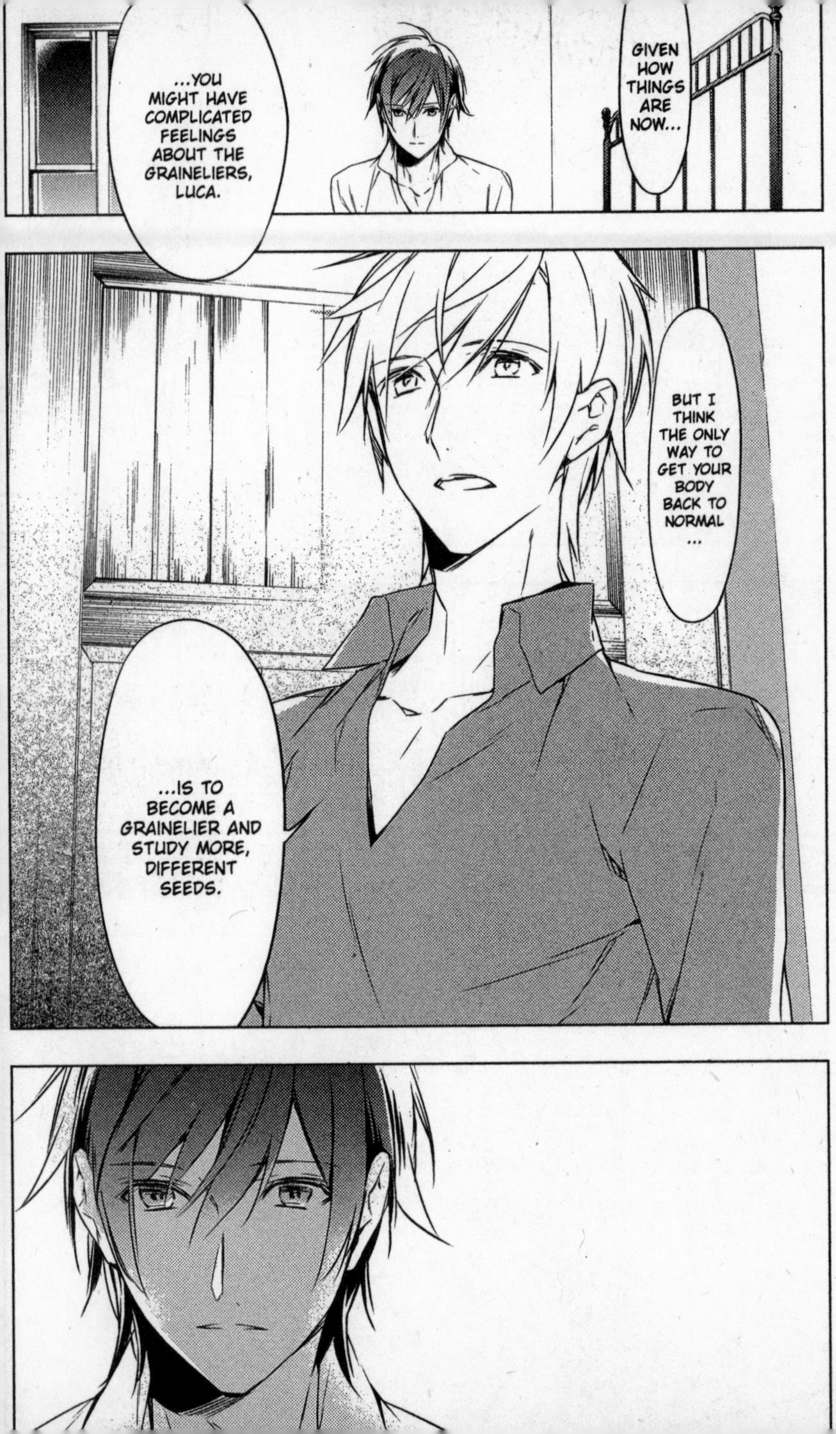
GIVEN HOW THINGS ARE NOW...
...YOU MIGHT HAVE COMPLICATED FEELINGS ABOUT THE GRAINELIERS, LUCA.
BUT I THINK THE ONLY WAY TO GET YOUR BODY BACK TO NORMAL...
...IS TO BECOME A GRAINELIER AND STUDY MORE, DIFFERENT SEEDS.

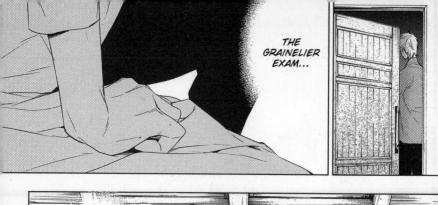

THE GRAINELIER EXAM...

WHAT SHOULD I DO, ABEL...?

I...

DAD...

...OOH!

NICE!

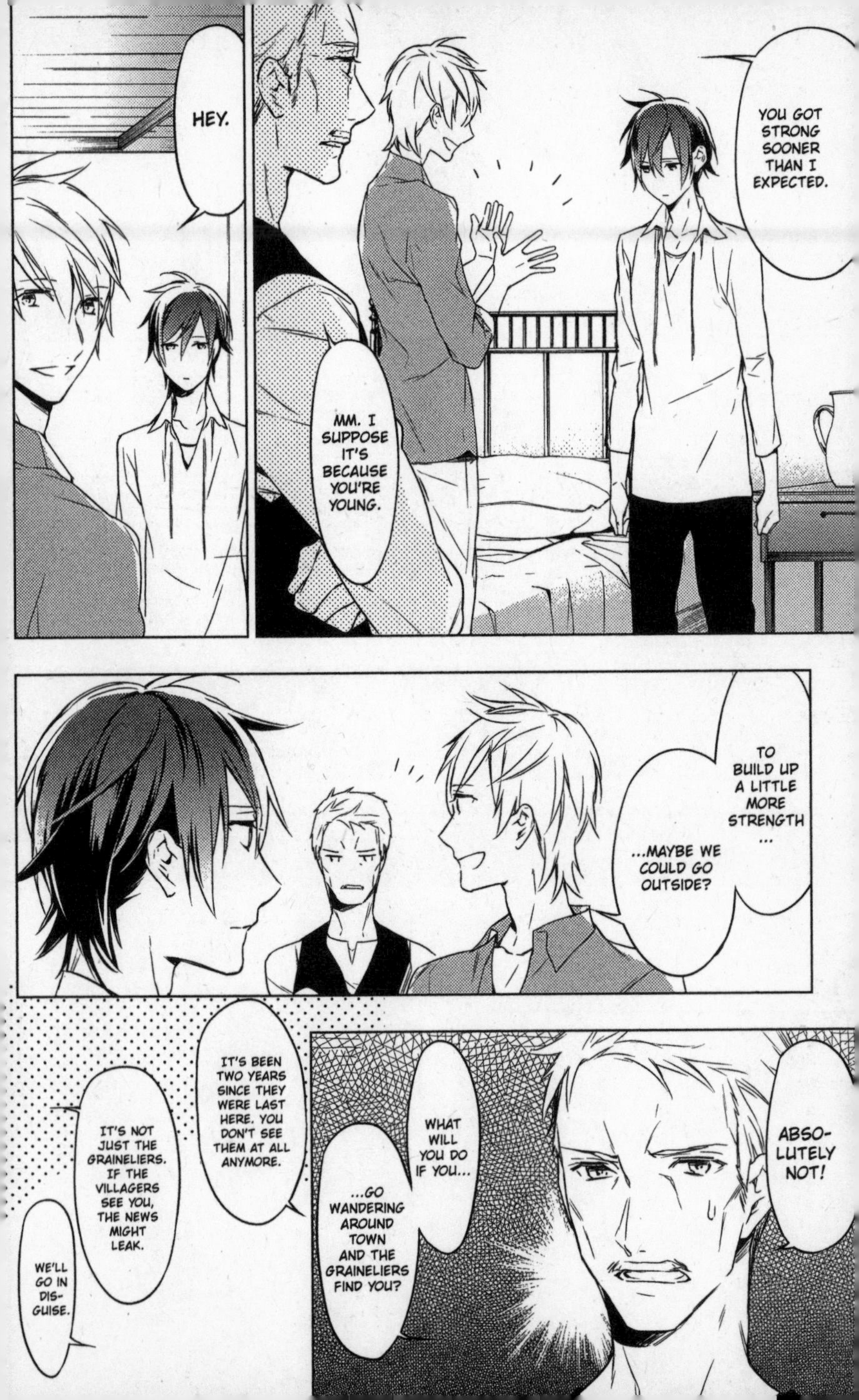
YOU GOT STRONG SOONER THAN I EXPECTED.
MM. I SUPPOSE IT'S BECAUSE YOU'RE YOUNG.
HEY.
TO BUILD UP A LITTLE MORE STRENGTH...
...MAYBE WE COULD GO OUTSIDE?
ABSO-LUTELY NOT!
WHAT WILL YOU DO IF YOU...
...GO WANDERING AROUND TOWN AND THE GRAINELIERS FIND YOU?
IT'S BEEN TWO YEARS SINCE THEY WERE LAST HERE. YOU DON'T SEE THEM AT ALL ANYMORE.
IT'S NOT JUST THE GRAINELIERS. IF THE VILLAGERS SEE YOU, THE NEWS MIGHT LEAK.
WE'LL GO IN DIS-GUISE.

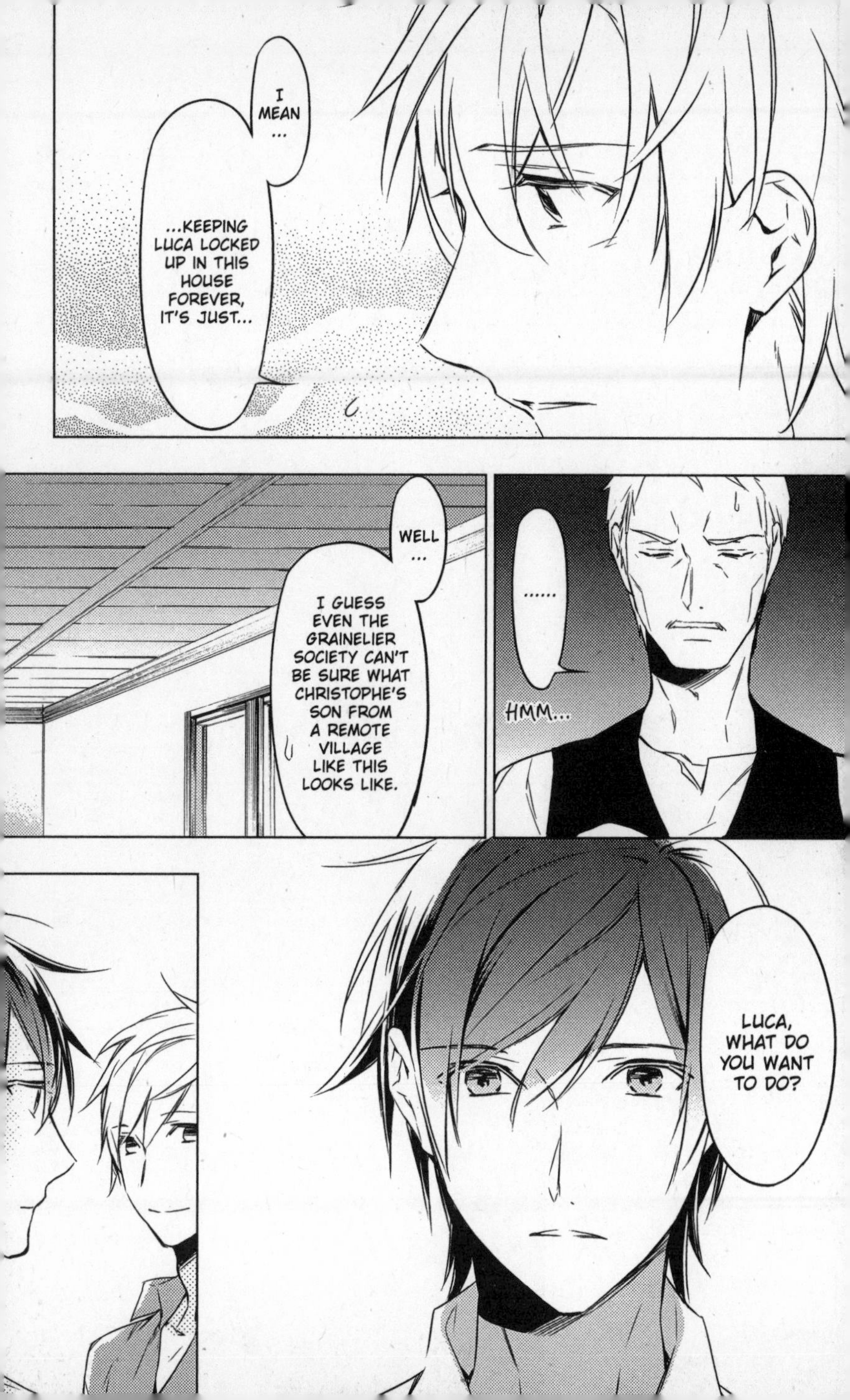
I MEAN ...
...KEEPING LUCA LOCKED UP IN THIS HOUSE FOREVER, IT'S JUST...
......
HMM...
WELL ...
I GUESS EVEN THE GRAINELIER SOCIETY CAN'T BE SURE WHAT CHRISTOPHE'S SON FROM A REMOTE VILLAGE LIKE THIS LOOKS LIKE.
LUCA, WHAT DO YOU WANT TO DO?

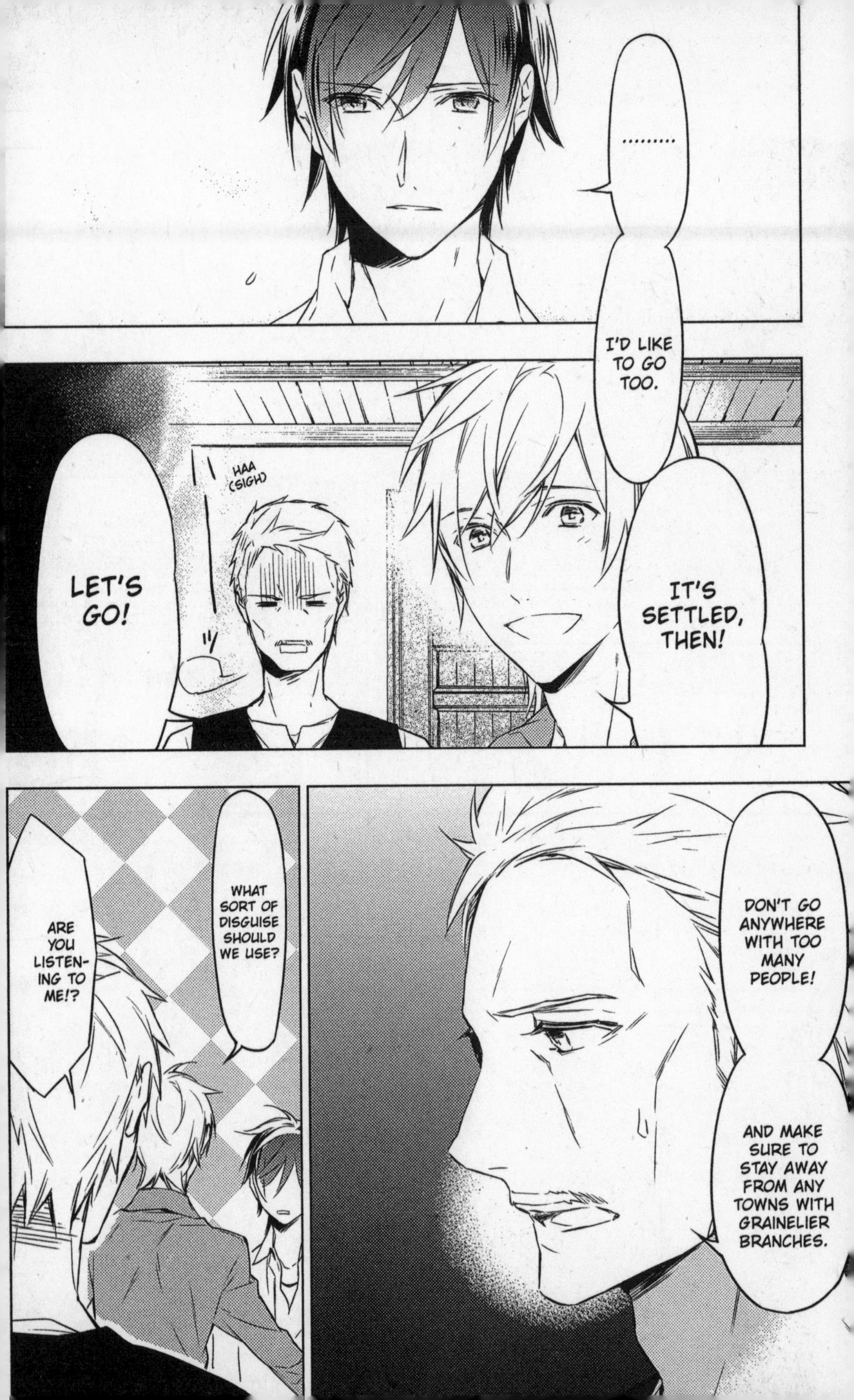
....
I'D LIKE TO GO TOO.
IT'S SETTLED, THEN!
HAA (SIGH)
LET'S GO!
DON'T GO ANYWHERE WITH TOO MANY PEOPLE!
AND MAKE SURE TO STAY AWAY FROM ANY TOWNS WITH GRAINELIER BRANCHES.
WHAT SORT OF DISGUISE SHOULD WE USE?
ARE YOU LISTEN-ING TO ME!?

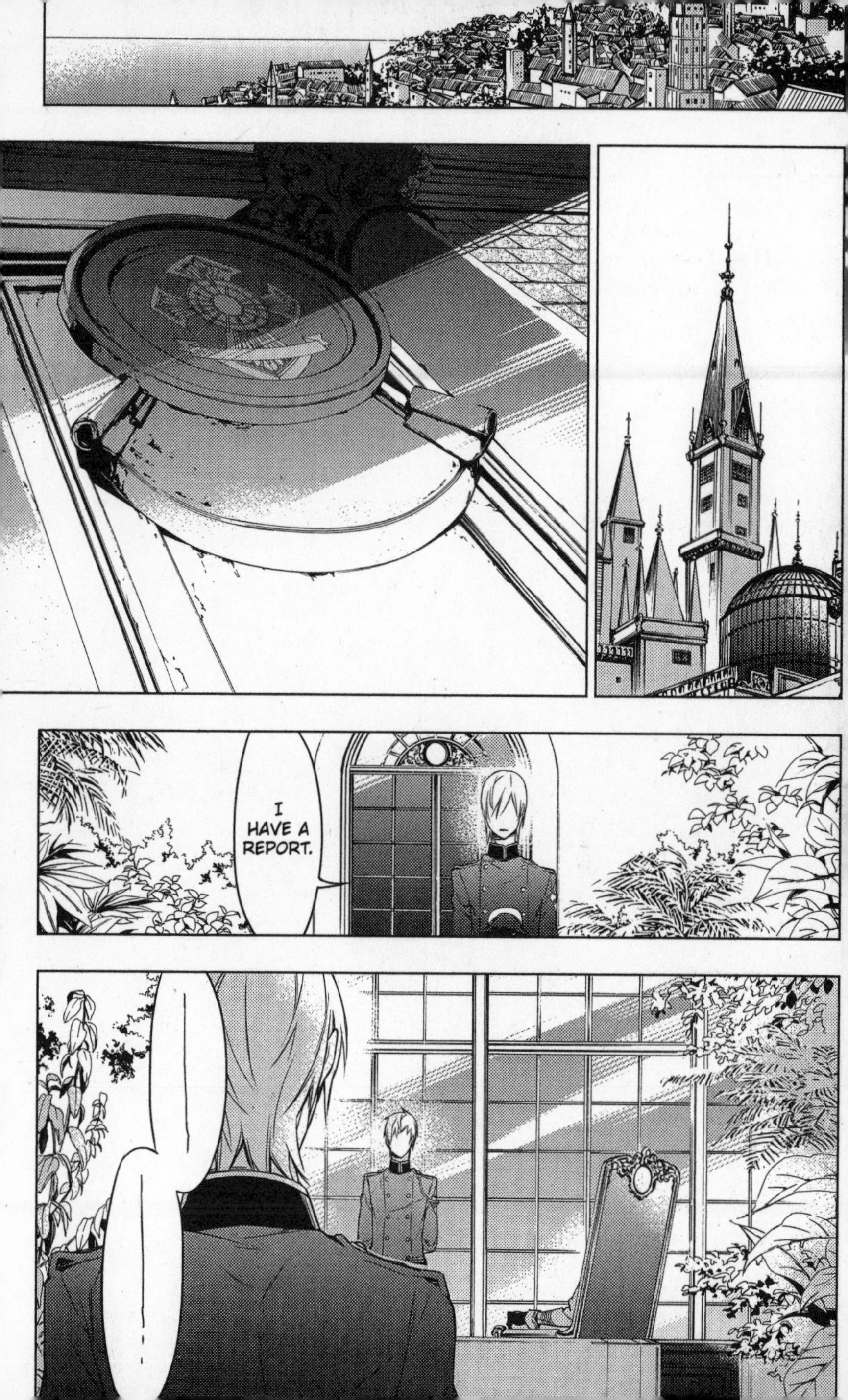
I HAVE A REPORT.

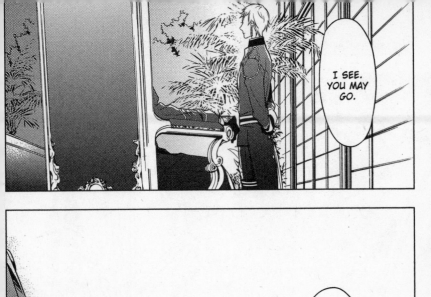

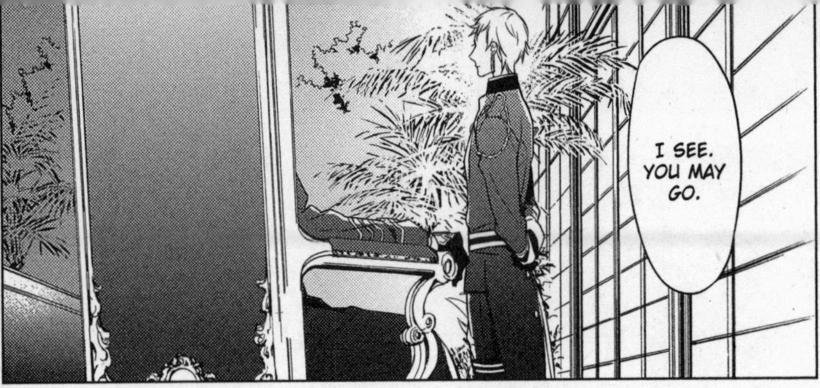
I SEE. YOU MAY GO.

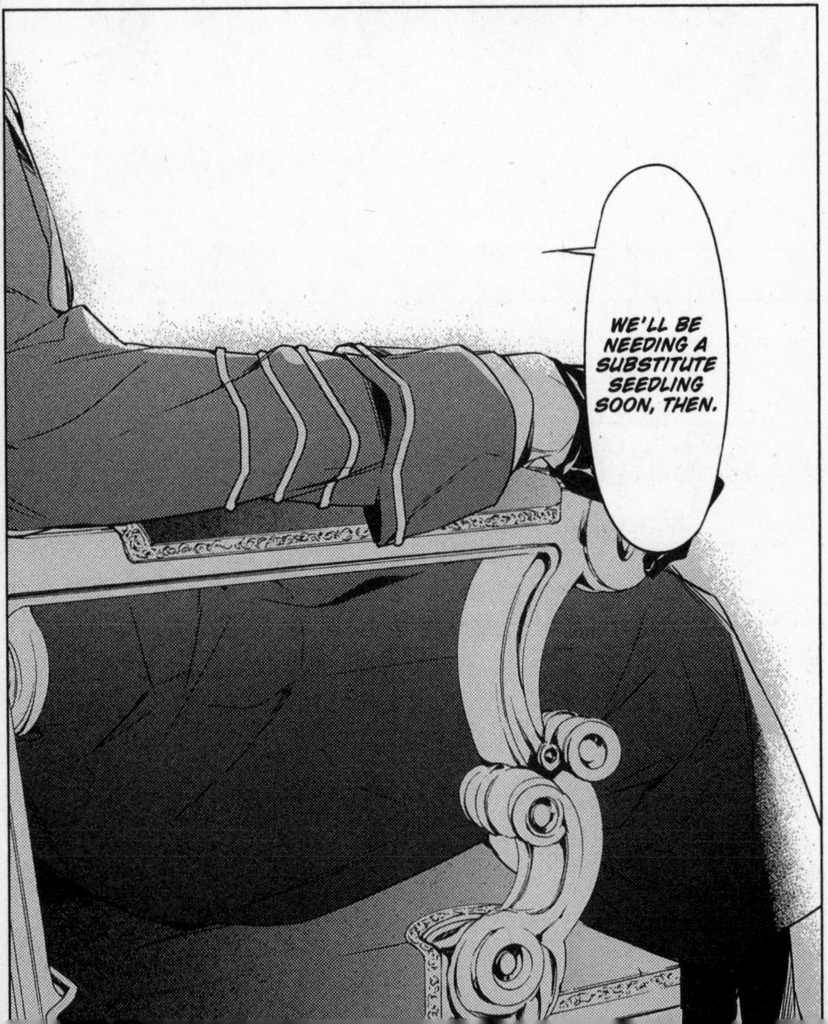
WE'LL BE NEEDING A SUBSTITUTE SEEDLING SOON, THEN.

GRAINELIERS

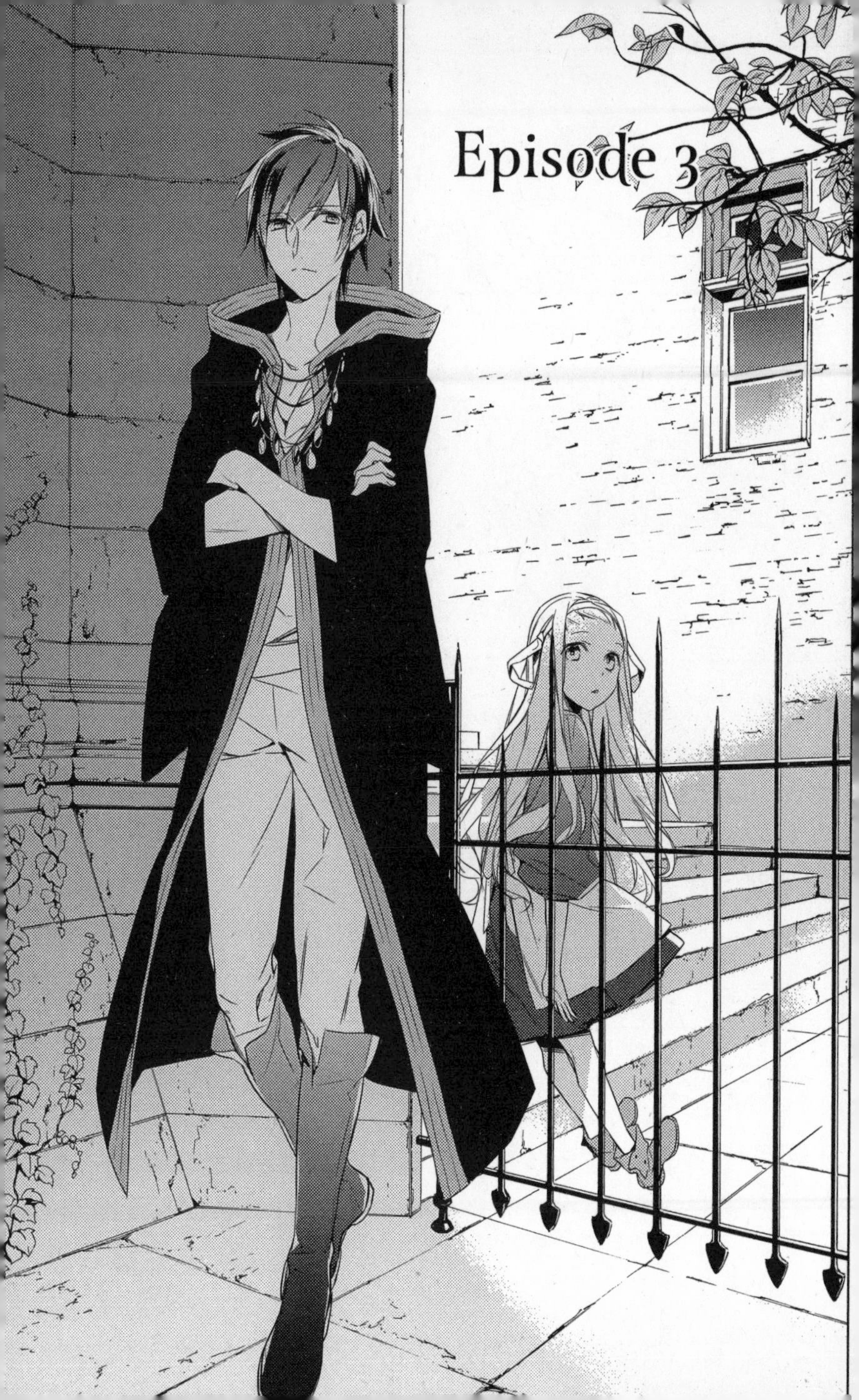
Episode 3

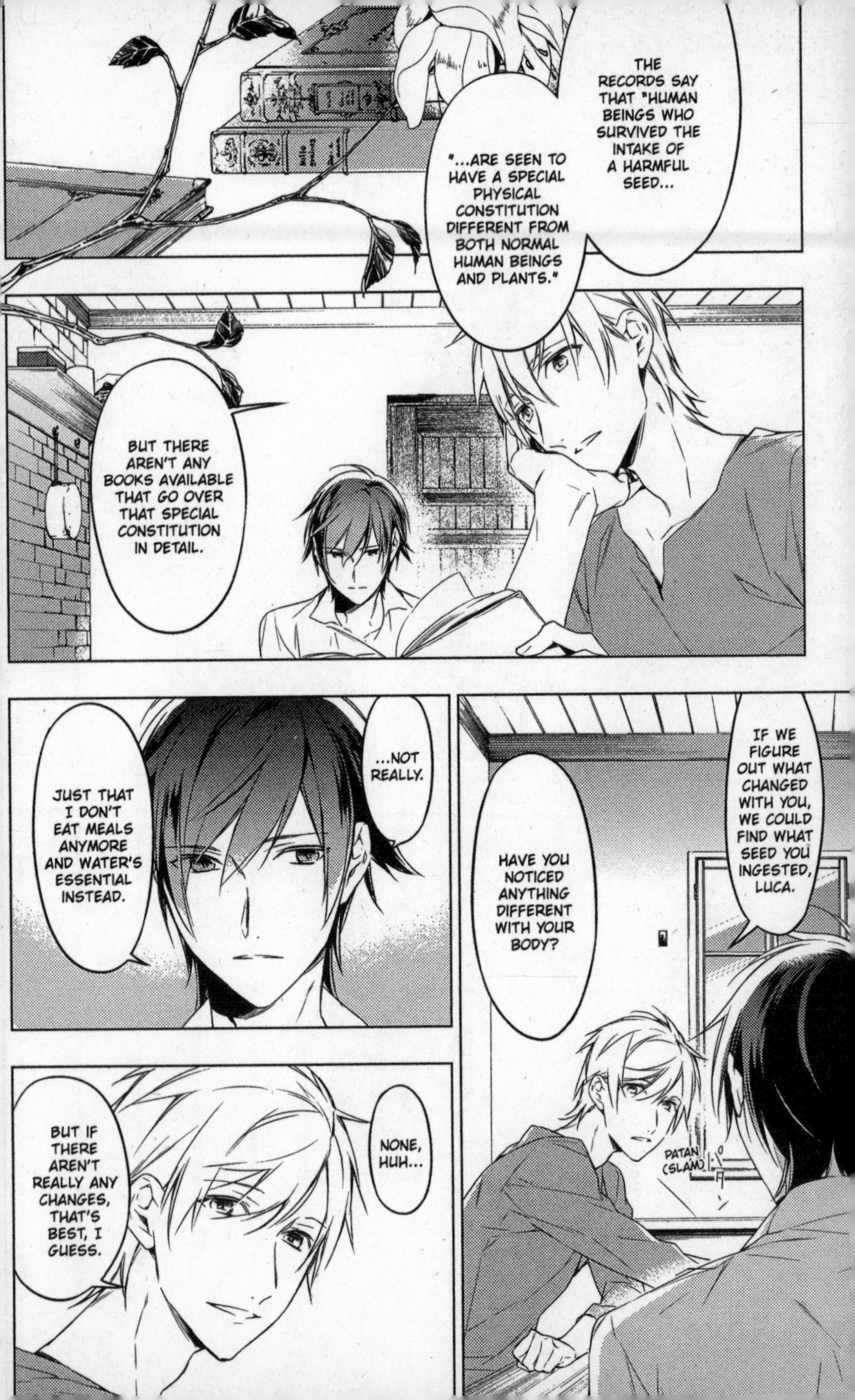
THE RECORDS SAY THAT "HUMAN BEINGS WHO SURVIVED THE INTAKE OF A HARMFUL SEED...
"...ARE SEEN TO HAVE A SPECIAL PHYSICAL CONSTITUTION DIFFERENT FROM BOTH NORMAL HUMAN BEINGS AND PLANTS."
BUT THERE AREN'T ANY BOOKS AVAILABLE THAT GO OVER THAT SPECIAL CONSTITUTION IN DETAIL.
IF WE FIGURE OUT WHAT CHANGED WITH YOU, WE COULD FIND WHAT SEED YOU INGESTED, LUCA.
HAVE YOU NOTICED ANYTHING DIFFERENT WITH YOUR BODY?
PATAN (SLAM)
...NOT REALLY.
JUST THAT I DON'T EAT MEALS ANYMORE AND WATER'S ESSENTIAL INSTEAD.
NONE, HUH...
BUT IF THERE AREN'T REALLY ANY CHANGES, THAT'S BEST, I GUESS.

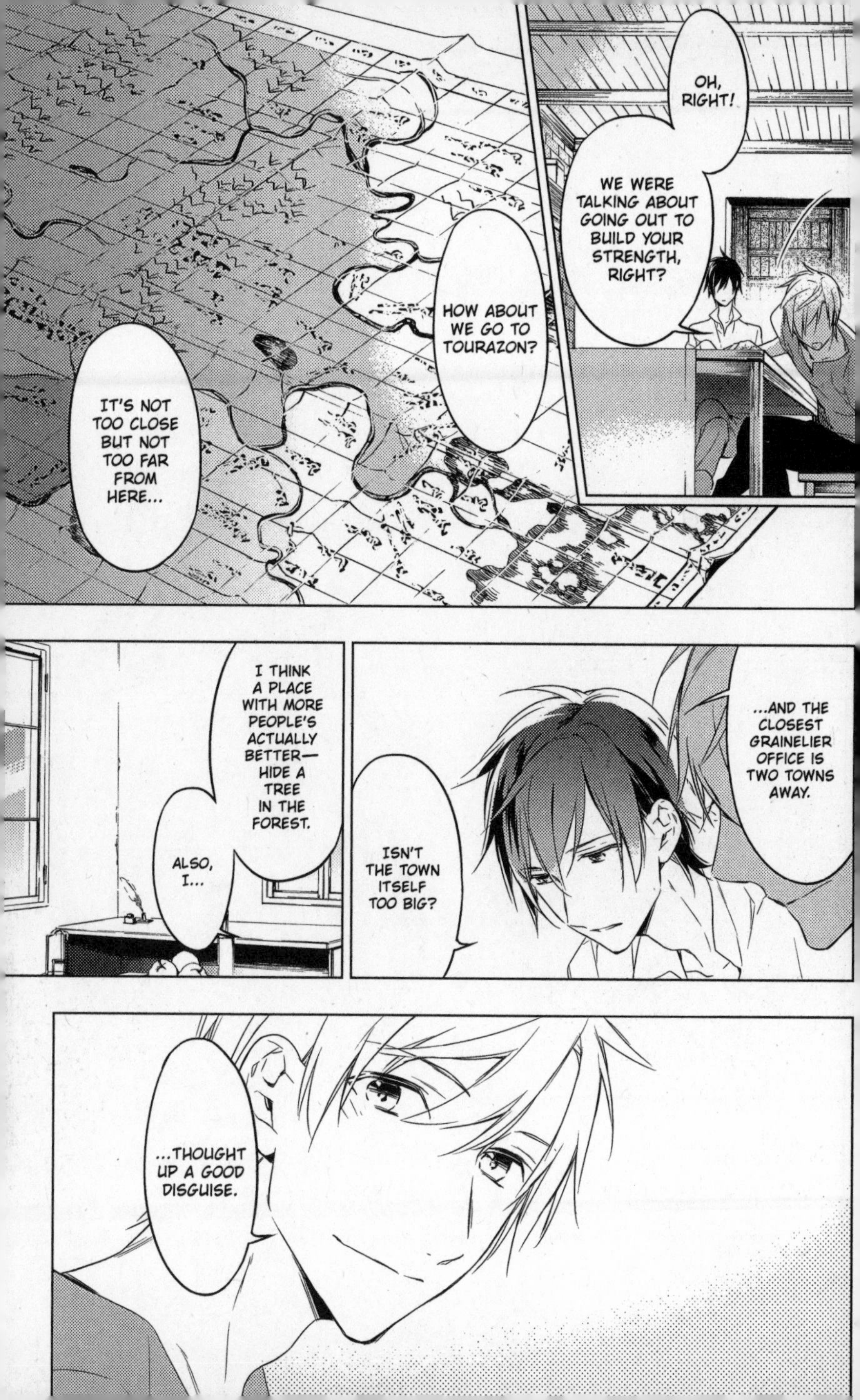
OH, RIGHT!
WE WERE TALKING ABOUT GOING OUT TO BUILD YOUR STRENGTH, RIGHT?
HOW ABOUT WE GO TO TOURAZON?
IT'S NOT TOO CLOSE BUT NOT TOO FAR FROM HERE...
...AND THE CLOSEST GRAINELIER OFFICE IS TWO TOWNS AWAY.
ISN'T THE TOWN ITSELF TOO BIG?
I THINK A PLACE WITH MORE PEOPLE'S ACTUALLY BETTER—HIDE A TREE IN THE FOREST.
ALSO, I...
...THOUGHT UP A GOOD DISGUISE.

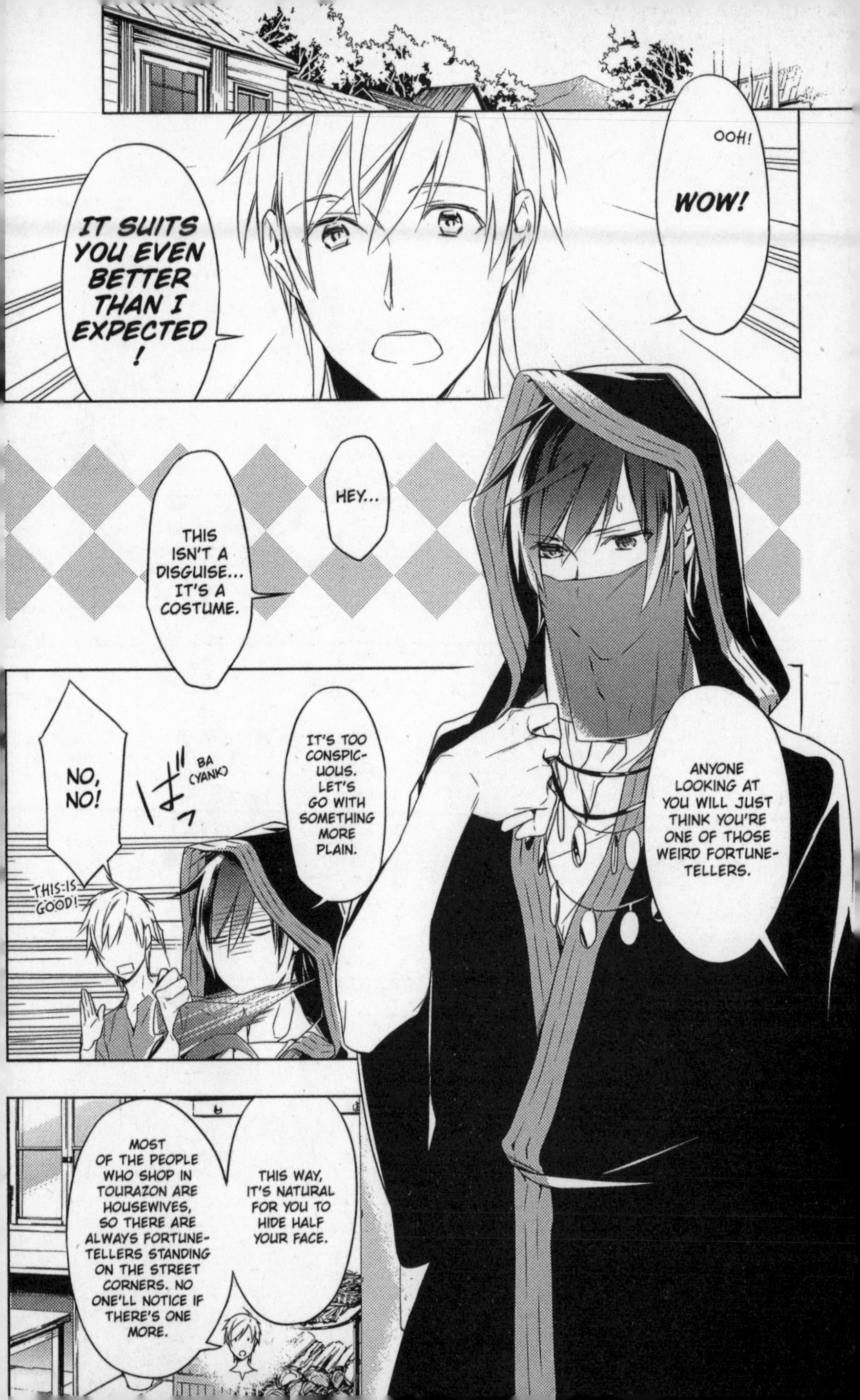

OOH!
WOW!
IT SUITS YOU EVEN BETTER THAN I EXPECTED!
HEY...
THIS ISN'T A DISGUISE... IT'S A COSTUME.
ANYONE LOOKING AT YOU WILL JUST THINK YOU'RE ONE OF THOSE WEIRD FORTUNE-TELLERS.
IT'S TOO CONSPICUOUS. LET'S GO WITH SOMETHING MORE PLAIN.
BA (YANK)
NO, NO!
THIS IS GOOD!
THIS WAY, IT'S NATURAL FOR YOU TO HIDE HALF YOUR FACE.
MOST OF THE PEOPLE WHO SHOP IN TOURAZON ARE HOUSEWIVES, SO THERE ARE ALWAYS FORTUNE-TELLERS STANDING ON THE STREET CORNERS. NO ONE'LL NOTICE IF THERE'S ONE MORE.

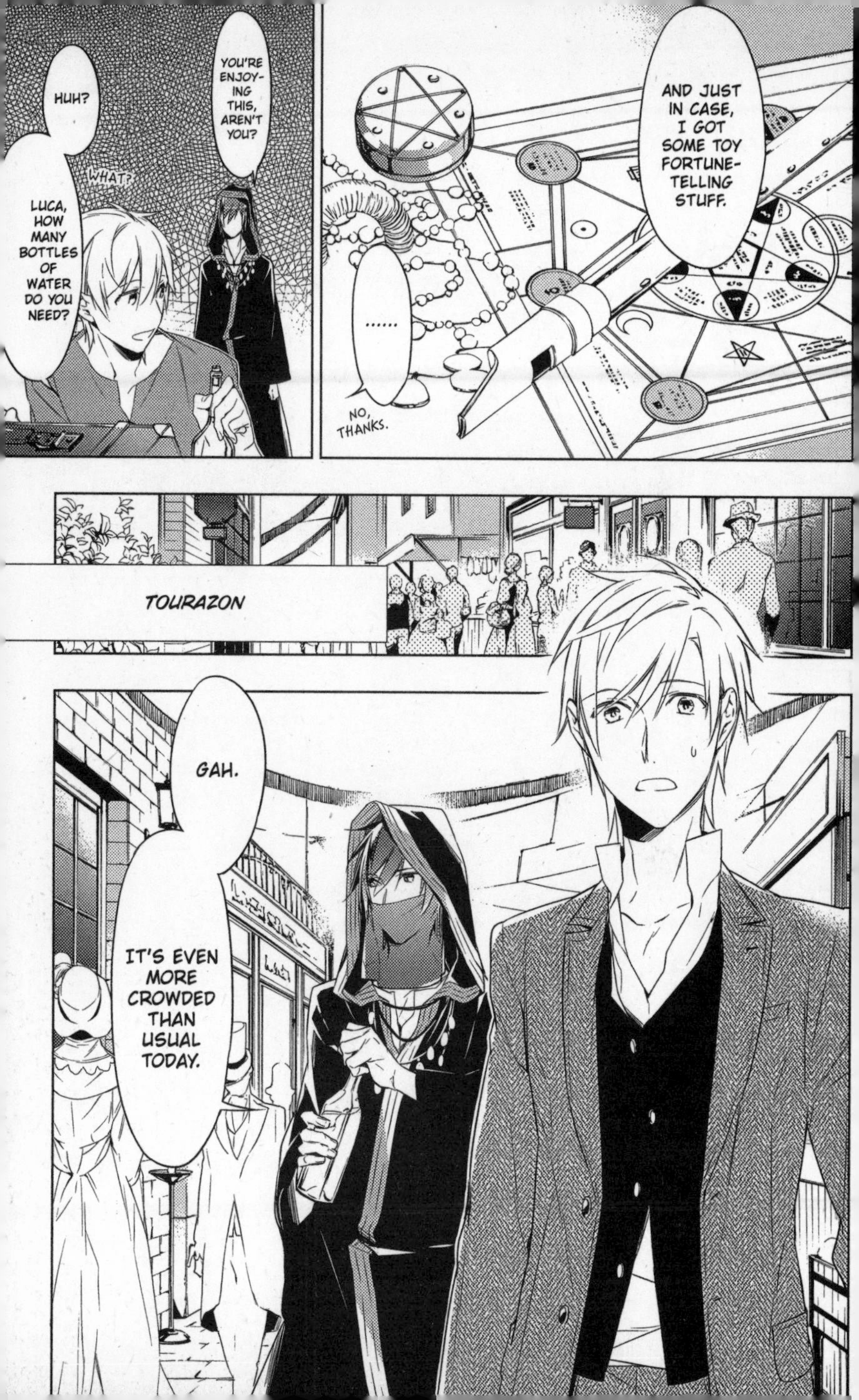
AND JUST IN CASE, I GOT SOME TOY FORTUNE-TELLING STUFF.
......
NO, THANKS.
YOU'RE ENJOYING THIS, AREN'T YOU?
HUH?
WHAT?
LUCA, HOW MANY BOTTLES OF WATER DO YOU NEED?
TOURAZON
GAH.
IT'S EVEN MORE CROWDED THAN USUAL TODAY.

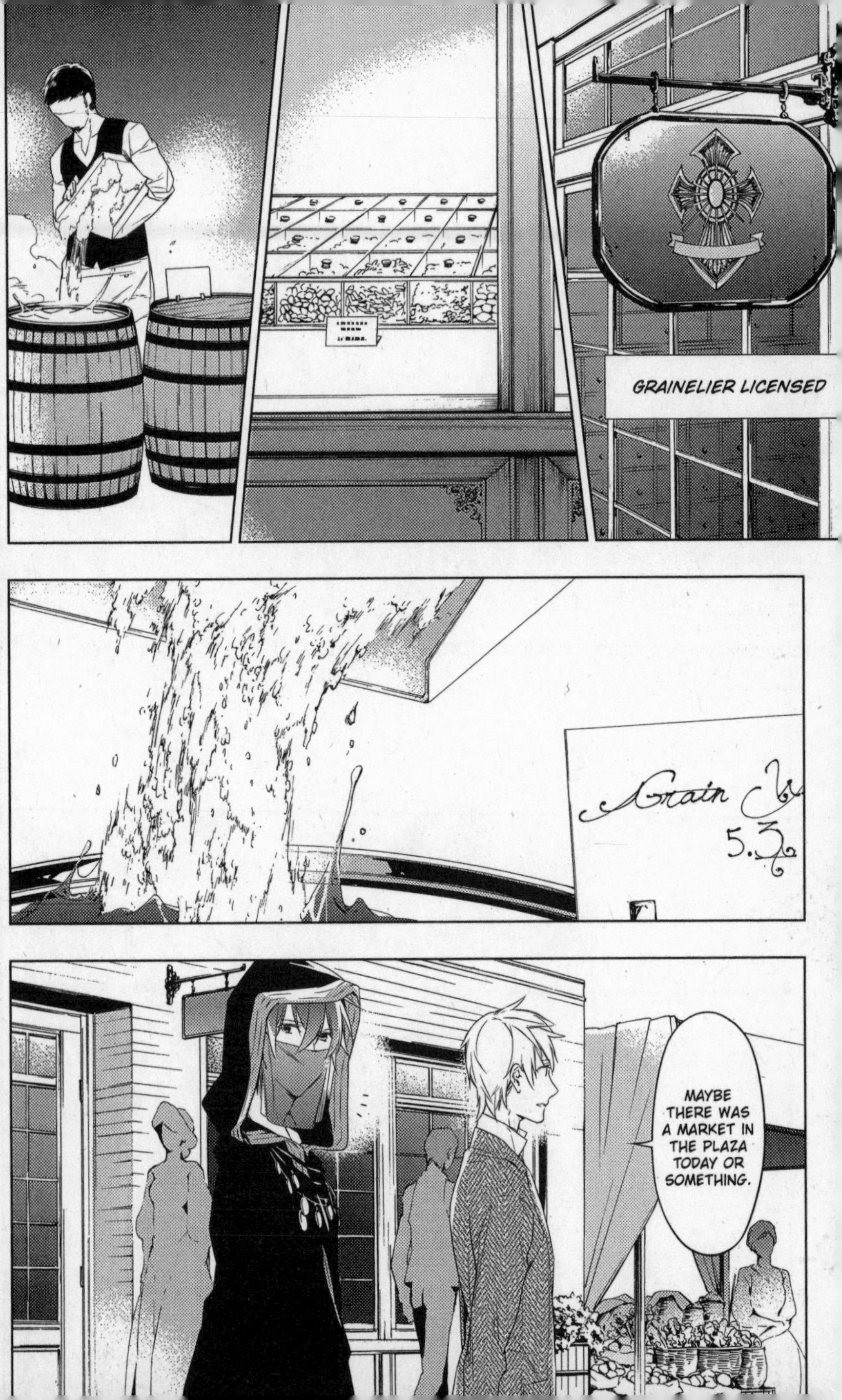
GRAINELIER LICENSED
Grain
5.3
MAYBE THERE WAS A MARKET IN THE PLAZA TODAY OR SOMETHING.

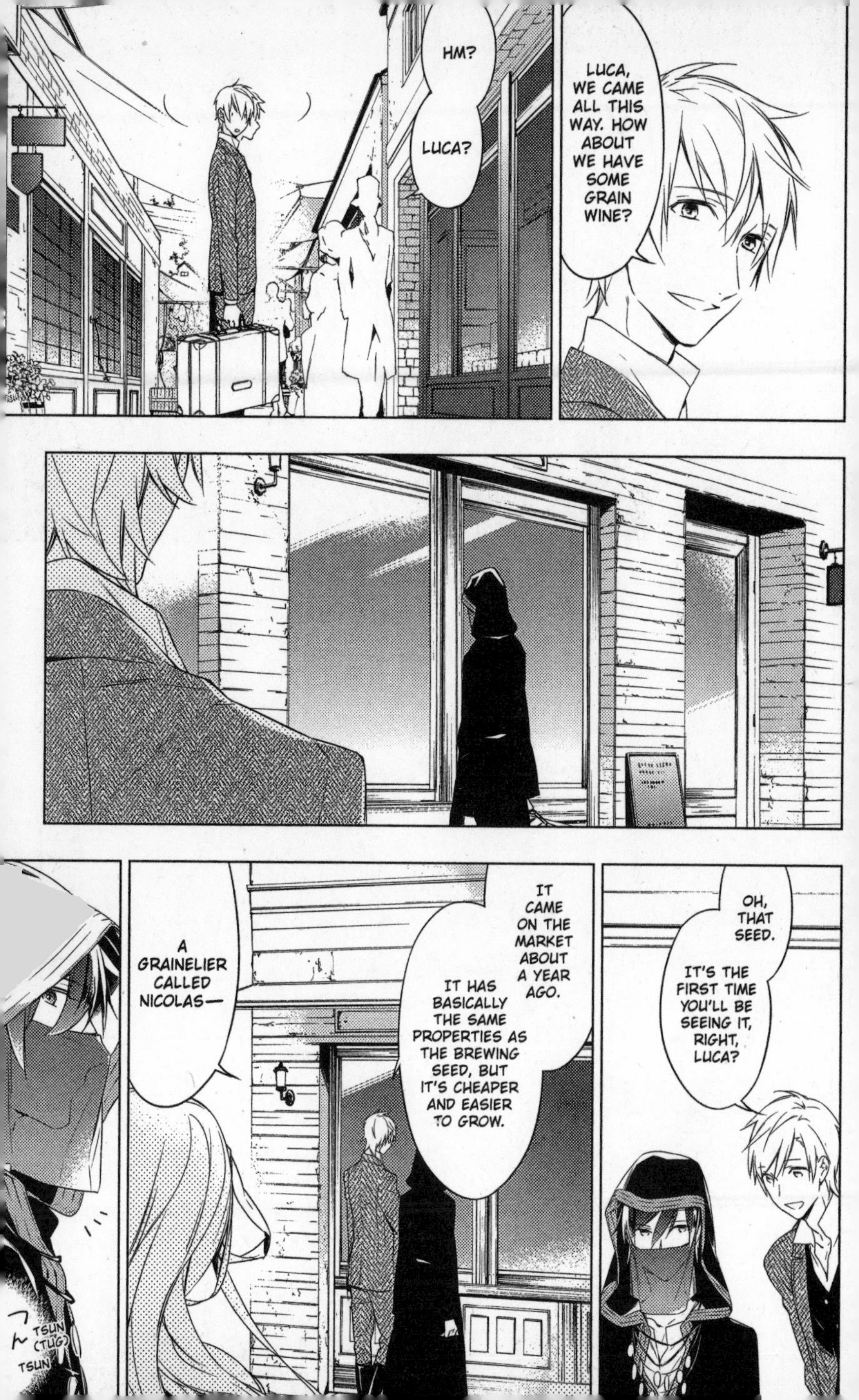
LUCA, WE CAME ALL THIS WAY. HOW ABOUT WE HAVE SOME GRAIN WINE?
HM?
LUCA?
OH, THAT SEED.
IT'S THE FIRST TIME YOU'LL BE SEEING IT, RIGHT, LUCA?
IT CAME ON THE MARKET ABOUT A YEAR AGO.
IT HAS BASICALLY THE SAME PROPERTIES AS THE BREWING SEED, BUT IT'S CHEAPER AND EASIER TO GROW.
A GRAINELIER CALLED NICOLAS—
TSUN (TUG) TSUN

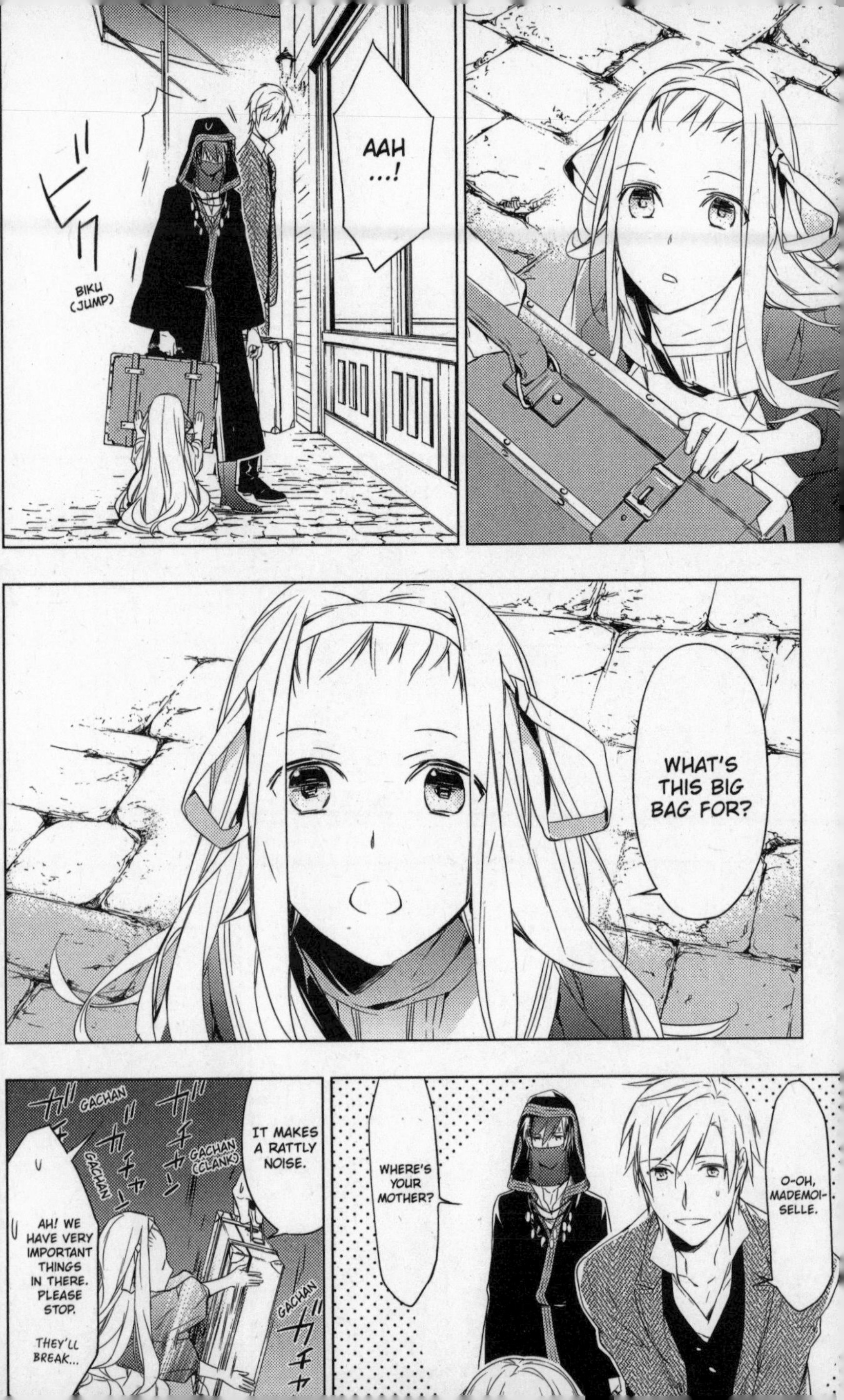
AAH ...!
BIKU (JUMP)
WHAT'S THIS BIG BAG FOR?
O-OH, MADEMOISELLE.
WHERE'S YOUR MOTHER?
IT MAKES A RATTLY NOISE.
GACHAN (CLANK)
GACHAN
GACHAN
AH! WE HAVE VERY IMPORTANT THINGS IN THERE. PLEASE STOP.
THEY'LL BREAK...
GACHAN

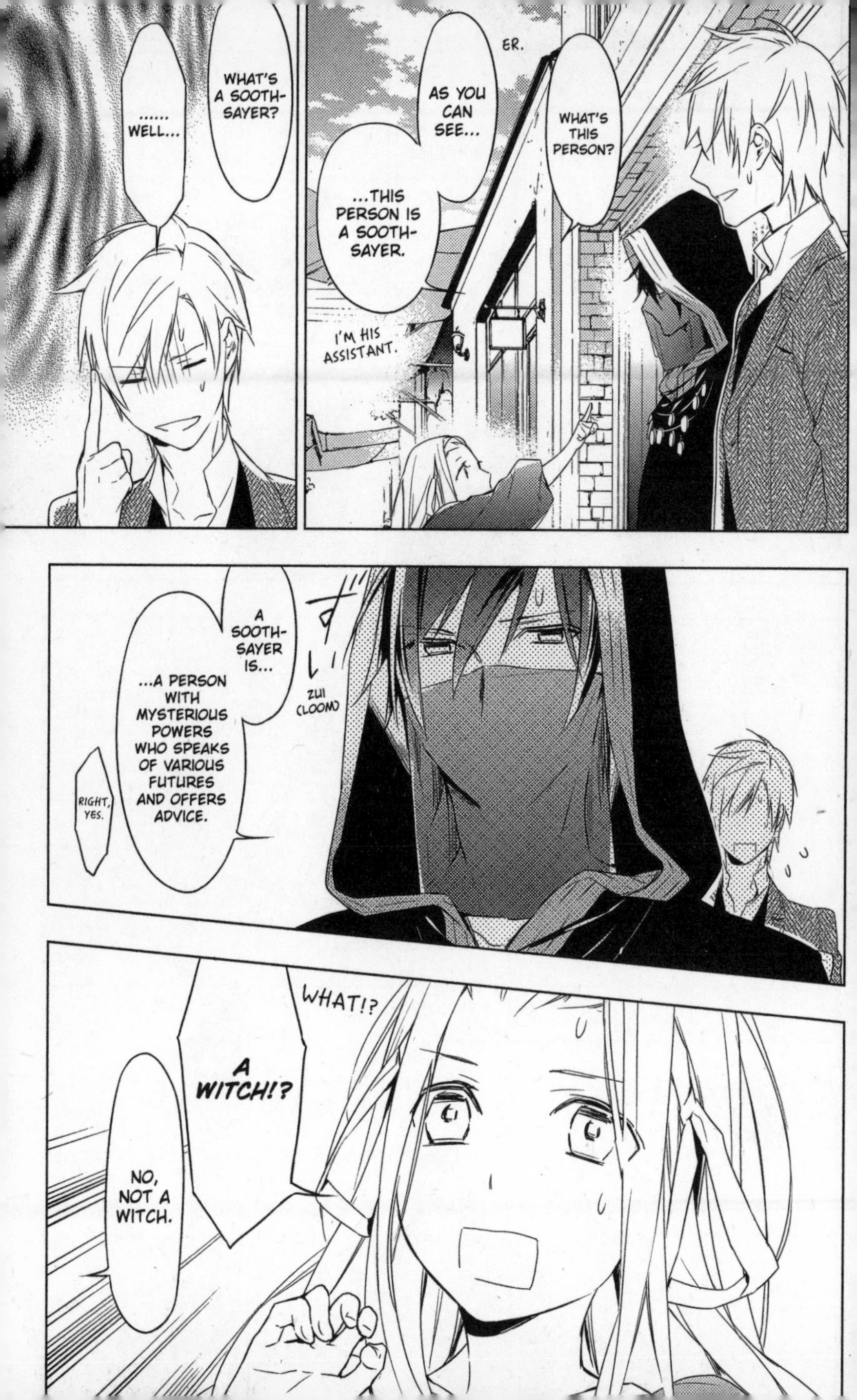
ER.
WHAT'S THIS PERSON?
AS YOU CAN SEE...
...THIS PERSON IS A SOOTHSAYER.
I'M HIS ASSISTANT.
WHAT'S A SOOTHSAYER?
...... WELL...
ZUI (LOOM)
A SOOTHSAYER IS...
...A PERSON WITH MYSTERIOUS POWERS WHO SPEAKS OF VARIOUS FUTURES AND OFFERS ADVICE.
RIGHT, YES.
WHAT!?
A WITCH!?
NO, NOT A WITCH.

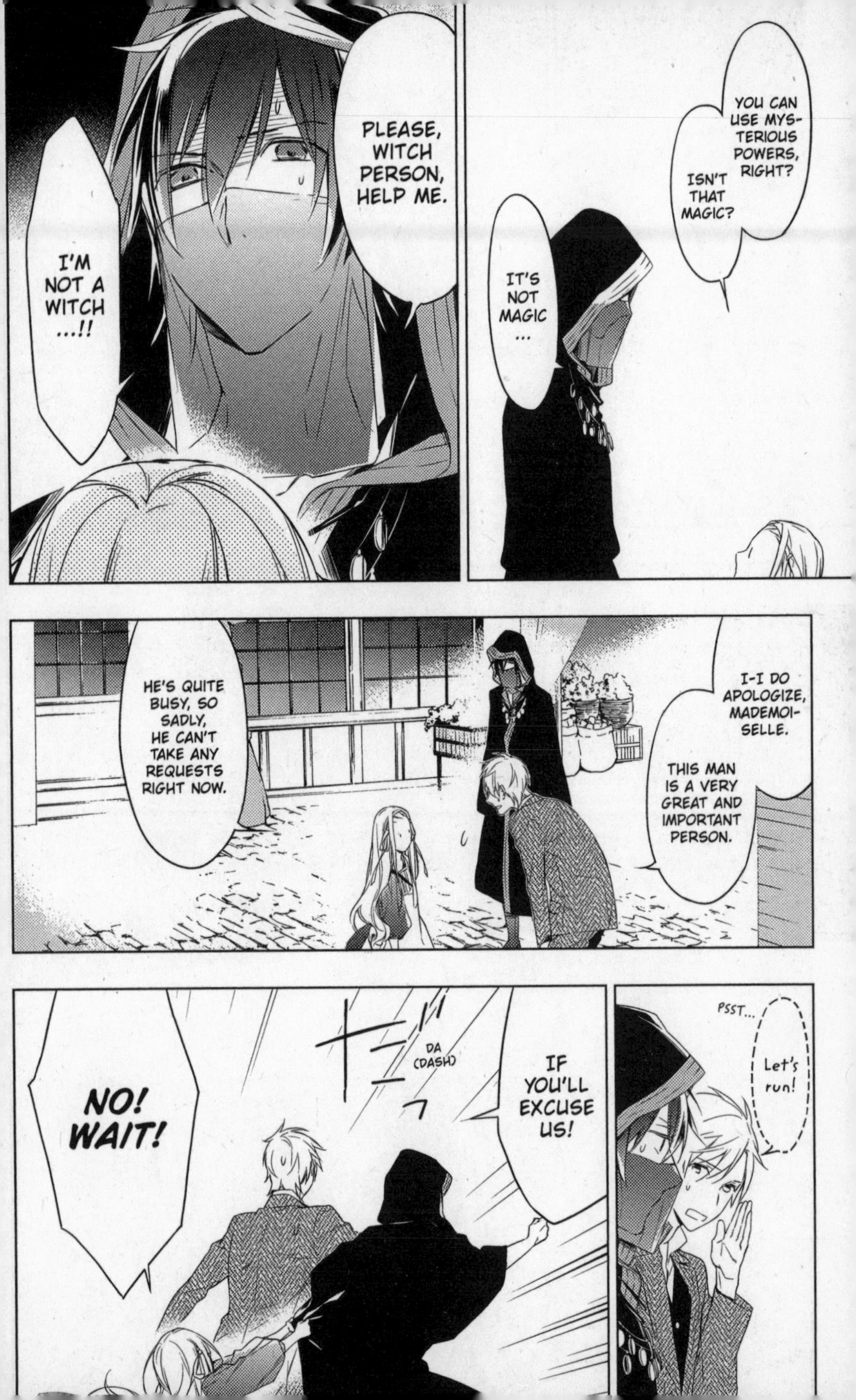
YOU CAN USE MYS-TERIOUS POWERS, RIGHT?
ISN'T THAT MAGIC?
IT'S NOT MAGIC ...
PLEASE, WITCH PERSON, HELP ME.
I'M NOT A WITCH ...!!
I-I DO APOLOGIZE, MADEMOISELLE.
THIS MAN IS A VERY GREAT AND IMPORTANT PERSON.
HE'S QUITE BUSY, SO SADLY, HE CAN'T TAKE ANY REQUESTS RIGHT NOW.
PSST...
Let's run!
IF YOU'LL EXCUSE US!
DA (DASH)
NO! WAIT!

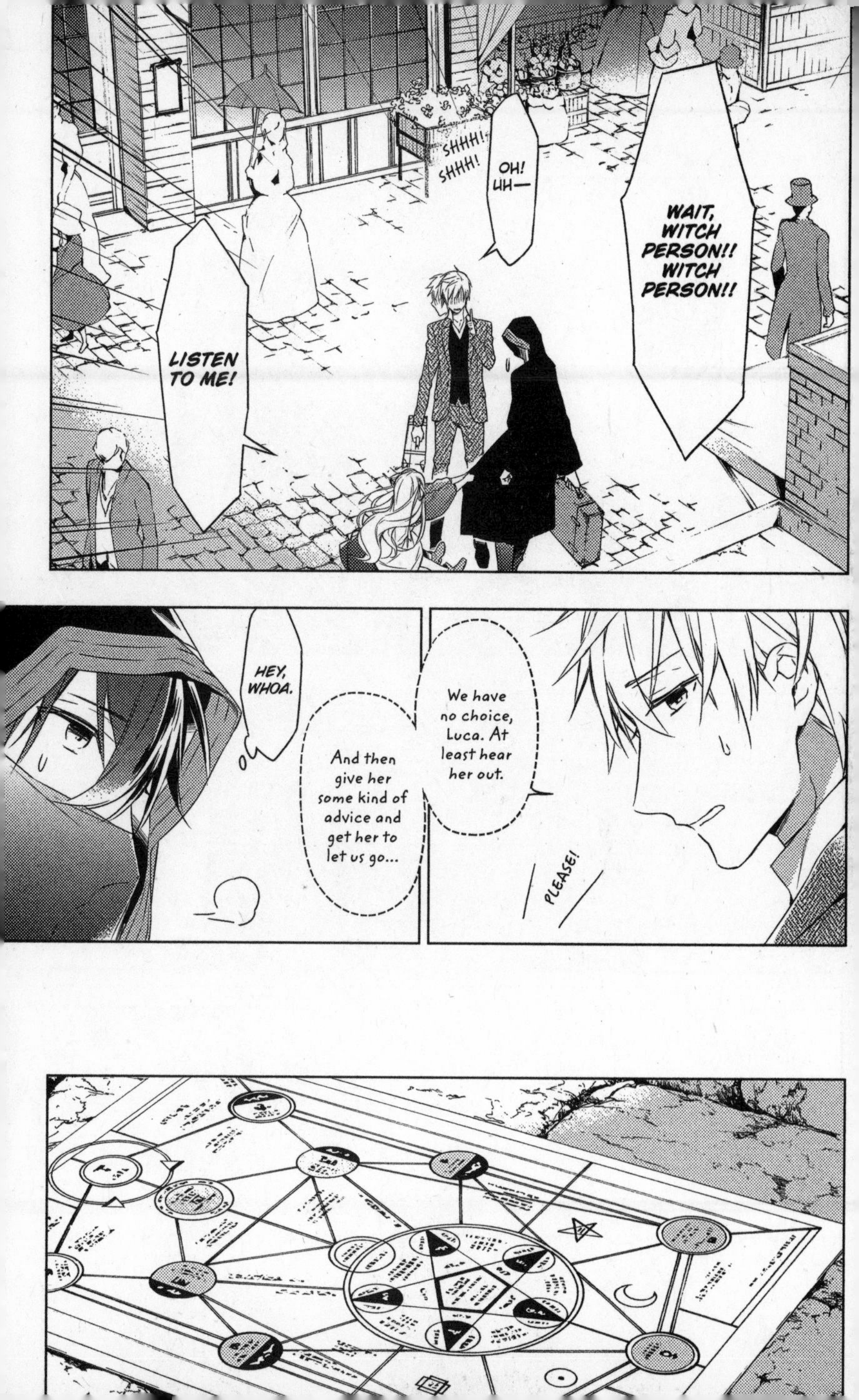
WAIT, WITCH PERSON!! WITCH PERSON!!
OH! UH—
SHHH! SHHH!
LISTEN TO ME!
We have no choice, Luca. At least hear her out.
PLEASE!
HEY, WHOA.
And then give her some kind of advice and get her to let us go...

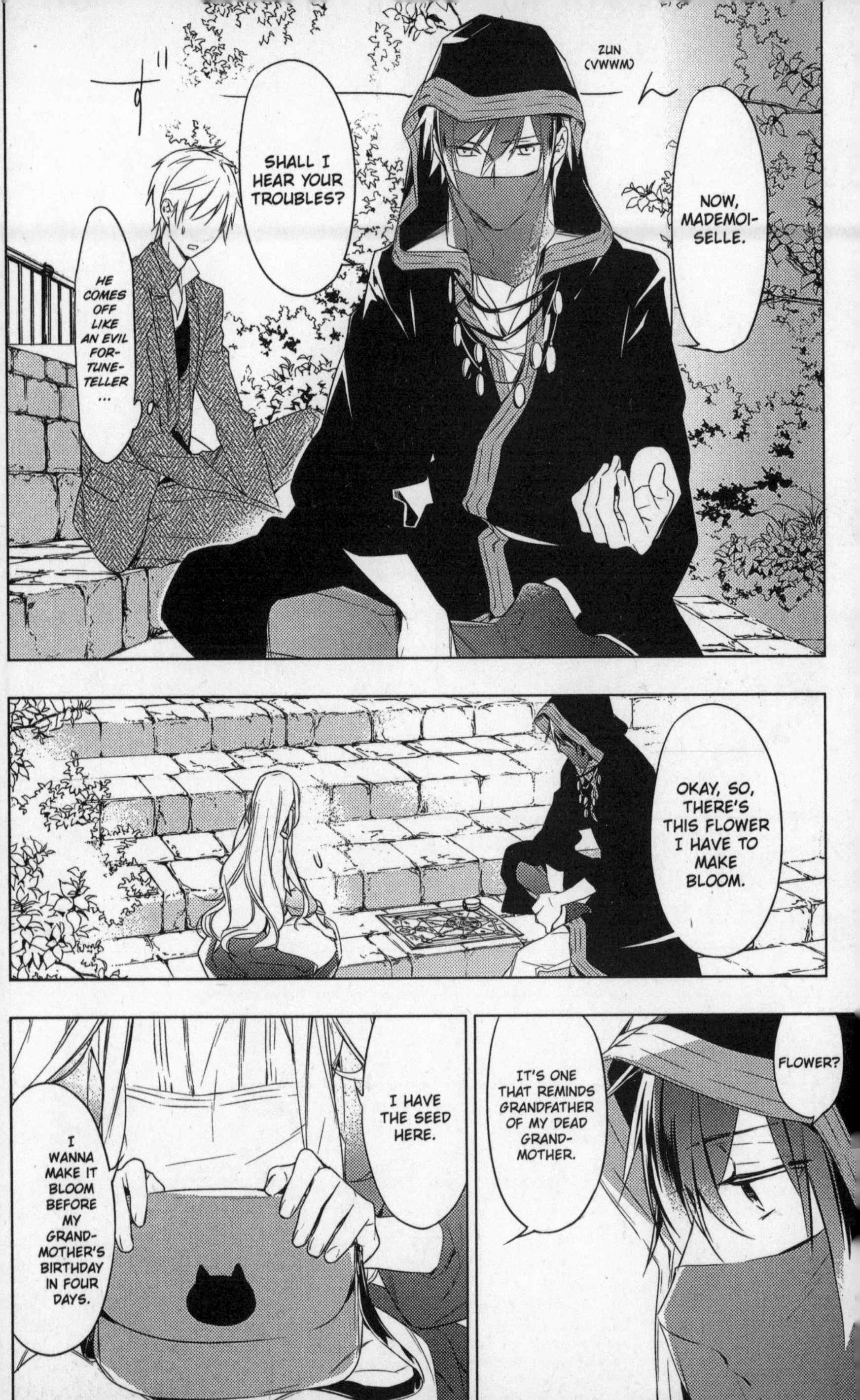
ZUN (VWWM)
NOW, MADEMOISELLE.
SHALL I HEAR YOUR TROUBLES?
HE COMES OFF LIKE AN EVIL FORTUNE-TELLER...
OKAY, SO, THERE'S THIS FLOWER I HAVE TO MAKE BLOOM.
FLOWER?
IT'S ONE THAT REMINDS GRANDFATHER OF MY DEAD GRANDMOTHER.
I HAVE THE SEED HERE.
I WANNA MAKE IT BLOOM BEFORE MY GRANDMOTHER'S BIRTHDAY IN FOUR DAYS.

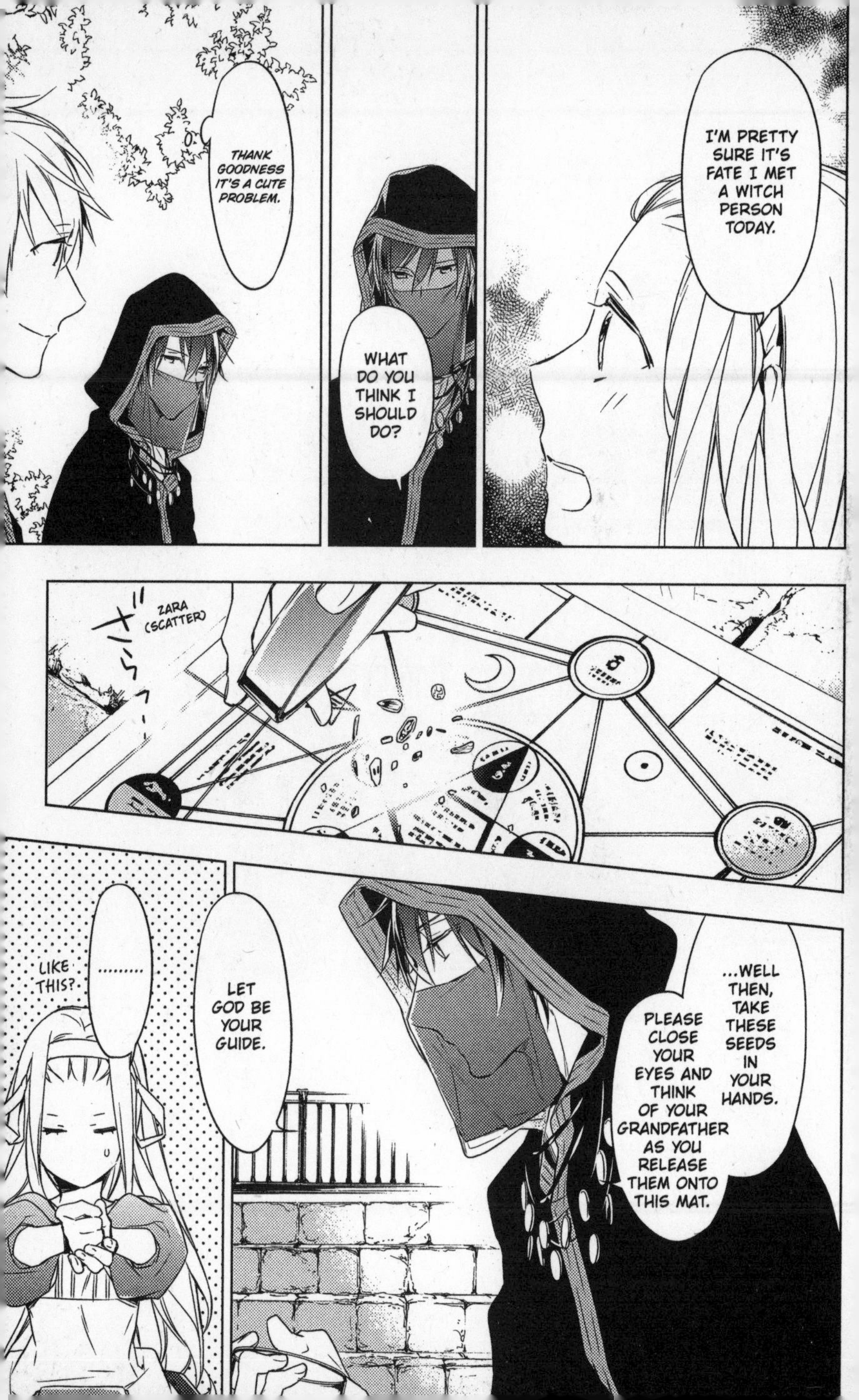
I'M PRETTY SURE IT'S FATE I MET A WITCH PERSON TODAY.
WHAT DO YOU THINK I SHOULD DO?
THANK GOODNESS IT'S A CUTE PROBLEM.
ZARA (SCATTER)
...WELL THEN, TAKE THESE SEEDS IN YOUR HANDS.
PLEASE CLOSE YOUR EYES AND THINK OF YOUR GRANDFATHER AS YOU RELEASE THEM ONTO THIS MAT.
LET GOD BE YOUR GUIDE.
....
LIKE THIS?

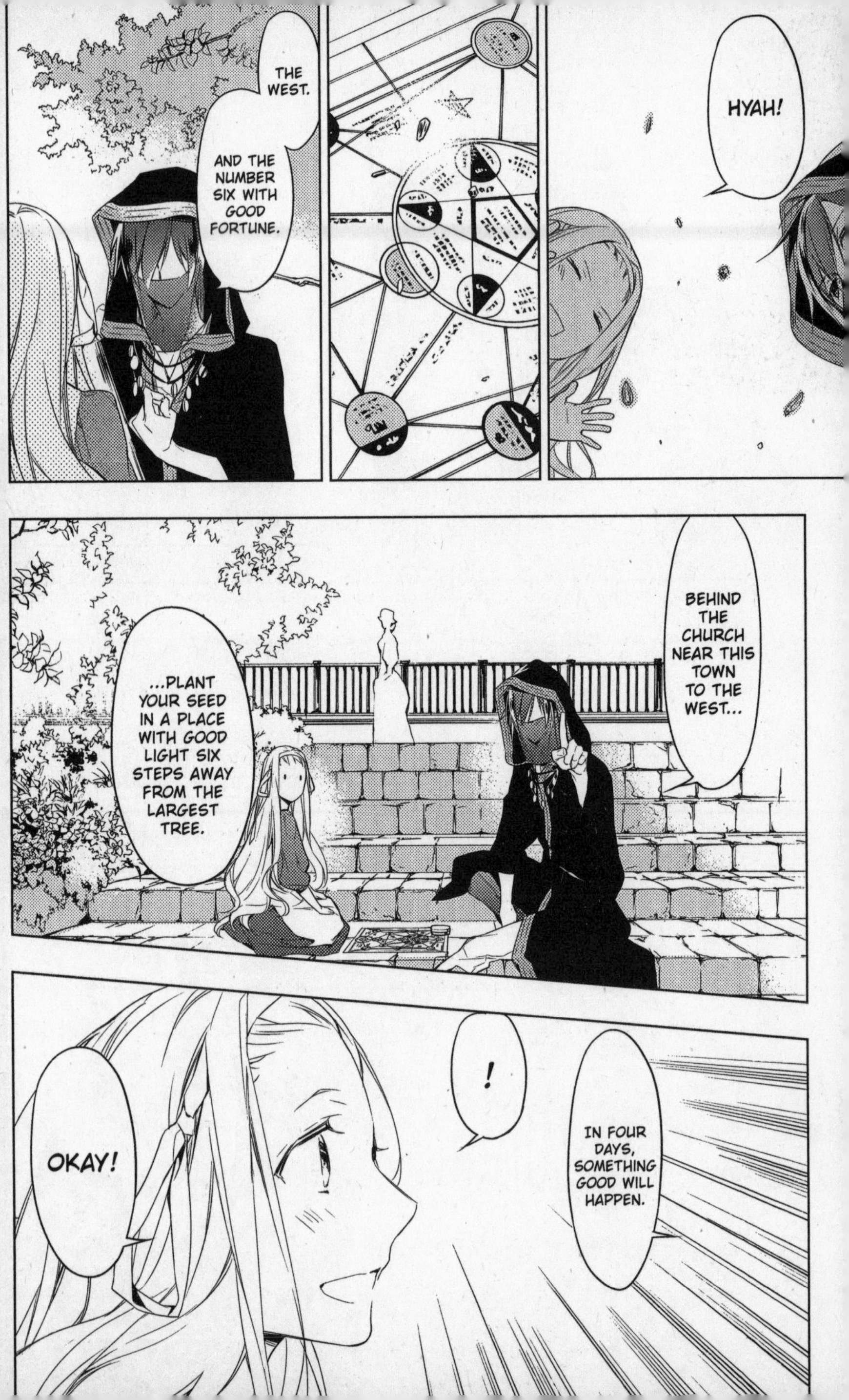
HYAH!
THE WEST.
AND THE NUMBER SIX WITH GOOD FORTUNE.
BEHIND THE CHURCH NEAR THIS TOWN TO THE WEST...
...PLANT YOUR SEED IN A PLACE WITH GOOD LIGHT SIX STEPS AWAY FROM THE LARGEST TREE.
IN FOUR DAYS, SOMETHING GOOD WILL HAPPEN.
!
OKAY!

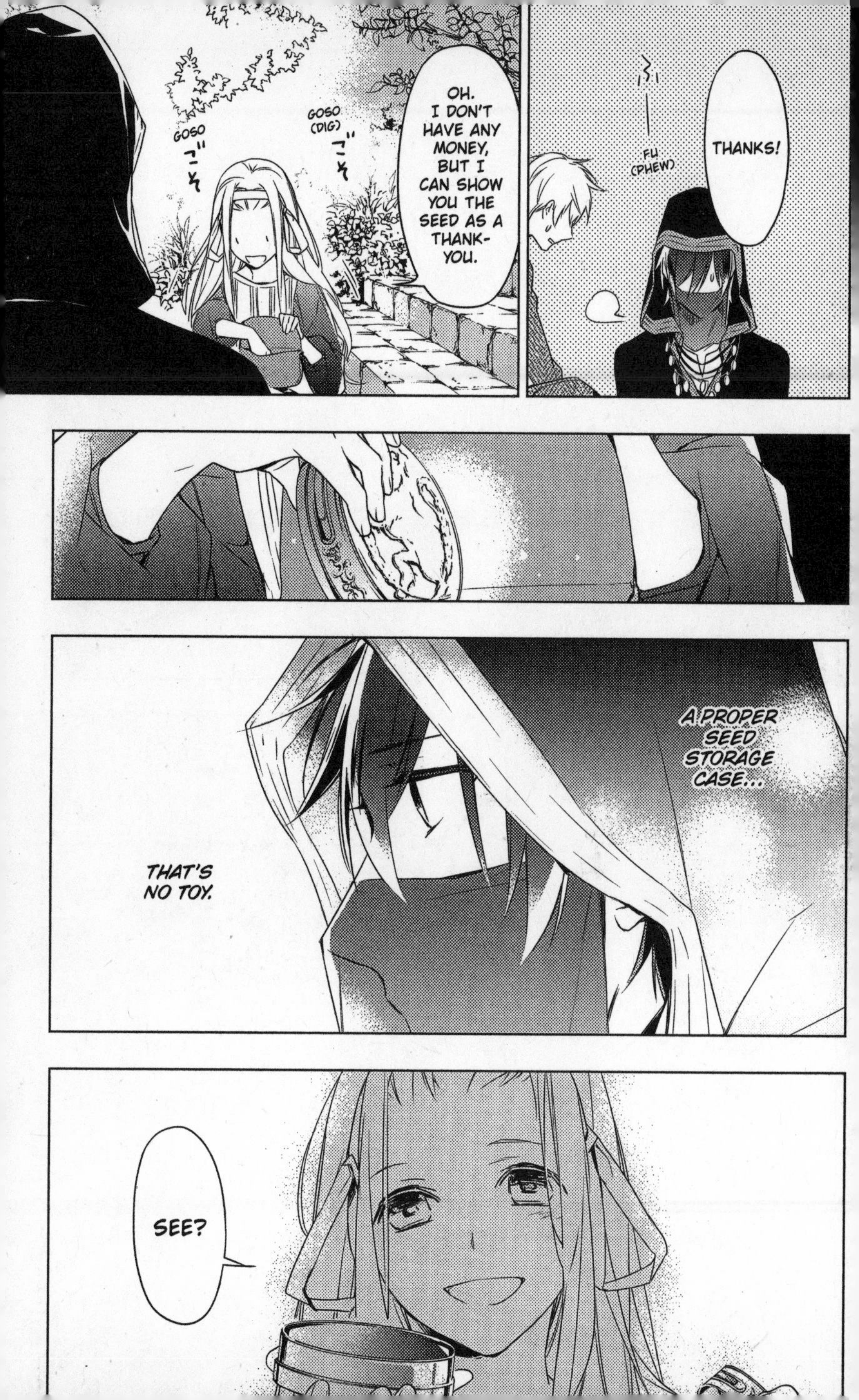

THANKS!
FU (PHEW)
OH. I DON'T HAVE ANY MONEY, BUT I CAN SHOW YOU THE SEED AS A THANK-YOU.
GOSO (DIG)
GOSO
A PROPER SEED STORAGE CASE...
THAT'S NO TOY.
SEE?

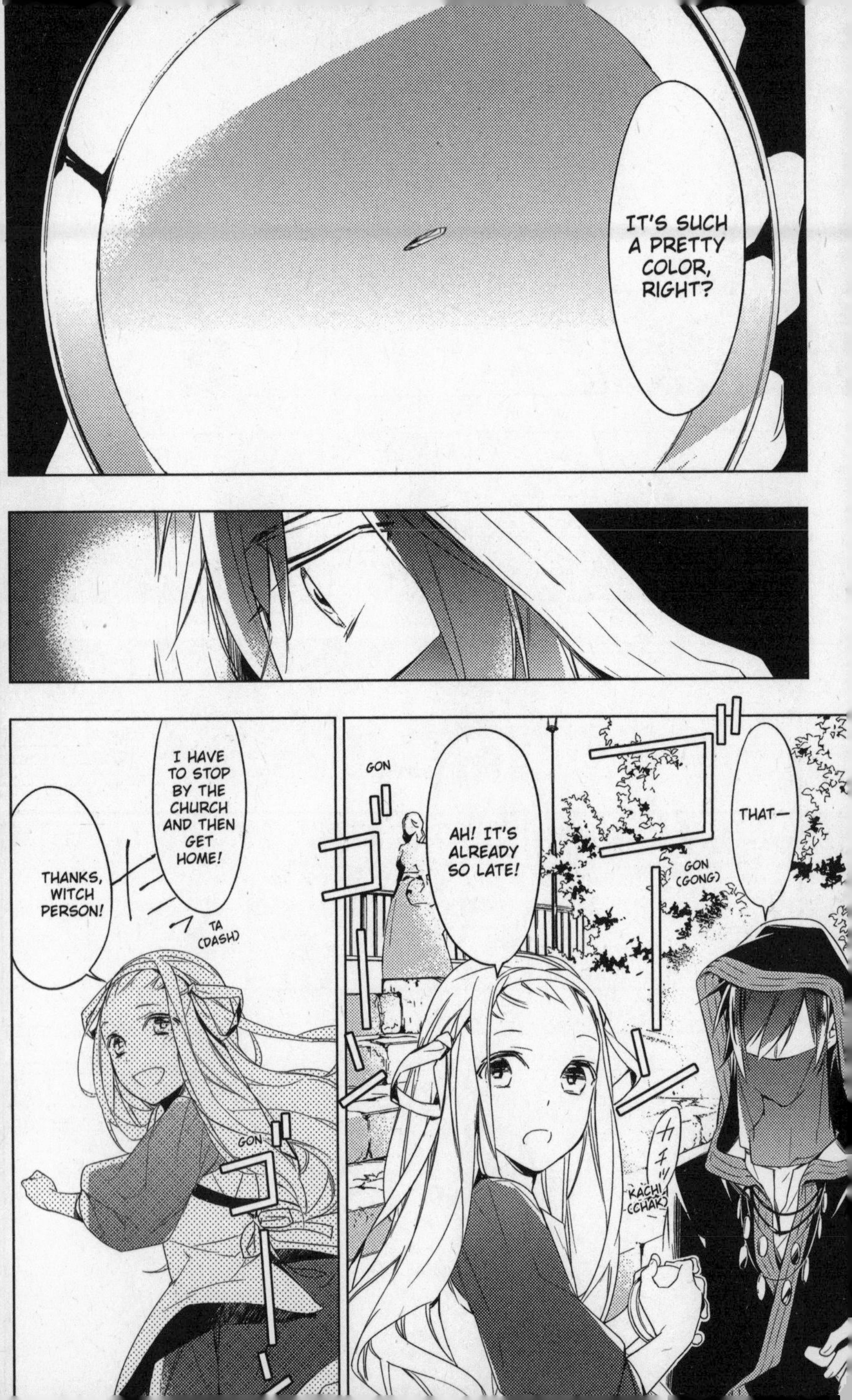
IT'S SUCH A PRETTY COLOR, RIGHT?
THAT—
GON (GONG)
AH! IT'S ALREADY SO LATE!
GON
KACHI (CHAK)
I HAVE TO STOP BY THE CHURCH AND THEN GET HOME!
THANKS, WITCH PERSON!
TA (DASH)
GON

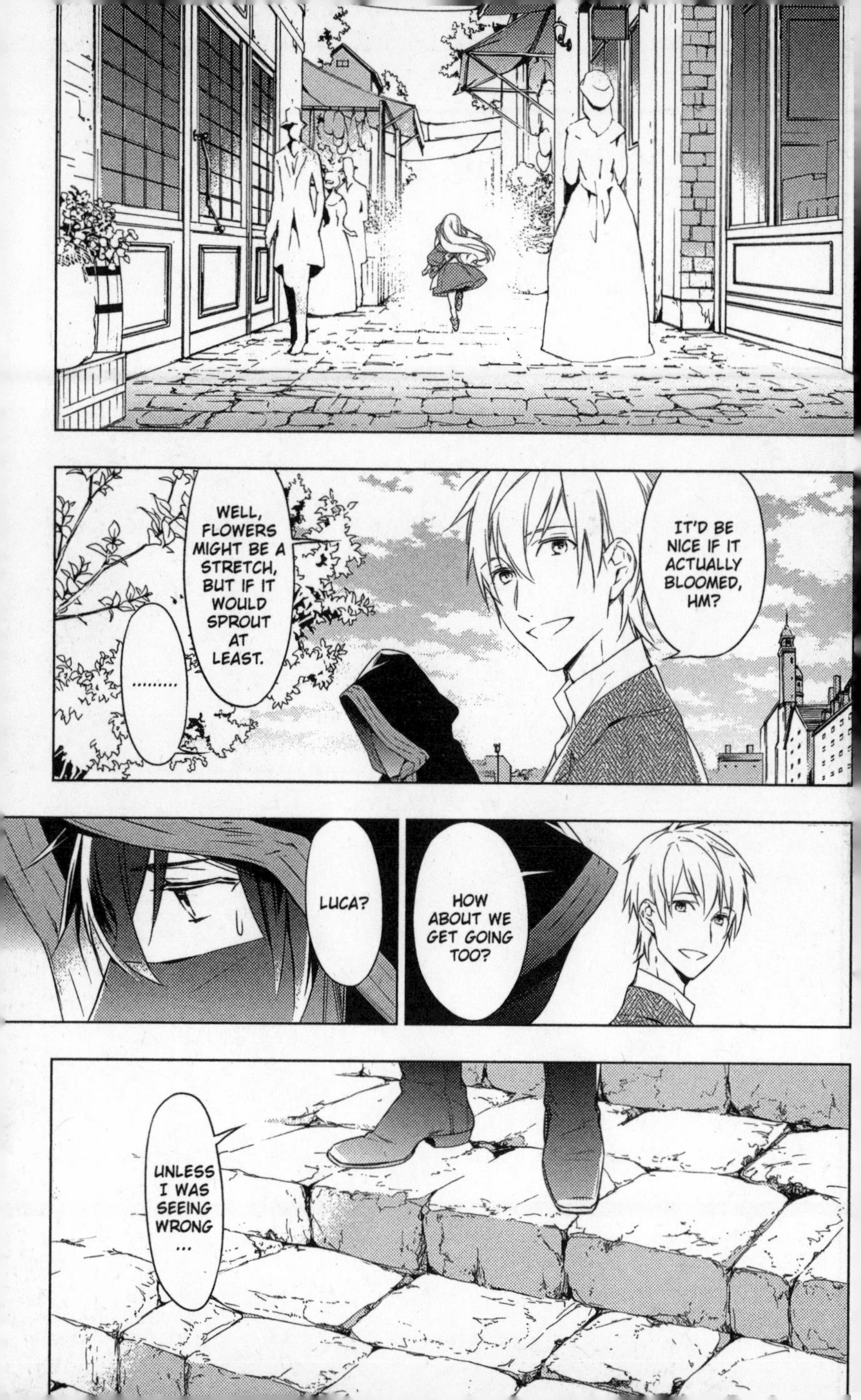
IT'D BE NICE IF IT ACTUALLY BLOOMED, HM?
WELL, FLOWERS MIGHT BE A STRETCH, BUT IF IT WOULD SPROUT AT LEAST.
....
HOW ABOUT WE GET GOING TOO?
LUCA?
UNLESS I WAS SEEING WRONG ...

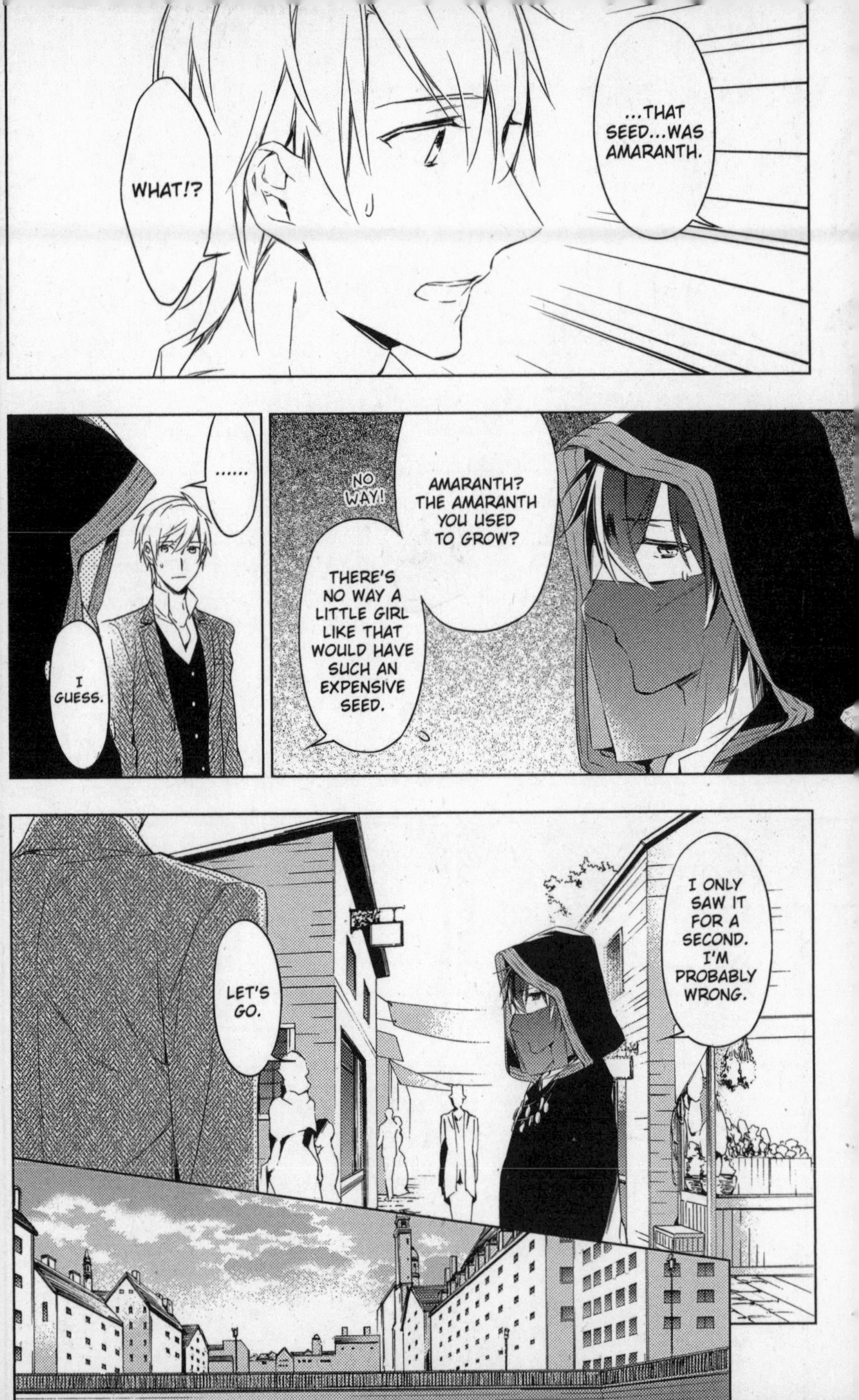
...THAT SEED...WAS AMARANTH.
WHAT!?
AMARANTH? THE AMARANTH YOU USED TO GROW?
NO WAY!
THERE'S NO WAY A LITTLE GIRL LIKE THAT WOULD HAVE SUCH AN EXPENSIVE SEED.
......
I GUESS.
I ONLY SAW IT FOR A SECOND. I'M PROBABLY WRONG.
LET'S GO.

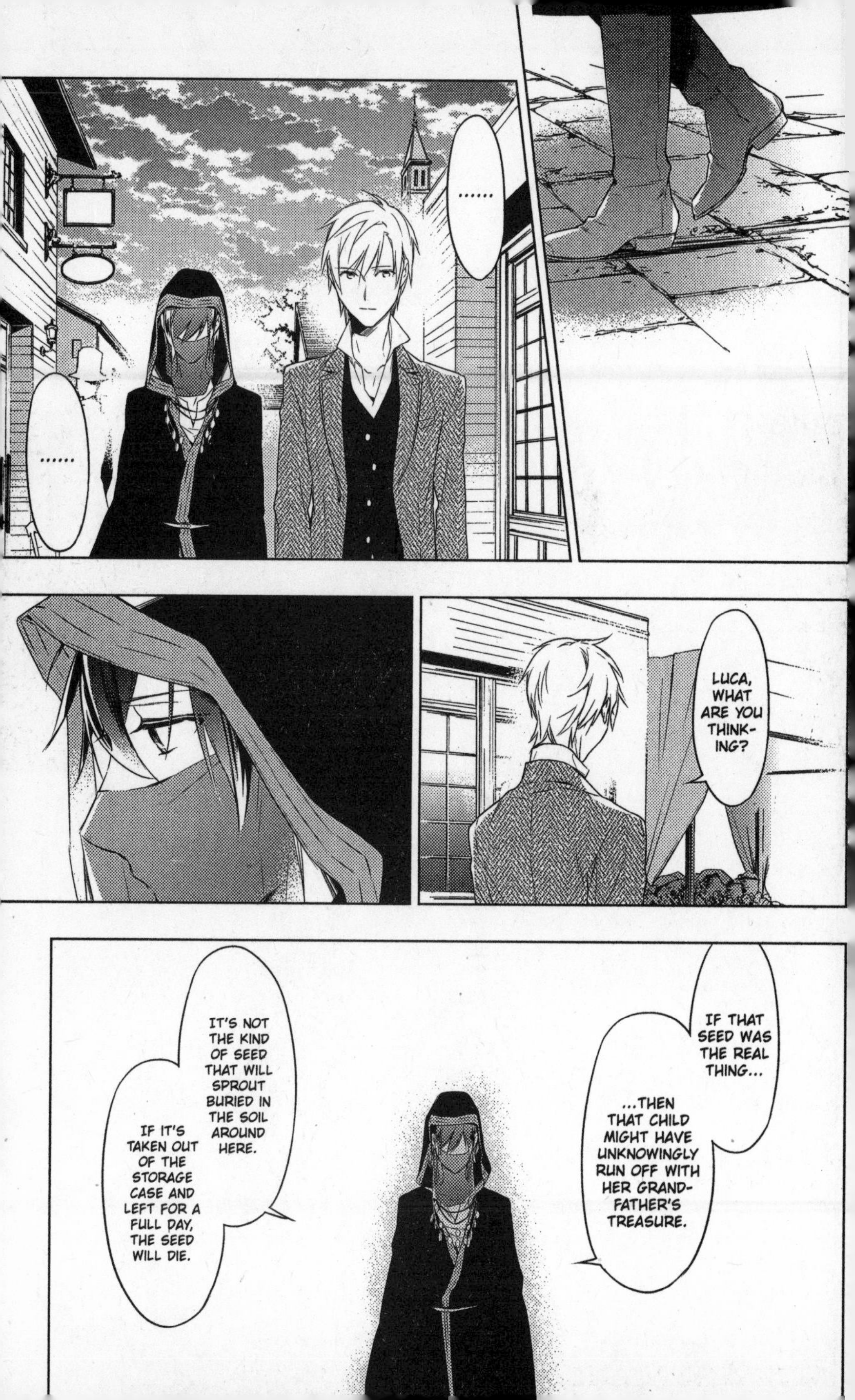
......
......
LUCA, WHAT ARE YOU THINKING?
IF THAT SEED WAS THE REAL THING...
...THEN THAT CHILD MIGHT HAVE UNKNOWINGLY RUN OFF WITH HER GRANDFATHER'S TREASURE.
IT'S NOT THE KIND OF SEED THAT WILL SPROUT BURIED IN THE SOIL AROUND HERE.
IF IT'S TAKEN OUT OF THE STORAGE CASE AND LEFT FOR A FULL DAY, THE SEED WILL DIE.

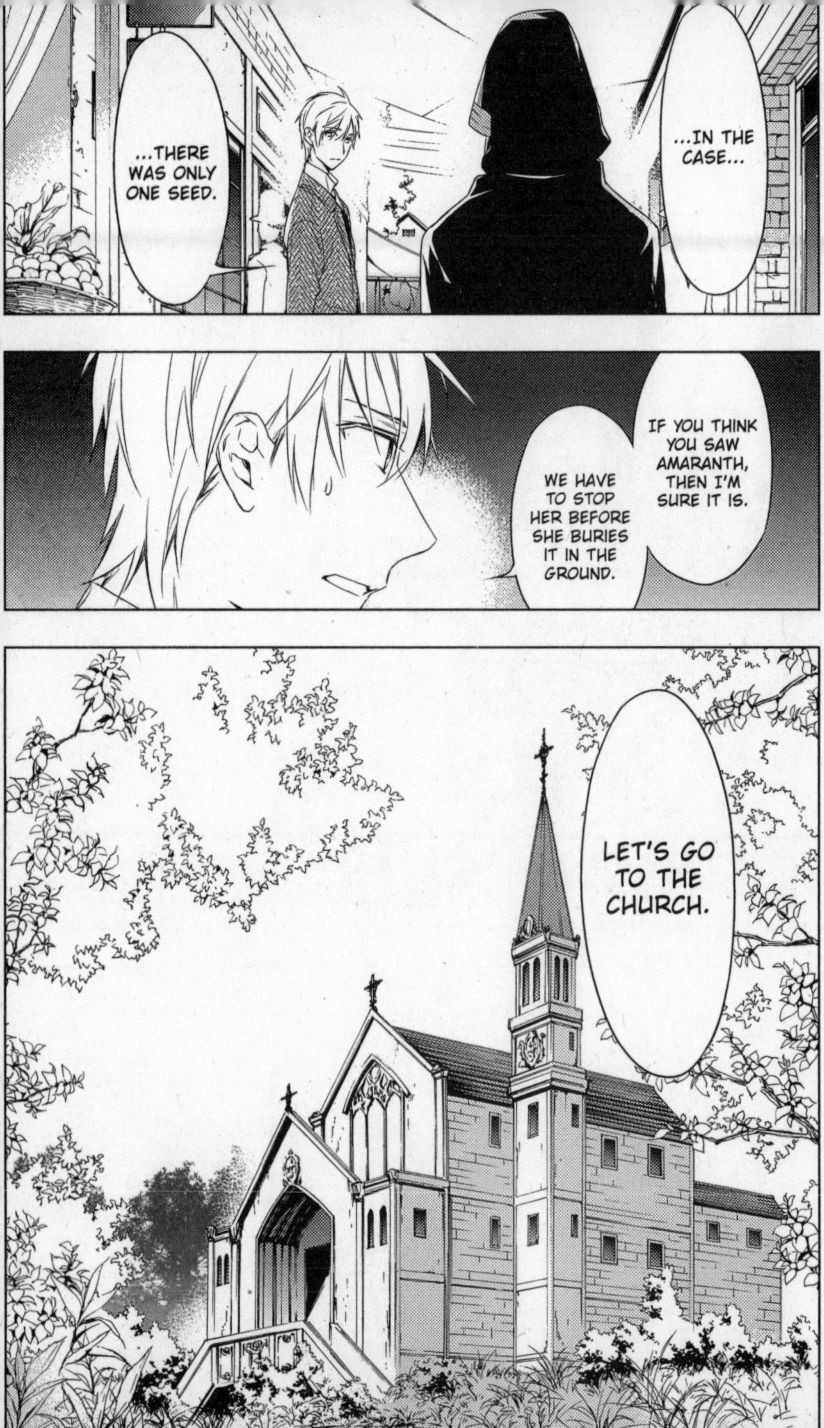
...IN THE CASE...
...THERE WAS ONLY ONE SEED.
IF YOU THINK YOU SAW AMARANTH, THEN I'M SURE IT IS.
WE HAVE TO STOP HER BEFORE SHE BURIES IT IN THE GROUND.
LET'S GO TO THE CHURCH.

GRAINELIERS

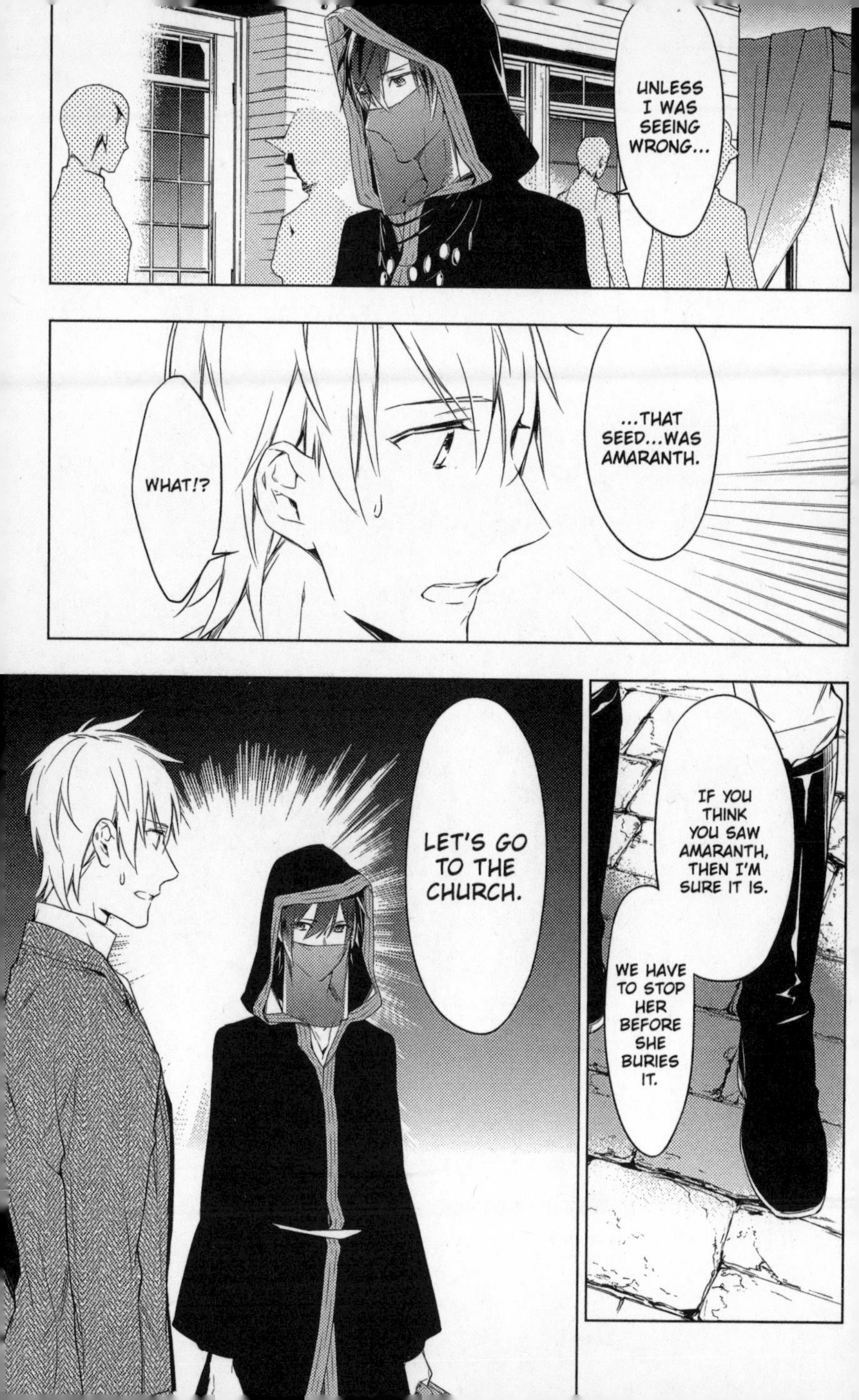
UNLESS I WAS SEEING WRONG...
...THAT SEED...WAS AMARANTH.
WHAT!?
IF YOU THINK YOU SAW AMARANTH, THEN I'M SURE IT IS.
WE HAVE TO STOP HER BEFORE SHE BURIES IT.
LET'S GO TO THE CHURCH.

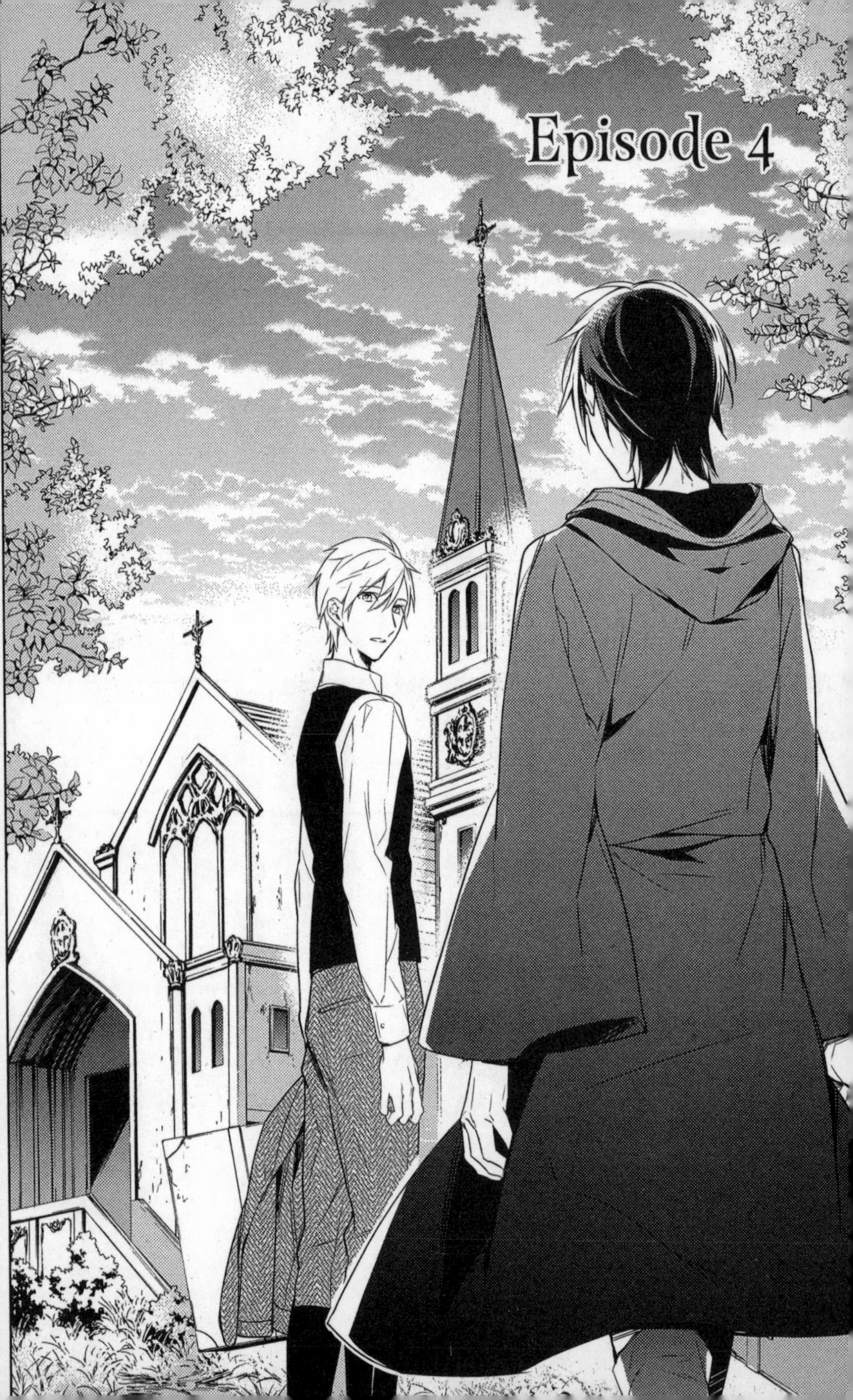
Episode 4

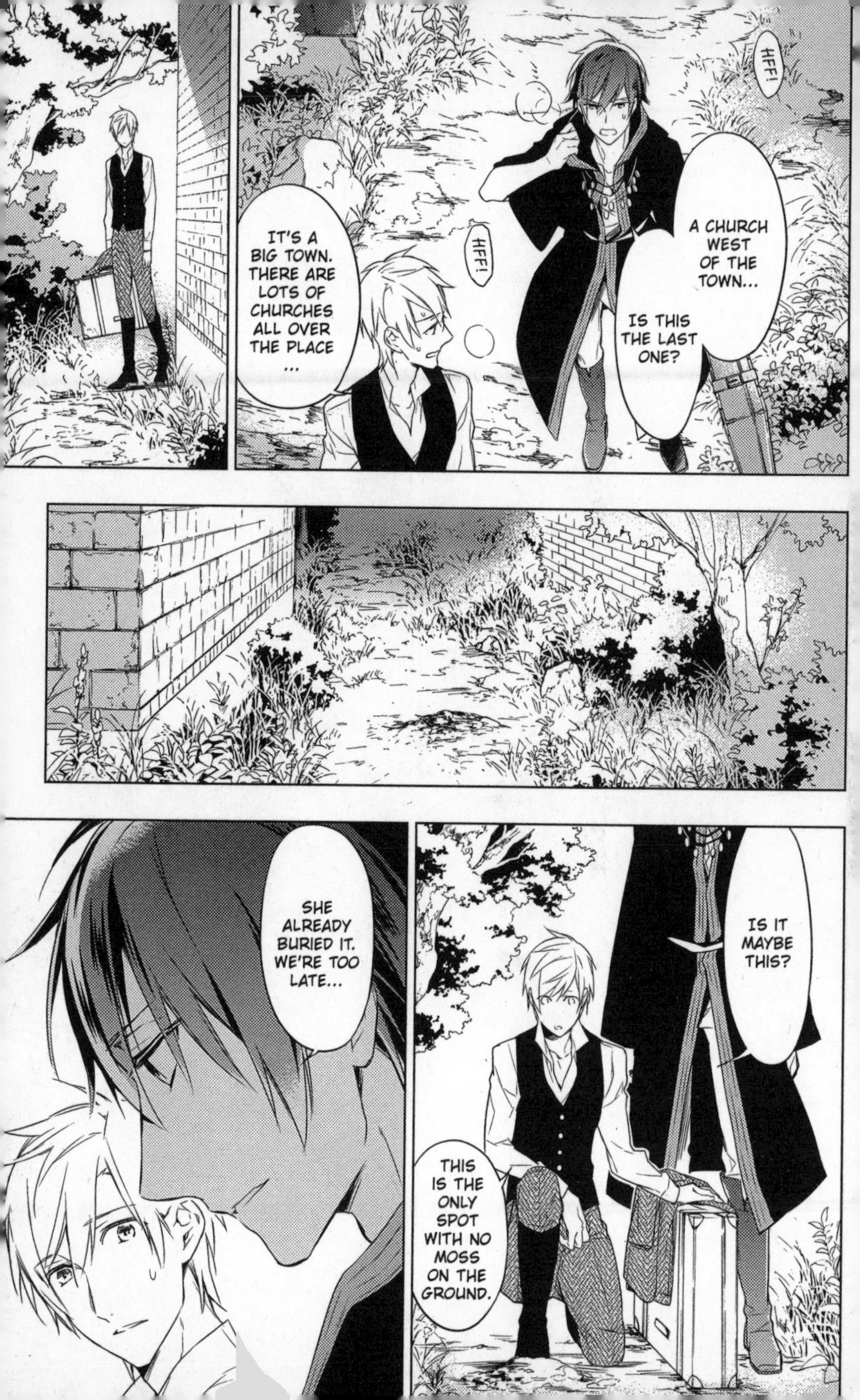
HFF!
A CHURCH WEST OF THE TOWN...
IS THIS THE LAST ONE?
HFF!
IT'S A BIG TOWN. THERE ARE LOTS OF CHURCHES ALL OVER THE PLACE...
IS IT MAYBE THIS?
THIS IS THE ONLY SPOT WITH NO MOSS ON THE GROUND.
SHE ALREADY BURIED IT. WE'RE TOO LATE...

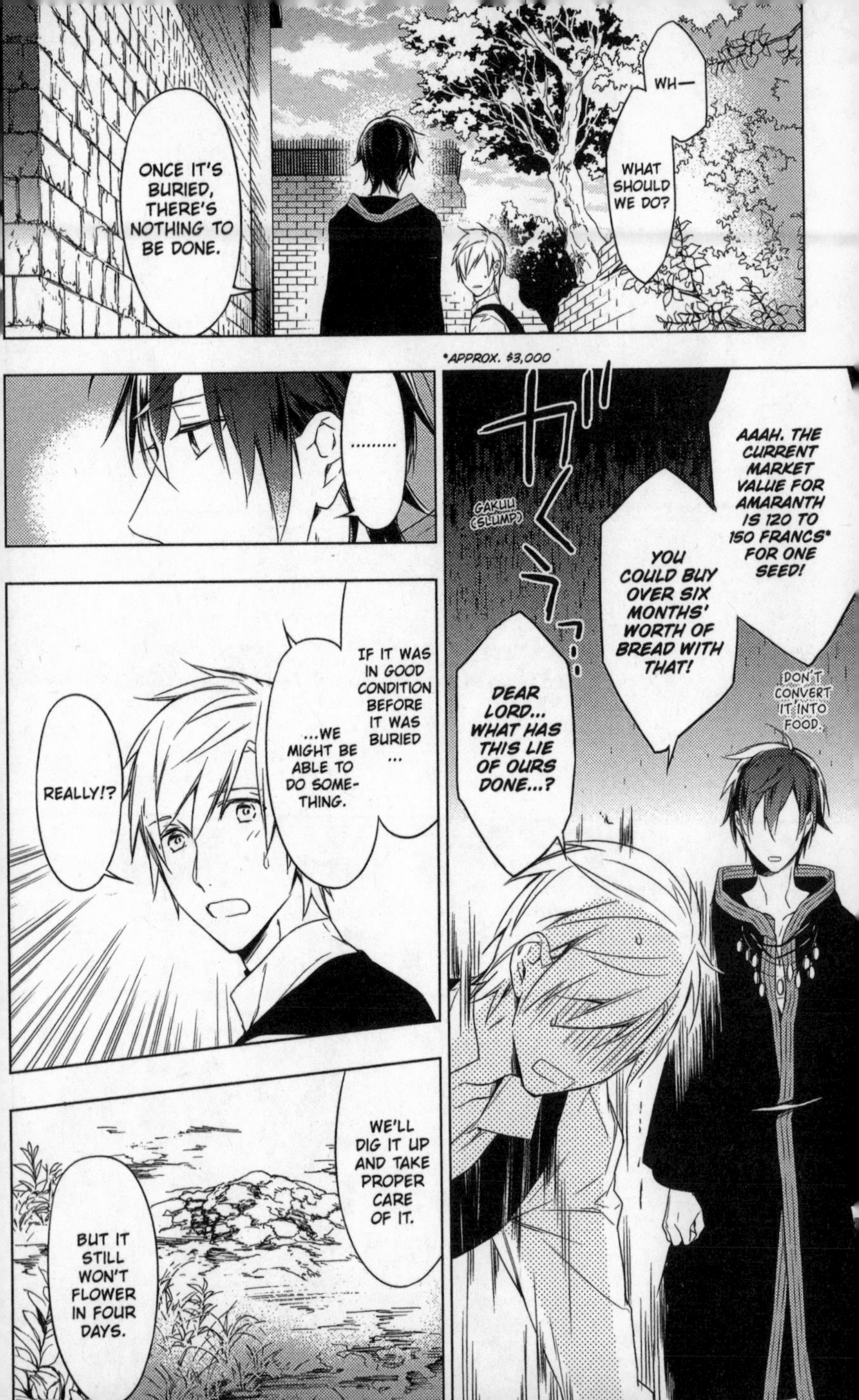
WH— WHAT SHOULD WE DO?
ONCE IT'S BURIED, THERE'S NOTHING TO BE DONE.
AAAH. THE CURRENT MARKET VALUE FOR AMARANTH IS 120 TO 150 FRANCS* FOR ONE SEED!
YOU COULD BUY OVER SIX MONTHS' WORTH OF BREAD WITH THAT!
GAKUU (SLUMP)
DEAR LORD... WHAT HAS THIS LIE OF OURS DONE...?
DON'T CONVERT IT INTO FOOD.
*APPROX. $3,000
....
IF IT WAS IN GOOD CONDITION BEFORE IT WAS BURIED ... ...WE MIGHT BE ABLE TO DO SOME-THING.
REALLY!?
WE'LL DIG IT UP AND TAKE PROPER CARE OF IT.
BUT IT STILL WON'T FLOWER IN FOUR DAYS.

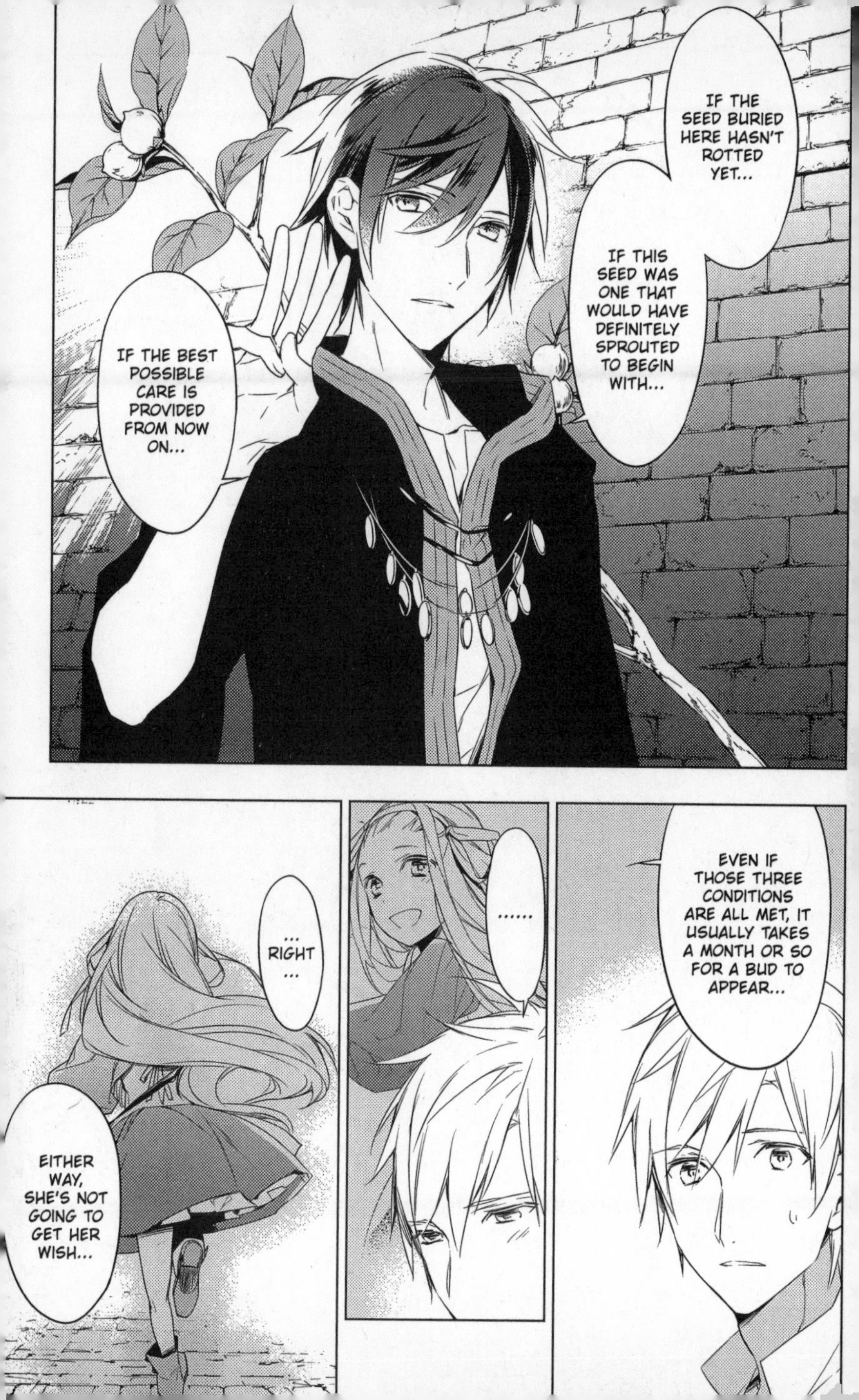
IF THE SEED BURIED HERE HASN'T ROTTED YET...
IF THIS SEED WAS ONE THAT WOULD HAVE DEFINITELY SPROUTED TO BEGIN WITH...
IF THE BEST POSSIBLE CARE IS PROVIDED FROM NOW ON...
EVEN IF THOSE THREE CONDITIONS ARE ALL MET, IT USUALLY TAKES A MONTH OR SO FOR A BUD TO APPEAR...
......
...RIGHT...
EITHER WAY, SHE'S NOT GOING TO GET HER WISH...

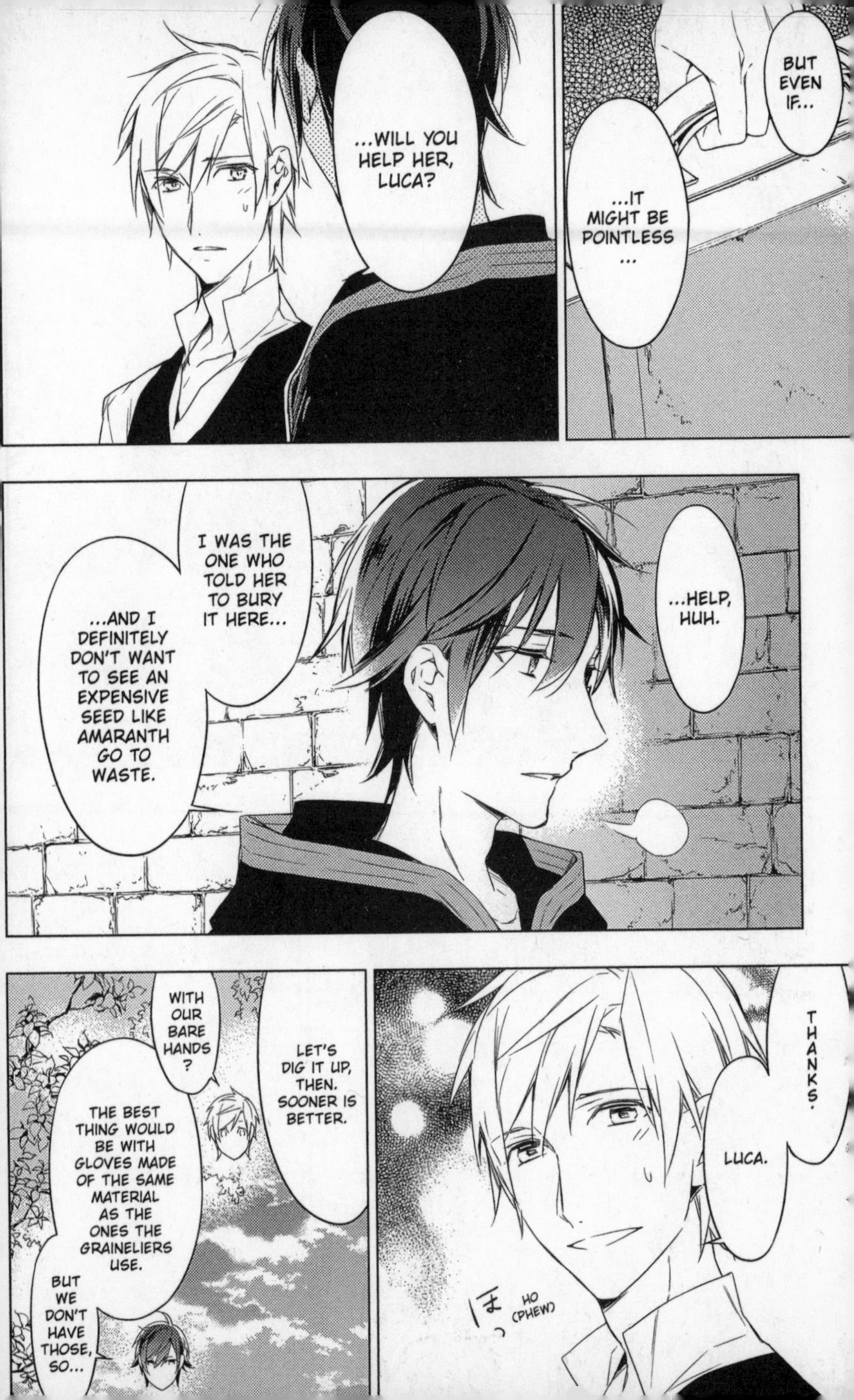
BUT EVEN IF...
...IT MIGHT BE POINTLESS...
...WILL YOU HELP HER, LUCA?
...HELP, HUH.
I WAS THE ONE WHO TOLD HER TO BURY IT HERE...
...AND I DEFINITELY DON'T WANT TO SEE AN EXPENSIVE SEED LIKE AMARANTH GO TO WASTE.
THANKS.
LUCA.
ほっ
HO (PHEW)
LET'S DIG IT UP, THEN. SOONER IS BETTER.
WITH OUR BARE HANDS?
THE BEST THING WOULD BE WITH GLOVES MADE OF THE SAME MATERIAL AS THE ONES THE GRAINELIERS USE.
BUT WE DON'T HAVE THOSE, SO...

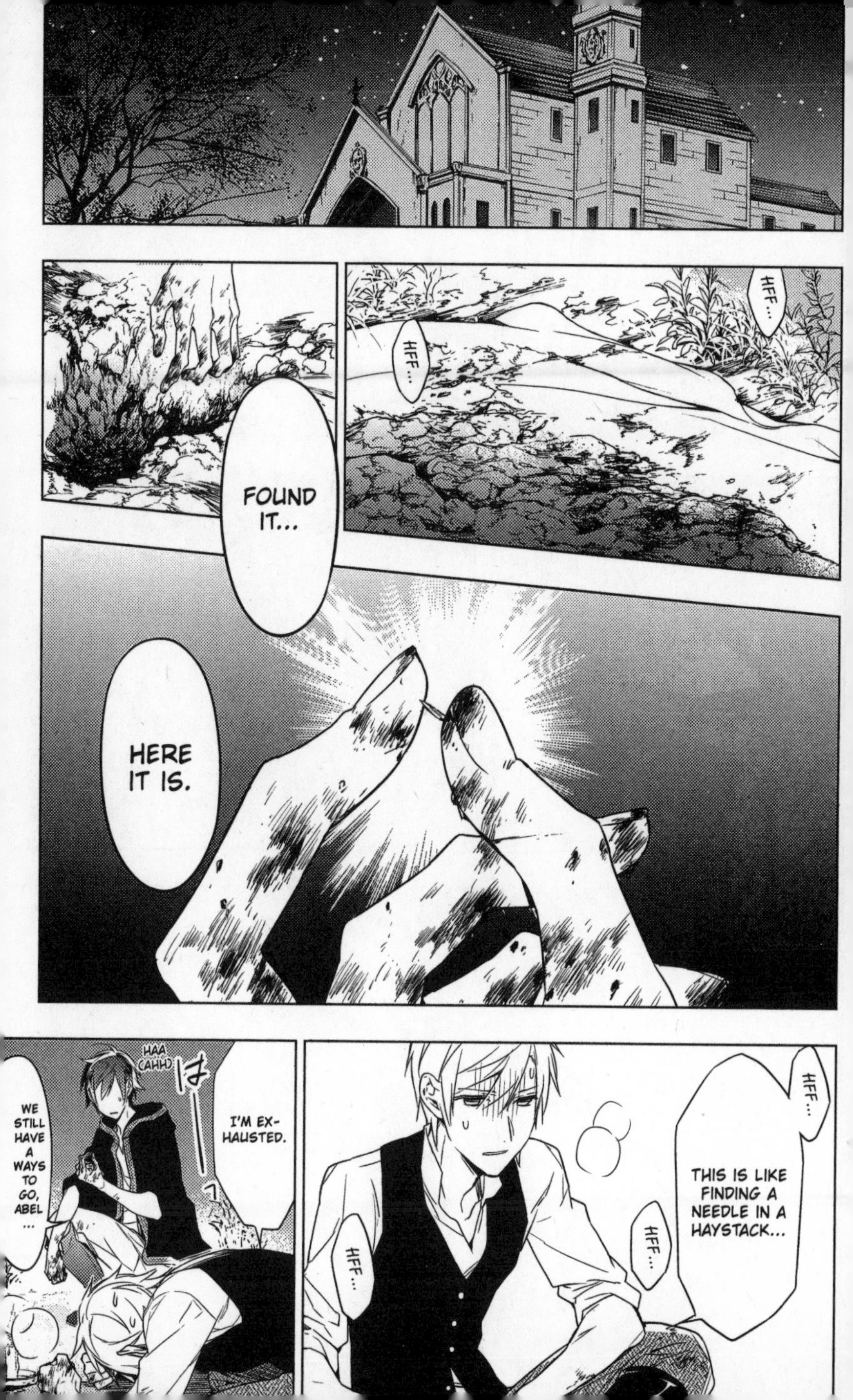
HFF...
HFF...
FOUND IT...
HERE IT IS.
HFF...
THIS IS LIKE FINDING A NEEDLE IN A HAYSTACK...
HFF...
HFF...
HAA (AHH)
I'M EX-HAUSTED.
WE STILL HAVE A WAYS TO GO, ABEL...

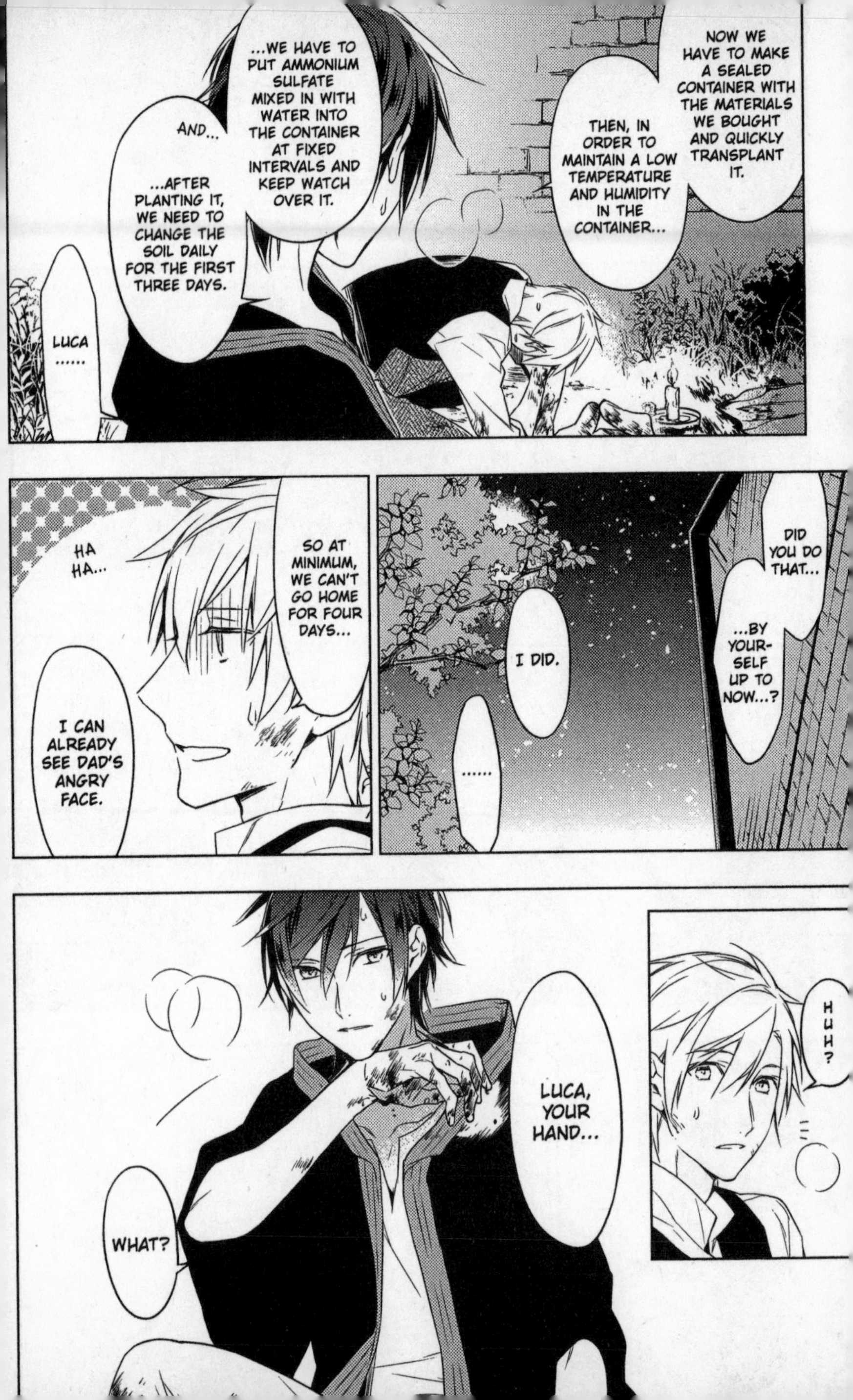
NOW WE HAVE TO MAKE A SEALED CONTAINER WITH THE MATERIALS WE BOUGHT AND QUICKLY TRANSPLANT IT.
THEN, IN ORDER TO MAINTAIN A LOW TEMPERATURE AND HUMIDITY IN THE CONTAINER...
...WE HAVE TO PUT AMMONIUM SULFATE MIXED IN WITH WATER INTO THE CONTAINER AT FIXED INTERVALS AND KEEP WATCH OVER IT.
AND...
...AFTER PLANTING IT, WE NEED TO CHANGE THE SOIL DAILY FOR THE FIRST THREE DAYS.
LUCA ......
DID YOU DO THAT...
...BY YOUR-SELF UP TO NOW...?
I DID.
......
SO AT MINIMUM, WE CAN'T GO HOME FOR FOUR DAYS...
HA HA...
I CAN ALREADY SEE DAD'S ANGRY FACE.
HUH?
LUCA, YOUR HAND...
WHAT?

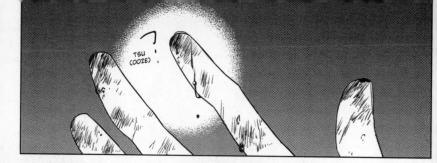

TSU (OOZE)
TCH! DAM-MIT.
IT'S SO DARK, I DIDN'T NOTICE ...!
WAS THERE A PIECE OF GLASS OR SOMETHING WHEN YOU WERE DIGGING IT UP?
ARE YOU OKAY?
A CUT LIKE THIS IS NO BIG DEAL.
I'M ACTU-ALLY...
...WORRIED THAT SOME BLOOD GOT ON THE SEED.
IT'S VERY DELICATE ...
ANYWAY, ONCE WE REPLANT IT...
...WE'LL TAKE TURNS WATCHING OVER IT. WE'LL STAY IN THIS CHURCH.

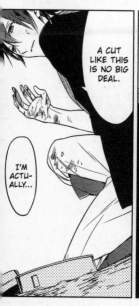

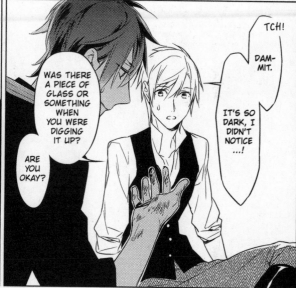

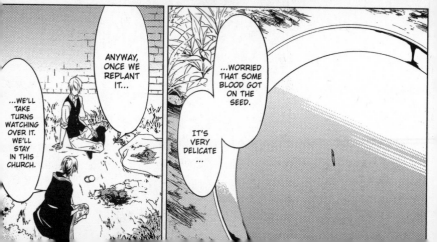

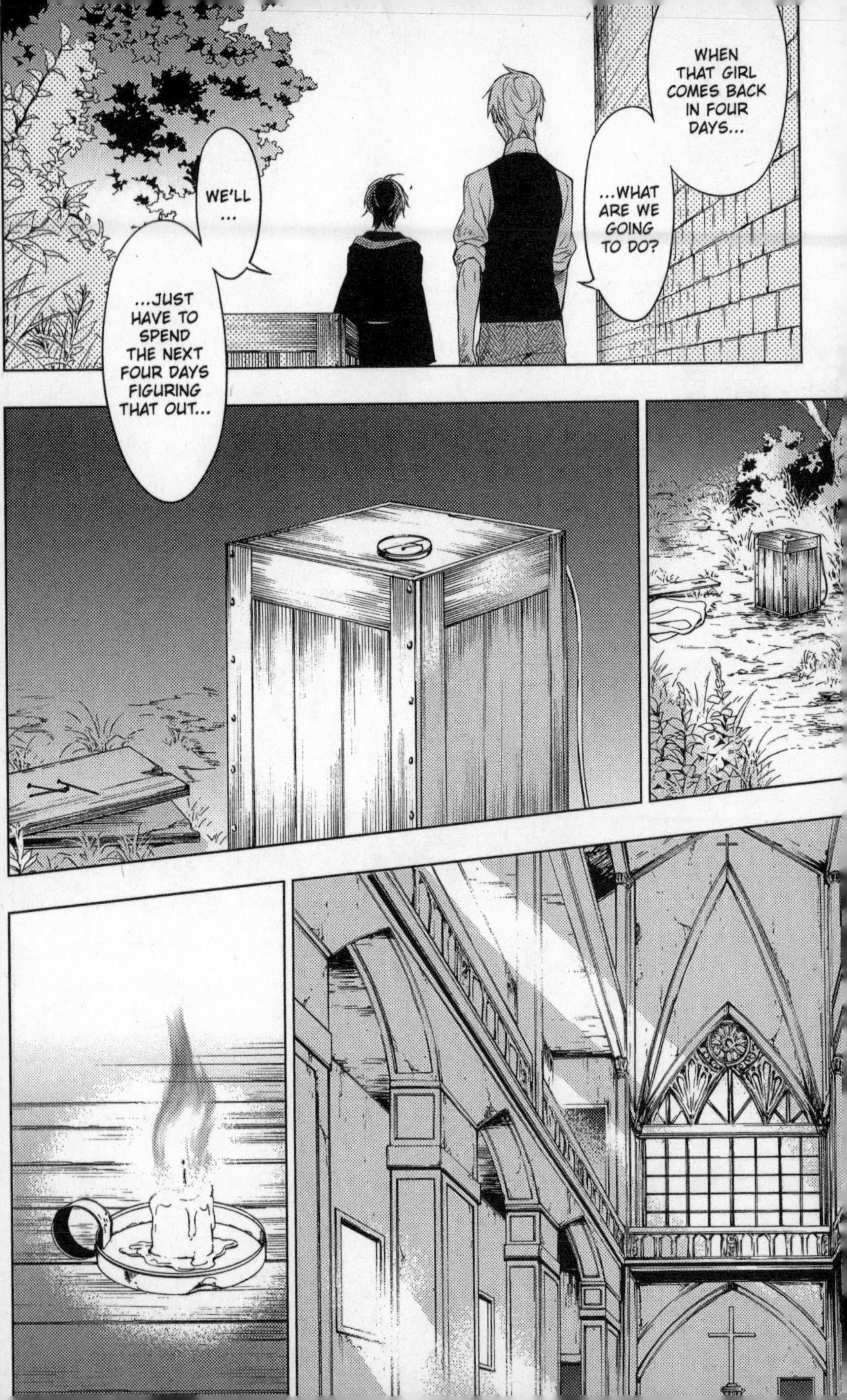
WHEN THAT GIRL COMES BACK IN FOUR DAYS...
...WHAT ARE WE GOING TO DO?
WE'LL ...
...JUST HAVE TO SPEND THE NEXT FOUR DAYS FIGURING THAT OUT...

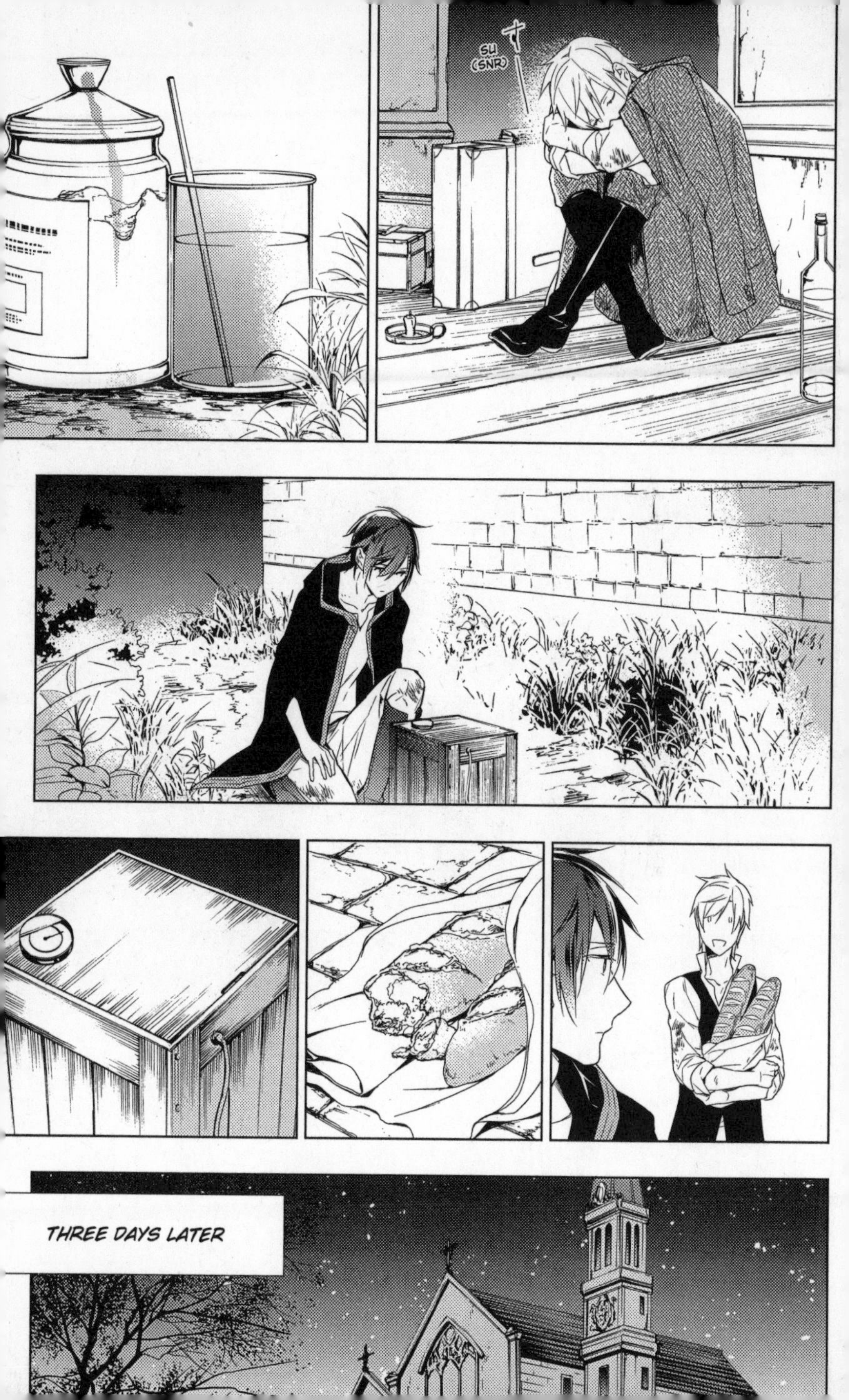
SU
(SNR)
THREE DAYS LATER

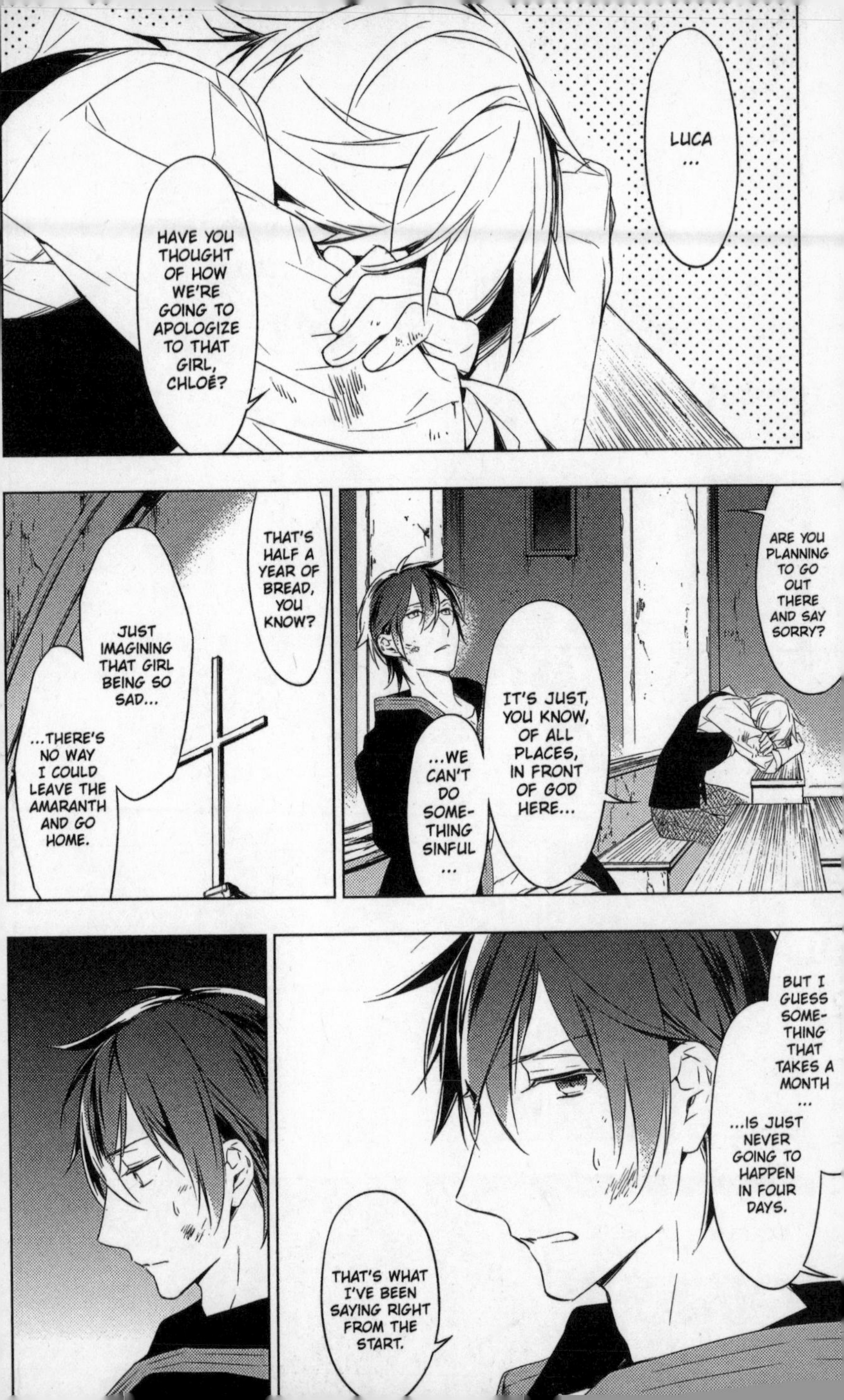
LUCA ...
HAVE YOU THOUGHT OF HOW WE'RE GOING TO APOLOGIZE TO THAT GIRL, CHLOÉ?
ARE YOU PLANNING TO GO OUT THERE AND SAY SORRY?
IT'S JUST, YOU KNOW, OF ALL PLACES, IN FRONT OF GOD HERE...
...WE CAN'T DO SOME-THING SINFUL ...
THAT'S HALF A YEAR OF BREAD, YOU KNOW?
JUST IMAGINING THAT GIRL BEING SO SAD...
...THERE'S NO WAY I COULD LEAVE THE AMARANTH AND GO HOME.
BUT I GUESS SOME-THING THAT TAKES A MONTH ...
...IS JUST NEVER GOING TO HAPPEN IN FOUR DAYS.
THAT'S WHAT I'VE BEEN SAYING RIGHT FROM THE START.

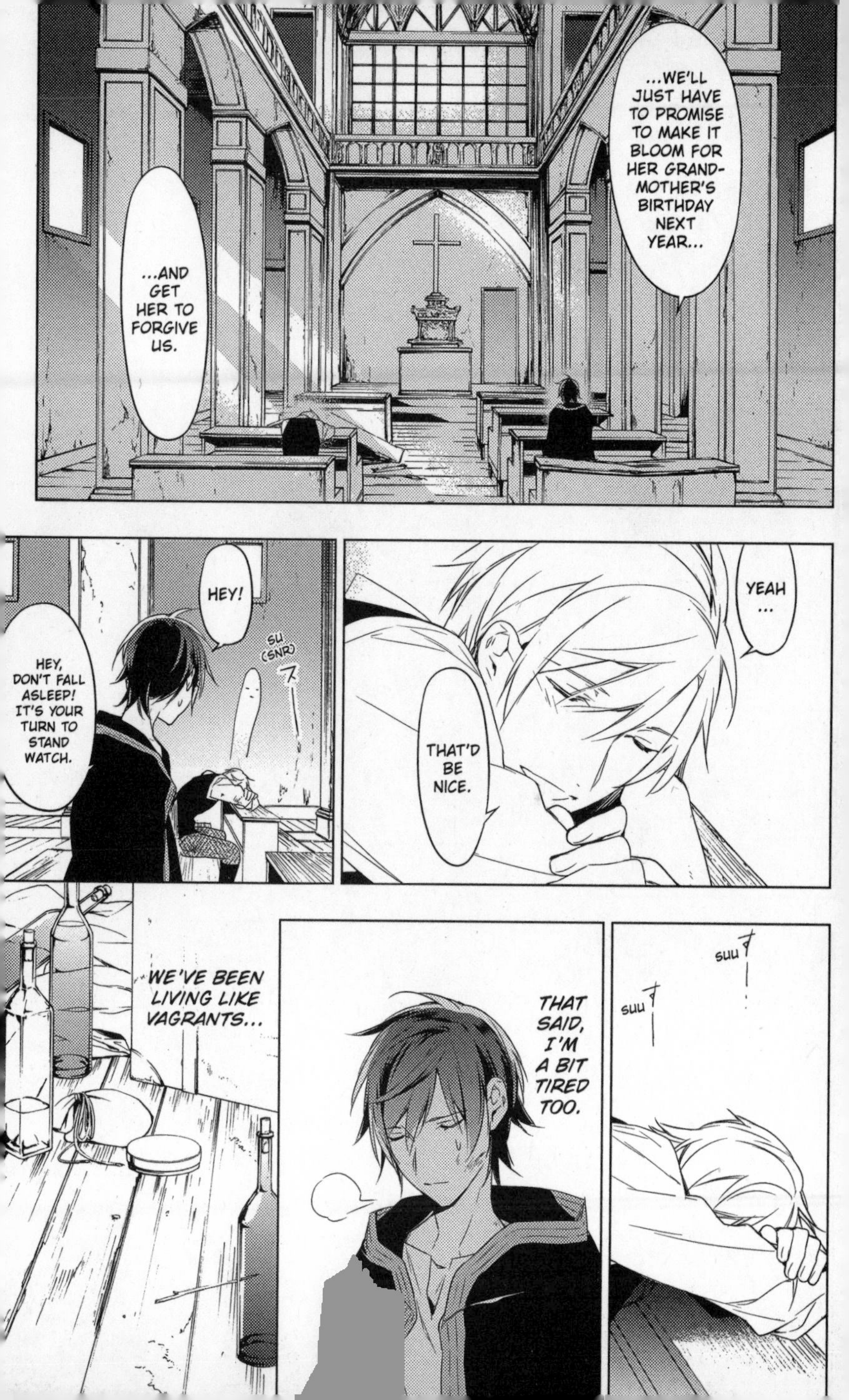
...WE'LL JUST HAVE TO PROMISE TO MAKE IT BLOOM FOR HER GRAND-MOTHER'S BIRTHDAY NEXT YEAR...
...AND GET HER TO FORGIVE US.
YEAH ...
THAT'D BE NICE.
HEY!
SU (SNR)
ス
HEY, DON'T FALL ASLEEP! IT'S YOUR TURN TO STAND WATCH.
SUU
SUU
THAT SAID, I'M A BIT TIRED TOO.
WE'VE BEEN LIVING LIKE VAGRANTS...

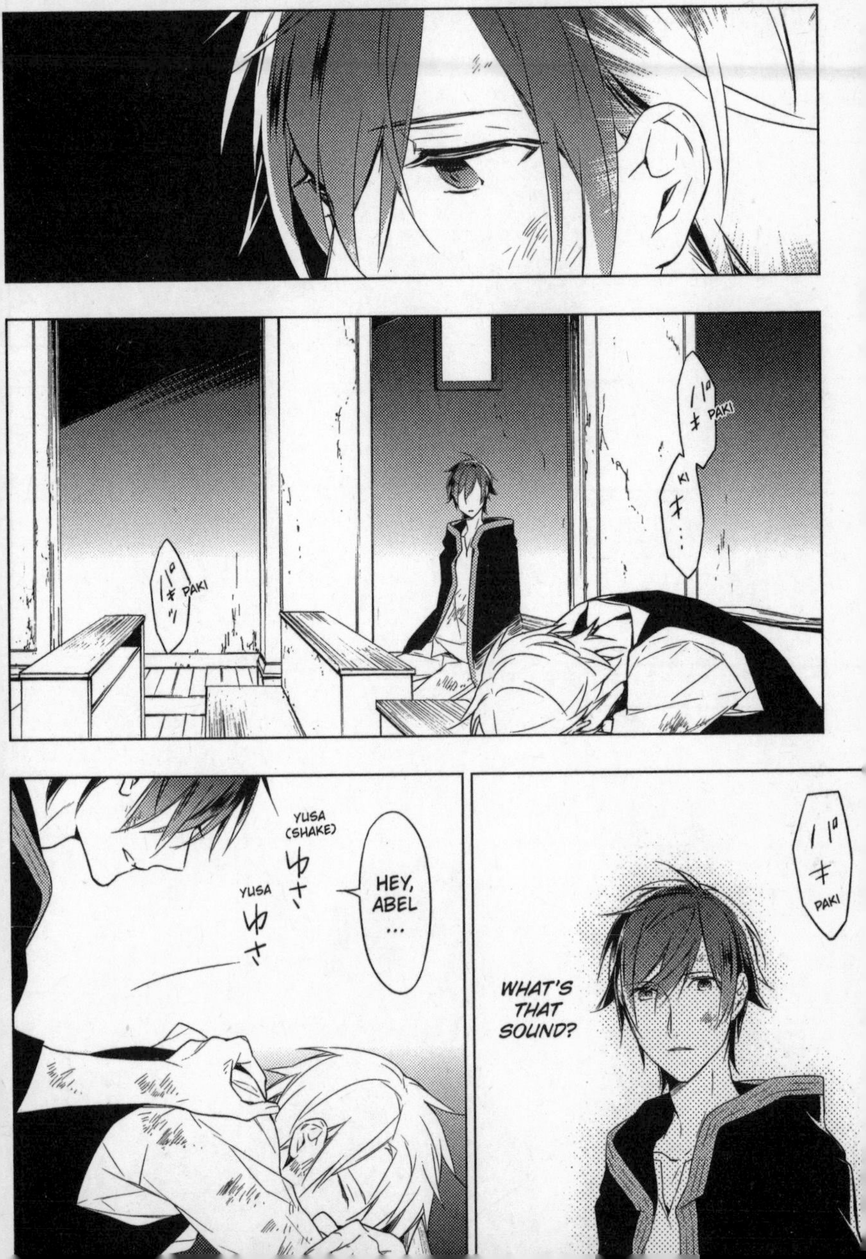
パキ PAKI
キ… KI
パキッ PAKI
パキ PAKI
WHAT'S THAT SOUND?
YUSA (SHAKE) ゆさ、
YUSA ゆさ
HEY, ABEL...

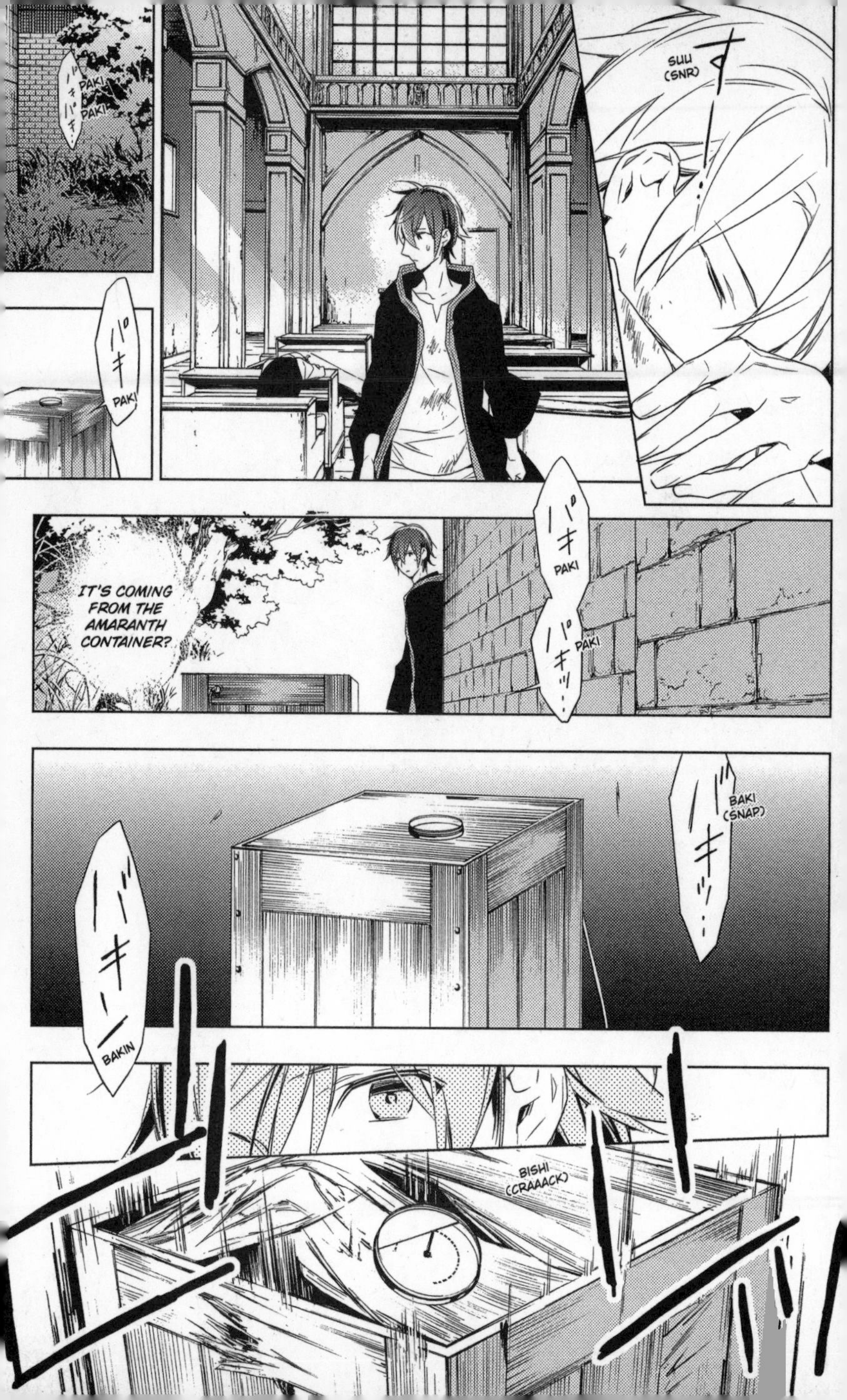
SUU (SNR)
PAKI PAKI
PAKI
PAKI
PAKI
IT'S COMING FROM THE AMARANTH CONTAINER?
BAKI (SNAP)
BAKIN
BISHI (CRAAACK)

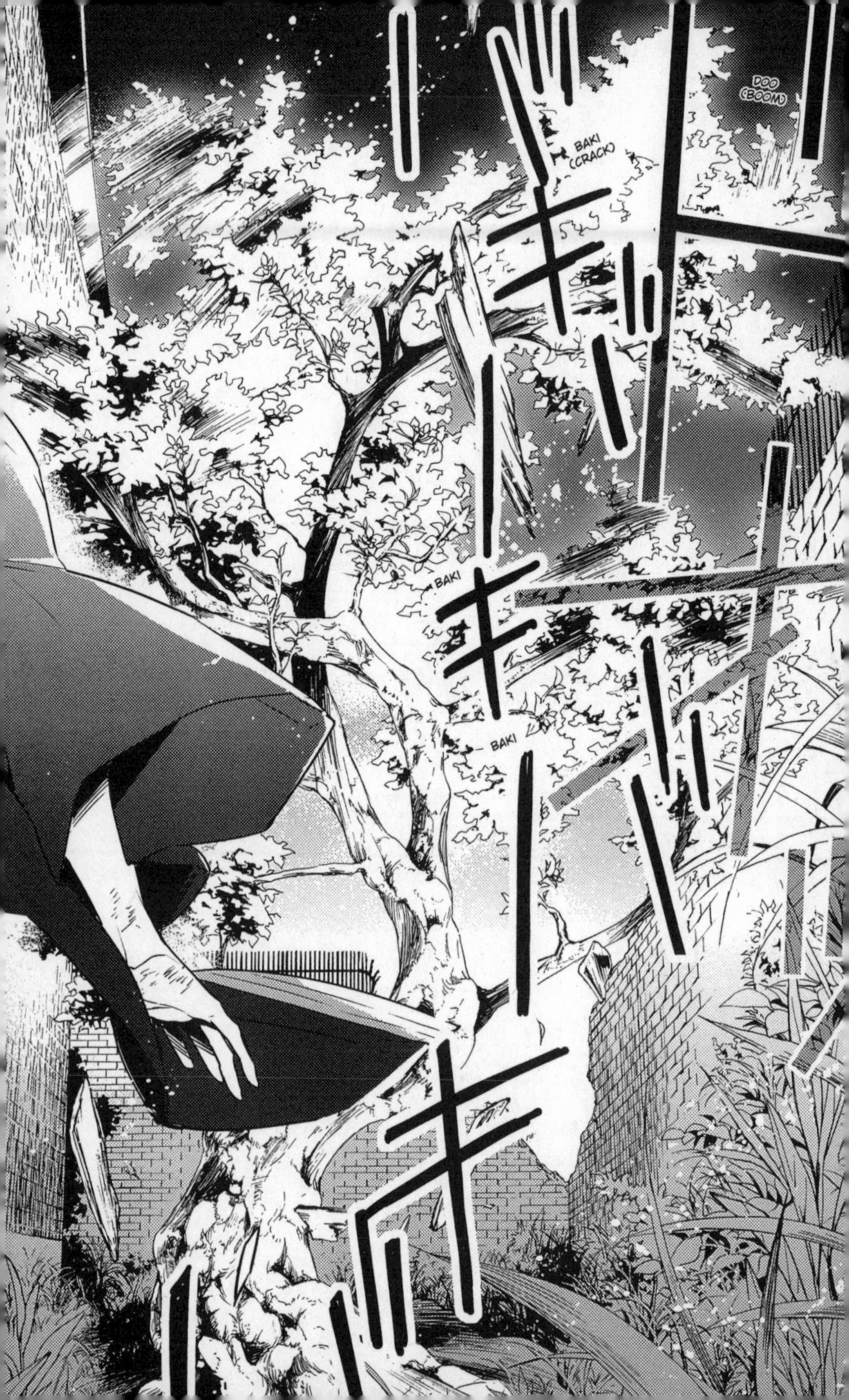
DOO (BOOM)
BAKI (CRACK)
BAKI
BAKI

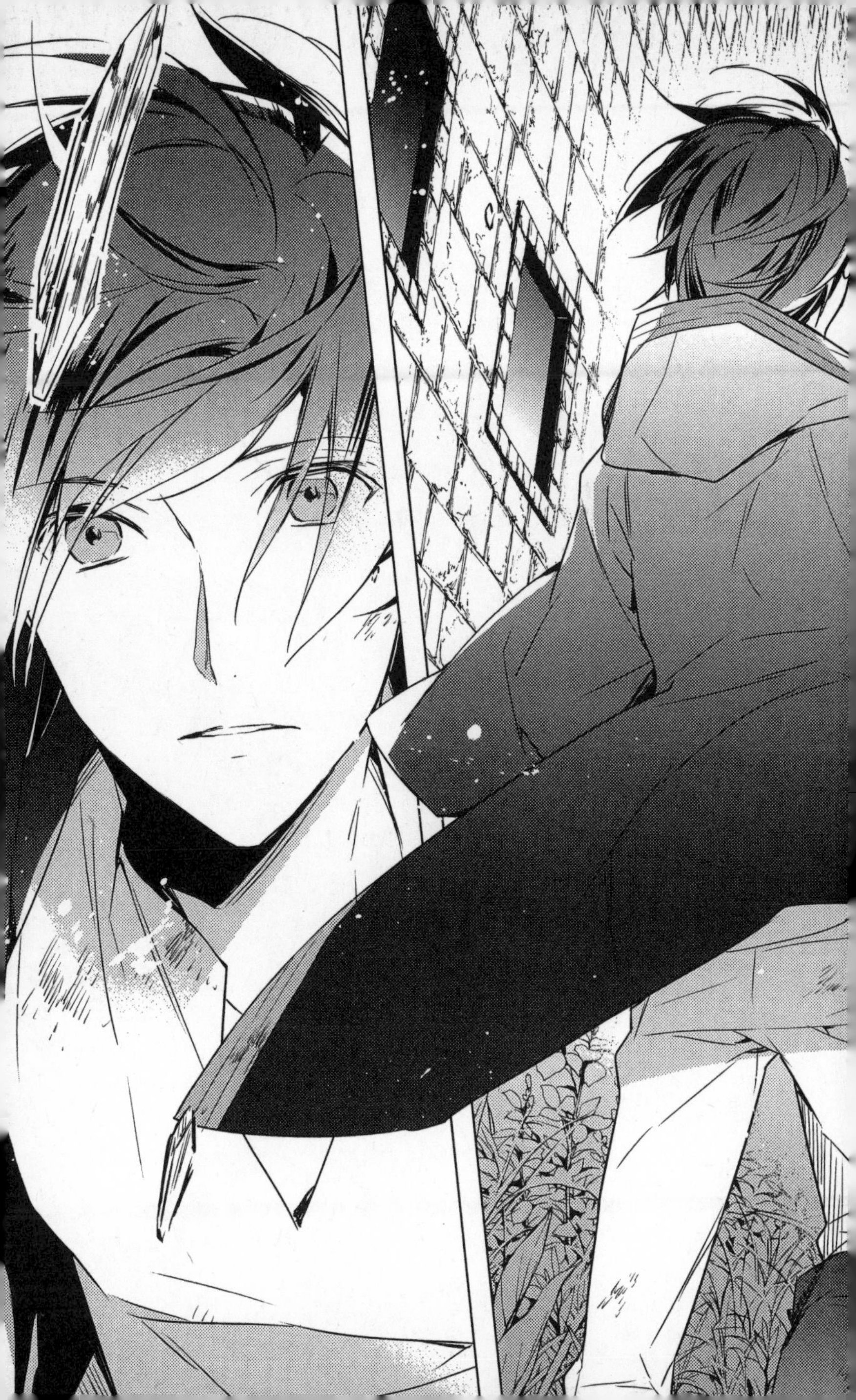

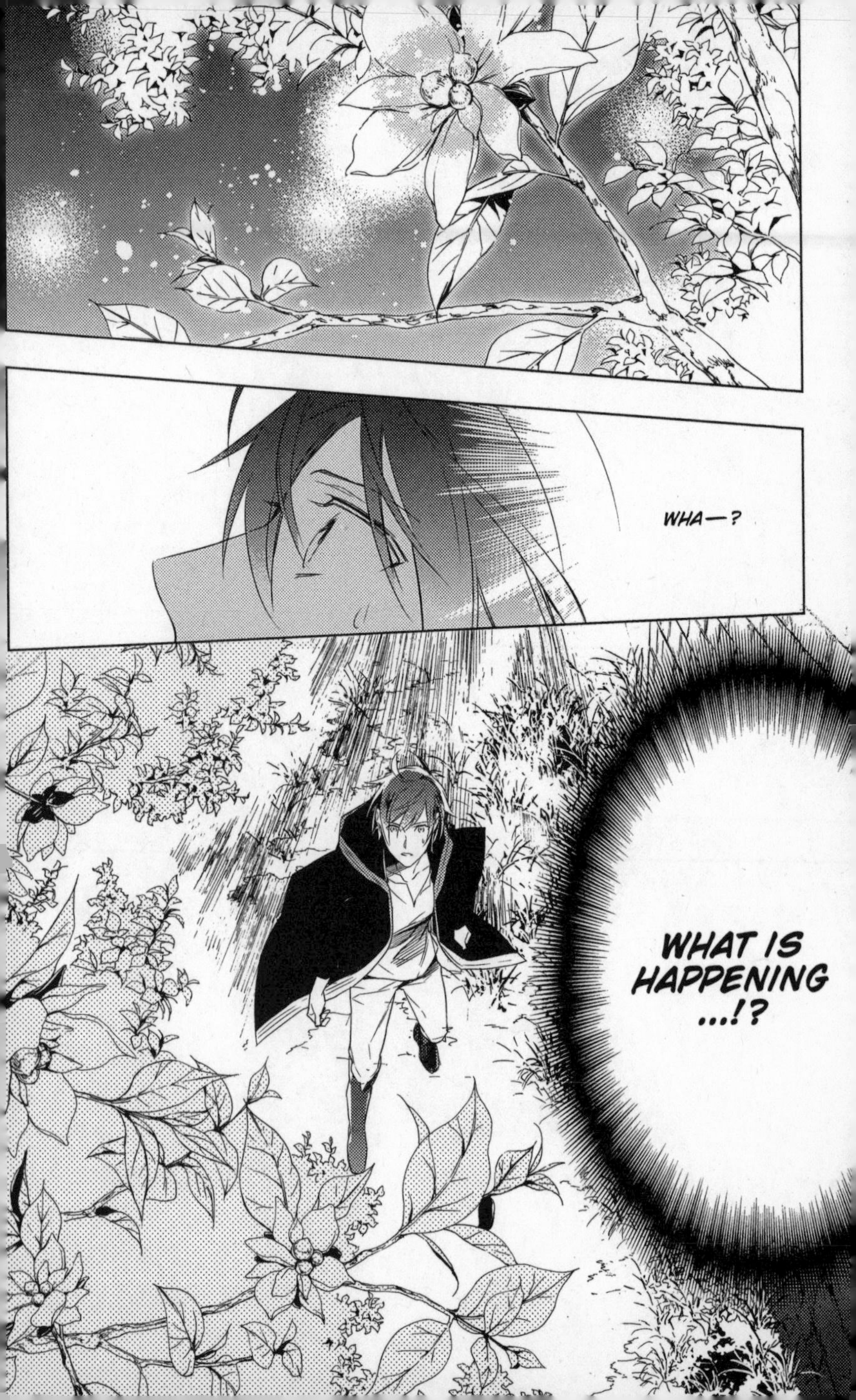
WHA—?
WHAT IS HAPPENING ...!?

GRAINELIERS

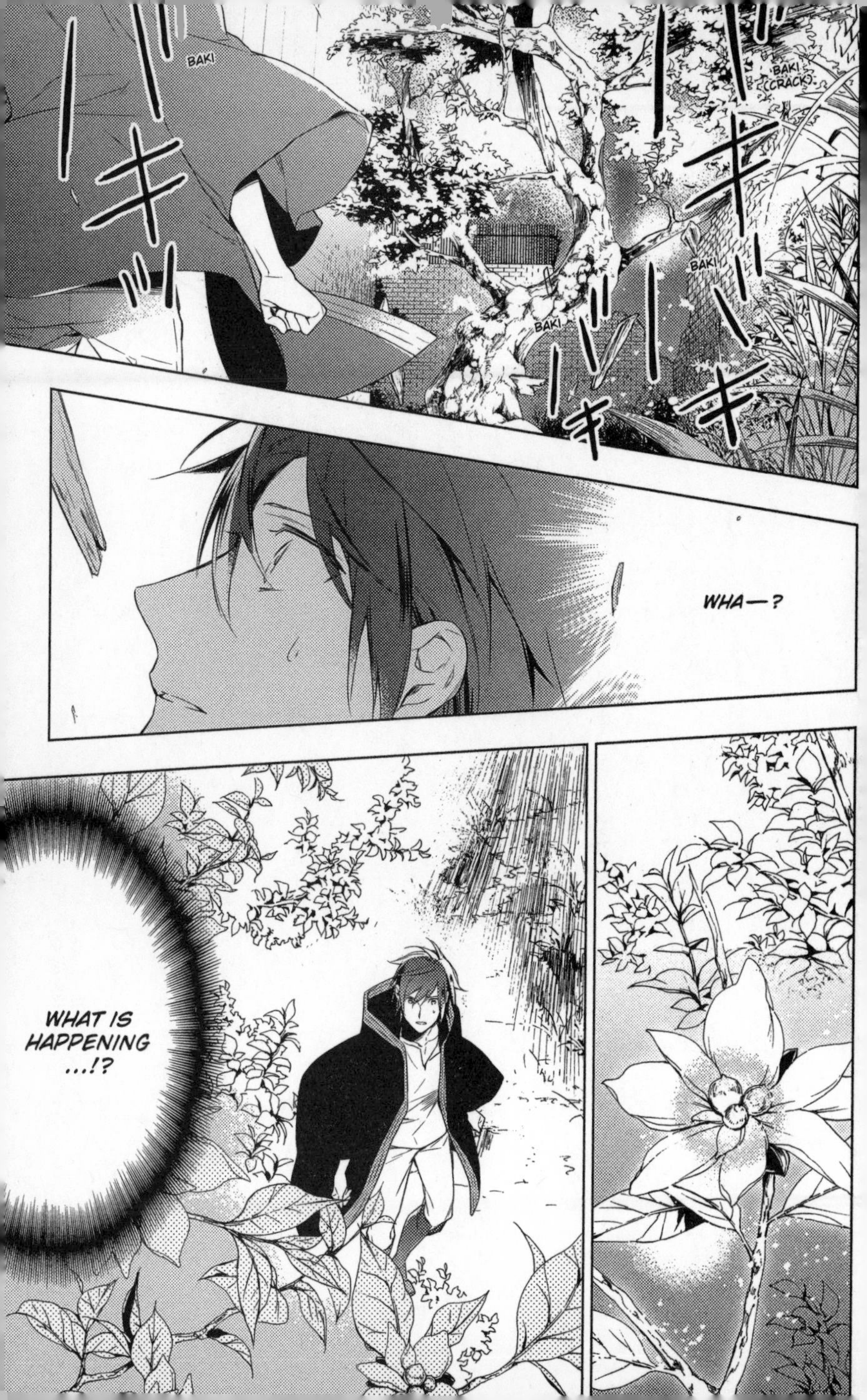
BAKI (CRACK)
BAKI
BAKI
BAKI
WHA—?
WHAT IS HAPPENING ...!?

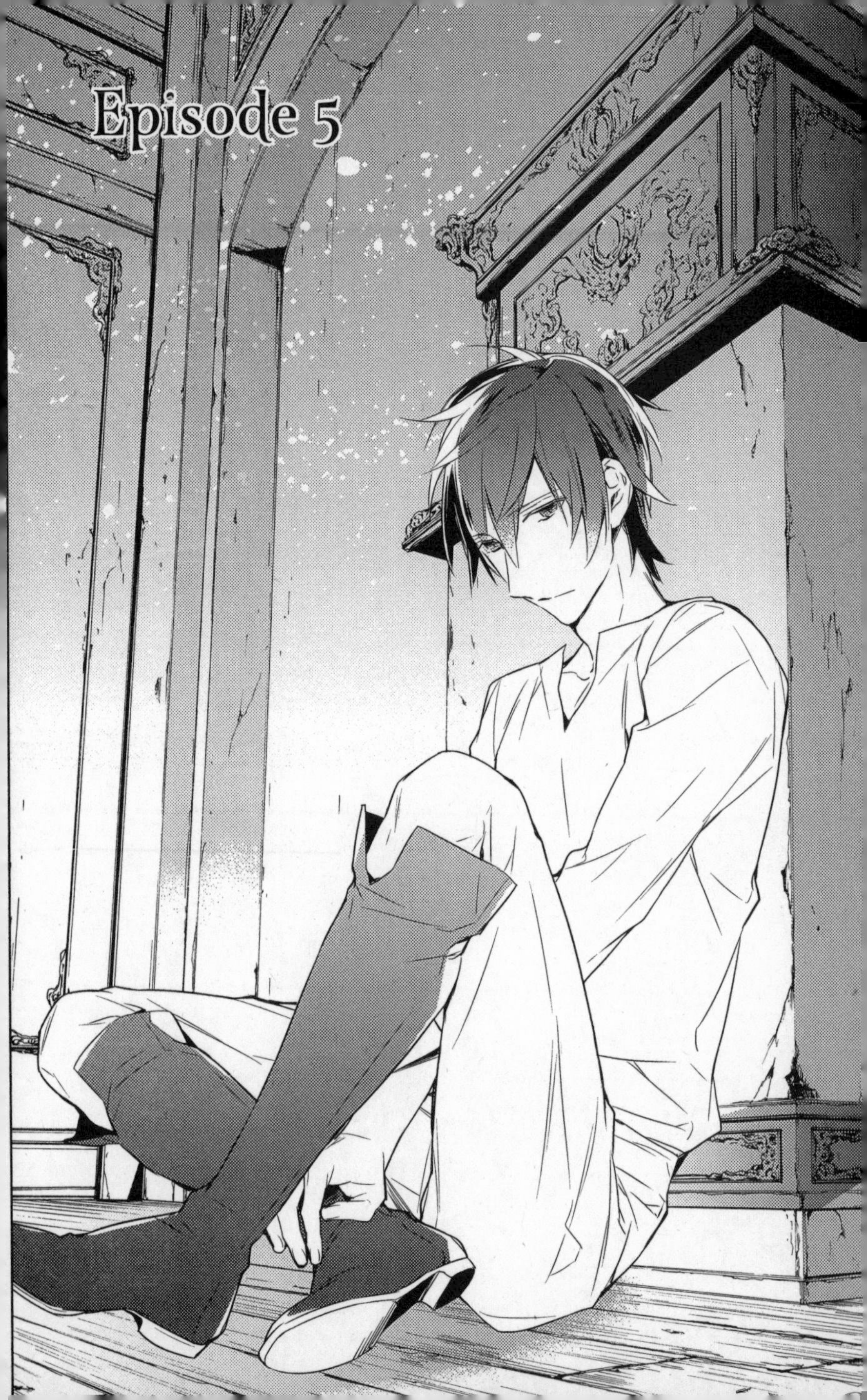
Episode 5

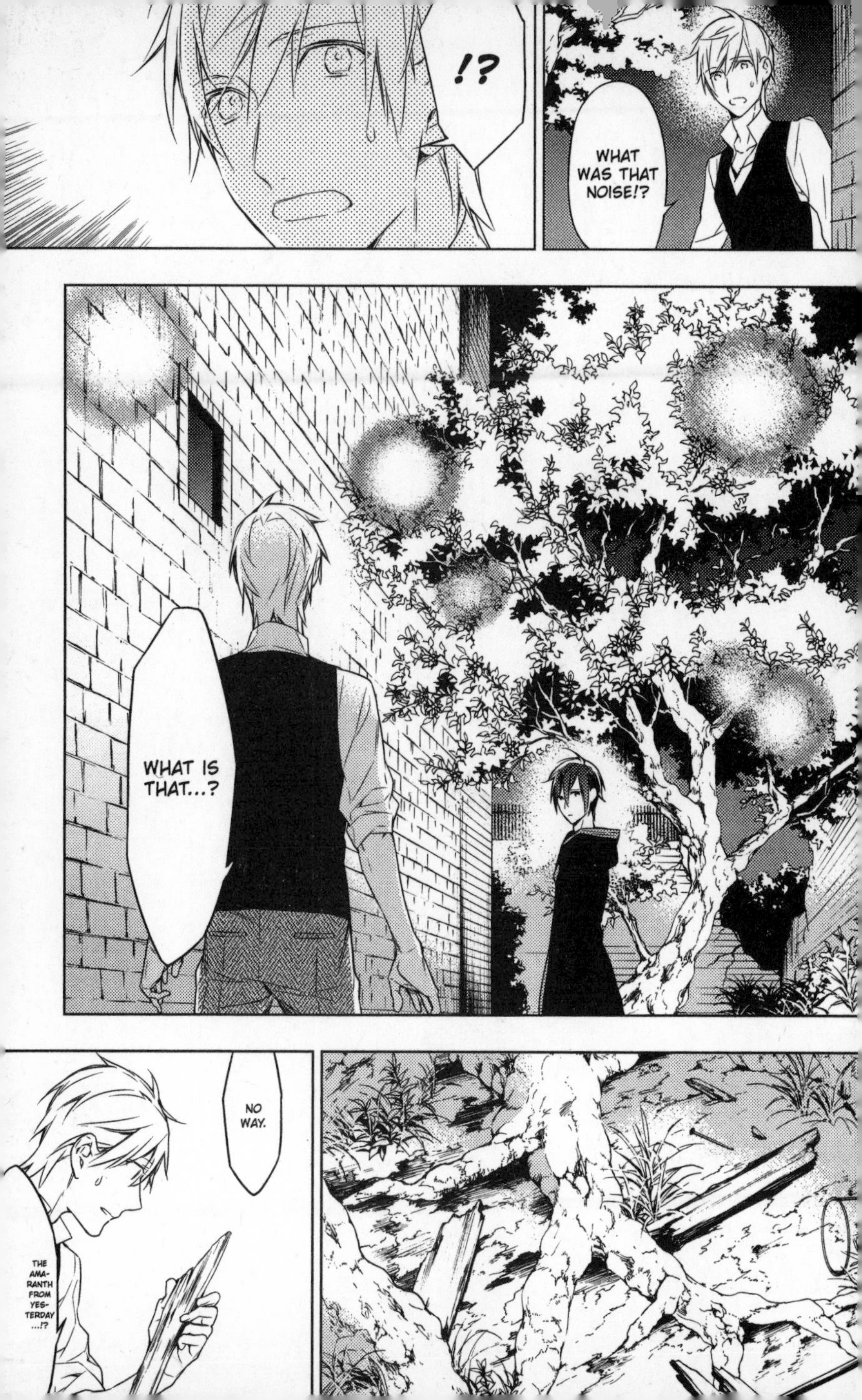
WHAT WAS THAT NOISE!?
!?
WHAT IS THAT...?
NO WAY.
THE AMARANTH FROM YESTERDAY...!?

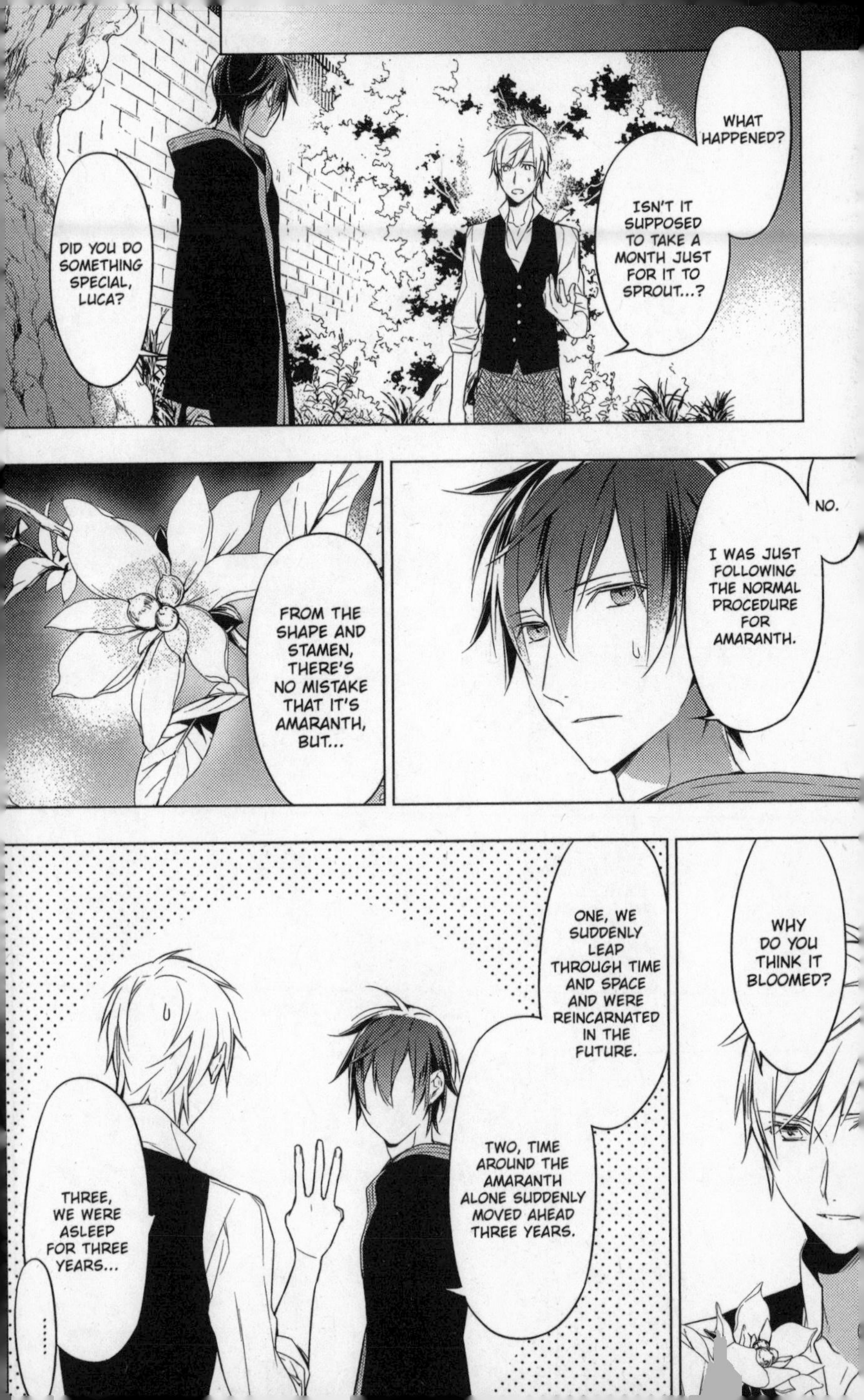
WHAT HAPPENED? ISN'T IT SUPPOSED TO TAKE A MONTH JUST FOR IT TO SPROUT...?
DID YOU DO SOMETHING SPECIAL, LUCA?
NO. I WAS JUST FOLLOWING THE NORMAL PROCEDURE FOR AMARANTH.
FROM THE SHAPE AND STAMEN, THERE'S NO MISTAKE THAT IT'S AMARANTH, BUT...
WHY DO YOU THINK IT BLOOMED?
ONE, WE SUDDENLY LEAP THROUGH TIME AND SPACE AND WERE REINCARNATED IN THE FUTURE.
TWO, TIME AROUND THE AMARANTH ALONE SUDDENLY MOVED AHEAD THREE YEARS.
THREE, WE WERE ASLEEP FOR THREE YEARS...
......

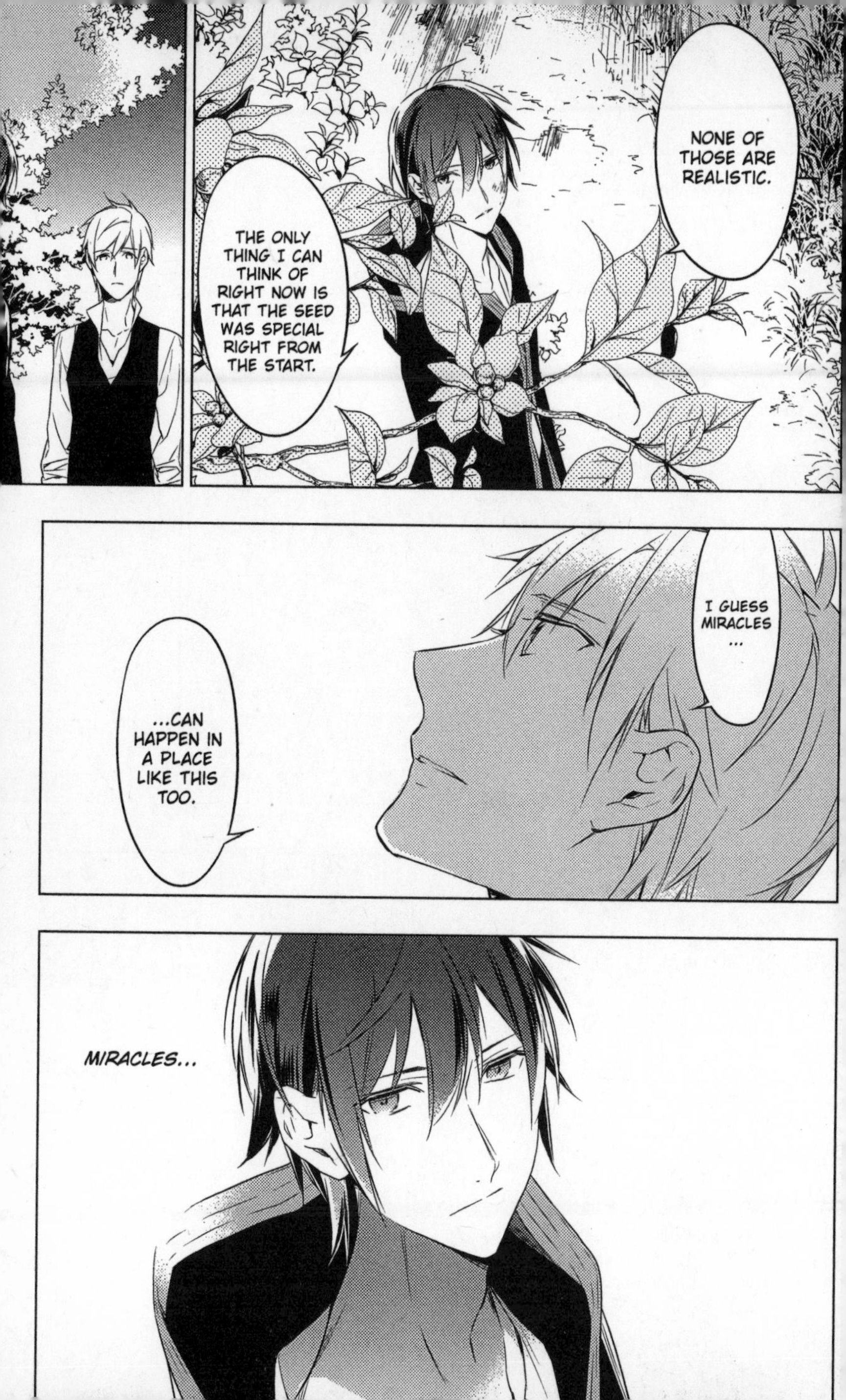
NONE OF THOSE ARE REALISTIC.
THE ONLY THING I CAN THINK OF RIGHT NOW IS THAT THE SEED WAS SPECIAL RIGHT FROM THE START.
I GUESS MIRACLES ...
...CAN HAPPEN IN A PLACE LIKE THIS TOO.
MIRACLES...

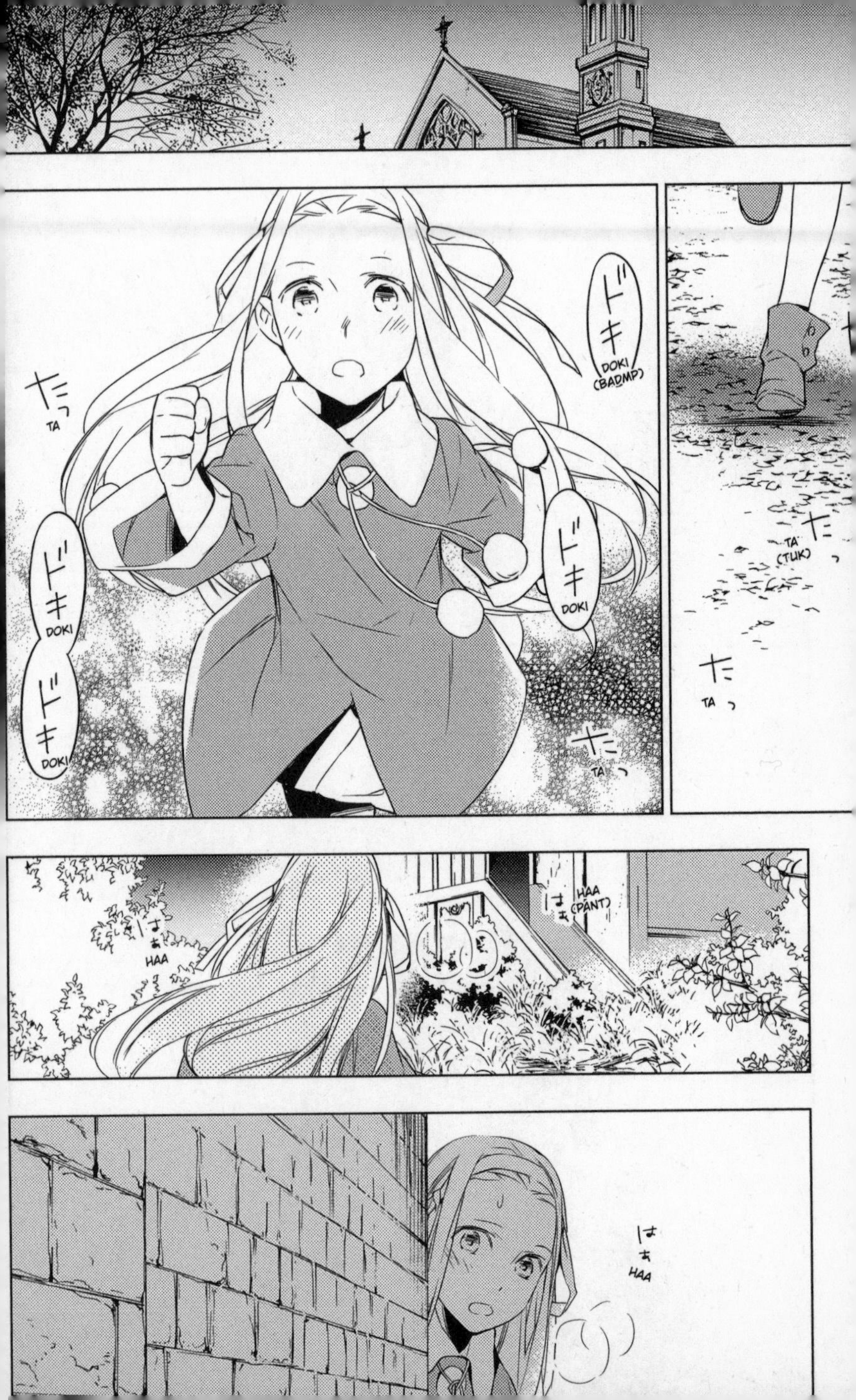
たっ
TA (TUK)
たっ
TA
ドキ
DOKI (BADMP)
ドキ
DOKI
たっ
TA
ドキ
DOKI
ドキ
DOKI
たっ
TA
はぁ
HAA (PANT)
はぁ
HAA
はぁ
HAA

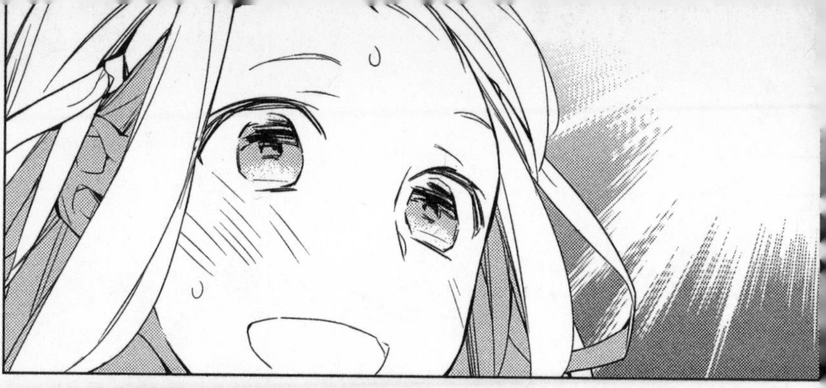
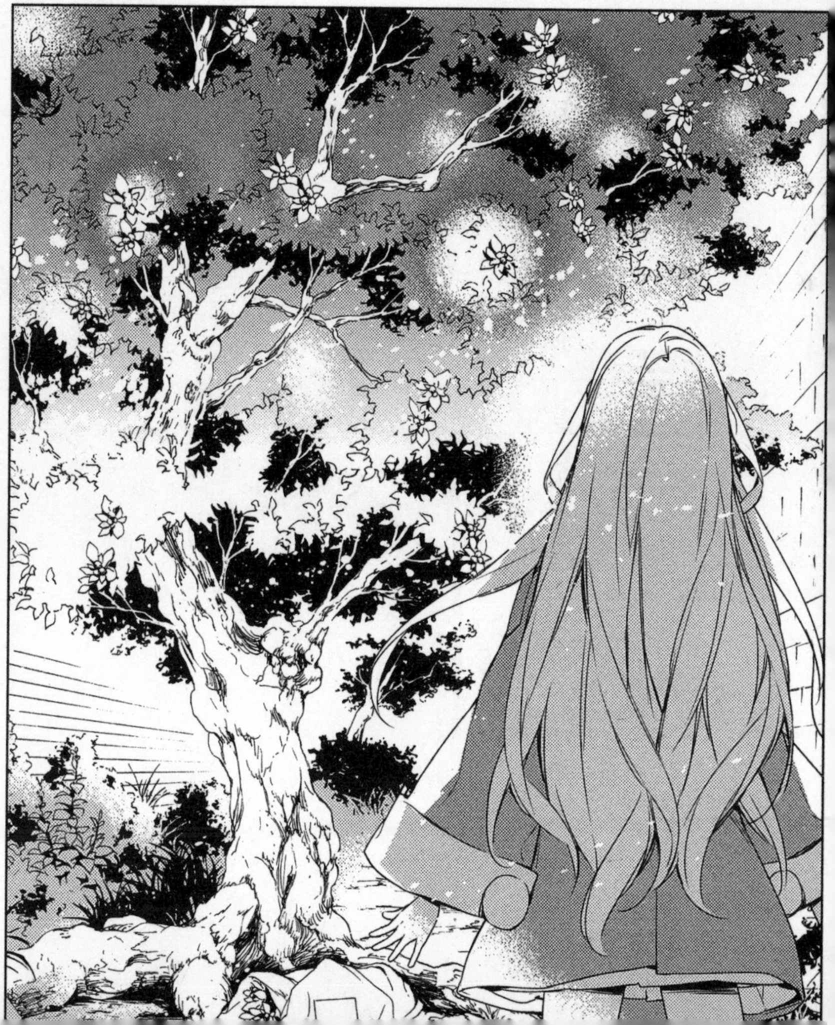

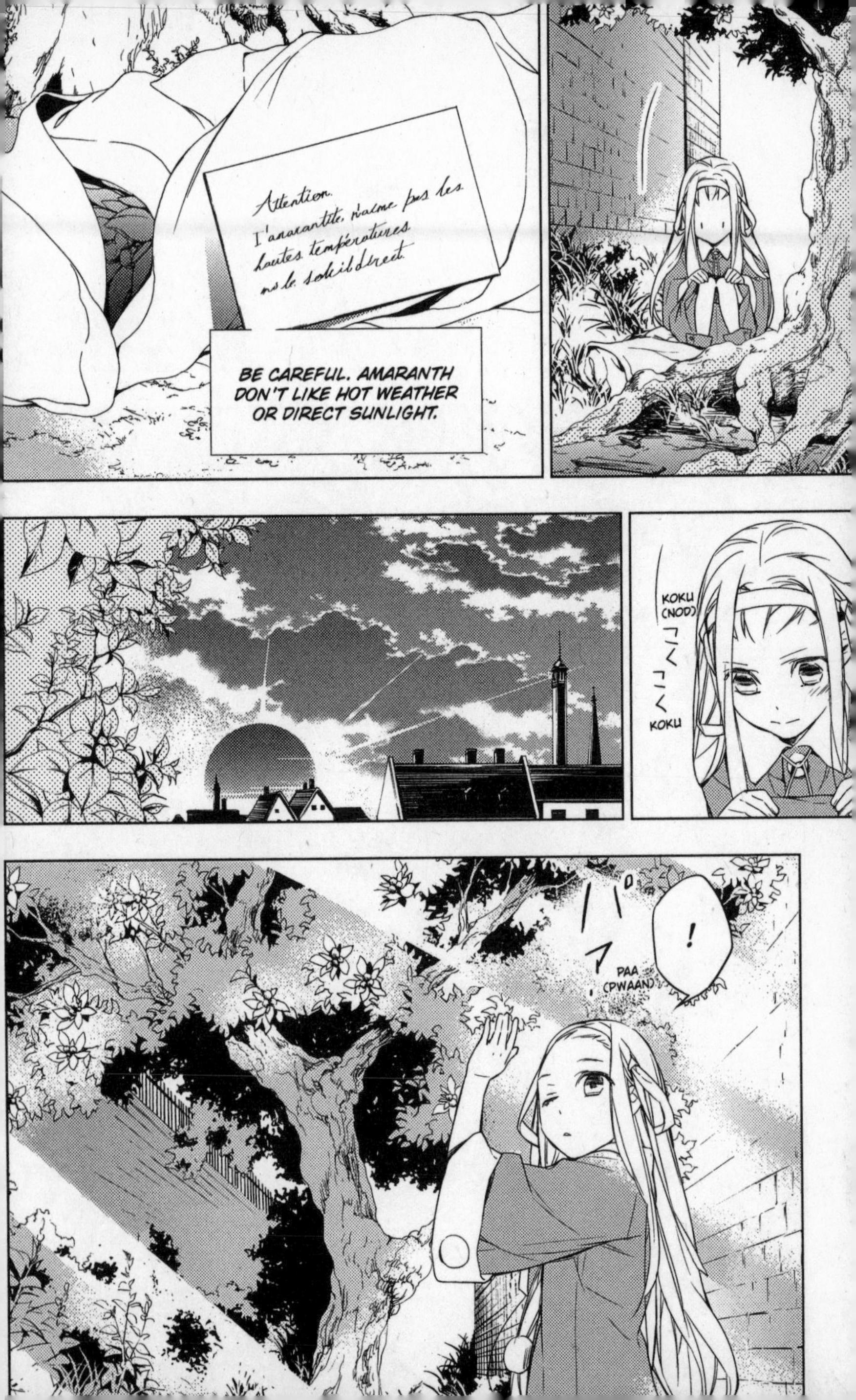
Attention. L'amarantite n'aime pas les hautes températures ni le soleil direct.
BE CAREFUL. AMARANTH DON'T LIKE HOT WEATHER OR DIRECT SUNLIGHT.
KOKU (NOD)
コク コク
KOKU
!
PAA (PWAAN)

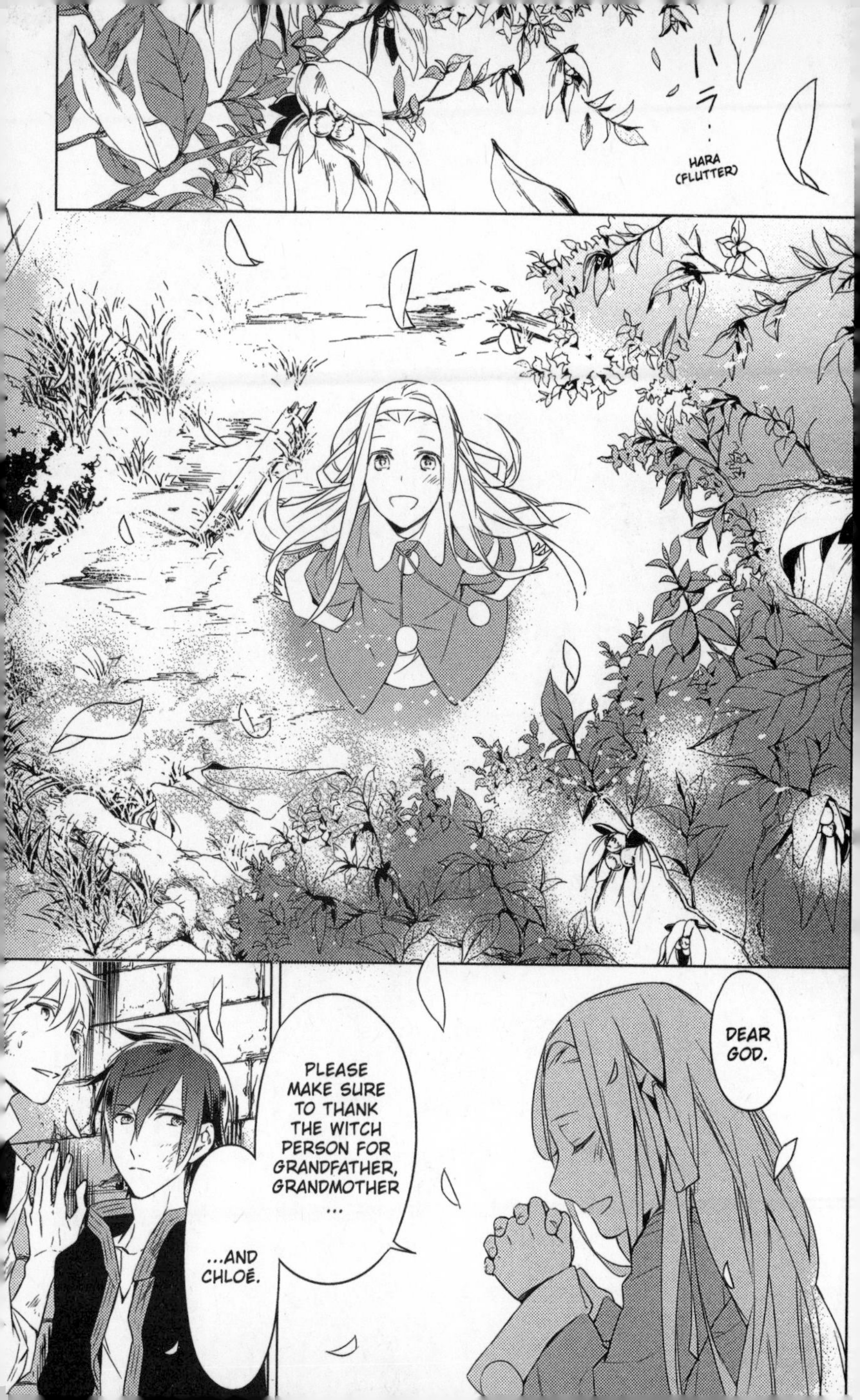
ハラ・・
HARA (FLUTTER)
DEAR GOD.
PLEASE MAKE SURE TO THANK THE WITCH PERSON FOR GRANDFATHER, GRANDMOTHER ...
...AND CHLOÉ.

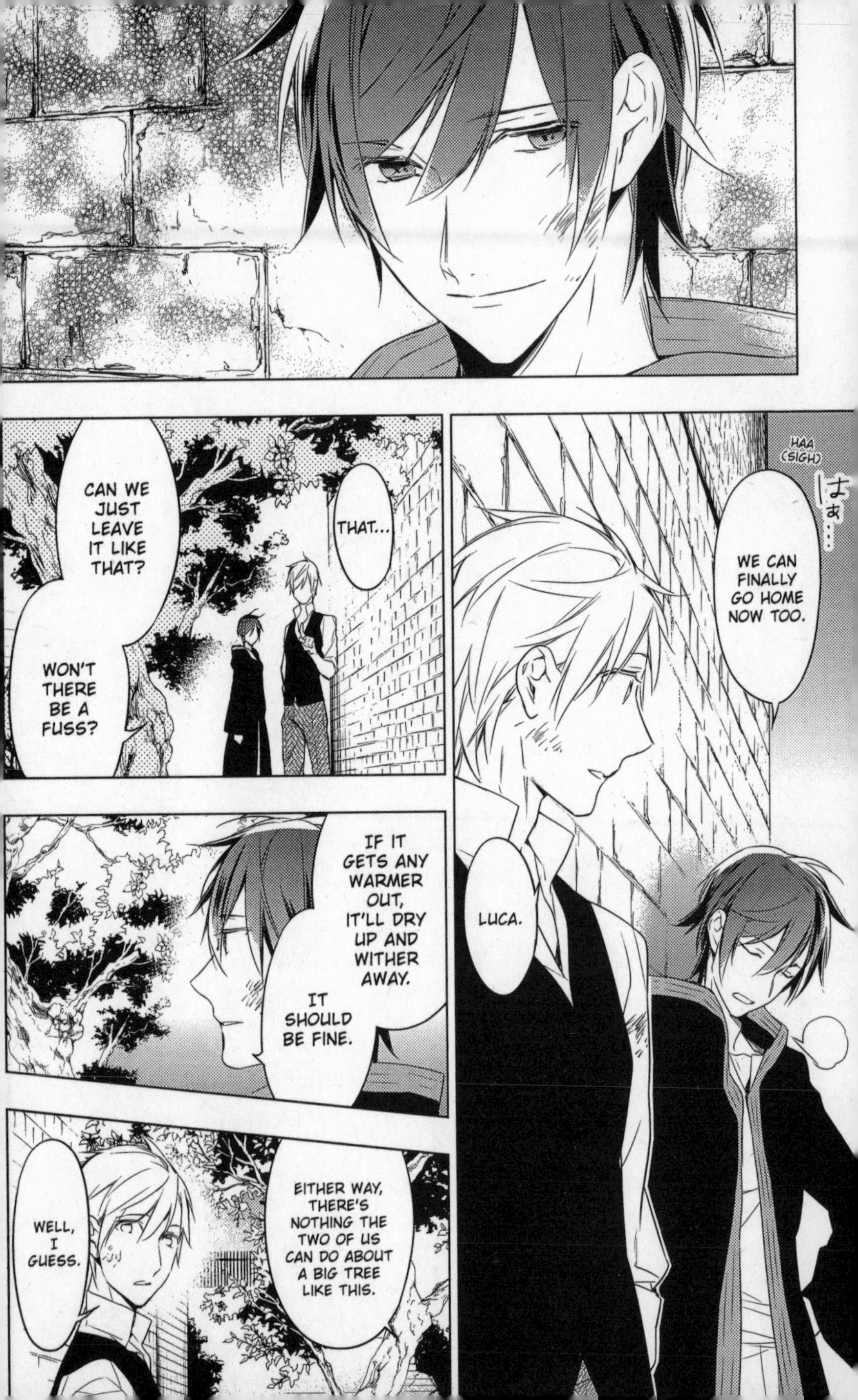
HAA (SIGH)
はぁ…
WE CAN FINALLY GO HOME NOW TOO.
LUCA.
THAT...
CAN WE JUST LEAVE IT LIKE THAT?
WON'T THERE BE A FUSS?
IF IT GETS ANY WARMER OUT, IT'LL DRY UP AND WITHER AWAY.
IT SHOULD BE FINE.
EITHER WAY, THERE'S NOTHING THE TWO OF US CAN DO ABOUT A BIG TREE LIKE THIS.
WELL, I GUESS.

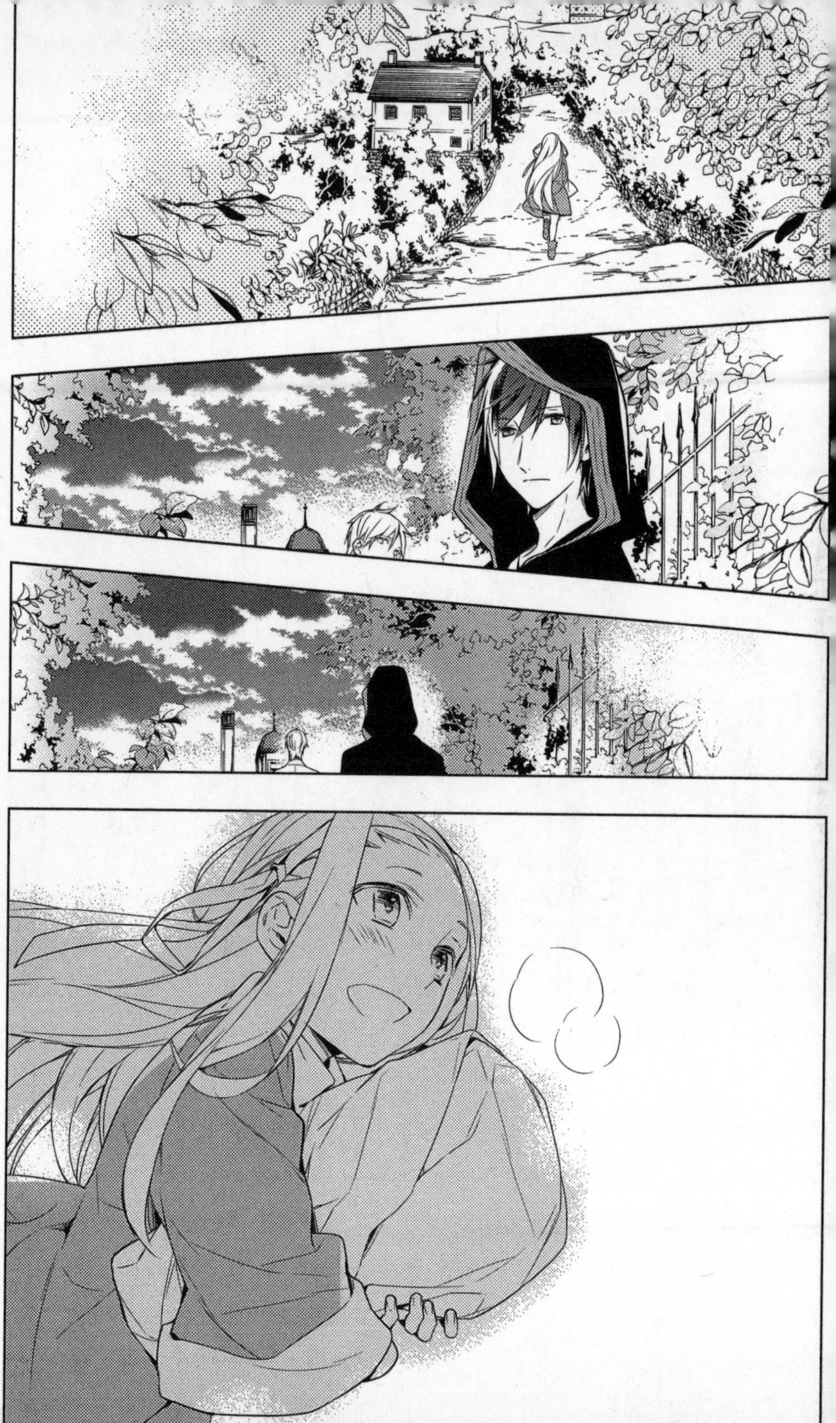

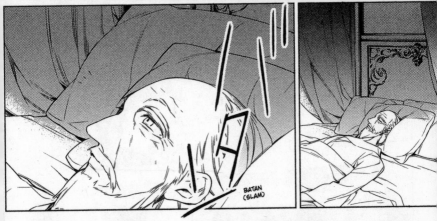

BATAN
(SLAM)

GRAND-
FATHER!

BATA

BATA

BATA

CHLOÉ.

BATA
(TROT)

KEEP
THROWING THE
DOOR OPEN
LIKE THAT,
AND YOU'LL
BREAK IT.

HFF!

HFF!

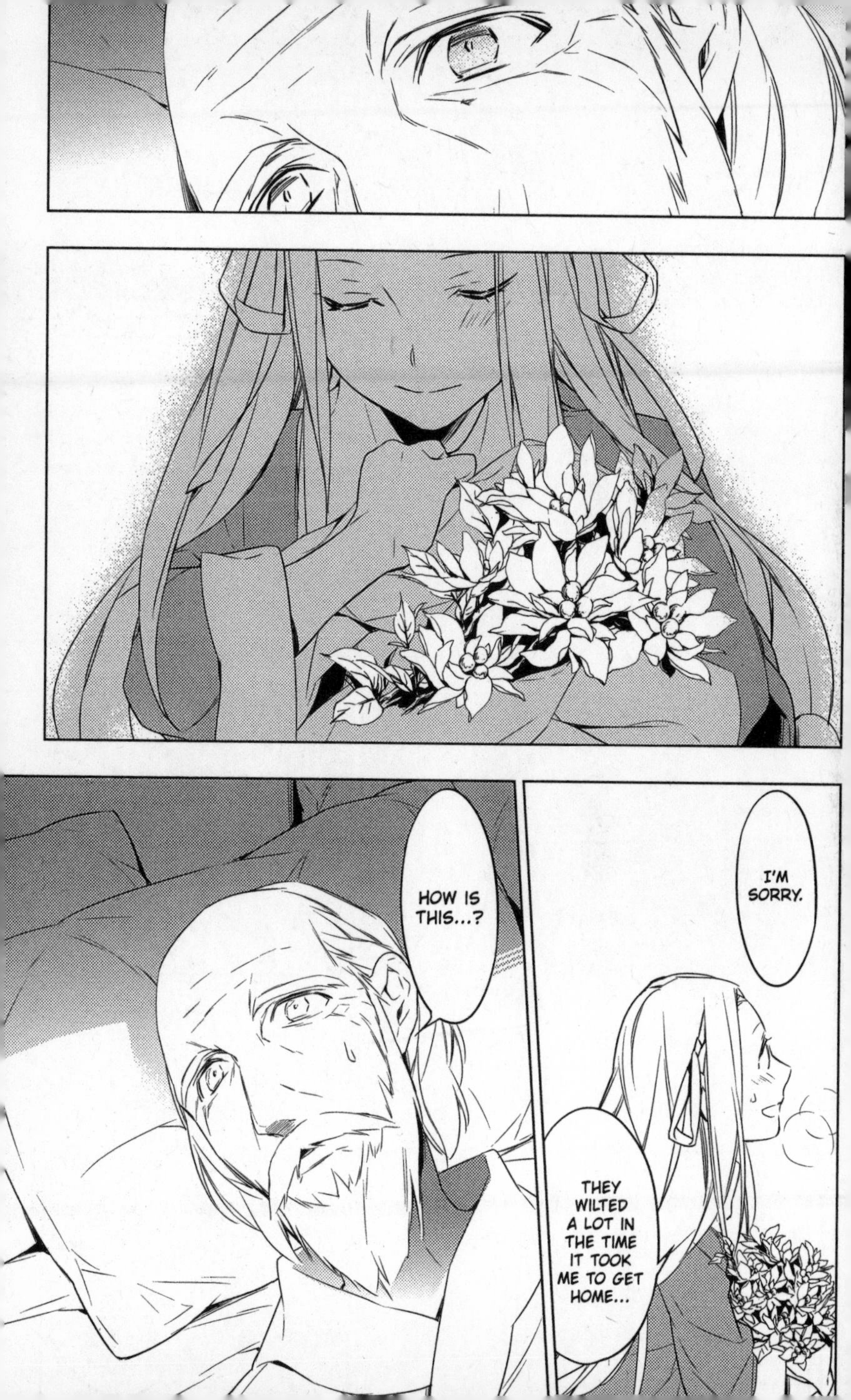
I'M SORRY.
THEY WILTED A LOT IN THE TIME IT TOOK ME TO GET HOME...
HOW IS THIS...?

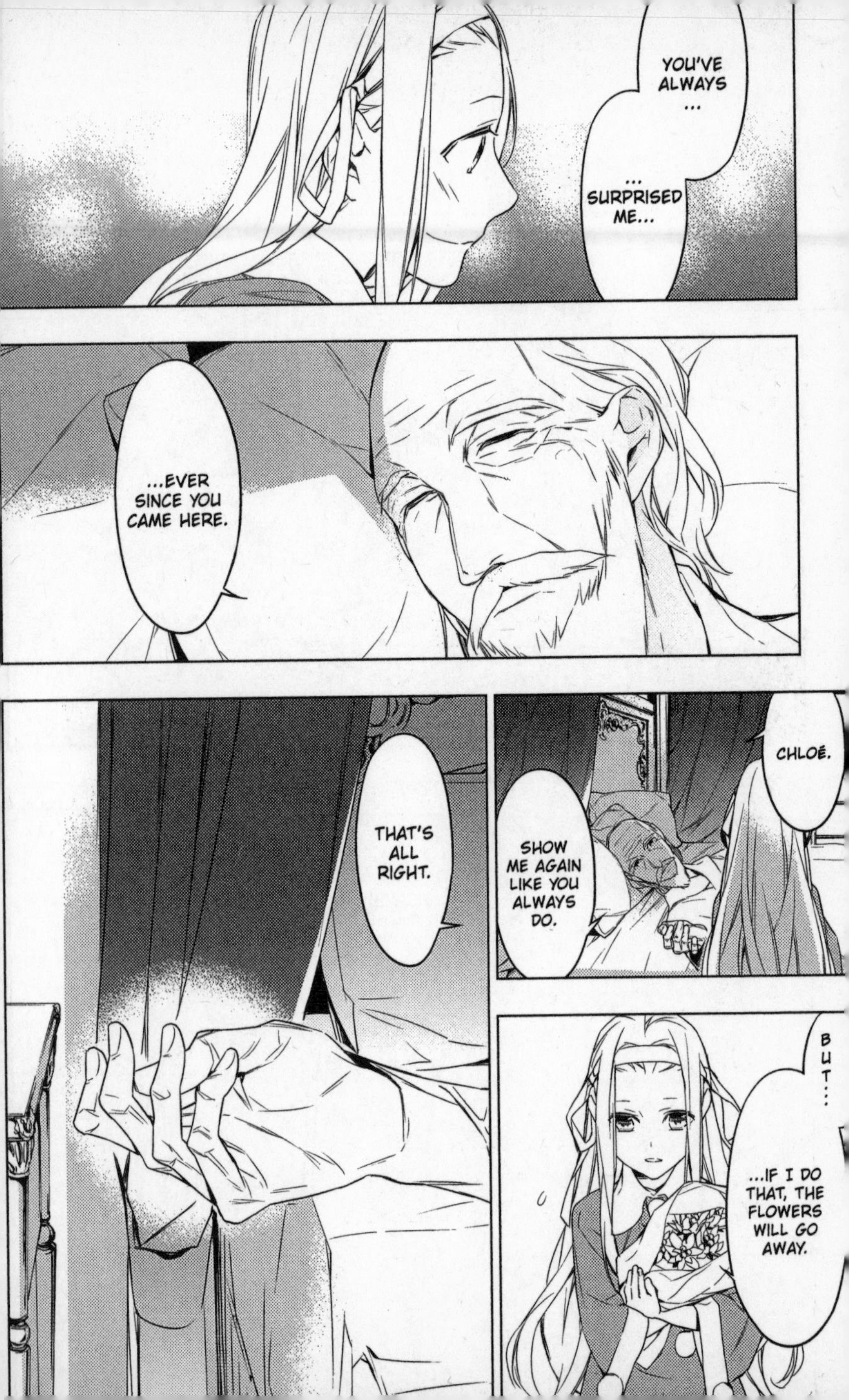
YOU'VE ALWAYS ...
... SURPRISED ME...
...EVER SINCE YOU CAME HERE.
CHLOÉ.
SHOW ME AGAIN LIKE YOU ALWAYS DO.
BUT...
...IF I DO THAT, THE FLOWERS WILL GO AWAY.
THAT'S ALL RIGHT.

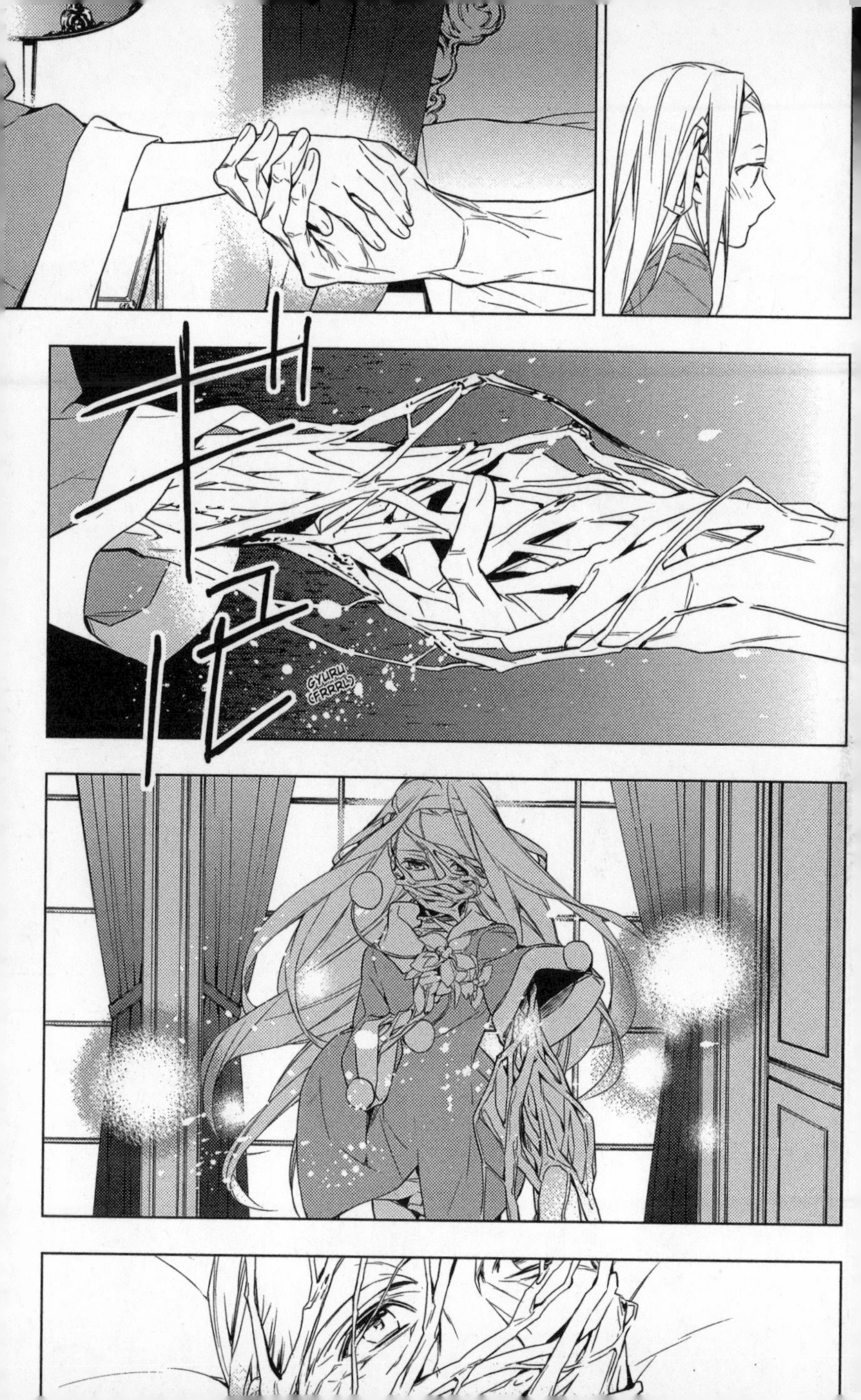
GYURU
(FRRRL)

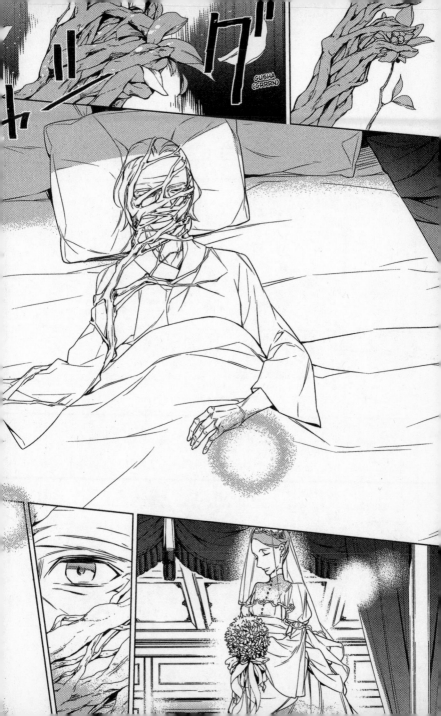

GUSHA
(GRRRN)

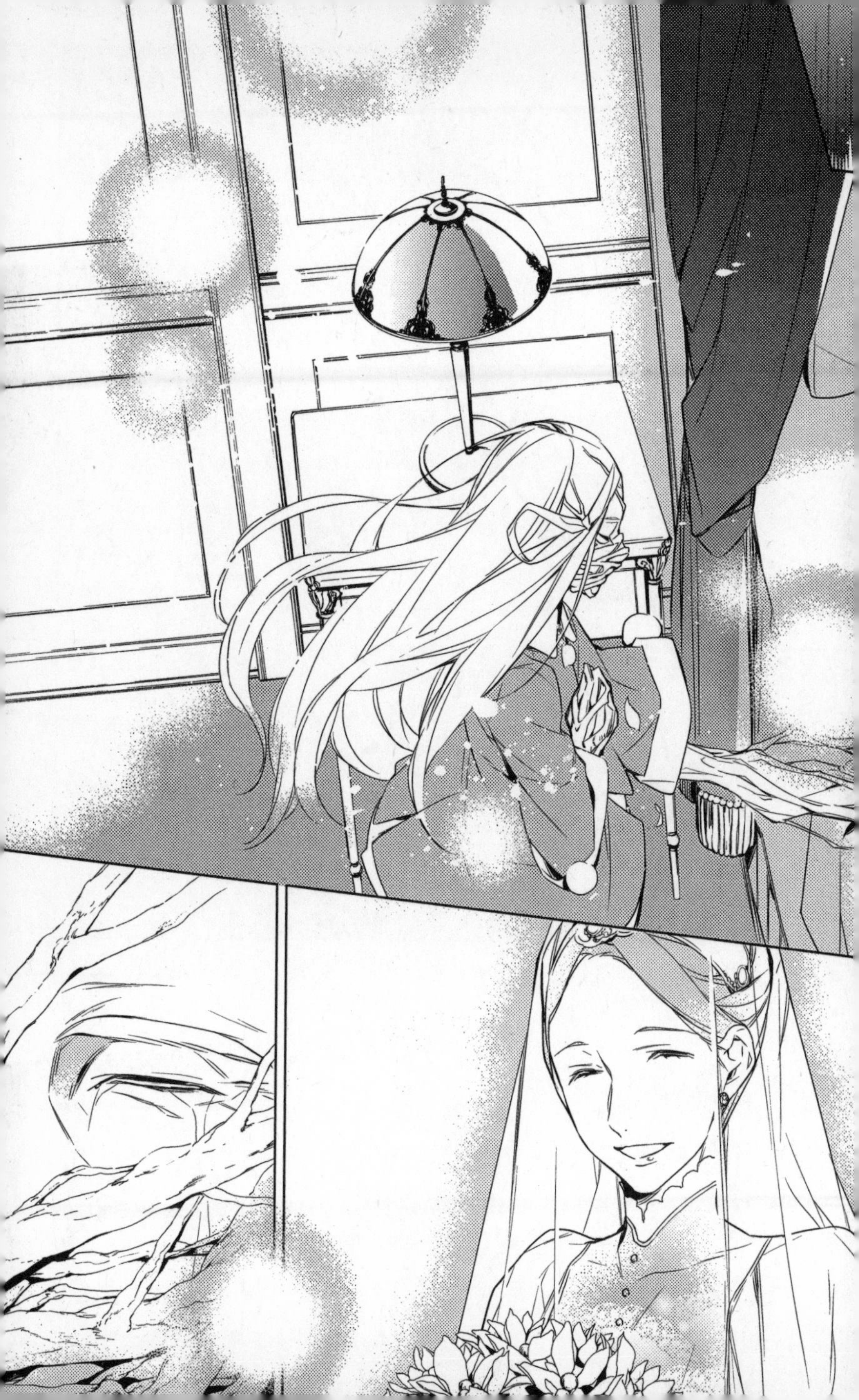

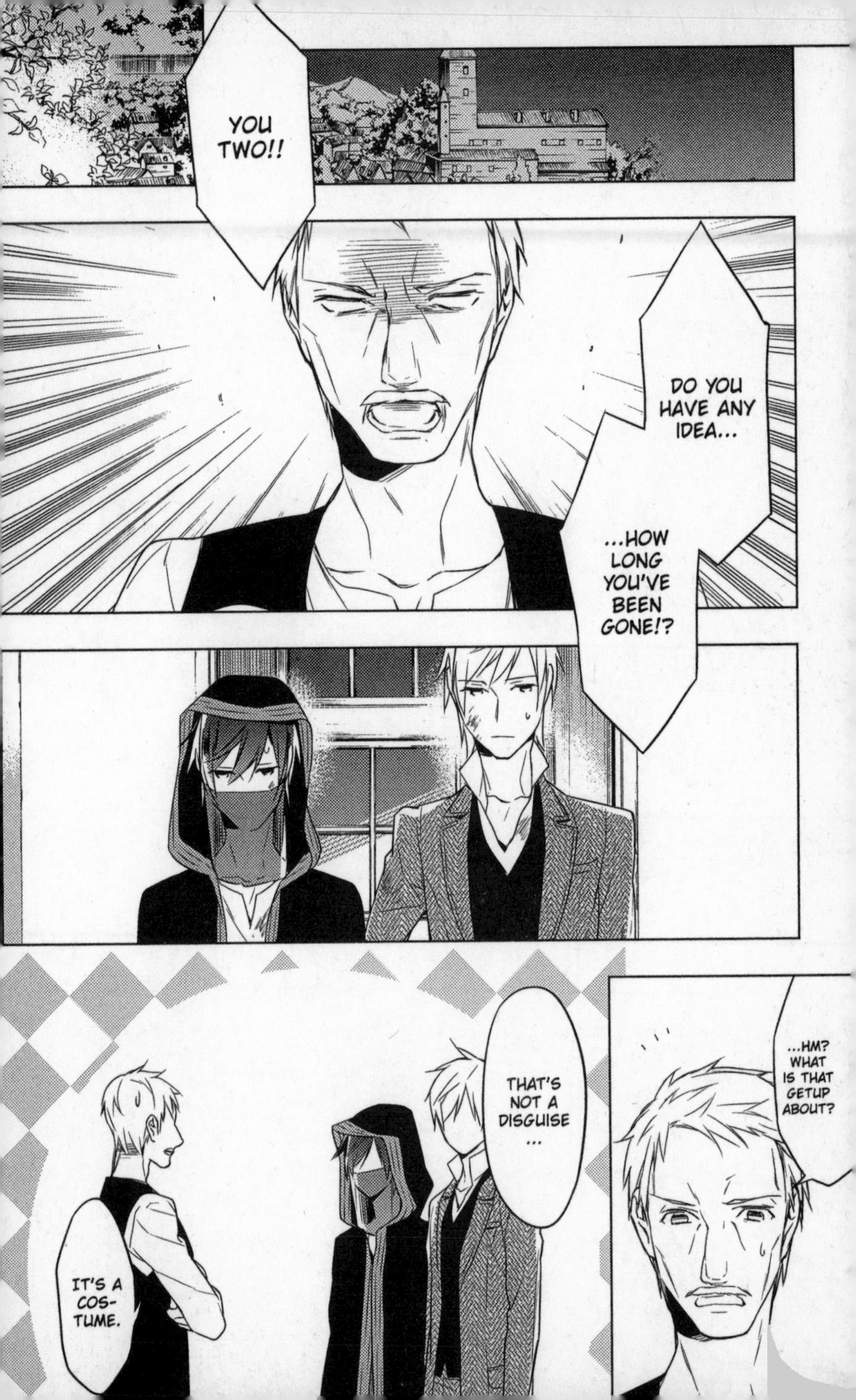
YOU TWO!!
DO YOU HAVE ANY IDEA...
...HOW LONG YOU'VE BEEN GONE!?
...HM? WHAT IS THAT GETUP ABOUT?
THAT'S NOT A DISGUISE ...
IT'S A COS- TUME.

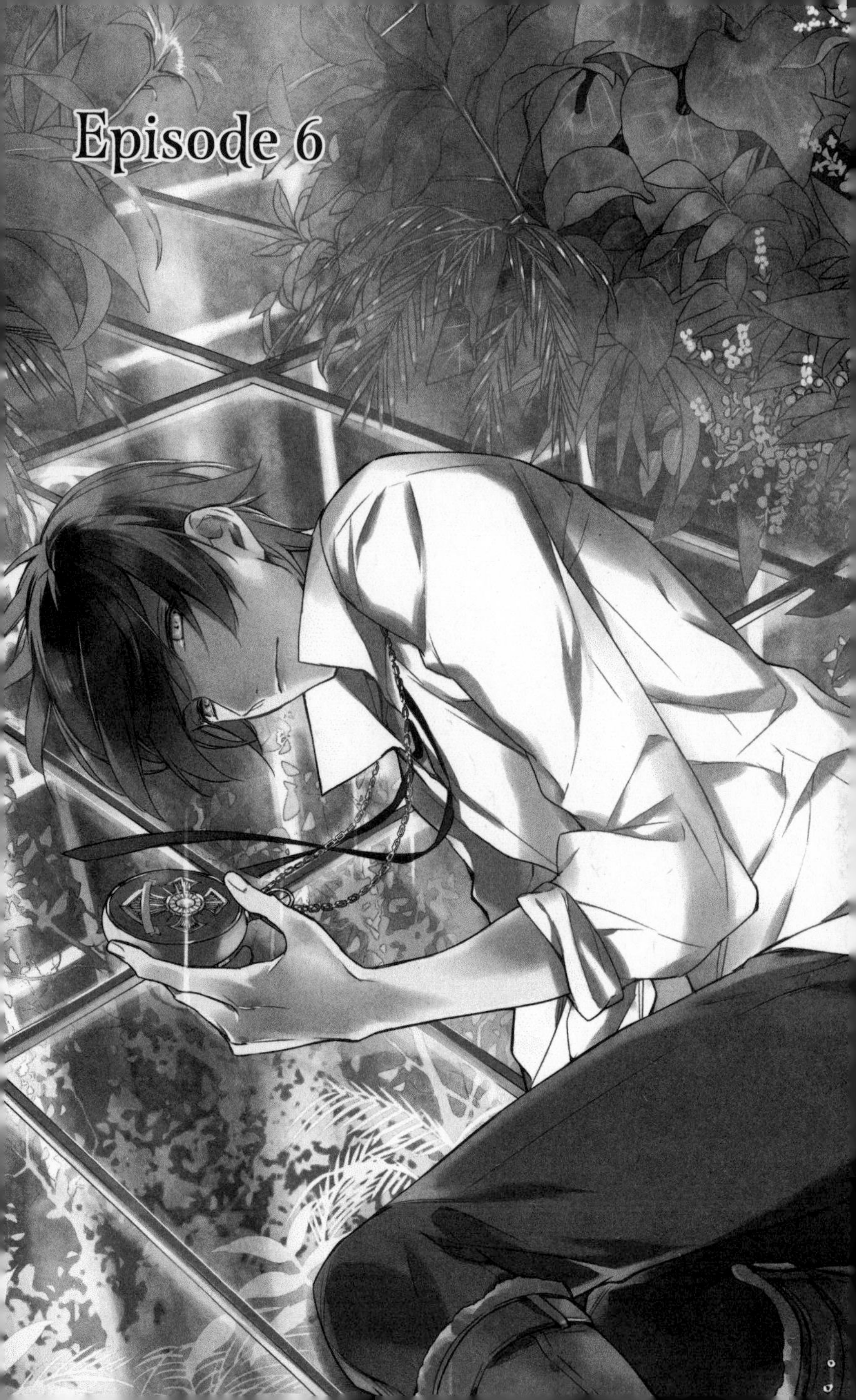
Episode 6

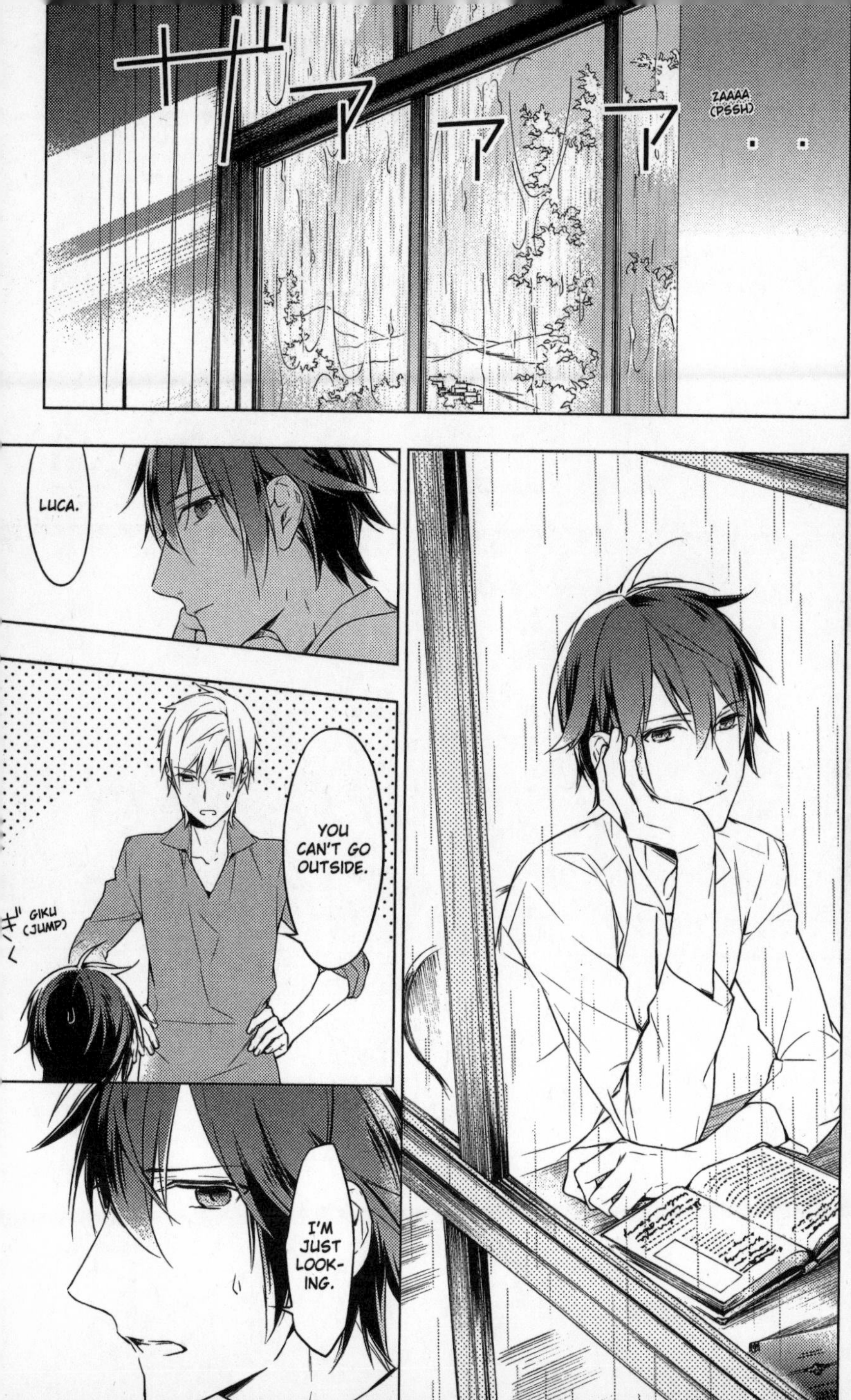
ZAAAA (PSSH)
· ·
LUCA.
YOU CAN'T GO OUTSIDE.
GIKU (JUMP)
I'M JUST LOOKING.

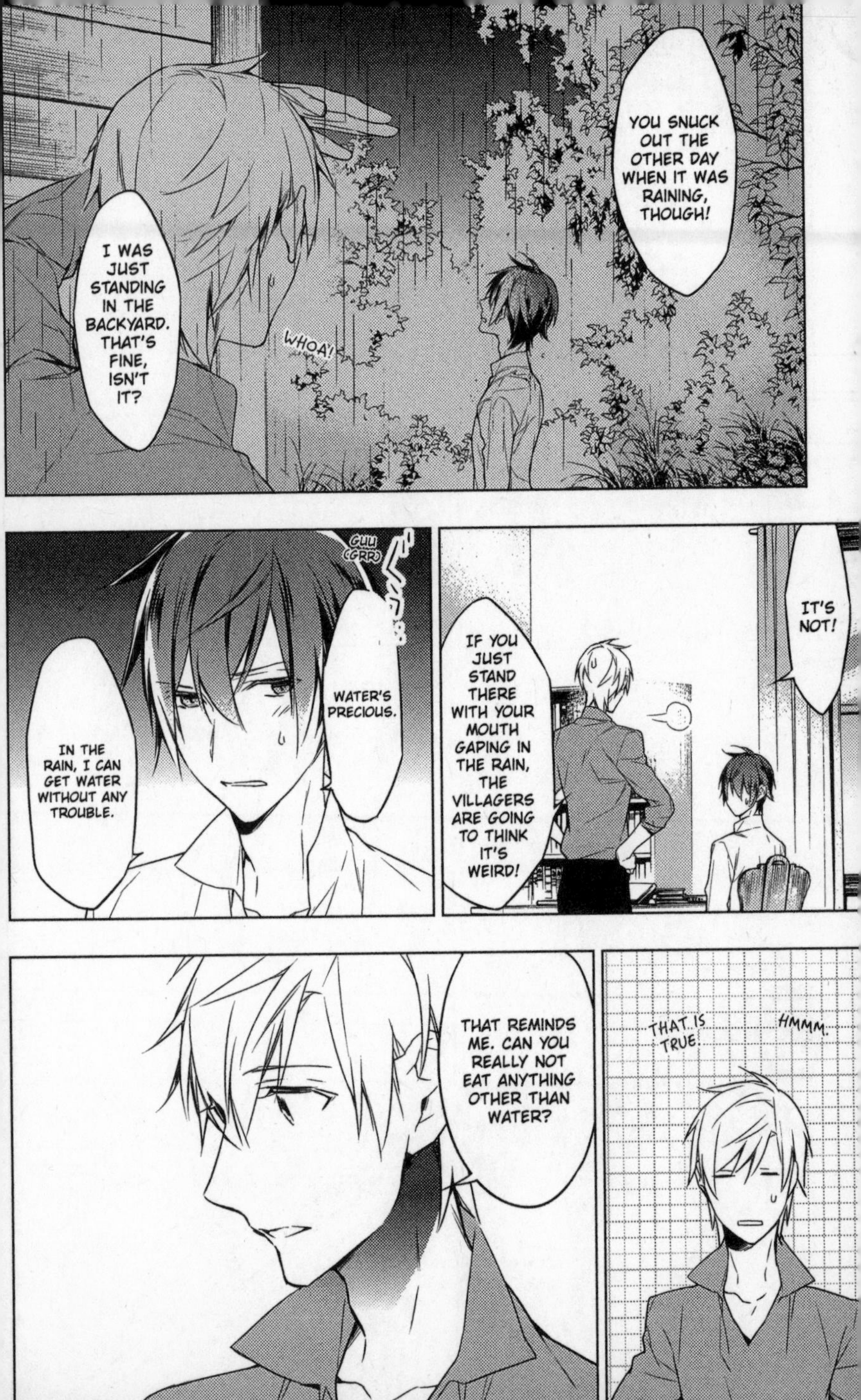
YOU SNUCK OUT THE OTHER DAY WHEN IT WAS RAINING, THOUGH!
WHOA!
I WAS JUST STANDING IN THE BACKYARD. THAT'S FINE, ISN'T IT?
IT'S NOT!
IF YOU JUST STAND THERE WITH YOUR MOUTH GAPING IN THE RAIN, THE VILLAGERS ARE GOING TO THINK IT'S WEIRD!
GUU (GRR)
WATER'S PRECIOUS.
IN THE RAIN, I CAN GET WATER WITHOUT ANY TROUBLE.
HMMM.
THAT IS TRUE.
THAT REMINDS ME. CAN YOU REALLY NOT EAT ANYTHING OTHER THAN WATER?

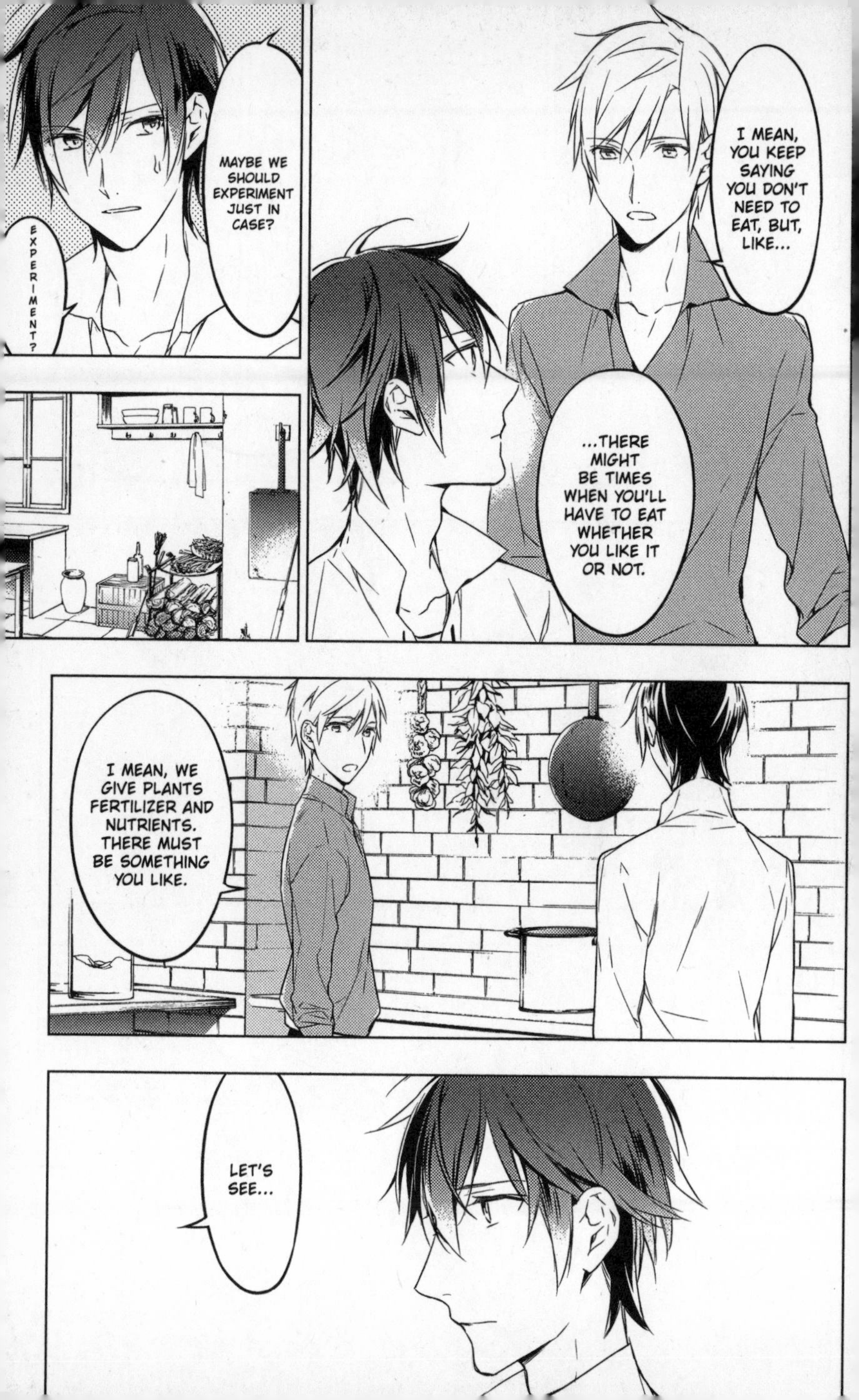
I MEAN, YOU KEEP SAYING YOU DON'T NEED TO EAT, BUT, LIKE...
...THERE MIGHT BE TIMES WHEN YOU'LL HAVE TO EAT WHETHER YOU LIKE IT OR NOT.
MAYBE WE SHOULD EXPERIMENT JUST IN CASE?
EXPERIMENT?
I MEAN, WE GIVE PLANTS FERTILIZER AND NUTRIENTS. THERE MUST BE SOMETHING YOU LIKE.
LET'S SEE...

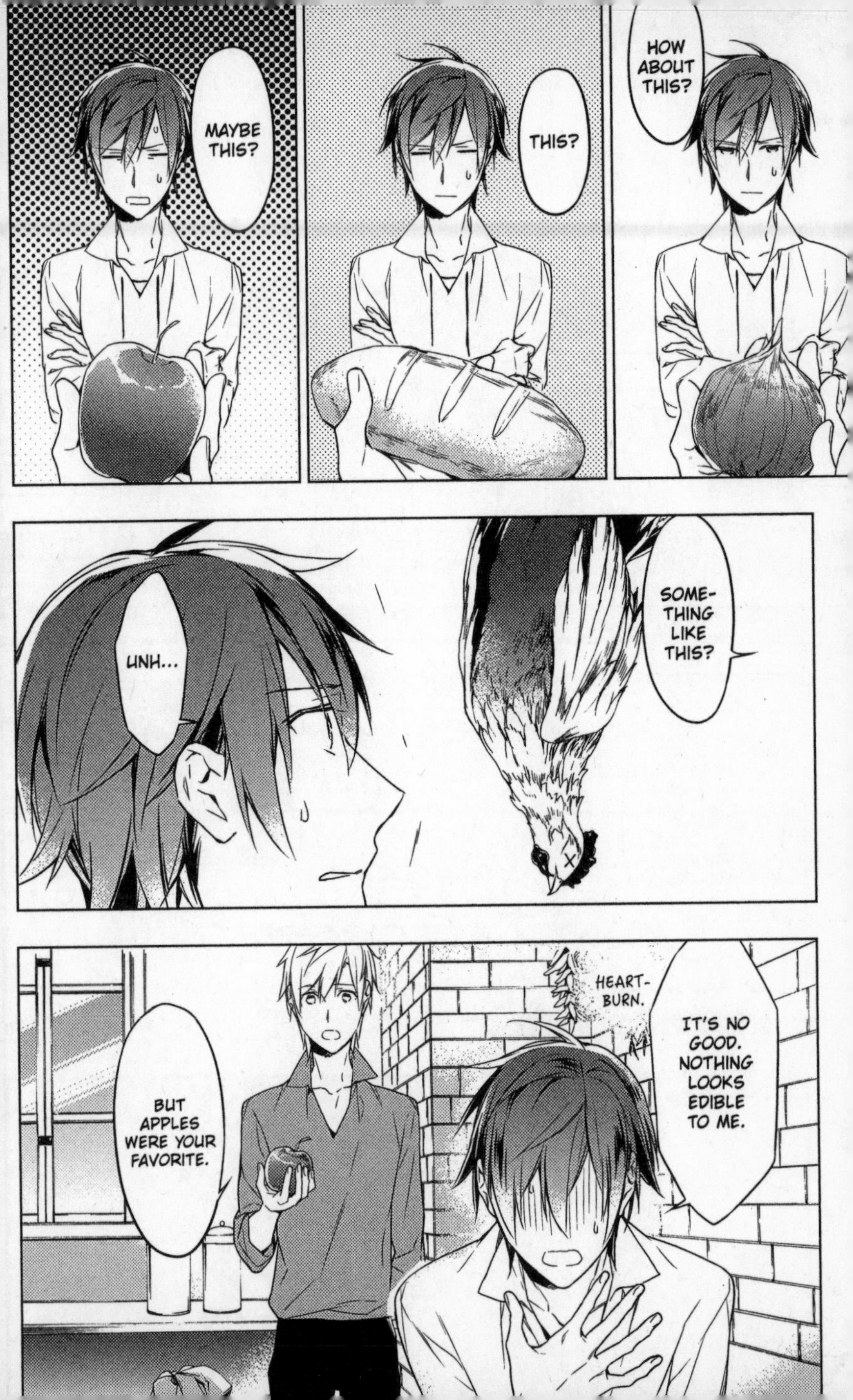
HOW ABOUT THIS?
THIS?
MAYBE THIS?
SOME-THING LIKE THIS?
UNH...
IT'S NO GOOD. NOTHING LOOKS EDIBLE TO ME.
HEART-BURN.
BUT APPLES WERE YOUR FAVORITE.

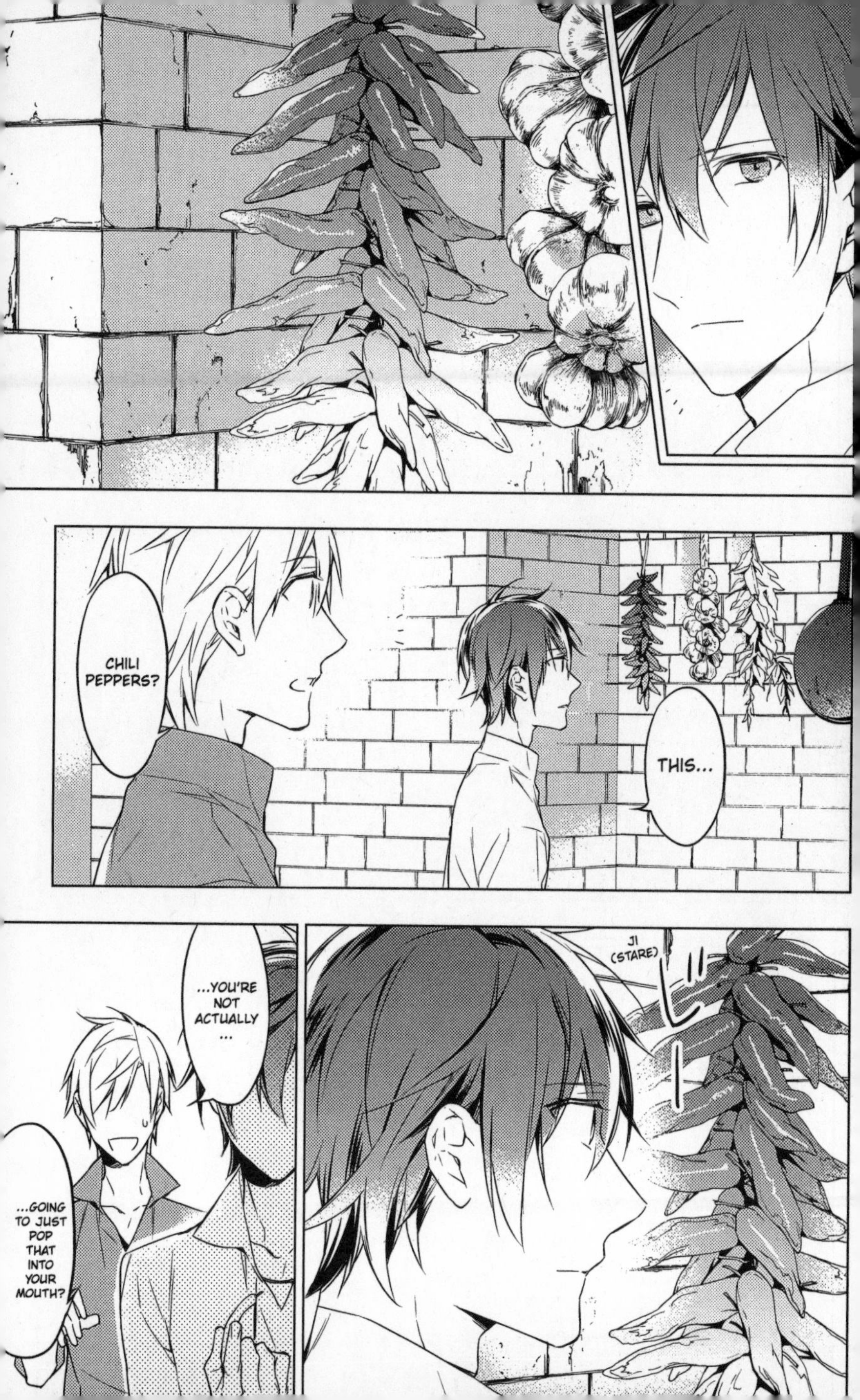
THIS...
CHILI PEPPERS?
JI (STARE)
...YOU'RE NOT ACTUALLY ...
...GOING TO JUST POP THAT INTO YOUR MOUTH?

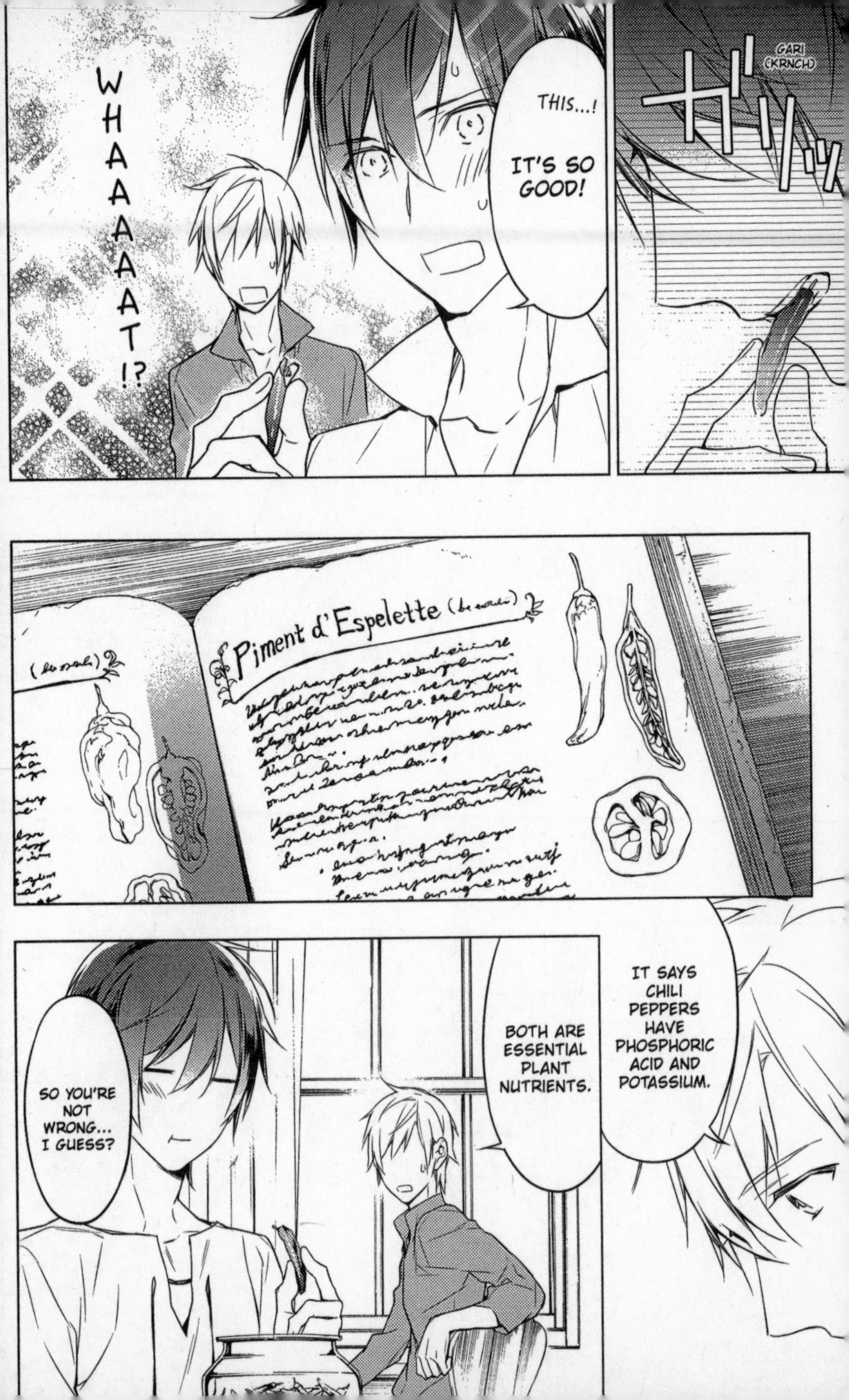

GARI (KRNCH)
THIS...! IT'S SO GOOD!
WHAAAAAT!?
Piment d'Espelette
IT SAYS CHILI PEPPERS HAVE PHOSPHORIC ACID AND POTASSIUM.
BOTH ARE ESSENTIAL PLANT NUTRIENTS.
SO YOU'RE NOT WRONG... I GUESS?

GRAINELIERS

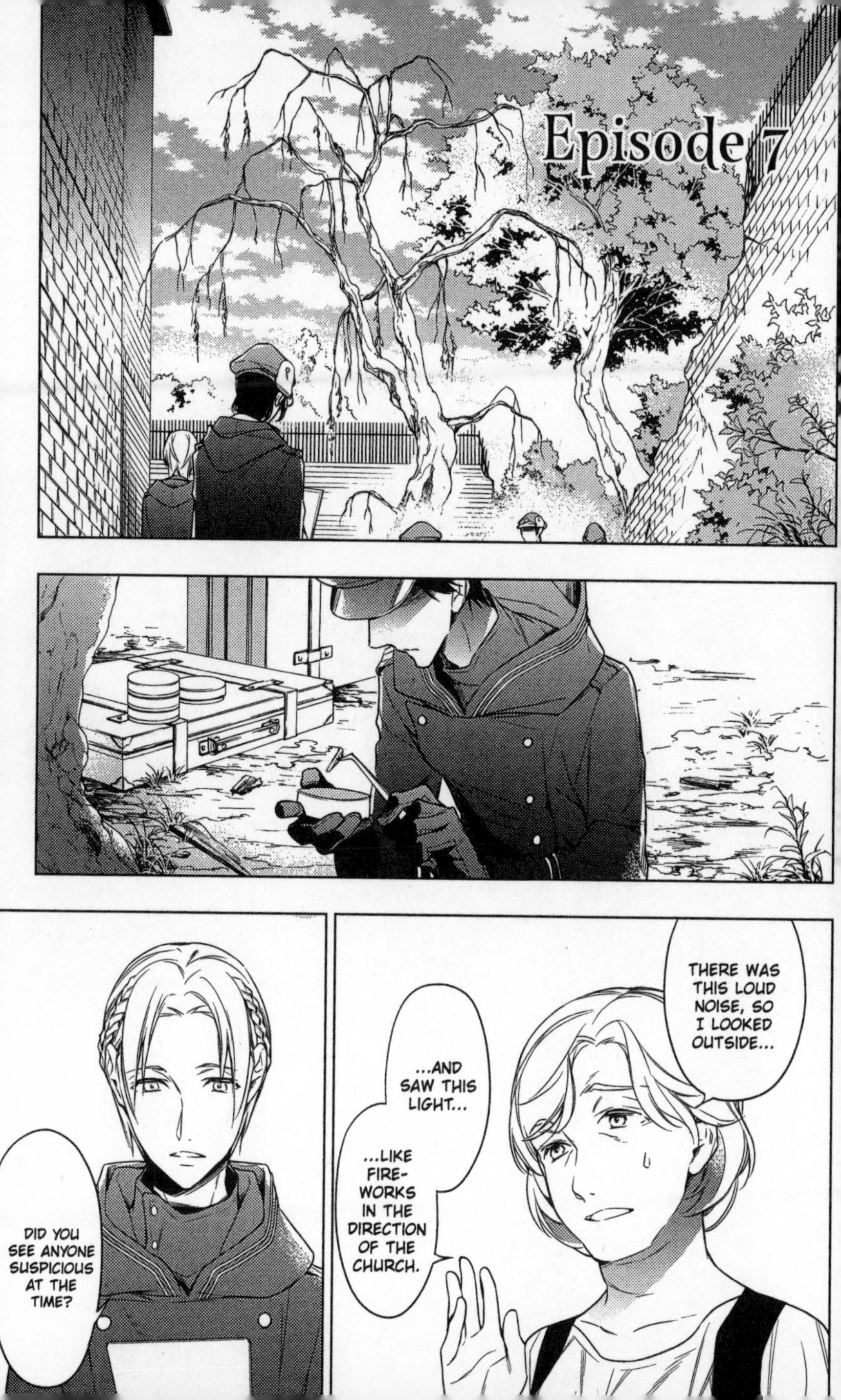
Episode 7
THERE WAS THIS LOUD NOISE, SO I LOOKED OUTSIDE...
...AND SAW THIS LIGHT...
...LIKE FIRE-WORKS IN THE DIRECTION OF THE CHURCH.
DID YOU SEE ANYONE SUSPICIOUS AT THE TIME?

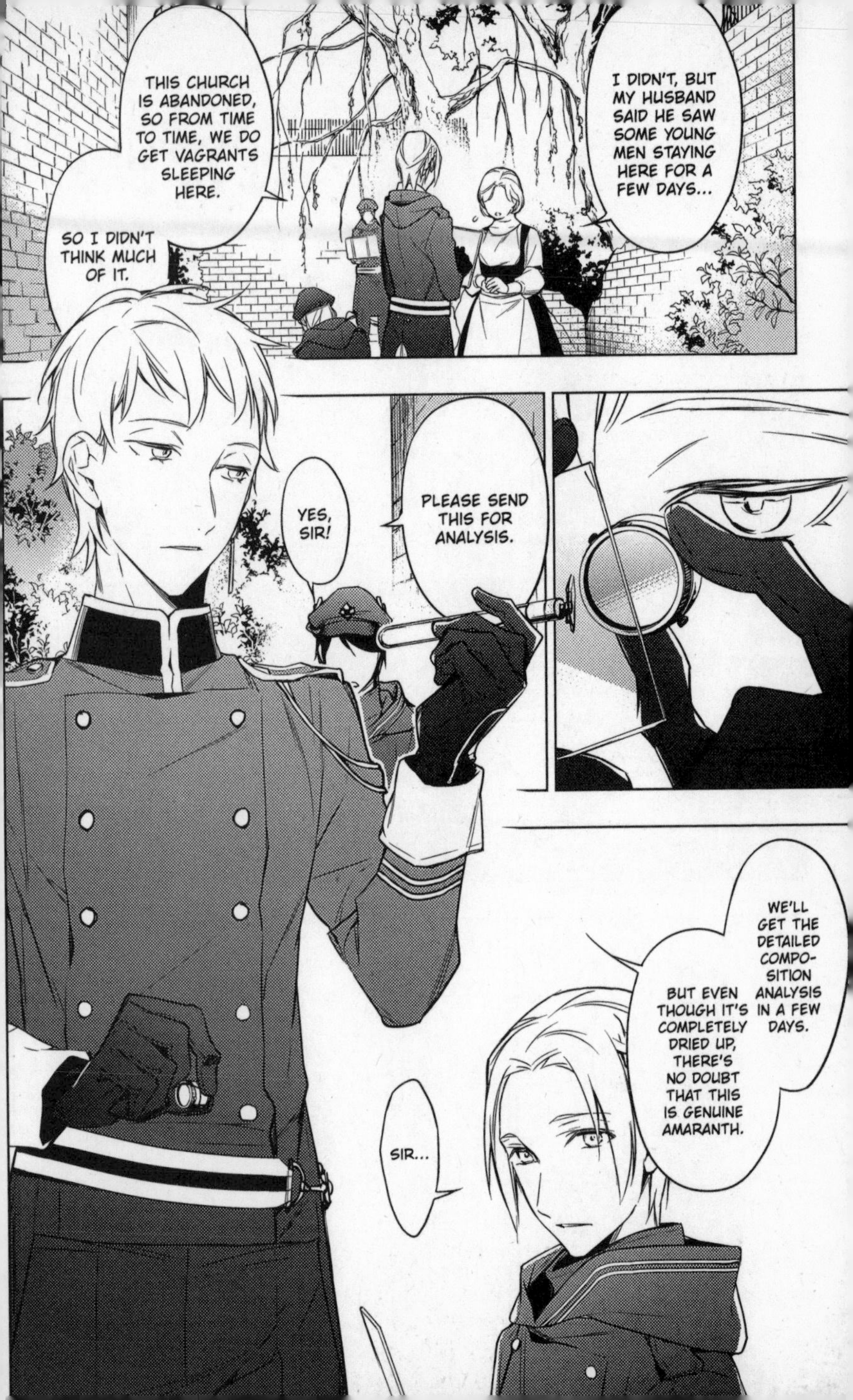
I DIDN'T, BUT MY HUSBAND SAID HE SAW SOME YOUNG MEN STAYING HERE FOR A FEW DAYS...
THIS CHURCH IS ABANDONED, SO FROM TIME TO TIME, WE DO GET VAGRANTS SLEEPING HERE.
SO I DIDN'T THINK MUCH OF IT.
PLEASE SEND THIS FOR ANALYSIS.
YES, SIR!
WE'LL GET THE DETAILED COMPO-SITION ANALYSIS IN A FEW DAYS.
BUT EVEN THOUGH IT'S COMPLETELY DRIED UP, THERE'S NO DOUBT THAT THIS IS GENUINE AMARANTH.
SIR...

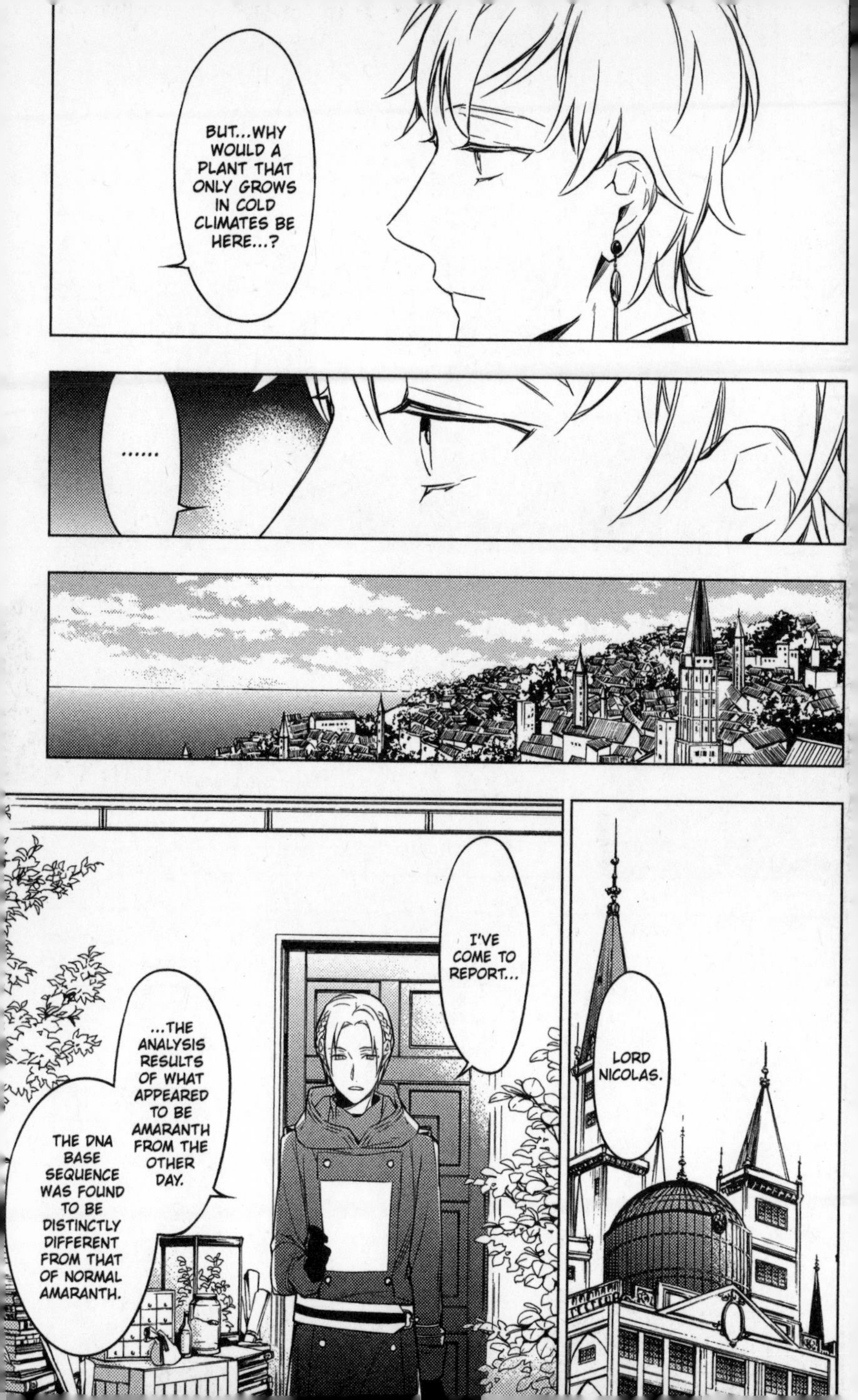
BUT...WHY WOULD A PLANT THAT ONLY GROWS IN COLD CLIMATES BE HERE...?
......
LORD NICOLAS.
I'VE COME TO REPORT...
...THE ANALYSIS RESULTS OF WHAT APPEARED TO BE AMARANTH FROM THE OTHER DAY.
THE DNA BASE SEQUENCE WAS FOUND TO BE DISTINCTLY DIFFERENT FROM THAT OF NORMAL AMARANTH.

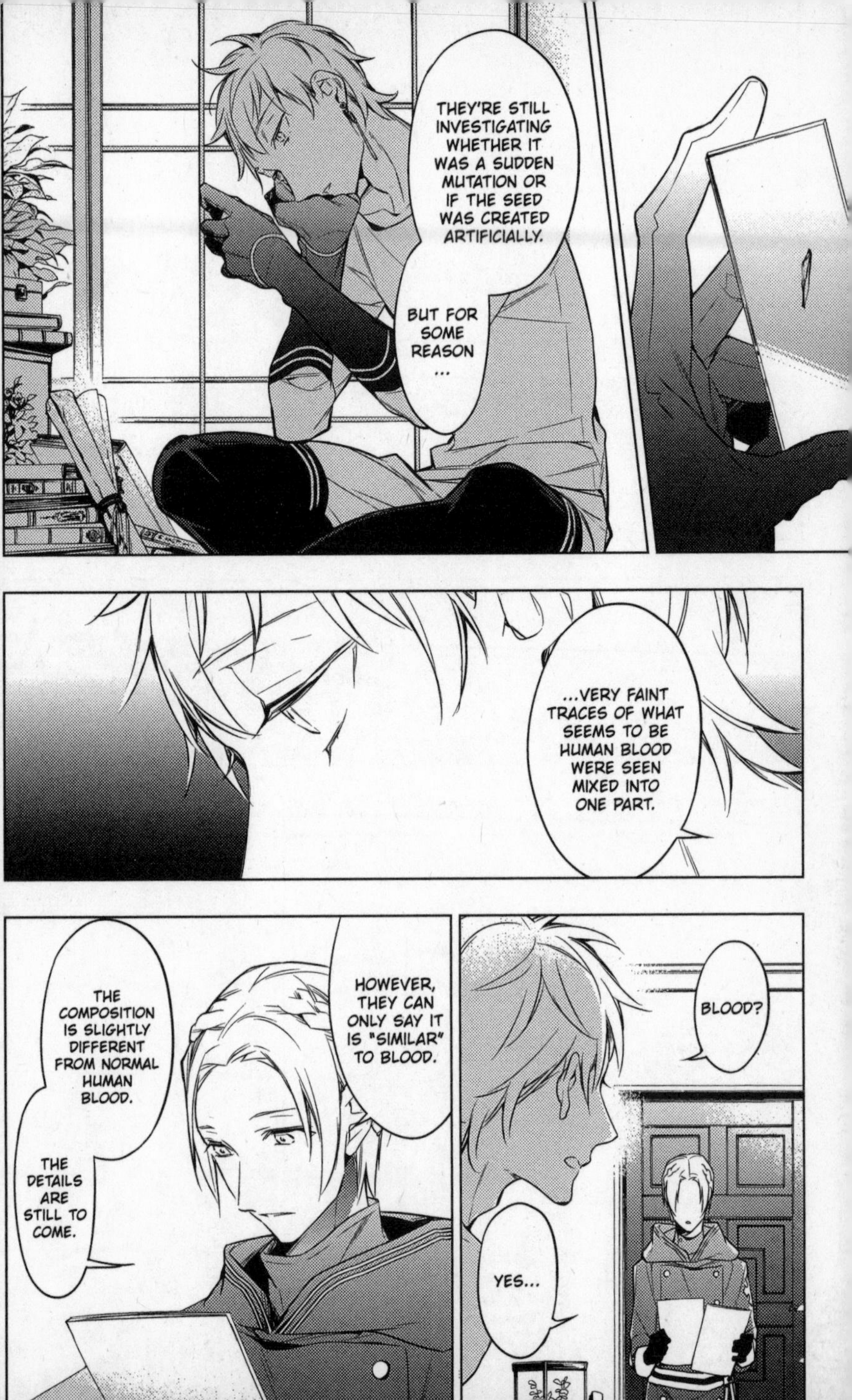
THEY'RE STILL INVESTIGATING WHETHER IT WAS A SUDDEN MUTATION OR IF THE SEED WAS CREATED ARTIFICIALLY.
BUT FOR SOME REASON...
...VERY FAINT TRACES OF WHAT SEEMS TO BE HUMAN BLOOD WERE SEEN MIXED INTO ONE PART.
BLOOD?
YES...
HOWEVER, THEY CAN ONLY SAY IT IS "SIMILAR" TO BLOOD.
THE COMPOSITION IS SLIGHTLY DIFFERENT FROM NORMAL HUMAN BLOOD.
THE DETAILS ARE STILL TO COME.

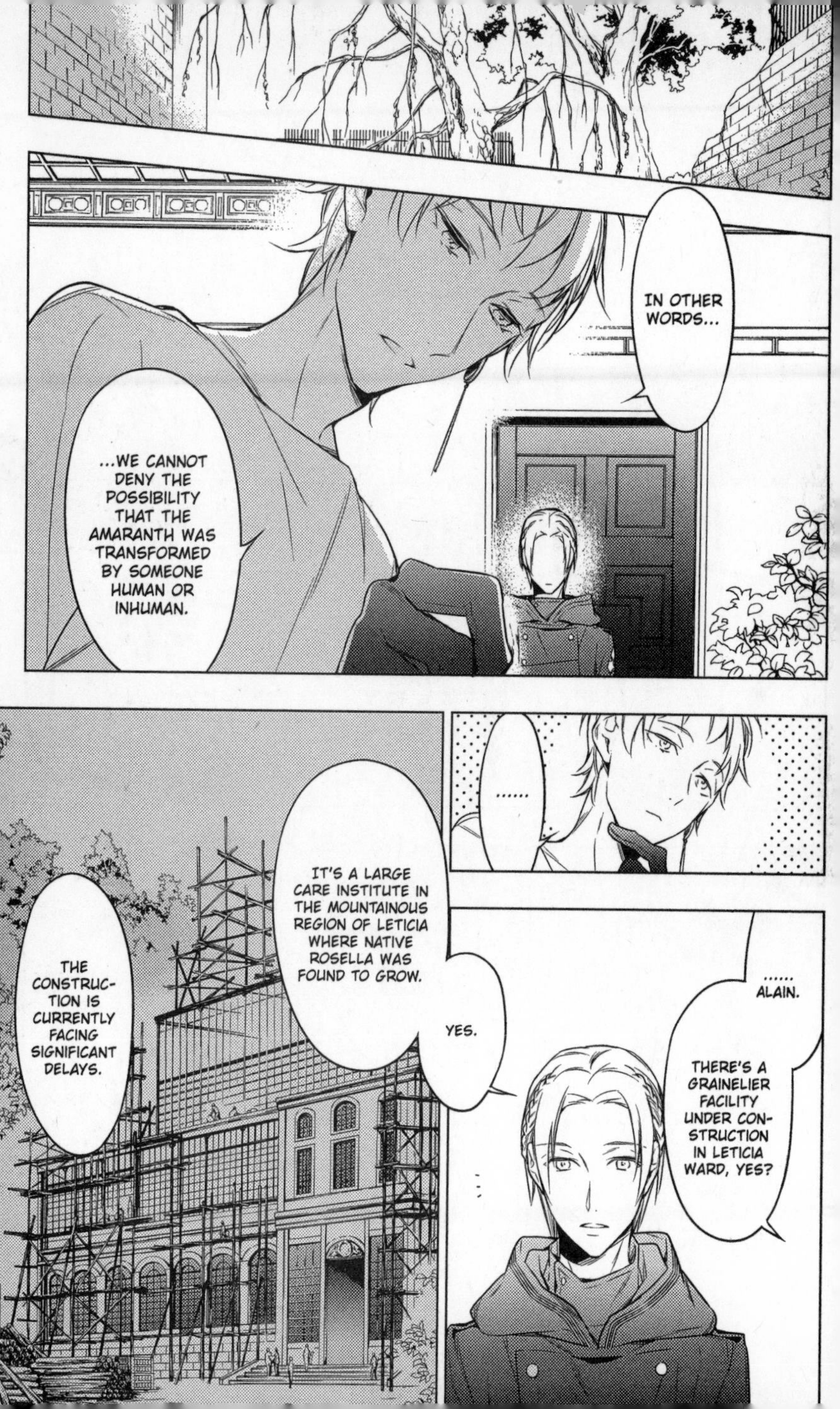
IN OTHER WORDS...
...WE CANNOT DENY THE POSSIBILITY THAT THE AMARANTH WAS TRANSFORMED BY SOMEONE HUMAN OR INHUMAN.
......
...... ALAIN.
THERE'S A GRAINELIER FACILITY UNDER CONSTRUCTION IN LETICIA WARD, YES?
YES.
IT'S A LARGE CARE INSTITUTE IN THE MOUNTAINOUS REGION OF LETICIA WHERE NATIVE ROSELLA WAS FOUND TO GROW.
THE CONSTRUCTION IS CURRENTLY FACING SIGNIFICANT DELAYS.

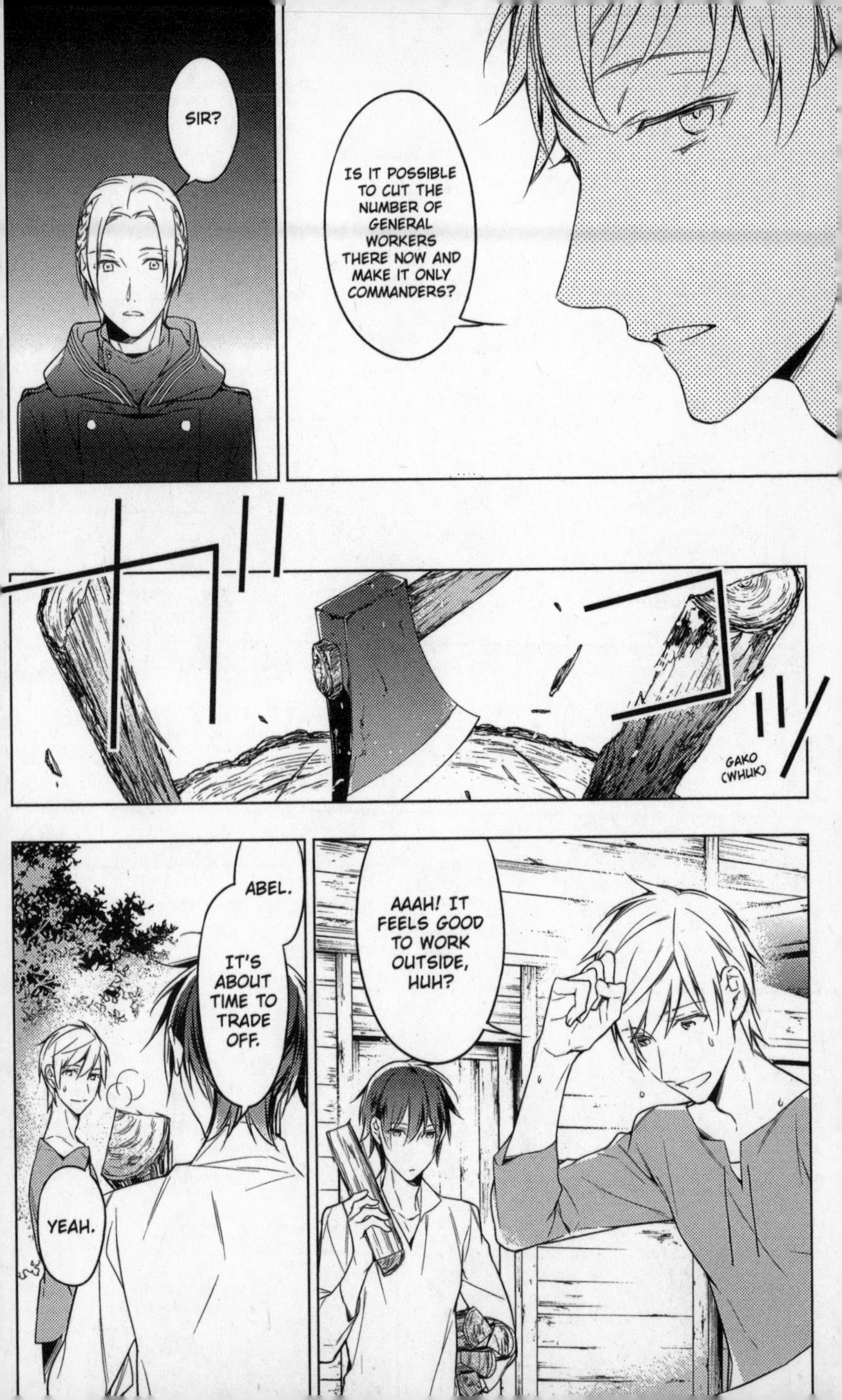
IS IT POSSIBLE TO CUT THE NUMBER OF GENERAL WORKERS THERE NOW AND MAKE IT ONLY COMMANDERS?
SIR?
GAKO (WHUK)
AAAH! IT FEELS GOOD TO WORK OUTSIDE, HUH?
ABEL.
IT'S ABOUT TIME TO TRADE OFF.
YEAH.

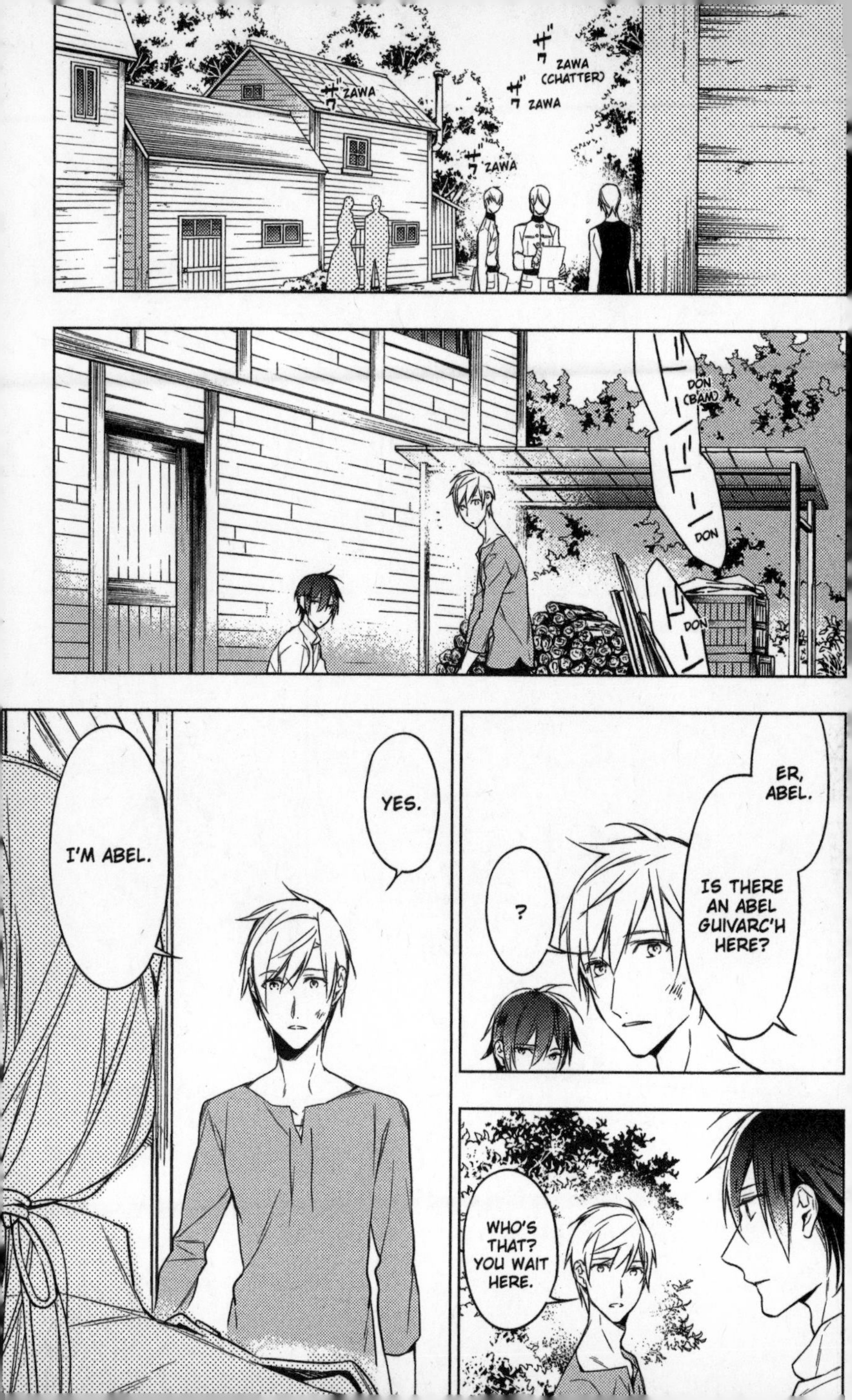
ZAWA (CHATTER)
ZAWA
ZAWA
ZAWA
DON (BAM)
DON
DON
ER, ABEL.
IS THERE AN ABEL GUIVARC'H HERE?
?
WHO'S THAT? YOU WAIT HERE.
YES.
I'M ABEL.

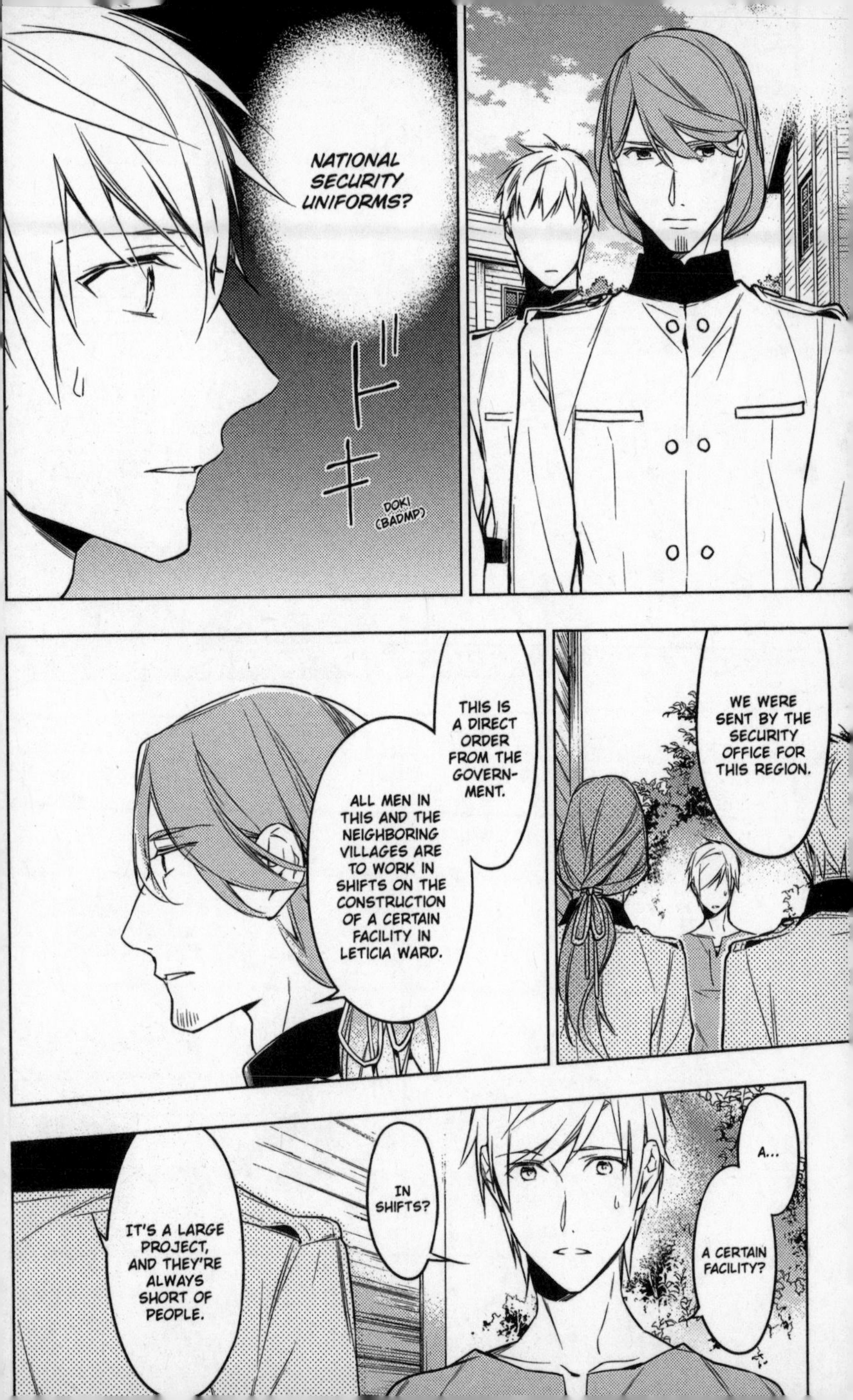
NATIONAL SECURITY UNIFORMS?
ドキ
DOKI (BADMP)
WE WERE SENT BY THE SECURITY OFFICE FOR THIS REGION.
THIS IS A DIRECT ORDER FROM THE GOVERNMENT.
ALL MEN IN THIS AND THE NEIGHBORING VILLAGES ARE TO WORK IN SHIFTS ON THE CONSTRUCTION OF A CERTAIN FACILITY IN LETICIA WARD.
A...
A CERTAIN FACILITY?
IN SHIFTS?
IT'S A LARGE PROJECT, AND THEY'RE ALWAYS SHORT OF PEOPLE.

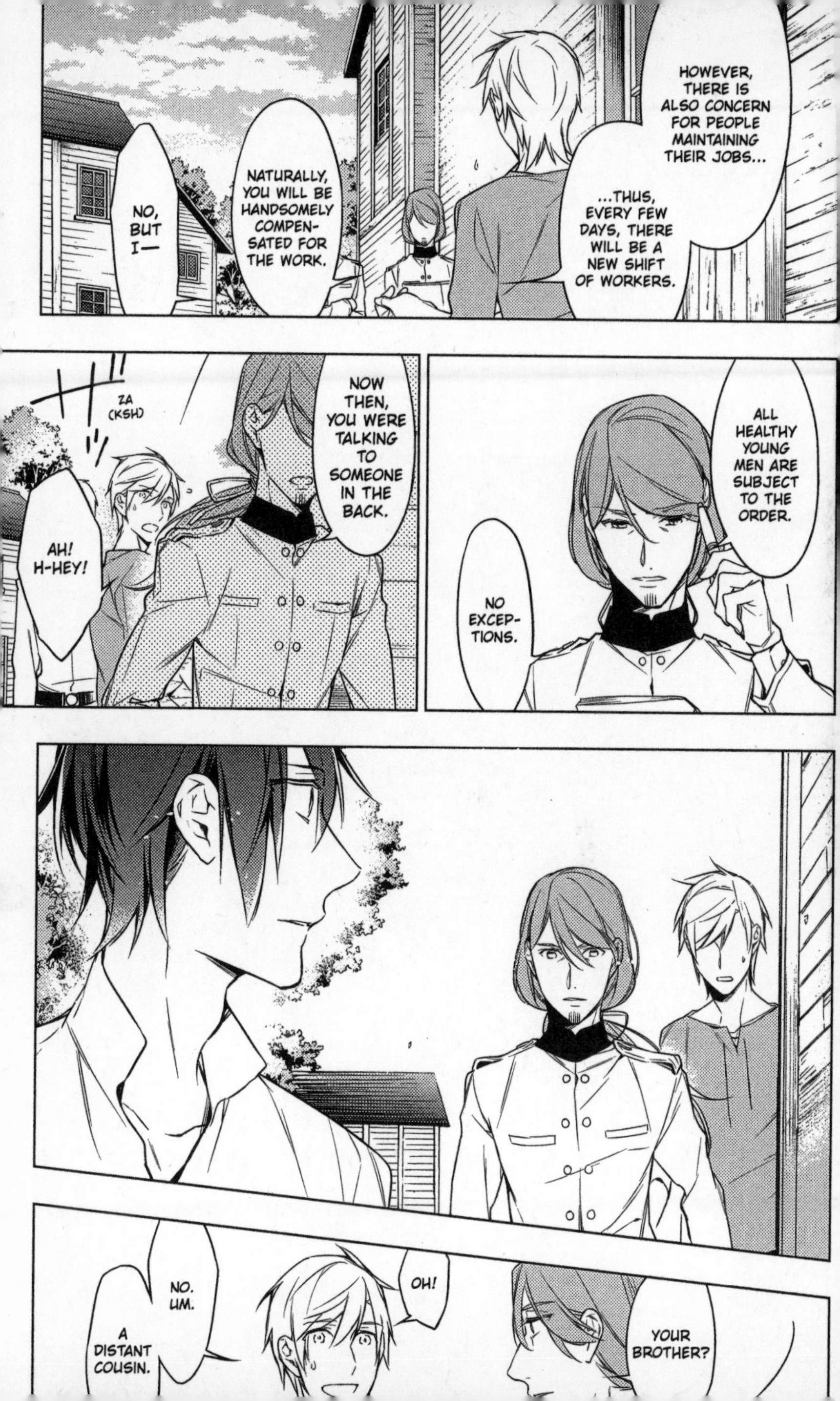
HOWEVER, THERE IS ALSO CONCERN FOR PEOPLE MAINTAINING THEIR JOBS...
...THUS, EVERY FEW DAYS, THERE WILL BE A NEW SHIFT OF WORKERS.
NATURALLY, YOU WILL BE HANDSOMELY COMPEN-SATED FOR THE WORK.
NO, BUT I—
ALL HEALTHY YOUNG MEN ARE SUBJECT TO THE ORDER.
NO EXCEP-TIONS.
NOW THEN, YOU WERE TALKING TO SOMEONE IN THE BACK.
ZA (KSH)
AH! H-HEY!
YOUR BROTHER?
OH!
NO. UM.
A DISTANT COUSIN.

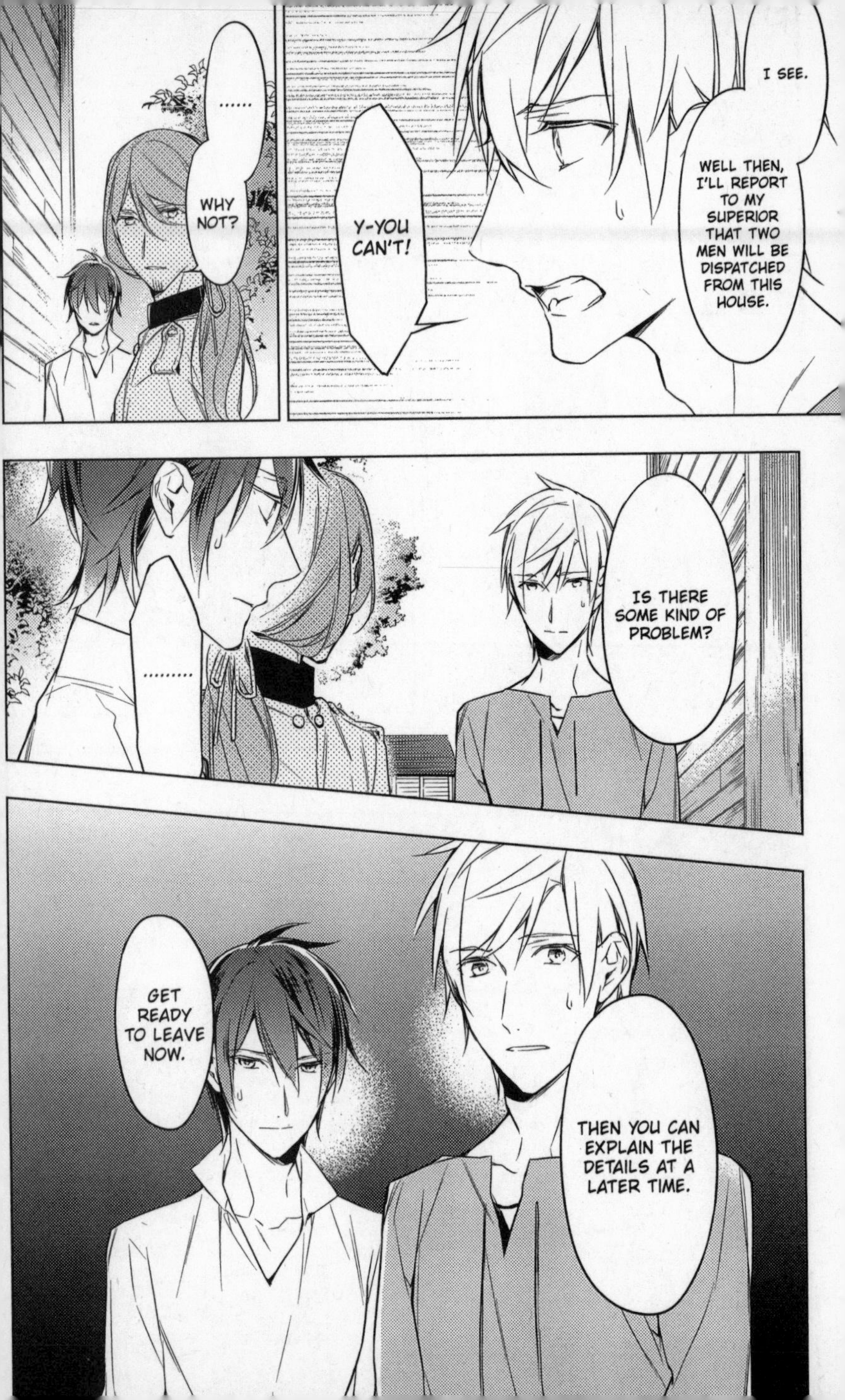
I SEE.
WELL THEN, I'LL REPORT TO MY SUPERIOR THAT TWO MEN WILL BE DISPATCHED FROM THIS HOUSE.
Y-YOU CAN'T!
......
WHY NOT?
IS THERE SOME KIND OF PROBLEM?
....
GET READY TO LEAVE NOW.
THEN YOU CAN EXPLAIN THE DETAILS AT A LATER TIME.

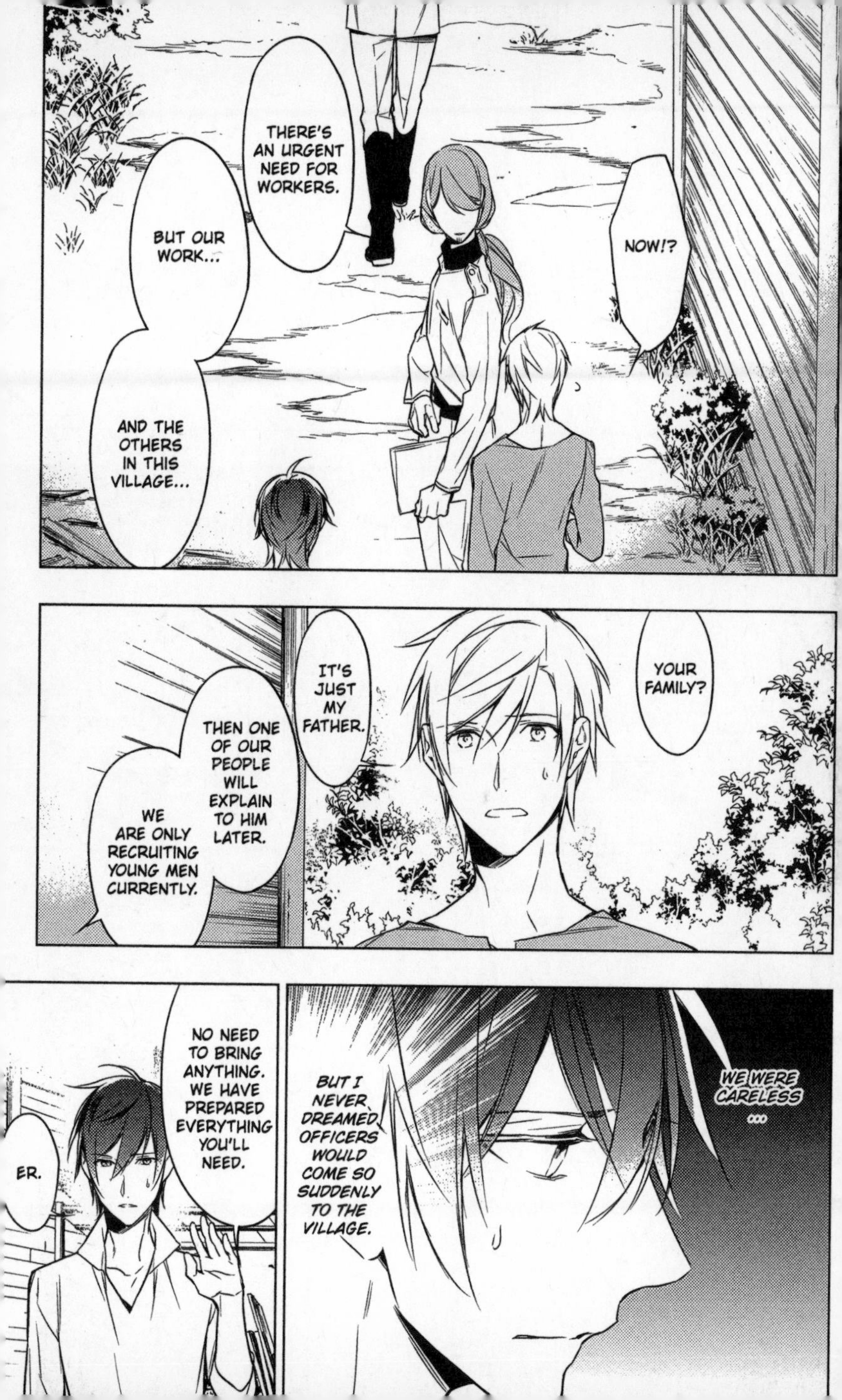
NOW!?
THERE'S AN URGENT NEED FOR WORKERS.
BUT OUR WORK...
AND THE OTHERS IN THIS VILLAGE...
YOUR FAMILY?
IT'S JUST MY FATHER.
THEN ONE OF OUR PEOPLE WILL EXPLAIN TO HIM LATER.
WE ARE ONLY RECRUITING YOUNG MEN CURRENTLY.
WE WERE CARELESS...
BUT I NEVER DREAMED OFFICERS WOULD COME SO SUDDENLY TO THE VILLAGE.
NO NEED TO BRING ANYTHING. WE HAVE PREPARED EVERYTHING YOU'LL NEED.
ER.

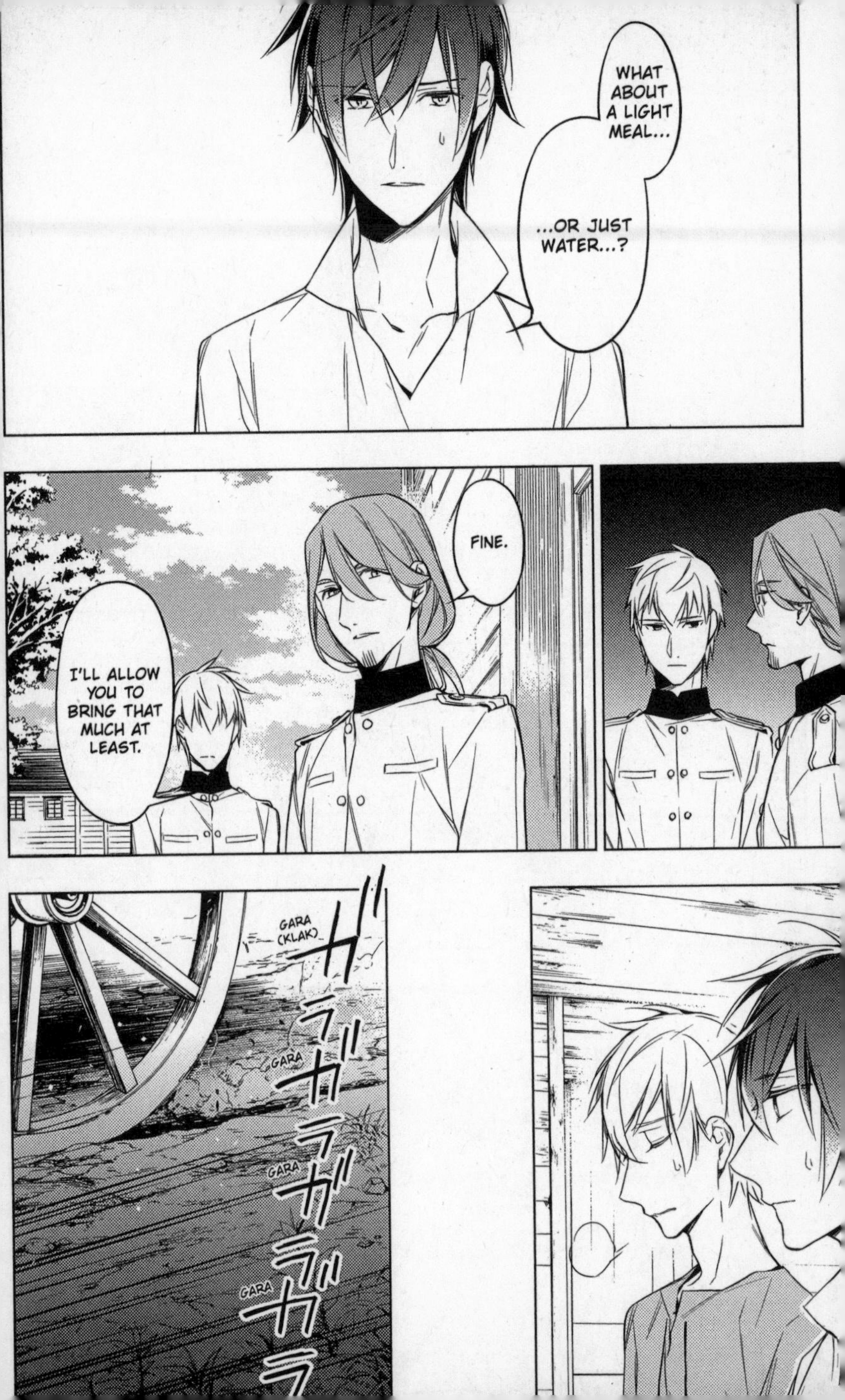
WHAT ABOUT A LIGHT MEAL...
...OR JUST WATER...?
FINE.
I'LL ALLOW YOU TO BRING THAT MUCH AT LEAST.
GARA (KLAK)
GARA
GARA
GARA

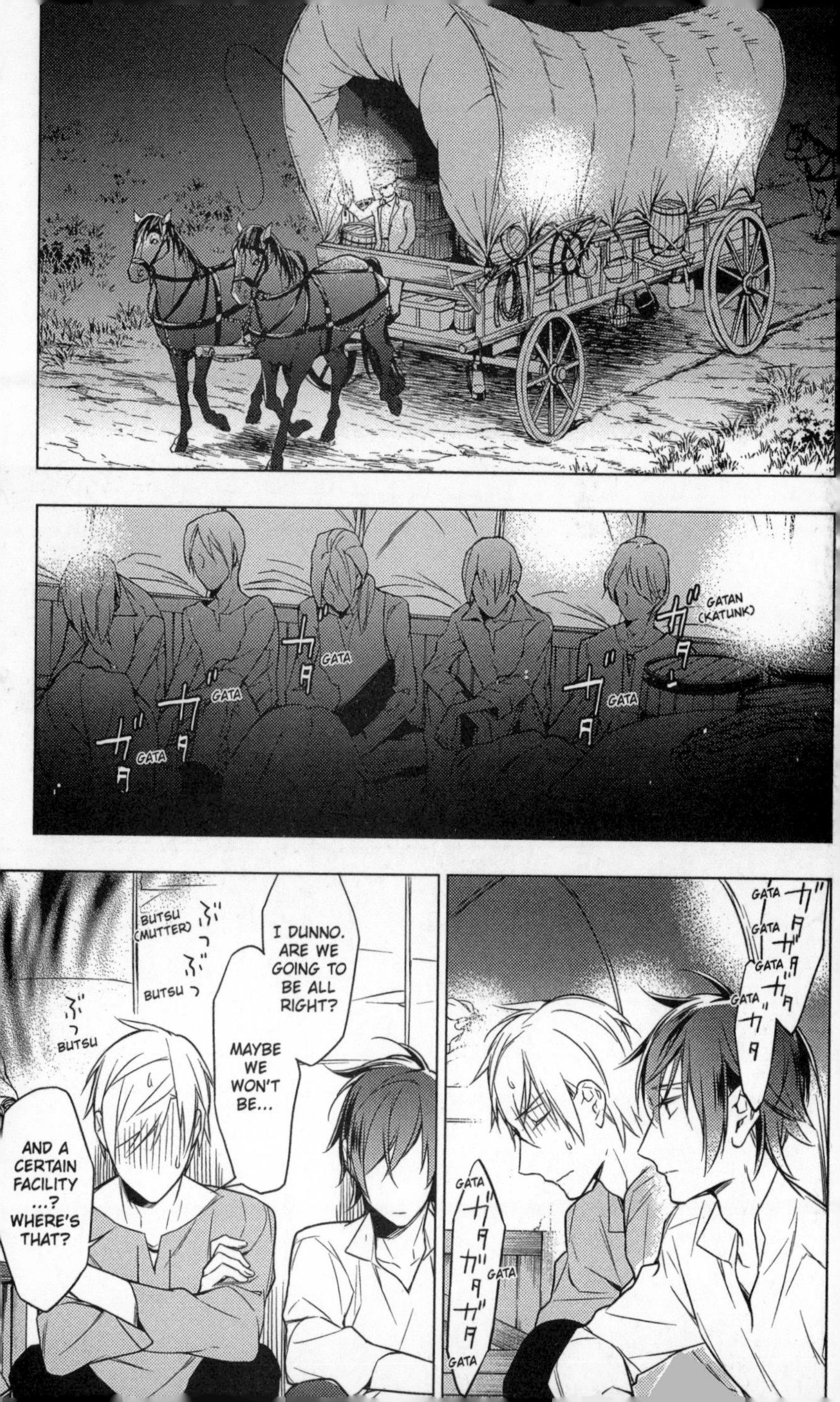
GATAN (KATUNK)
GATA
GATA
GATA
GATA
GATA
GATA
GATA
GATA
GATA
GATA
GATA
BUTSU (MUTTER)
BUTSU
BUTSU
AND A CERTAIN FACILITY ...? WHERE'S THAT?
I DUNNO. ARE WE GOING TO BE ALL RIGHT?
MAYBE WE WON'T BE...

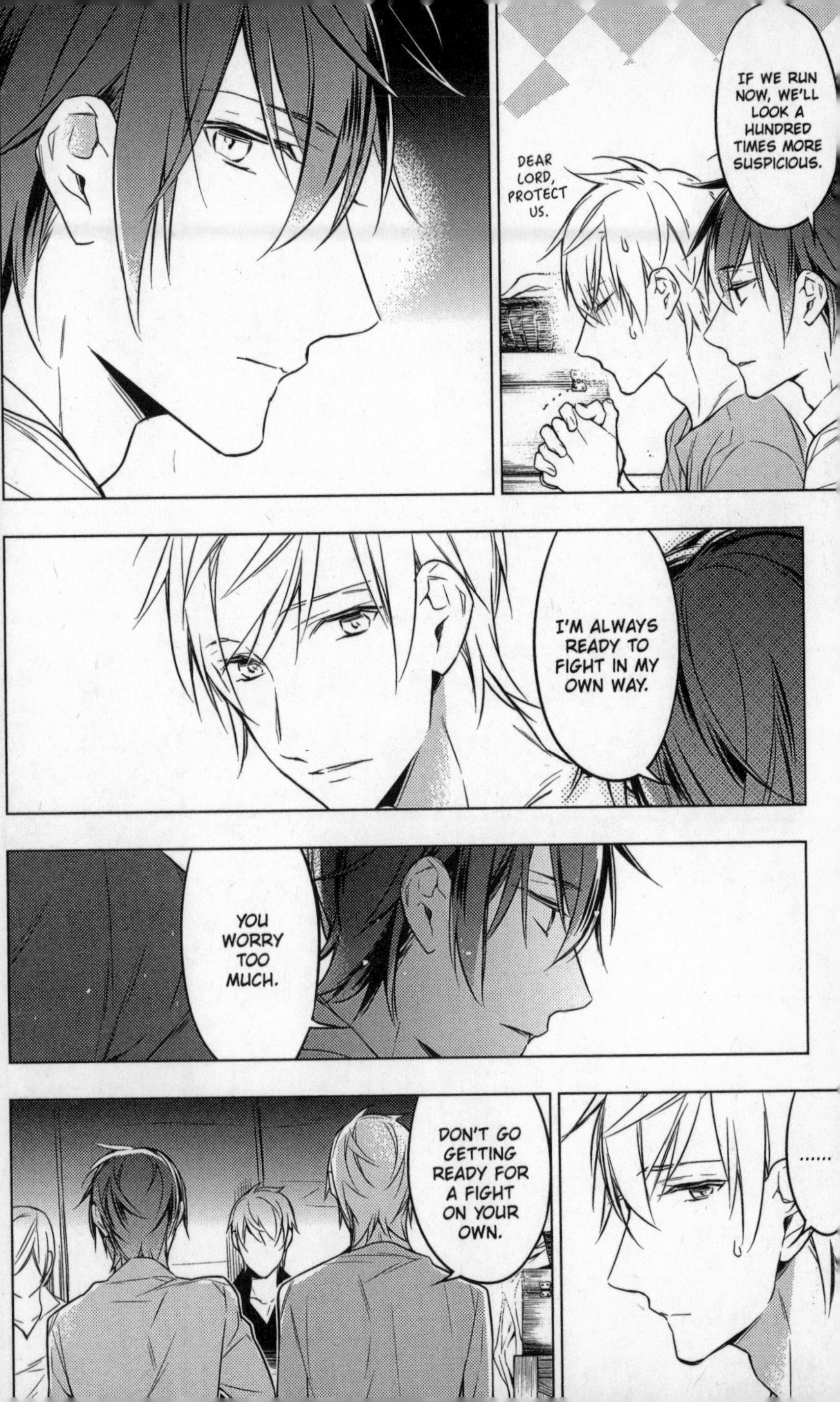
IF WE RUN NOW, WE'LL LOOK A HUNDRED TIMES MORE SUSPICIOUS.
DEAR LORD, PROTECT US.
I'M ALWAYS READY TO FIGHT IN MY OWN WAY.
YOU WORRY TOO MUCH.
......
DON'T GO GETTING READY FOR A FIGHT ON YOUR OWN.

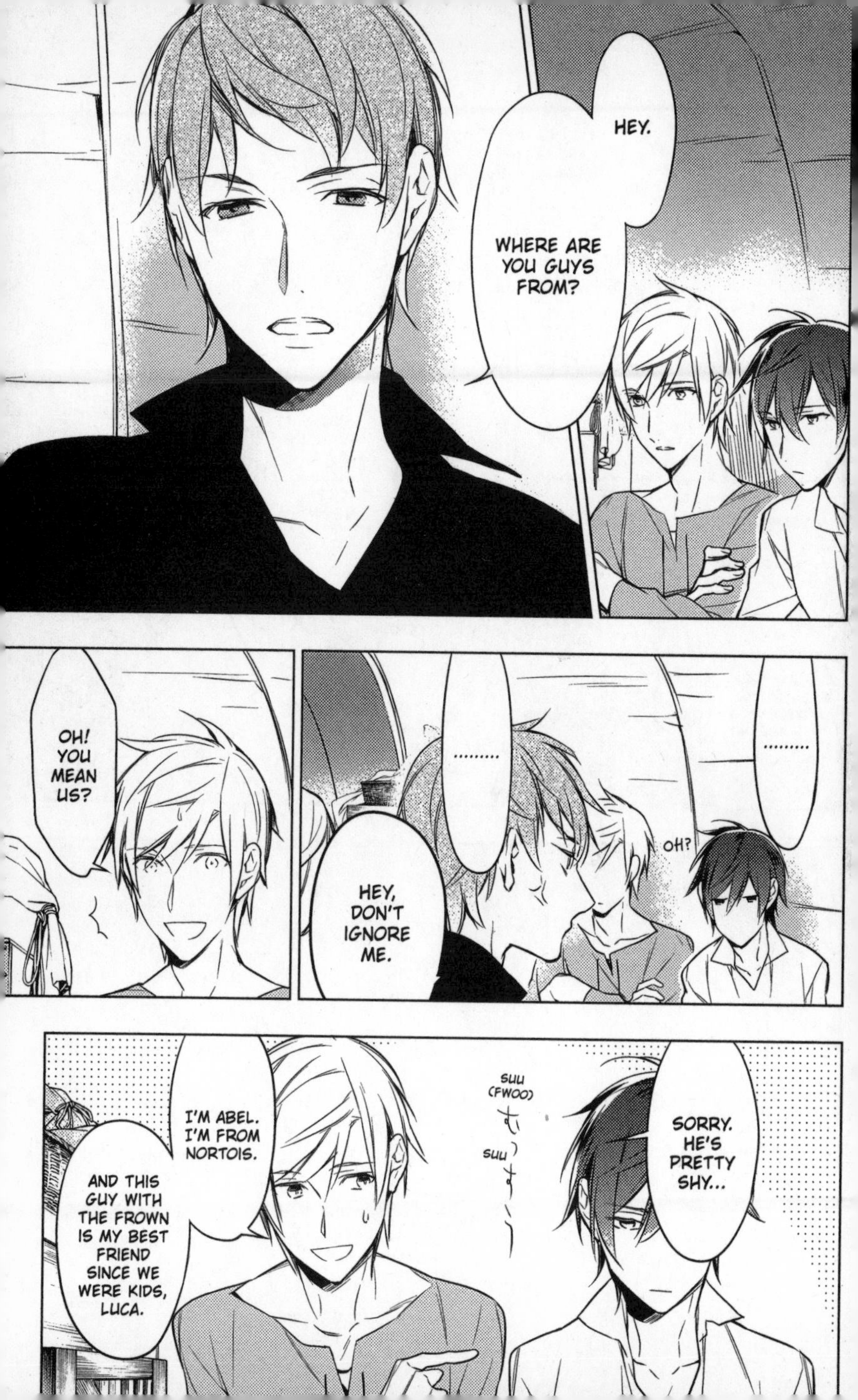
HEY.
WHERE ARE YOU GUYS FROM?
....
....
OH?
HEY, DON'T IGNORE ME.
OH! YOU MEAN US?
SORRY. HE'S PRETTY SHY...
SUU (FWOO)
SUU
I'M ABEL. I'M FROM NORTOIS.
AND THIS GUY WITH THE FROWN IS MY BEST FRIEND SINCE WE WERE KIDS, LUCA.

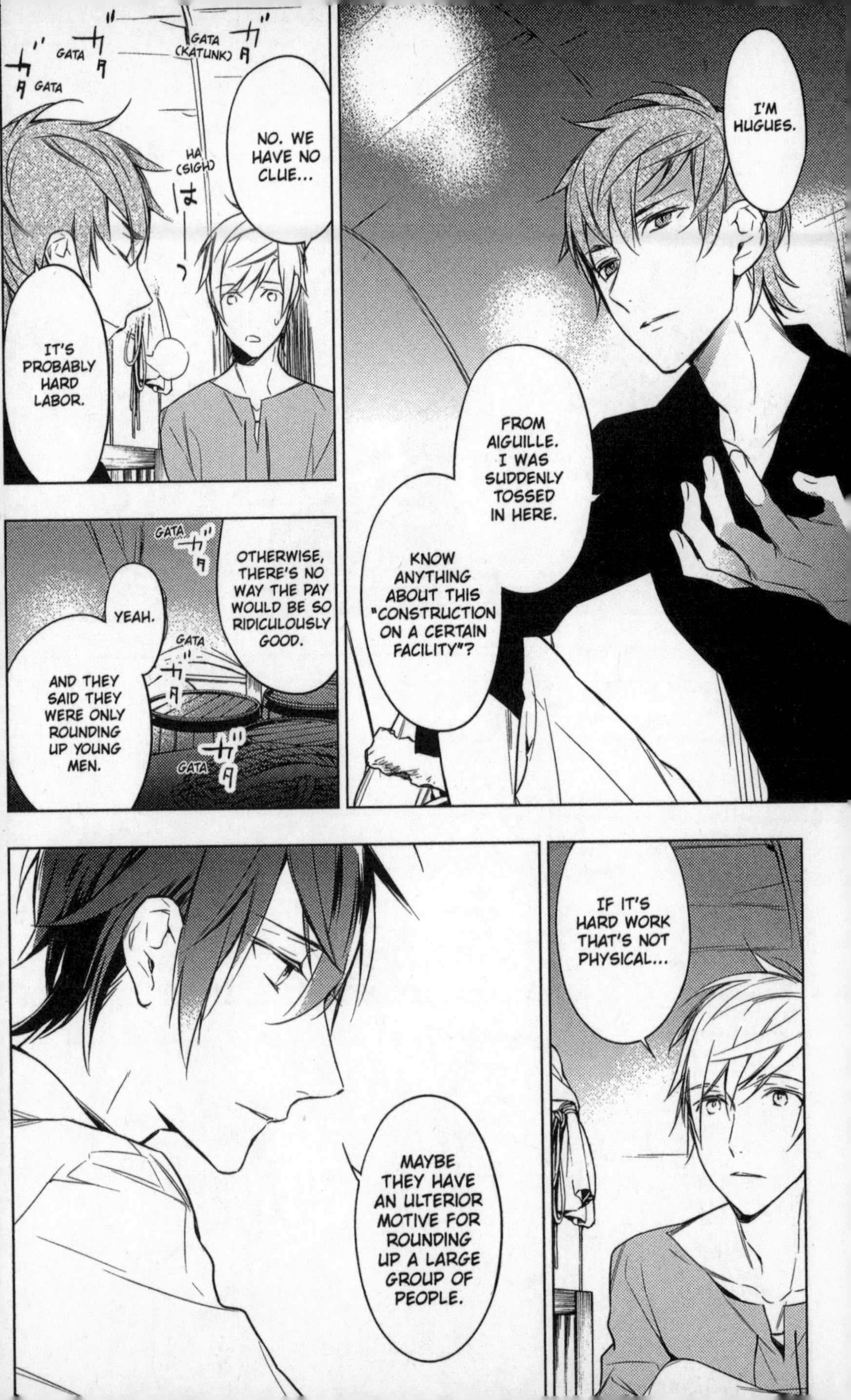
I'M HUGUES.
FROM AIGUILLE. I WAS SUDDENLY TOSSED IN HERE.
KNOW ANYTHING ABOUT THIS "CONSTRUCTION ON A CERTAIN FACILITY"?
GATA (KATUNK)
GATA
GATA
NO. WE HAVE NO CLUE...
HA (SIGH)
IT'S PROBABLY HARD LABOR.
GATA
OTHERWISE, THERE'S NO WAY THE PAY WOULD BE SO RIDICULOUSLY GOOD.
YEAH.
GATA
AND THEY SAID THEY WERE ONLY ROUNDING UP YOUNG MEN.
GATA
IF IT'S HARD WORK THAT'S NOT PHYSICAL...
MAYBE THEY HAVE AN ULTERIOR MOTIVE FOR ROUNDING UP A LARGE GROUP OF PEOPLE.

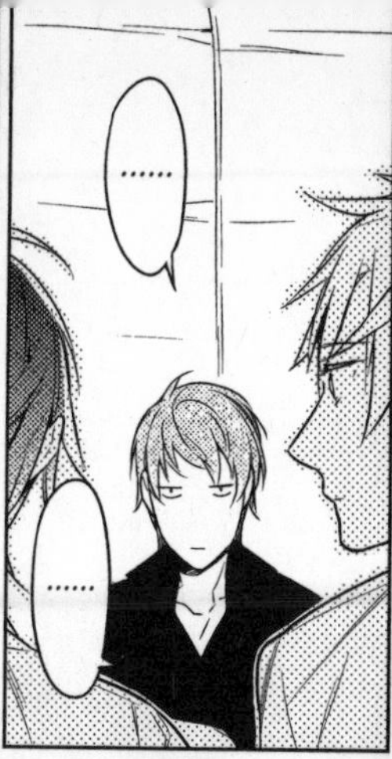
......
......

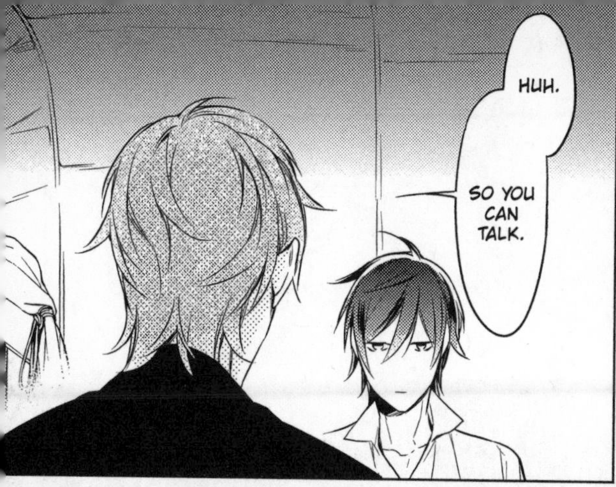
HUH.
SO YOU CAN TALK.

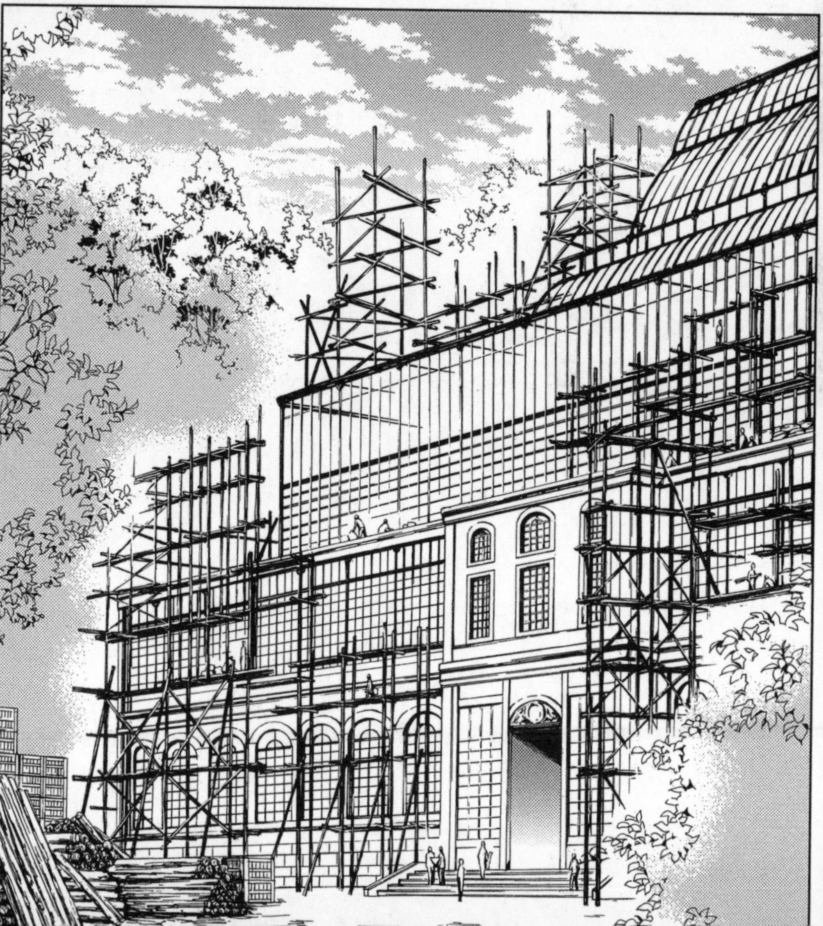

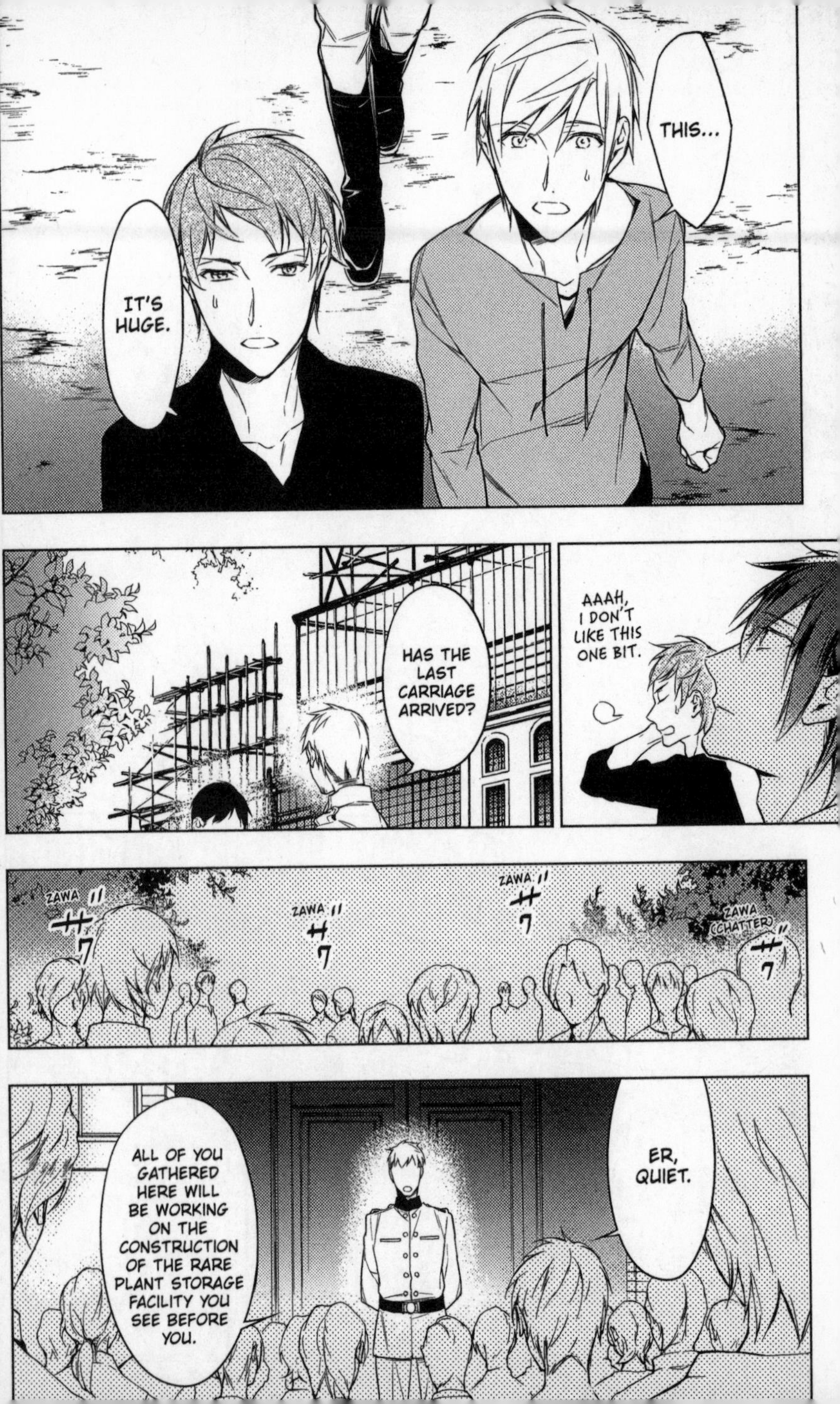
THIS...
IT'S HUGE.
AAAH, I DON'T LIKE THIS ONE BIT.
HAS THE LAST CARRIAGE ARRIVED?
ZAWA (CHATTER)
ZAWA
ZAWA
ZAWA
ER, QUIET.
ALL OF YOU GATHERED HERE WILL BE WORKING ON THE CONSTRUCTION OF THE RARE PLANT STORAGE FACILITY YOU SEE BEFORE YOU.

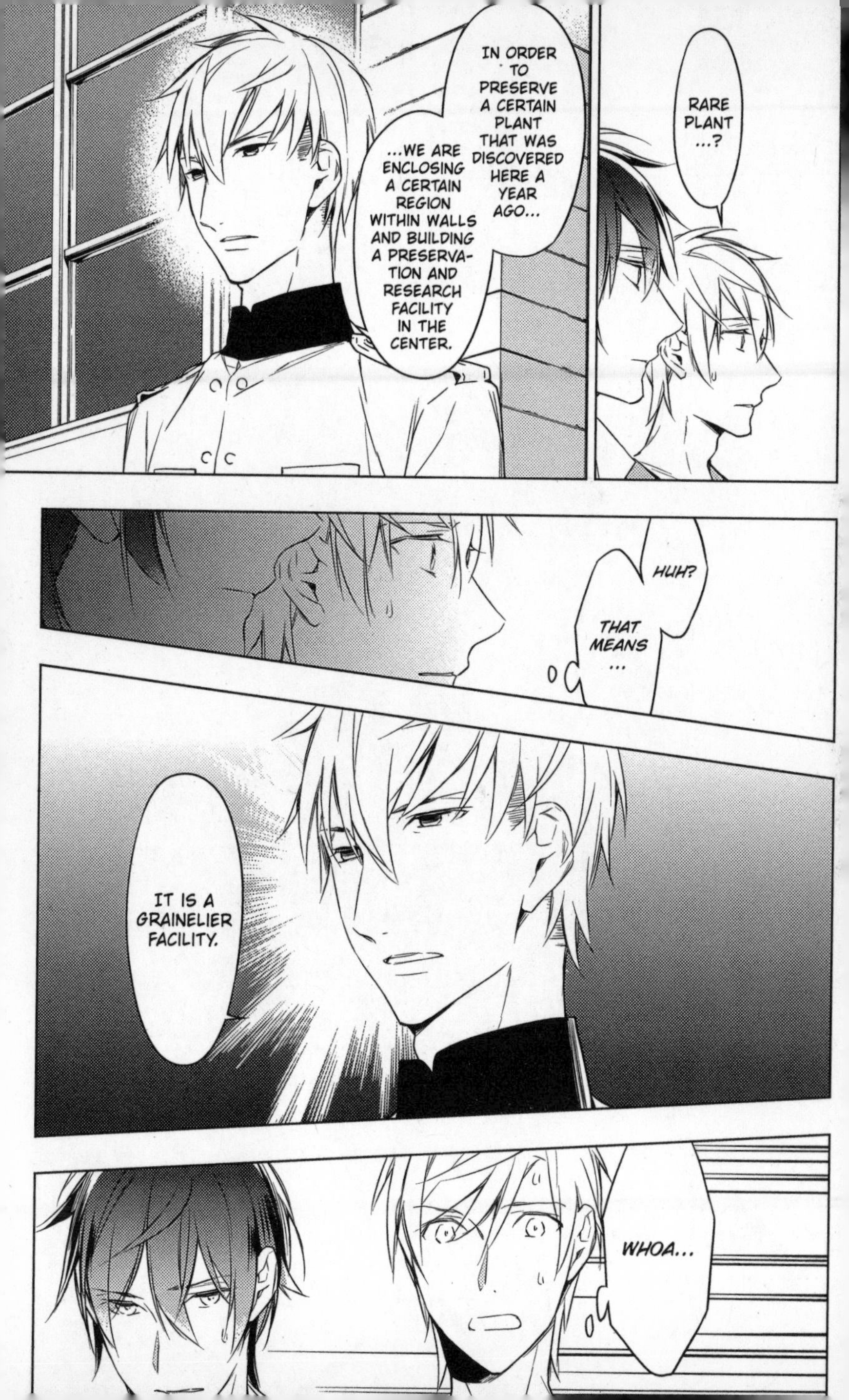
RARE PLANT ...?
IN ORDER TO PRESERVE A CERTAIN PLANT THAT WAS DISCOVERED HERE A YEAR AGO...
...WE ARE ENCLOSING A CERTAIN REGION WITHIN WALLS AND BUILDING A PRESERVATION AND RESEARCH FACILITY IN THE CENTER.
HUH?
THAT MEANS ...
IT IS A GRAINELIER FACILITY.
WHOA...

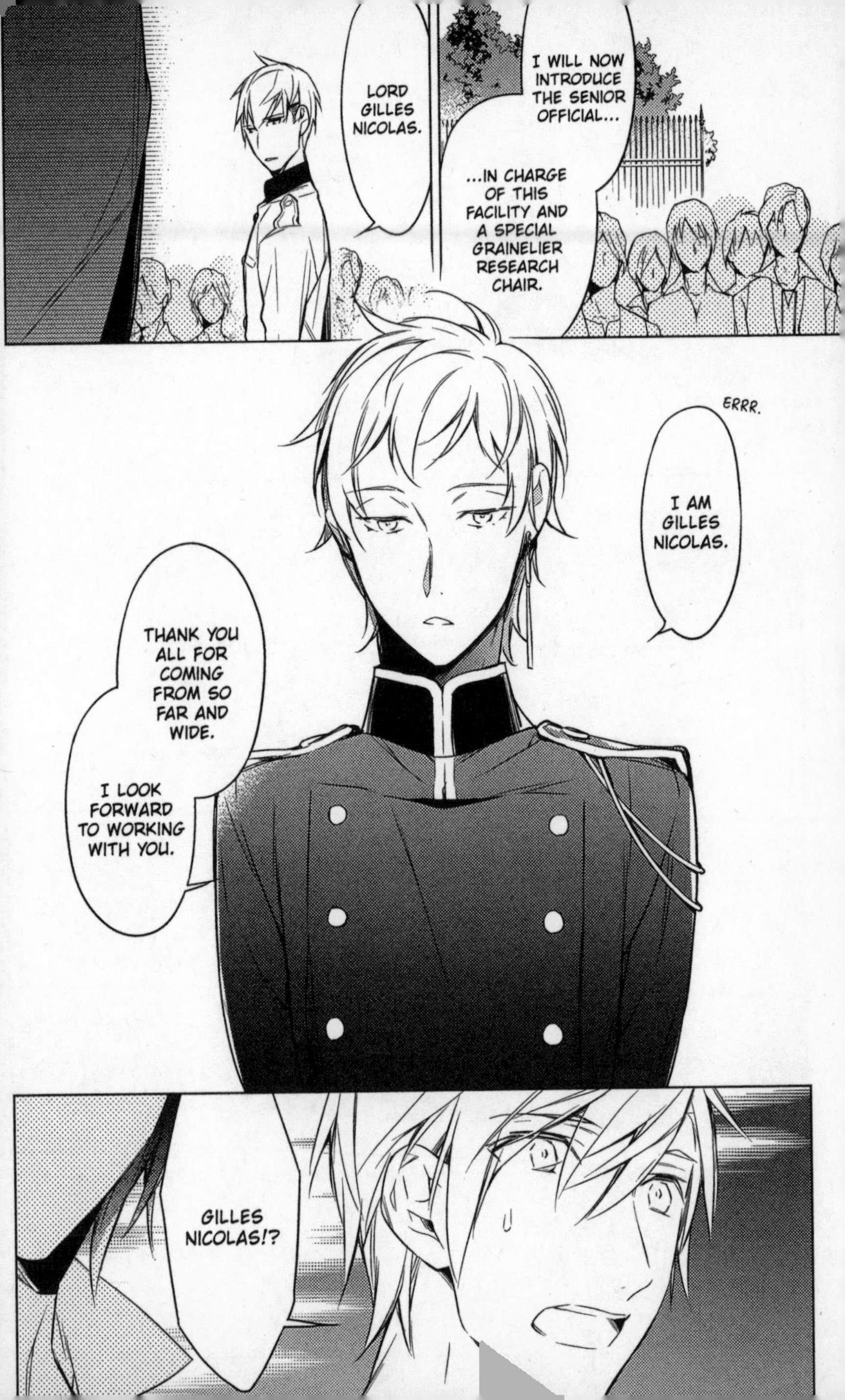
I WILL NOW INTRODUCE THE SENIOR OFFICIAL...
...IN CHARGE OF THIS FACILITY AND A SPECIAL GRAINELIER RESEARCH CHAIR.
LORD GILLES NICOLAS.
ERRR.
I AM GILLES NICOLAS.
THANK YOU ALL FOR COMING FROM SO FAR AND WIDE.
I LOOK FORWARD TO WORKING WITH YOU.
GILLES NICOLAS!?

GRAINELIERS

THE SENIOR OFFICIAL IN CHARGE OF THE CONSTRUCTION OF THIS FACILITY...

I AM GILLES NICOLAS.

...AND SPECIAL GRAINELIER RESEARCH CHAIR...

THANK YOU ALL FOR COMING FROM SO FAR AND WIDE.

...LORD GILLES NICOLAS.

I LOOK FORWARD TO WORKING WITH YOU.

GILLES NICOLAS ...!?

Episode 8

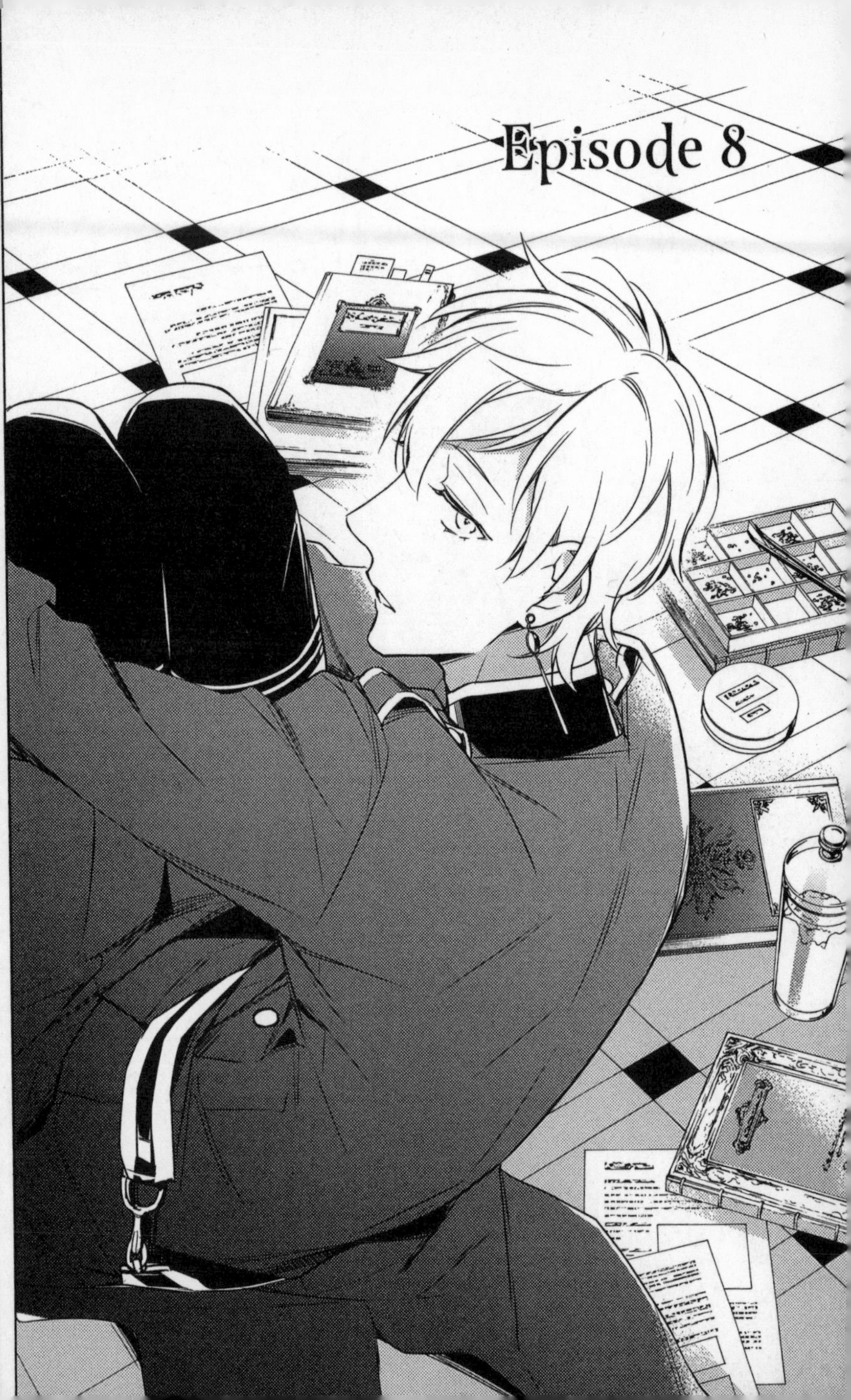

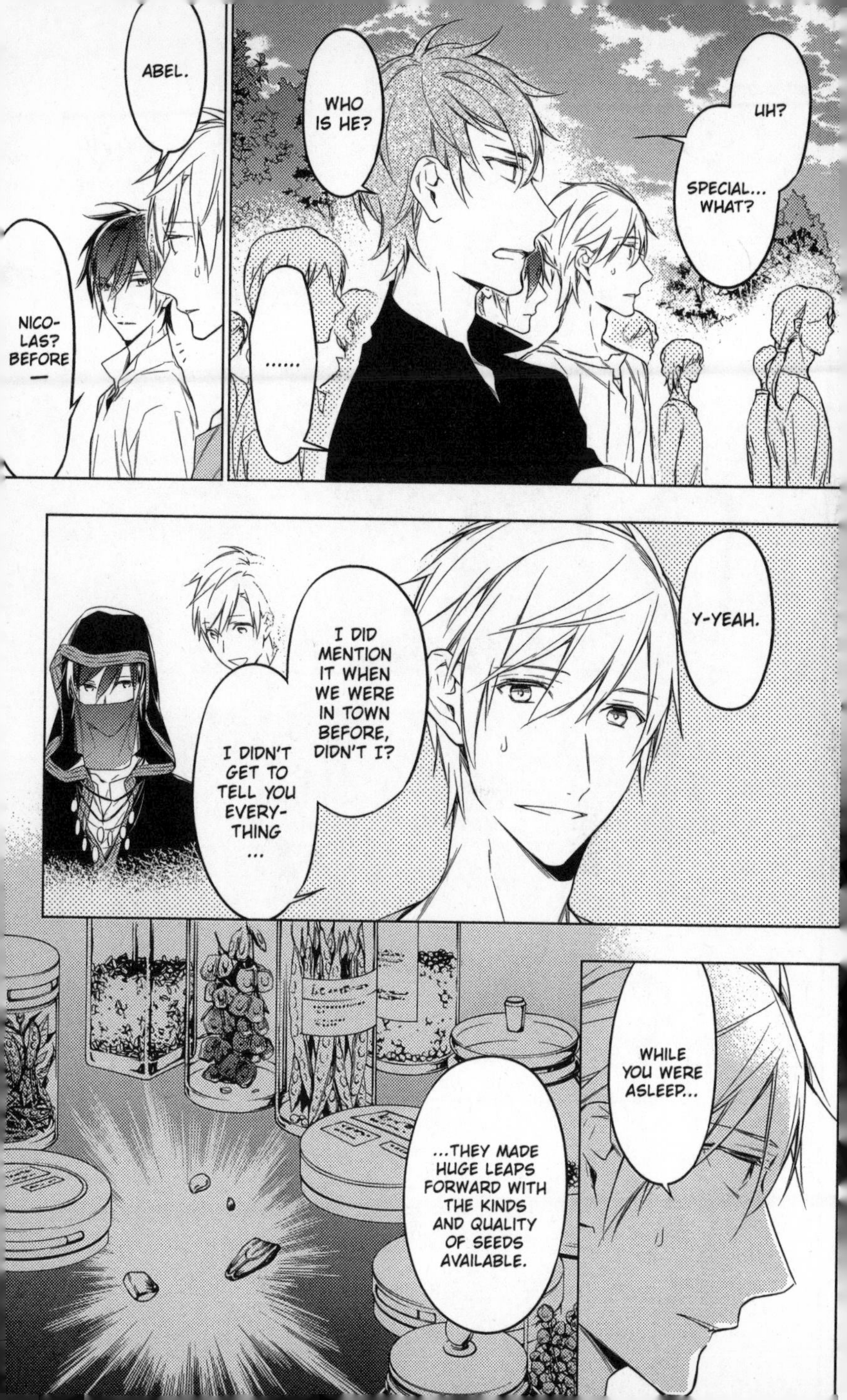
UH?
SPECIAL... WHAT?
WHO IS HE?
......
ABEL.
NICO-LAS? BEFORE —
Y-YEAH.
I DID MENTION IT WHEN WE WERE IN TOWN BEFORE, DIDN'T I?
I DIDN'T GET TO TELL YOU EVERY-THING ...
WHILE YOU WERE ASLEEP...
...THEY MADE HUGE LEAPS FORWARD WITH THE KINDS AND QUALITY OF SEEDS AVAILABLE.

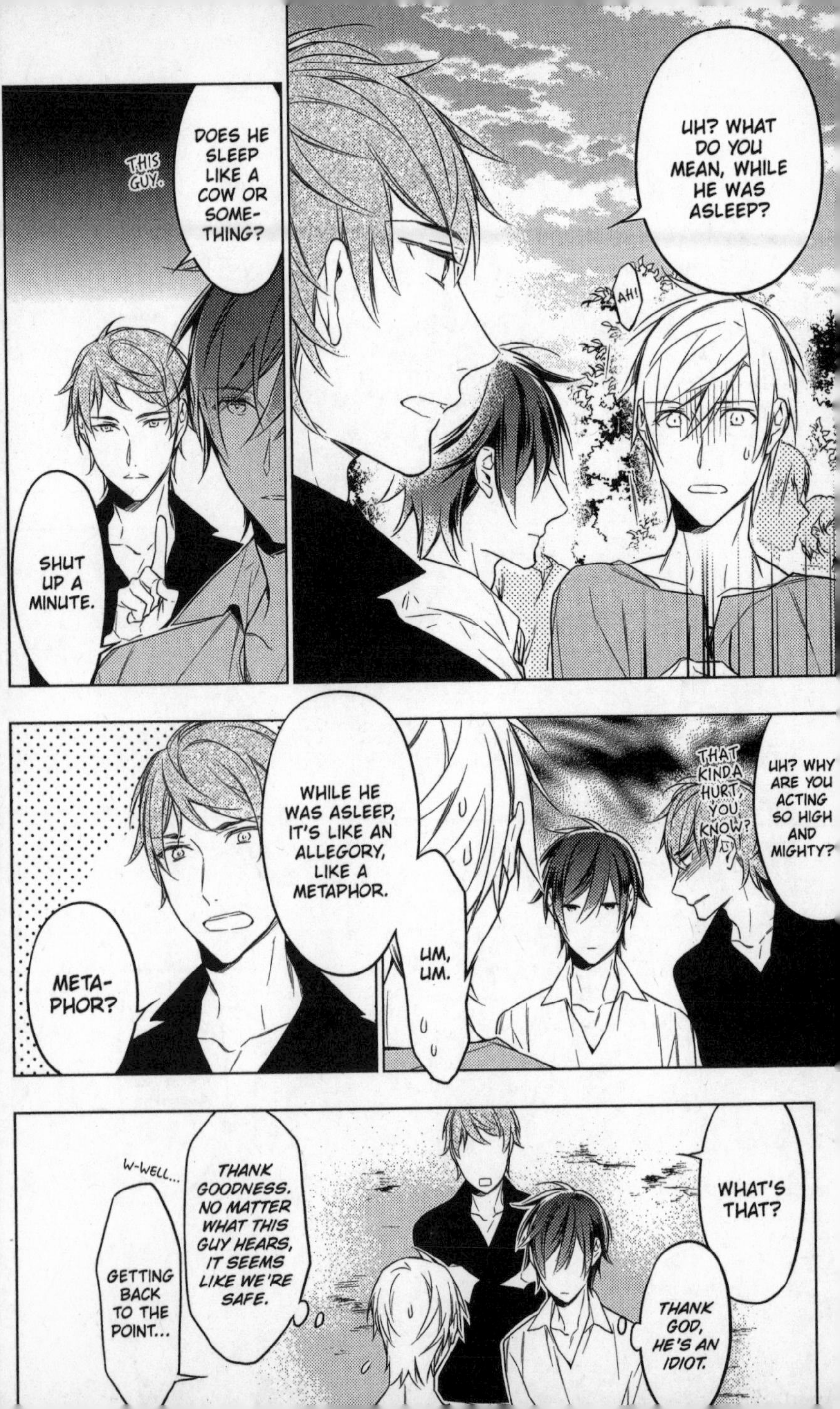
UH? WHAT DO YOU MEAN, WHILE HE WAS ASLEEP?
AH!
DOES HE SLEEP LIKE A COW OR SOME-THING?
THIS GUY.
SHUT UP A MINUTE.
UH? WHY ARE YOU ACTING SO HIGH AND MIGHTY?
THAT KINDA HURT, YOU KNOW?
UM, UM.
WHILE HE WAS ASLEEP, IT'S LIKE AN ALLEGORY, LIKE A METAPHOR.
META-PHOR?
WHAT'S THAT?
THANK GOD, HE'S AN IDIOT.
THANK GOODNESS. NO MATTER WHAT THIS GUY HEARS, IT SEEMS LIKE WE'RE SAFE.
W-WELL...
GETTING BACK TO THE POINT...

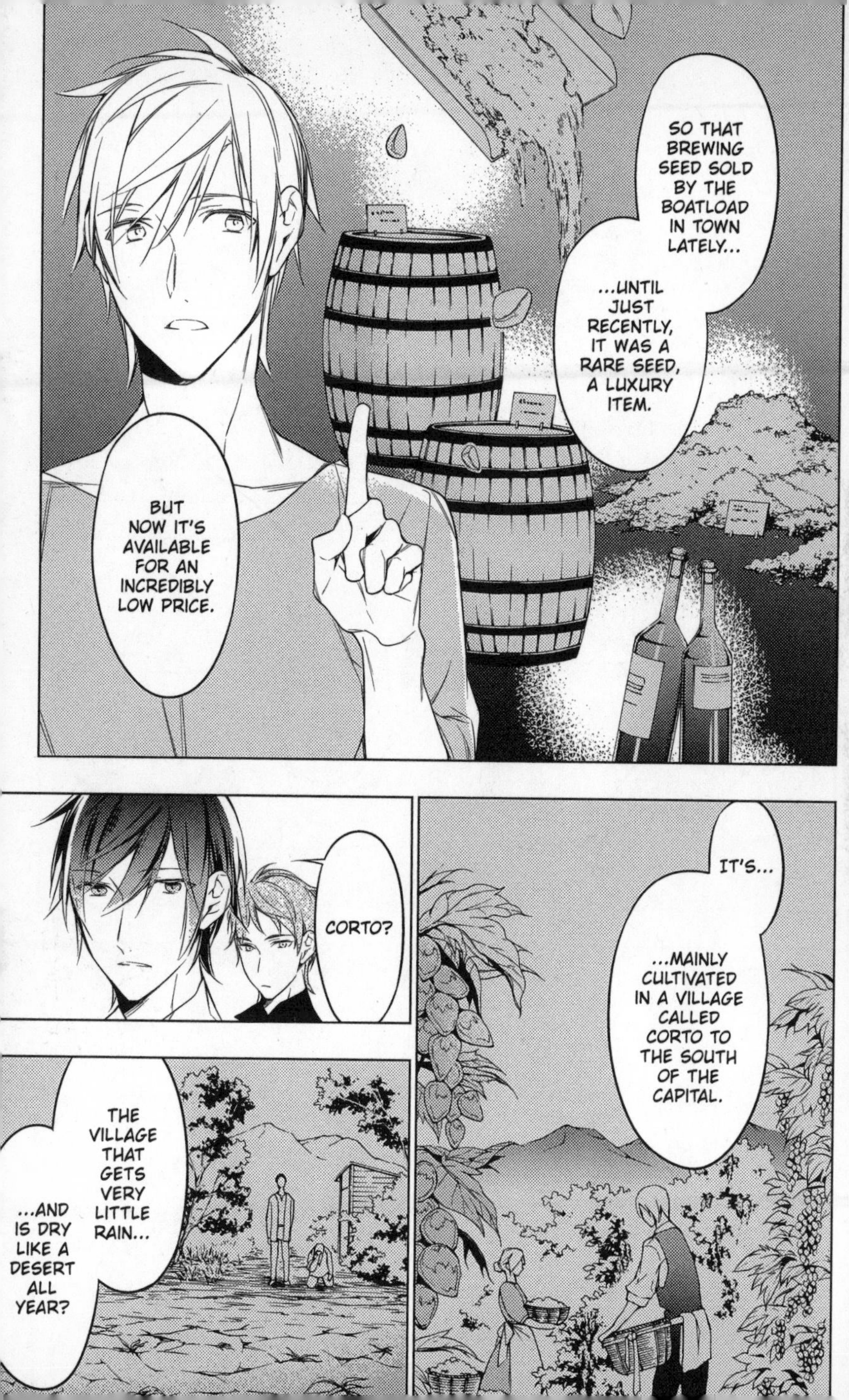
SO THAT BREWING SEED SOLD BY THE BOATLOAD IN TOWN LATELY...
...UNTIL JUST RECENTLY, IT WAS A RARE SEED, A LUXURY ITEM.
BUT NOW IT'S AVAILABLE FOR AN INCREDIBLY LOW PRICE.
IT'S...
...MAINLY CULTIVATED IN A VILLAGE CALLED CORTO TO THE SOUTH OF THE CAPITAL.
CORTO?
THE VILLAGE THAT GETS VERY LITTLE RAIN...
...AND IS DRY LIKE A DESERT ALL YEAR?

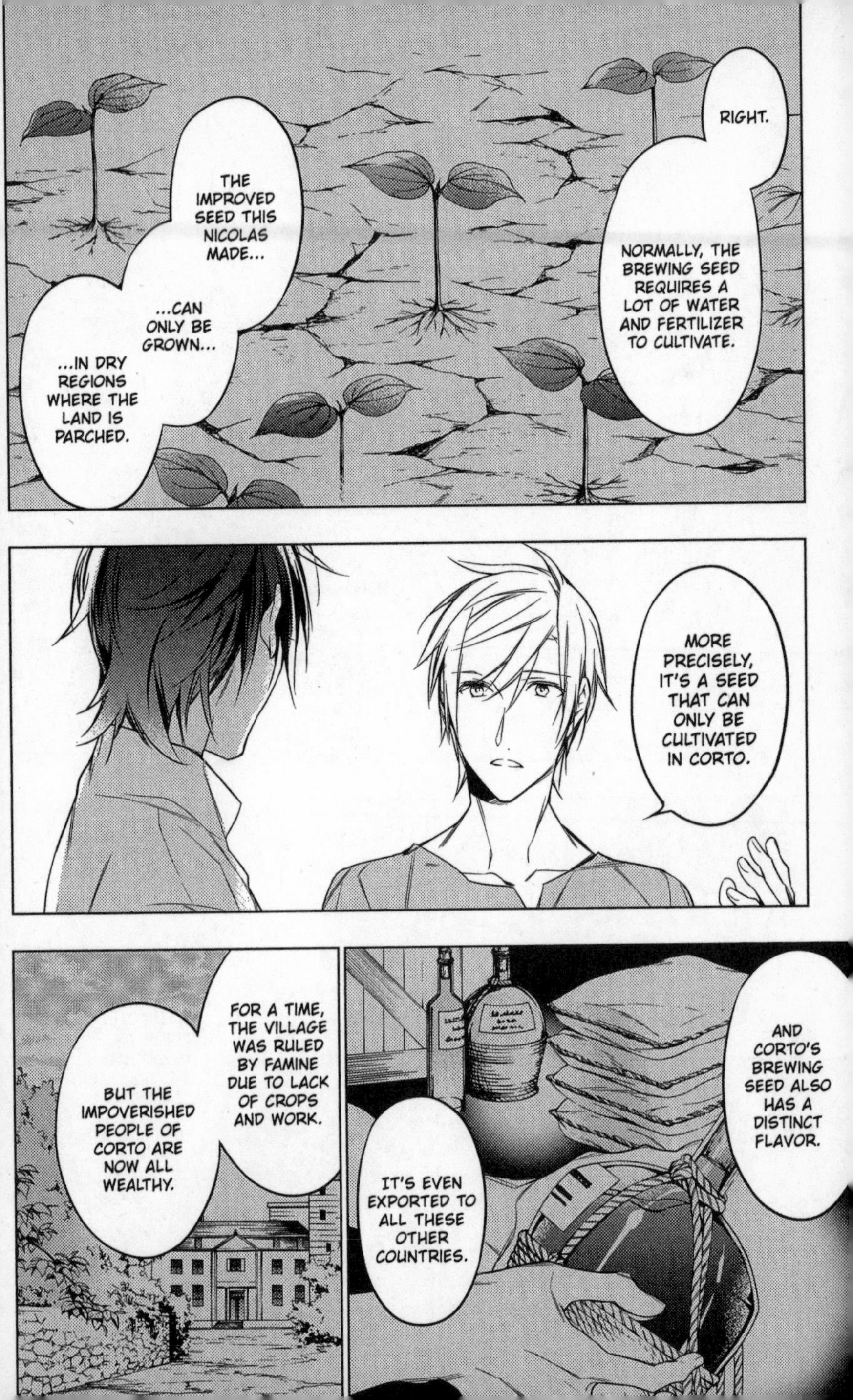
RIGHT.
NORMALLY, THE BREWING SEED REQUIRES A LOT OF WATER AND FERTILIZER TO CULTIVATE.
THE IMPROVED SEED THIS NICOLAS MADE...
...CAN ONLY BE GROWN...
...IN DRY REGIONS WHERE THE LAND IS PARCHED.
MORE PRECISELY, IT'S A SEED THAT CAN ONLY BE CULTIVATED IN CORTO.
AND CORTO'S BREWING SEED ALSO HAS A DISTINCT FLAVOR.
IT'S EVEN EXPORTED TO ALL THESE OTHER COUNTRIES.
FOR A TIME, THE VILLAGE WAS RULED BY FAMINE DUE TO LACK OF CROPS AND WORK.
BUT THE IMPOVERISHED PEOPLE OF CORTO ARE NOW ALL WEALTHY.

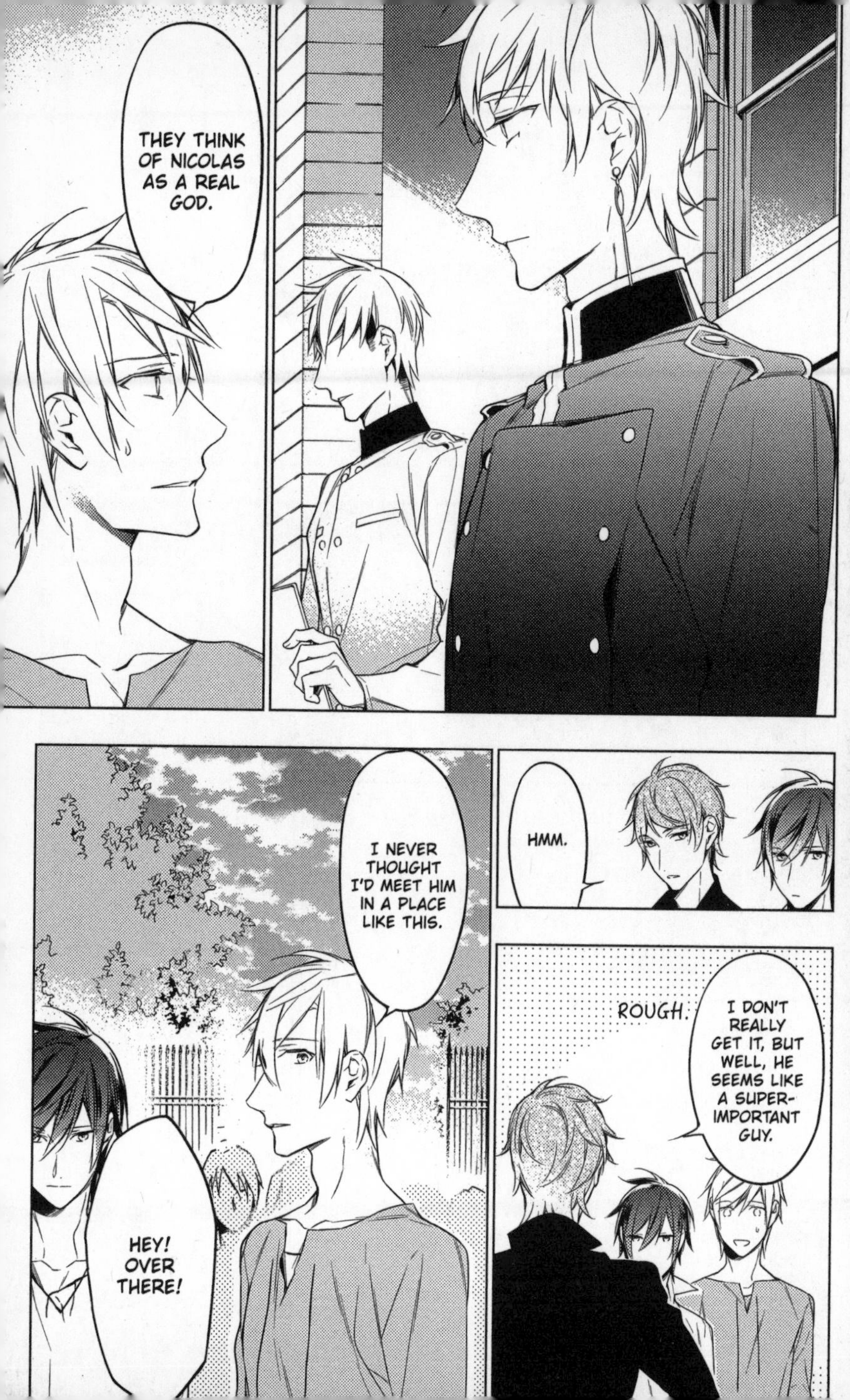
THEY THINK OF NICOLAS AS A REAL GOD.
HMM.
I DON'T REALLY GET IT, BUT WELL, HE SEEMS LIKE A SUPER-IMPORTANT GUY.
ROUGH.
I NEVER THOUGHT I'D MEET HIM IN A PLACE LIKE THIS.
HEY! OVER THERE!

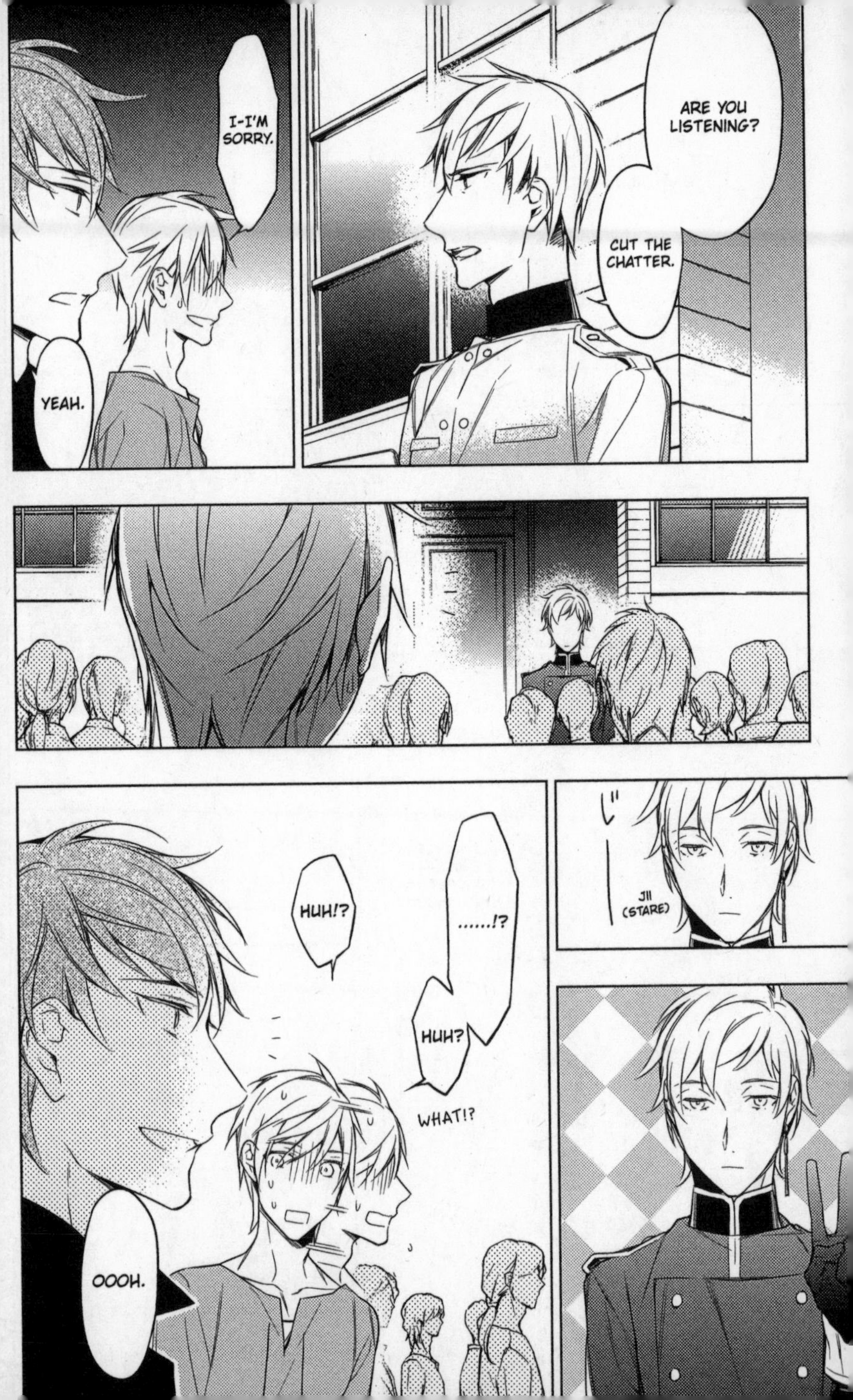
ARE YOU LISTENING?
CUT THE CHATTER.
I-I'M SORRY.
YEAH.
じ
JII (STARE)
......!?
HUH!?
HUH?
WHAT!?
OOOH.

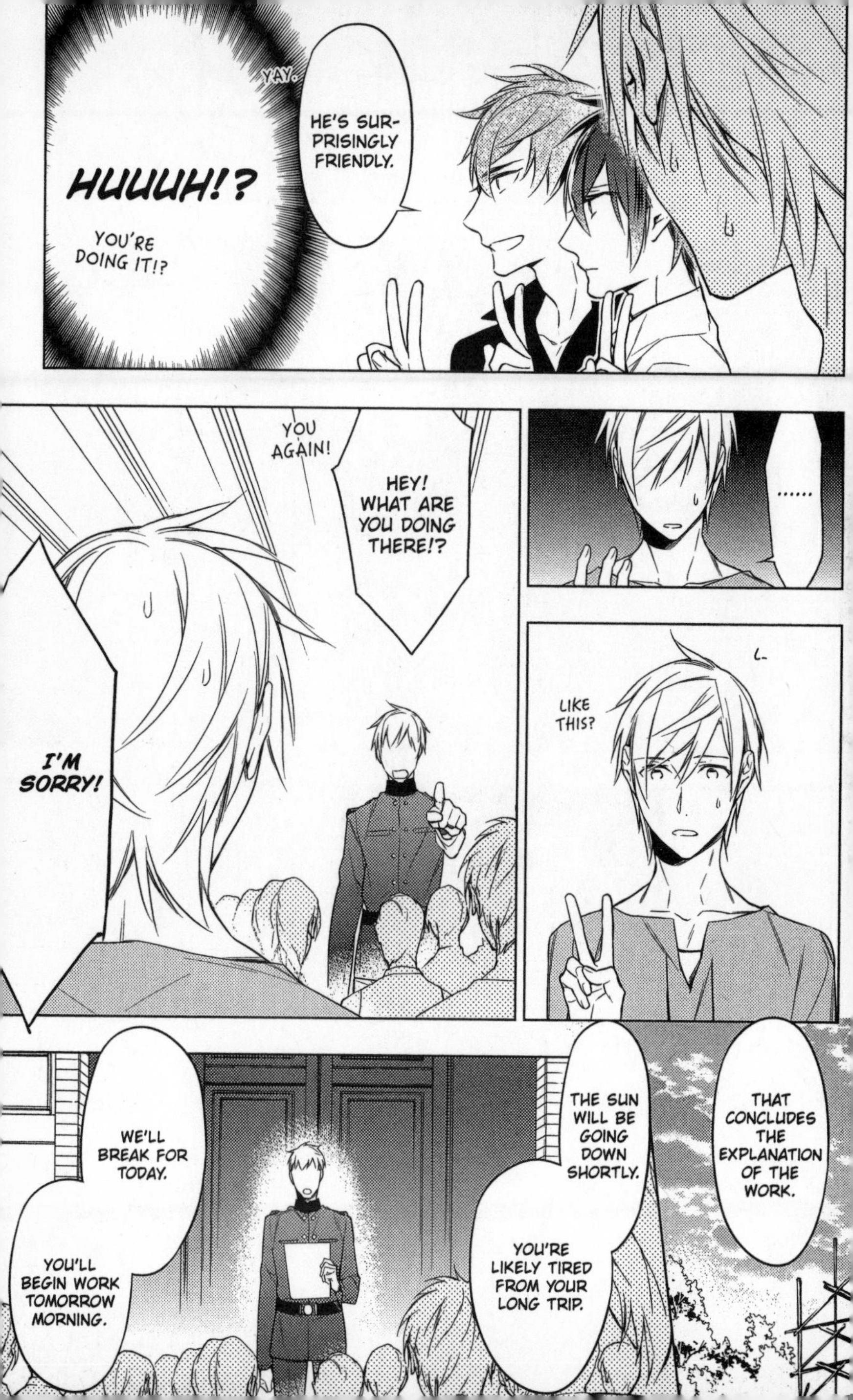
HE'S SUR-PRISINGLY FRIENDLY.
YAY.
HUUUH!?
YOU'RE DOING IT!?
......
LIKE THIS?
HEY! WHAT ARE YOU DOING THERE!?
YOU AGAIN!
I'M SORRY!
THAT CONCLUDES THE EXPLANATION OF THE WORK.
THE SUN WILL BE GOING DOWN SHORTLY.
YOU'RE LIKELY TIRED FROM YOUR LONG TRIP.
WE'LL BREAK FOR TODAY.
YOU'LL BEGIN WORK TOMORROW MORNING.

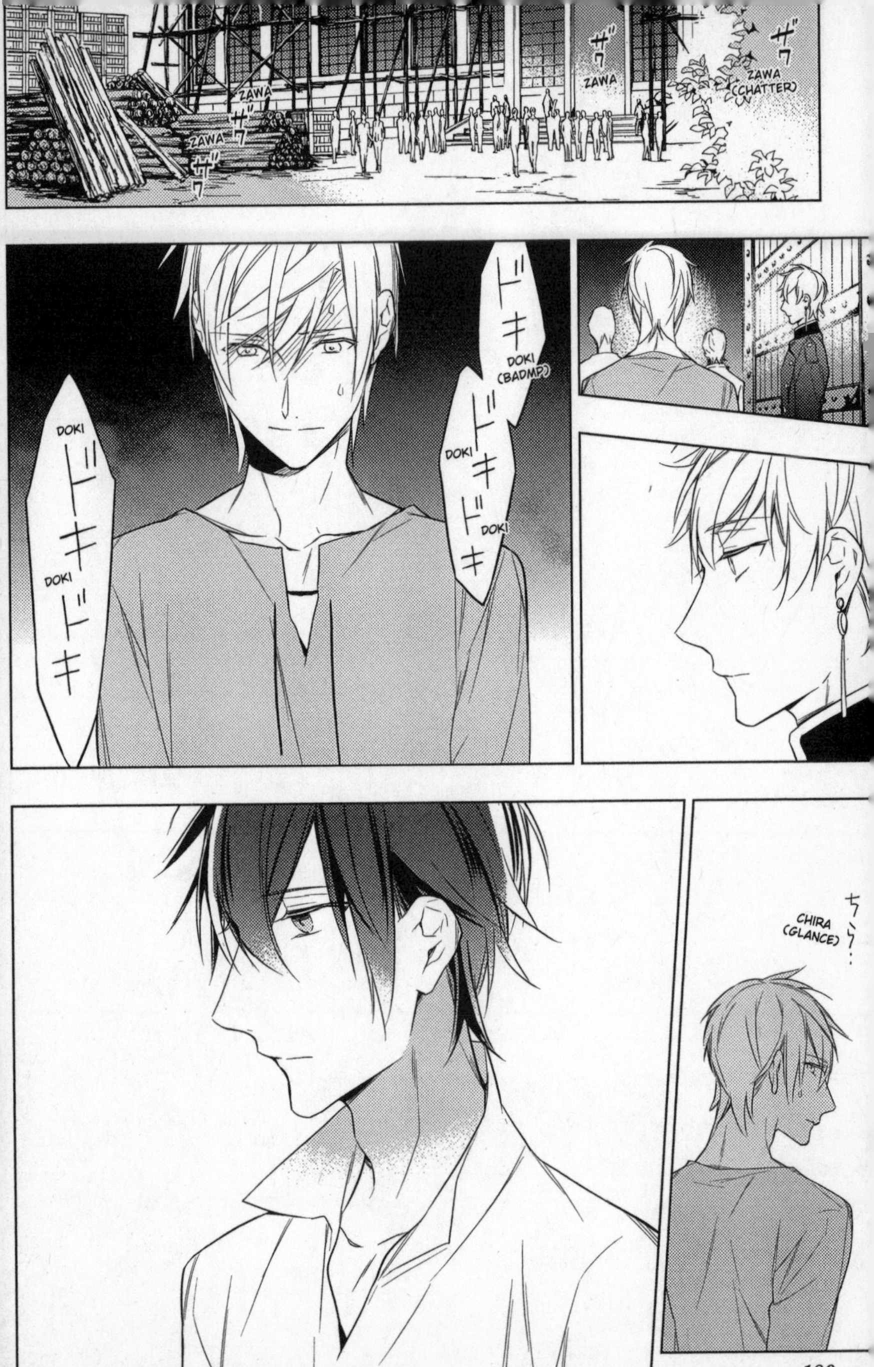
ザワ
ZAWA (CHATTER)
ザワ
ZAWA
ザワ
ZAWA
ザワ
ZAWA
ドキ
DOKI (BADMP)
ドキ
DOKI
ドキ
DOKI
ドキ
DOKI
ドキ
ちら…
CHIRA (GLANCE)

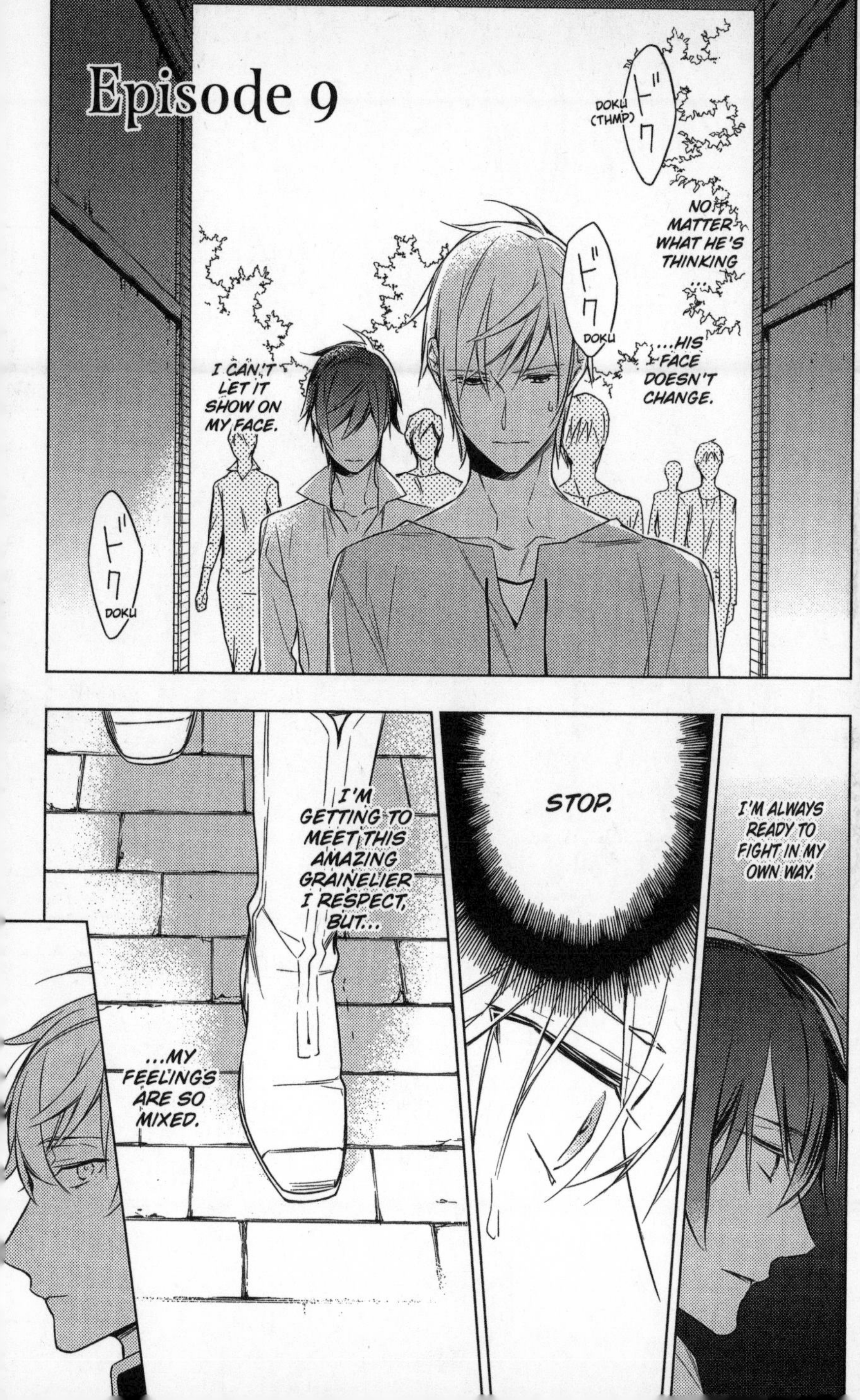
Episode 9
ドク
DOKU (THMP)
NO MATTER WHAT HE'S THINKING...
ドク
DOKU
...HIS FACE DOESN'T CHANGE.
I CAN'T LET IT SHOW ON MY FACE.
ドク
DOKU
I'M ALWAYS READY TO FIGHT IN MY OWN WAY.
STOP.
I'M GETTING TO MEET THIS AMAZING GRAINELIER I RESPECT, BUT...
...MY FEELINGS ARE SO MIXED.

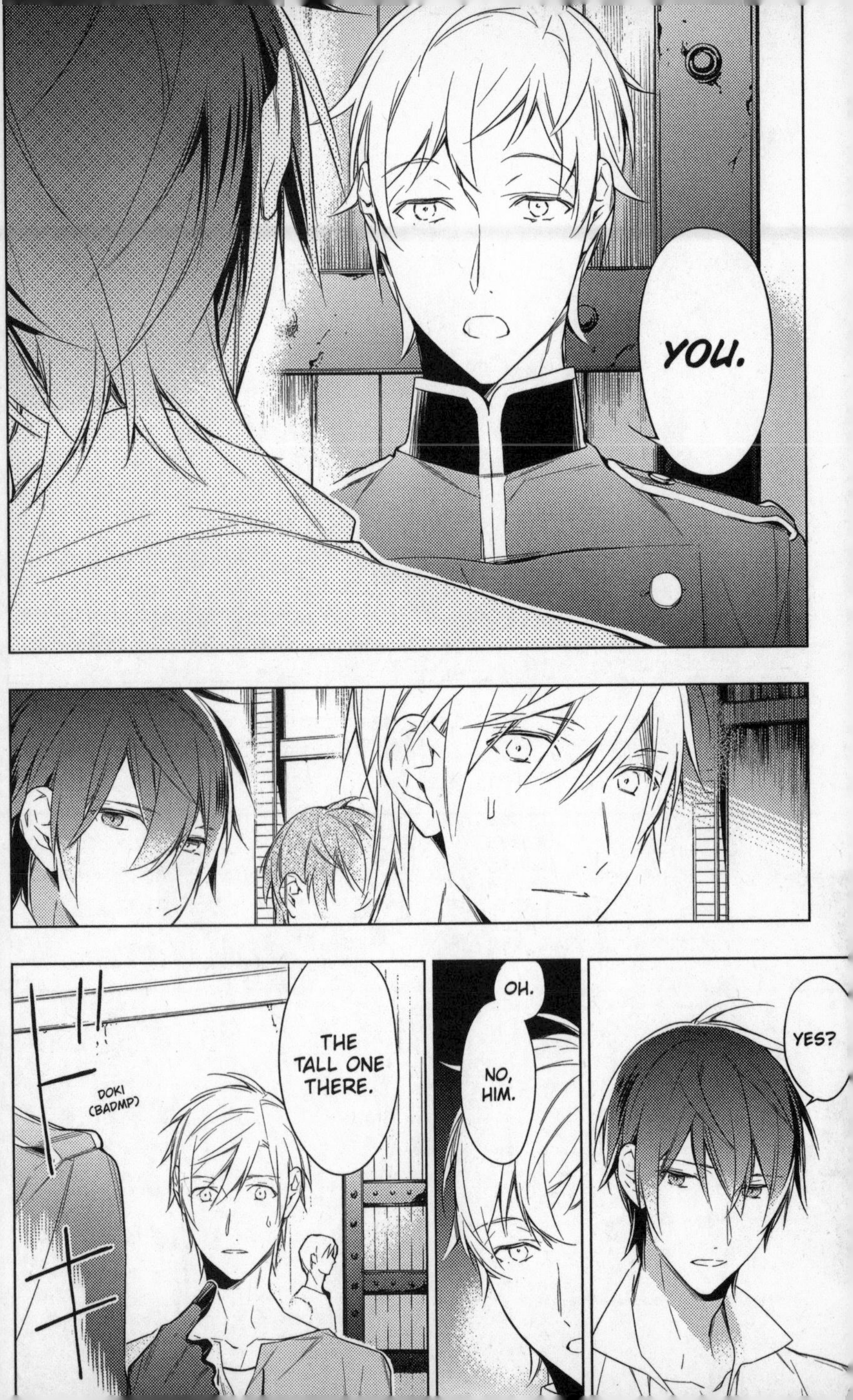
YOU.
YES?
OH.
NO, HIM.
THE TALL ONE THERE.
DOKI (BADMP)

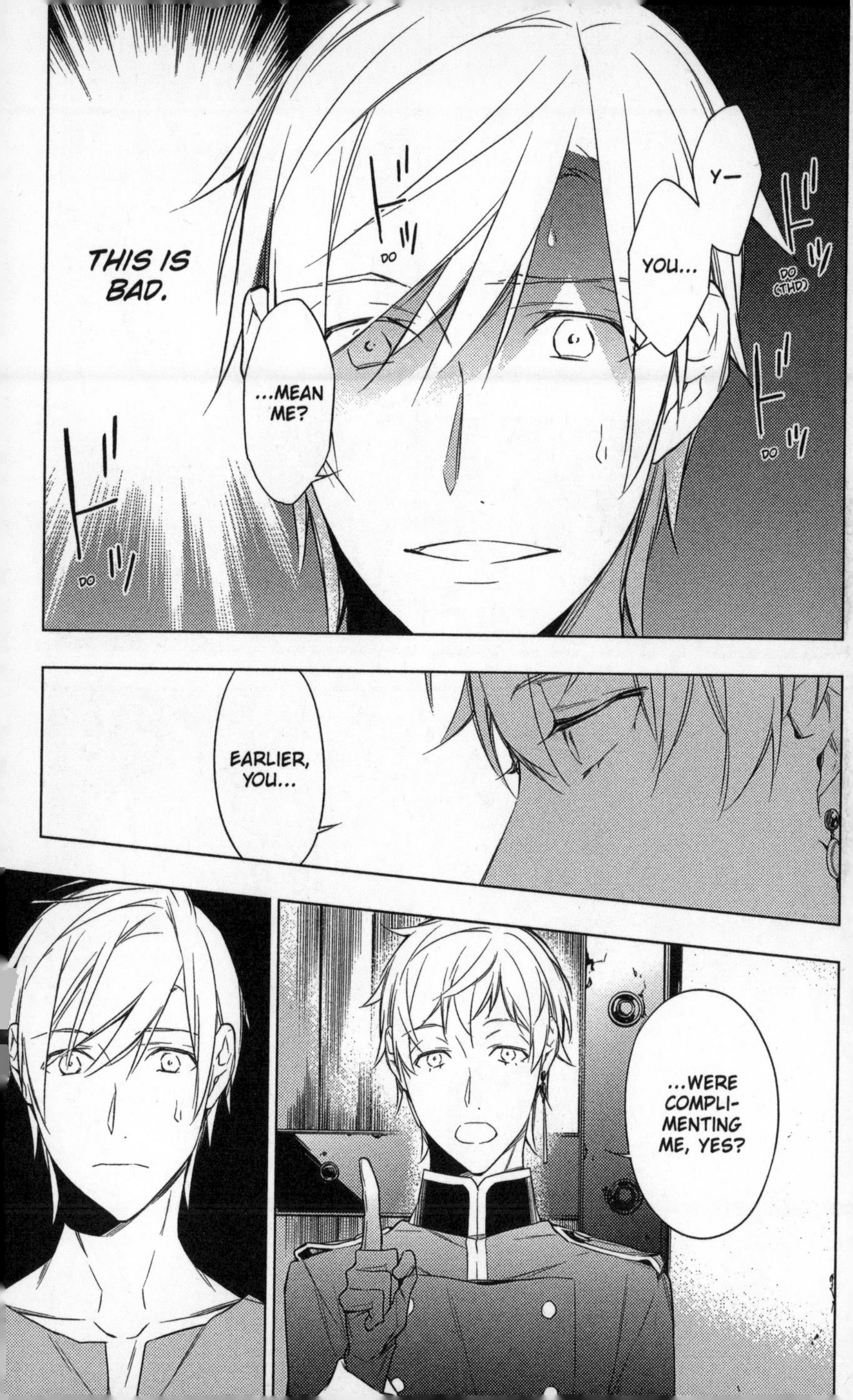
Y—
YOU...
DO (THD)
DO
DO
...MEAN ME?
THIS IS BAD.
DO
EARLIER, YOU...
...WERE COMPLI-MENTING ME, YES?

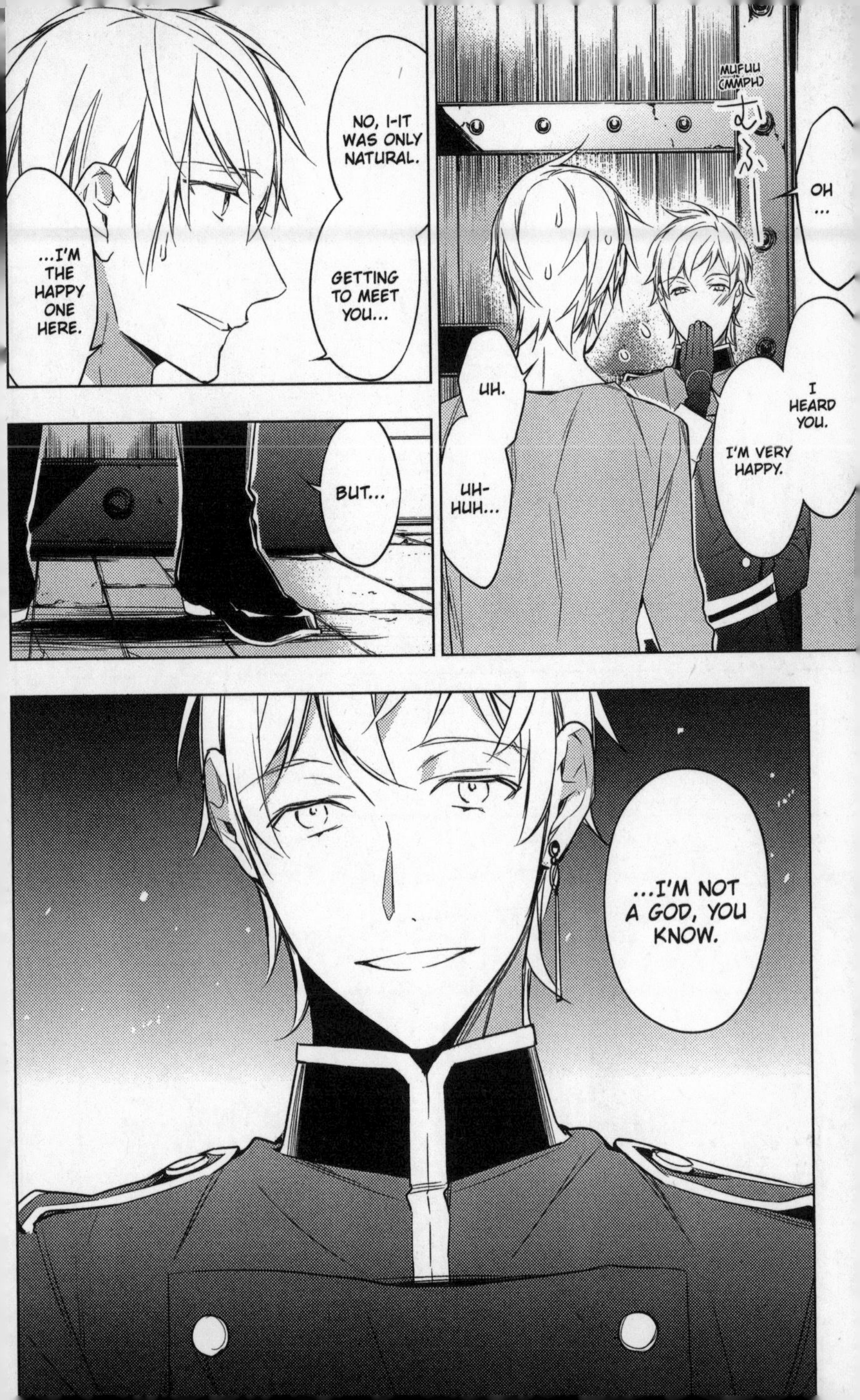
OH ...
MUFUU (MMPH)
I HEARD YOU.
I'M VERY HAPPY.
UH.
UH-HUH...
NO, I-IT WAS ONLY NATURAL.
GETTING TO MEET YOU...
...I'M THE HAPPY ONE HERE.
BUT...
...I'M NOT A GOD, YOU KNOW.

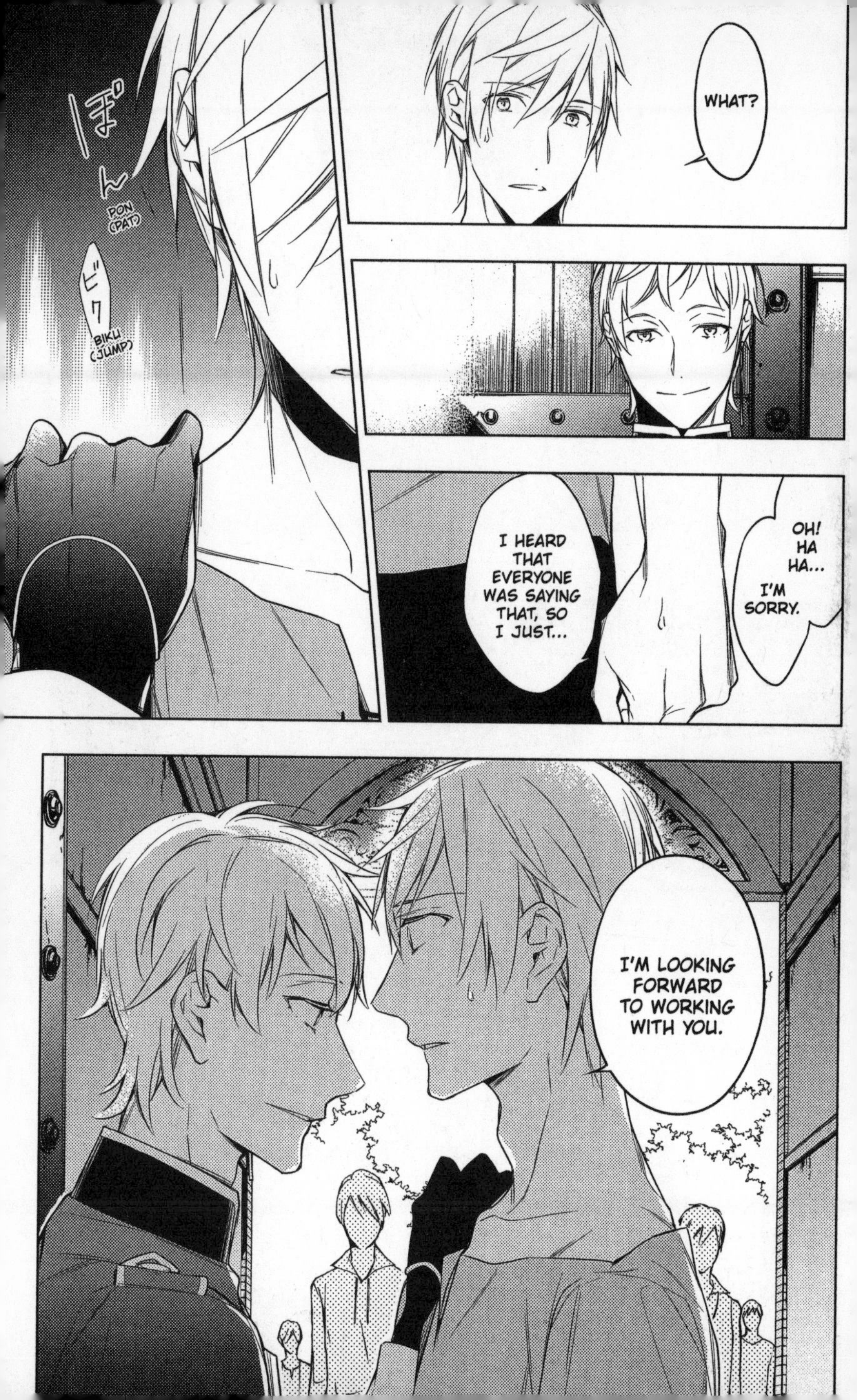
WHAT?
OH! HA HA... I'M SORRY.
I HEARD THAT EVERYONE WAS SAYING THAT, SO I JUST...
ぽん
PON (PAT)
ビク
BIKU (JUMP)
I'M LOOKING FORWARD TO WORKING WITH YOU.

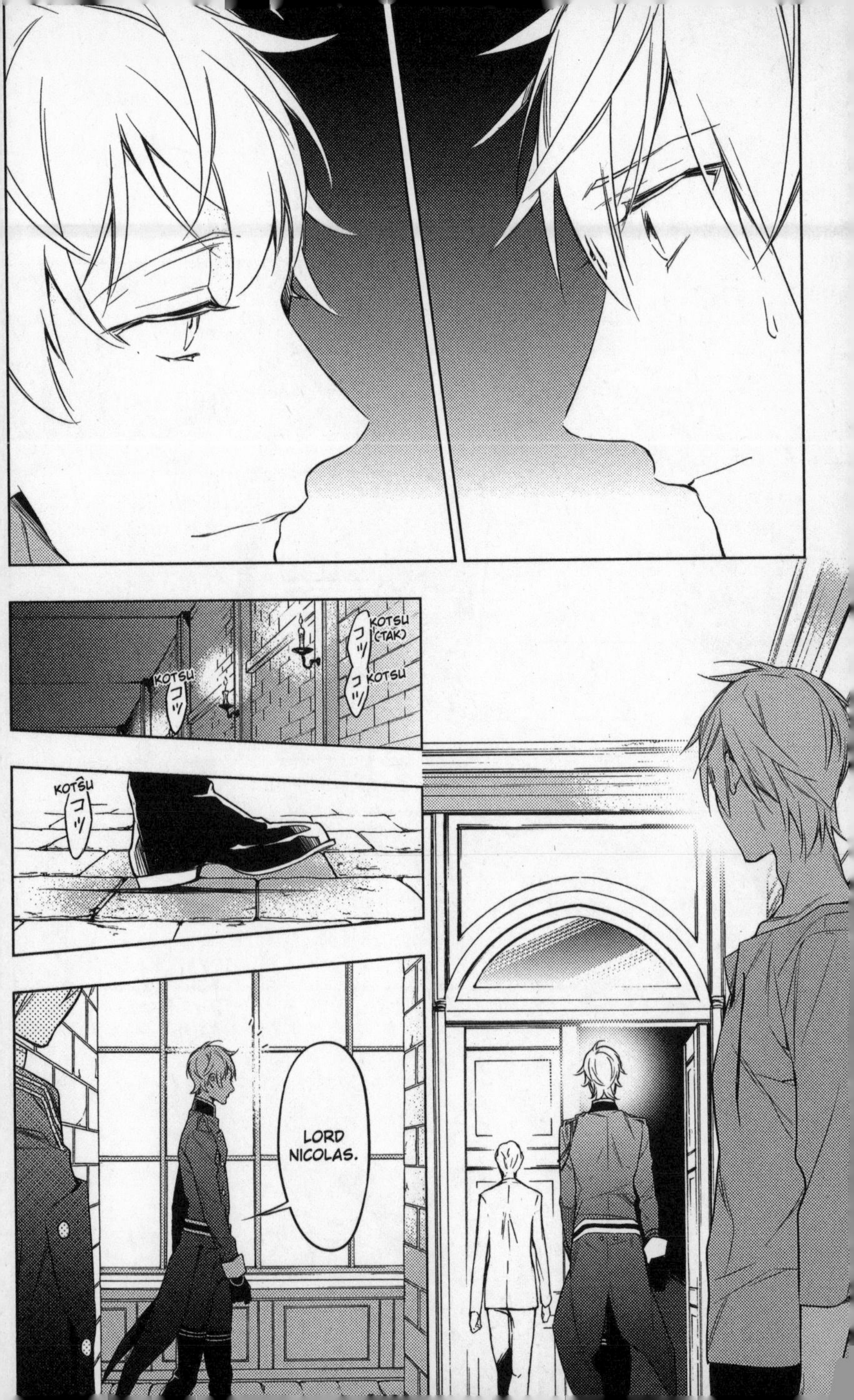
KOTSU (TAK)
KOTSU
KOTSU
KOTSU
LORD NICOLAS.

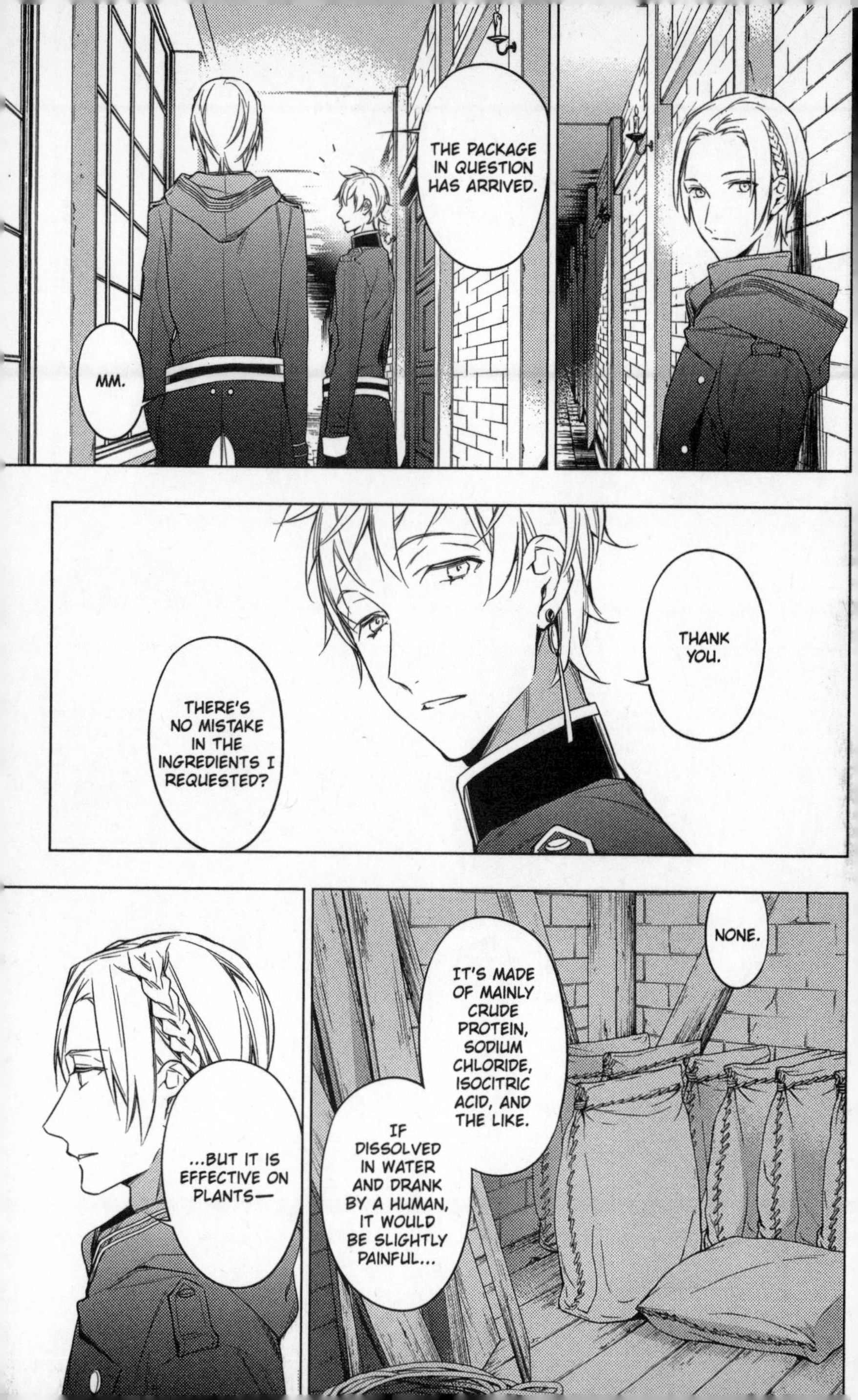
THE PACKAGE IN QUESTION HAS ARRIVED.
MM.
THANK YOU.
THERE'S NO MISTAKE IN THE INGREDIENTS I REQUESTED?
NONE.
IT'S MADE OF MAINLY CRUDE PROTEIN, SODIUM CHLORIDE, ISOCITRIC ACID, AND THE LIKE.
IF DISSOLVED IN WATER AND DRANK BY A HUMAN, IT WOULD BE SLIGHTLY PAINFUL...
...BUT IT IS EFFECTIVE ON PLANTS—

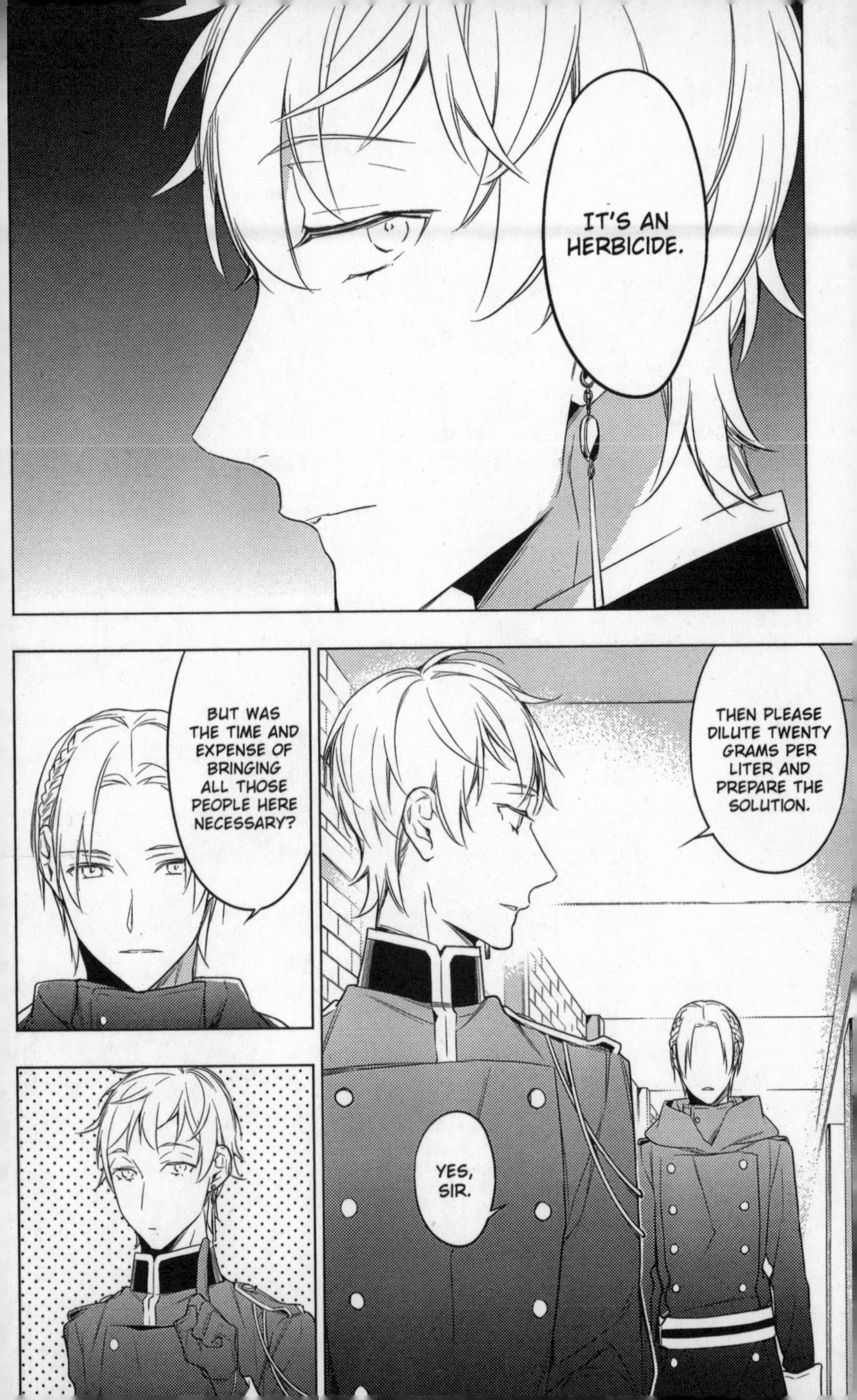
IT'S AN HERBICIDE.
THEN PLEASE DILUTE TWENTY GRAMS PER LITER AND PREPARE THE SOLUTION.
YES, SIR.
BUT WAS THE TIME AND EXPENSE OF BRINGING ALL THOSE PEOPLE HERE NECESSARY?

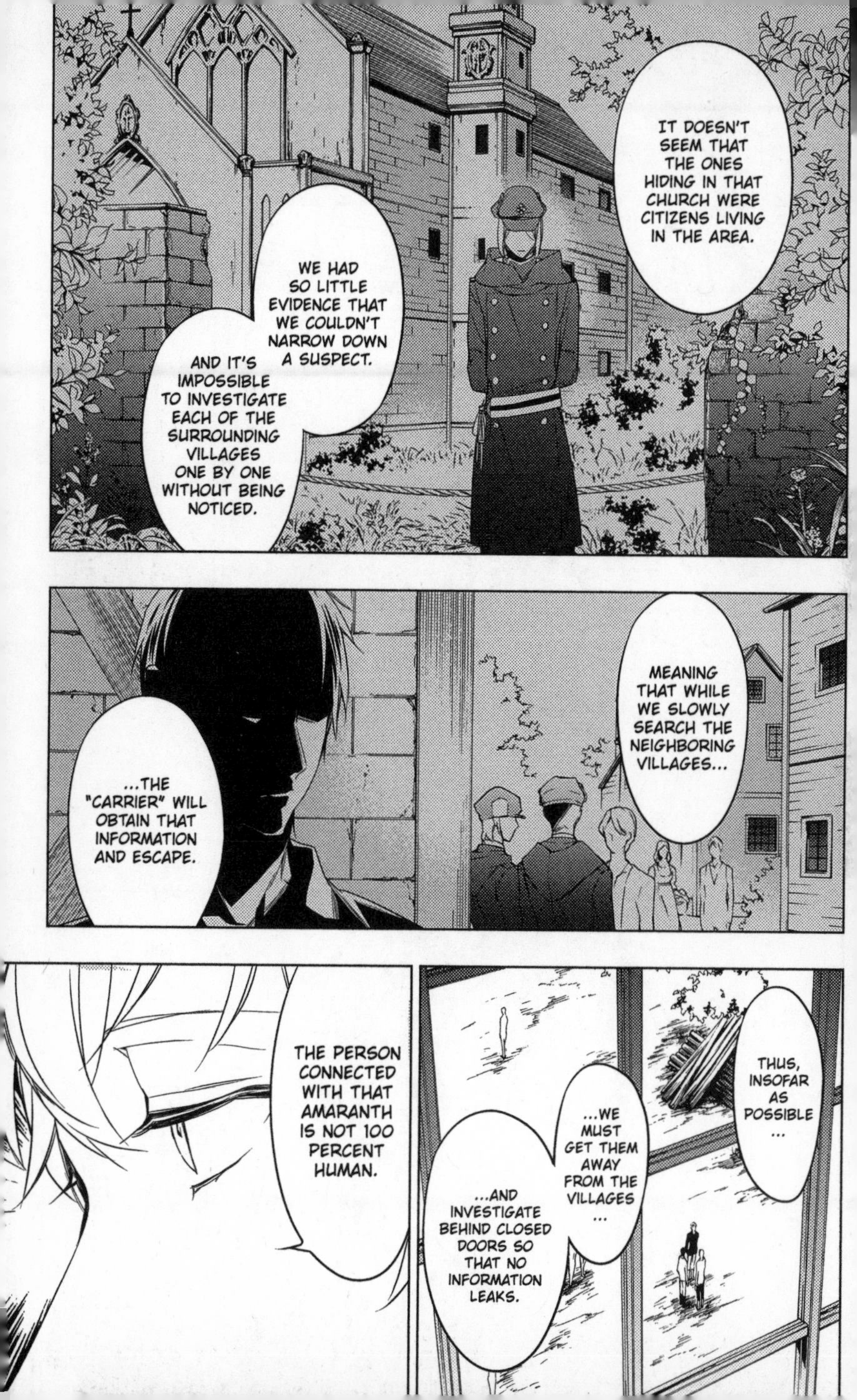
IT DOESN'T SEEM THAT THE ONES HIDING IN THAT CHURCH WERE CITIZENS LIVING IN THE AREA.
WE HAD SO LITTLE EVIDENCE THAT WE COULDN'T NARROW DOWN A SUSPECT.
AND IT'S IMPOSSIBLE TO INVESTIGATE EACH OF THE SURROUNDING VILLAGES ONE BY ONE WITHOUT BEING NOTICED.
MEANING THAT WHILE WE SLOWLY SEARCH THE NEIGHBORING VILLAGES...
..."CARRIER" WILL OBTAIN THAT INFORMATION AND ESCAPE.
THUS, INSOFAR AS POSSIBLE...
...WE MUST GET THEM AWAY FROM THE VILLAGES...
...AND INVESTIGATE BEHIND CLOSED DOORS SO THAT NO INFORMATION LEAKS.
THE PERSON CONNECTED WITH THAT AMARANTH IS NOT 100 PERCENT HUMAN.

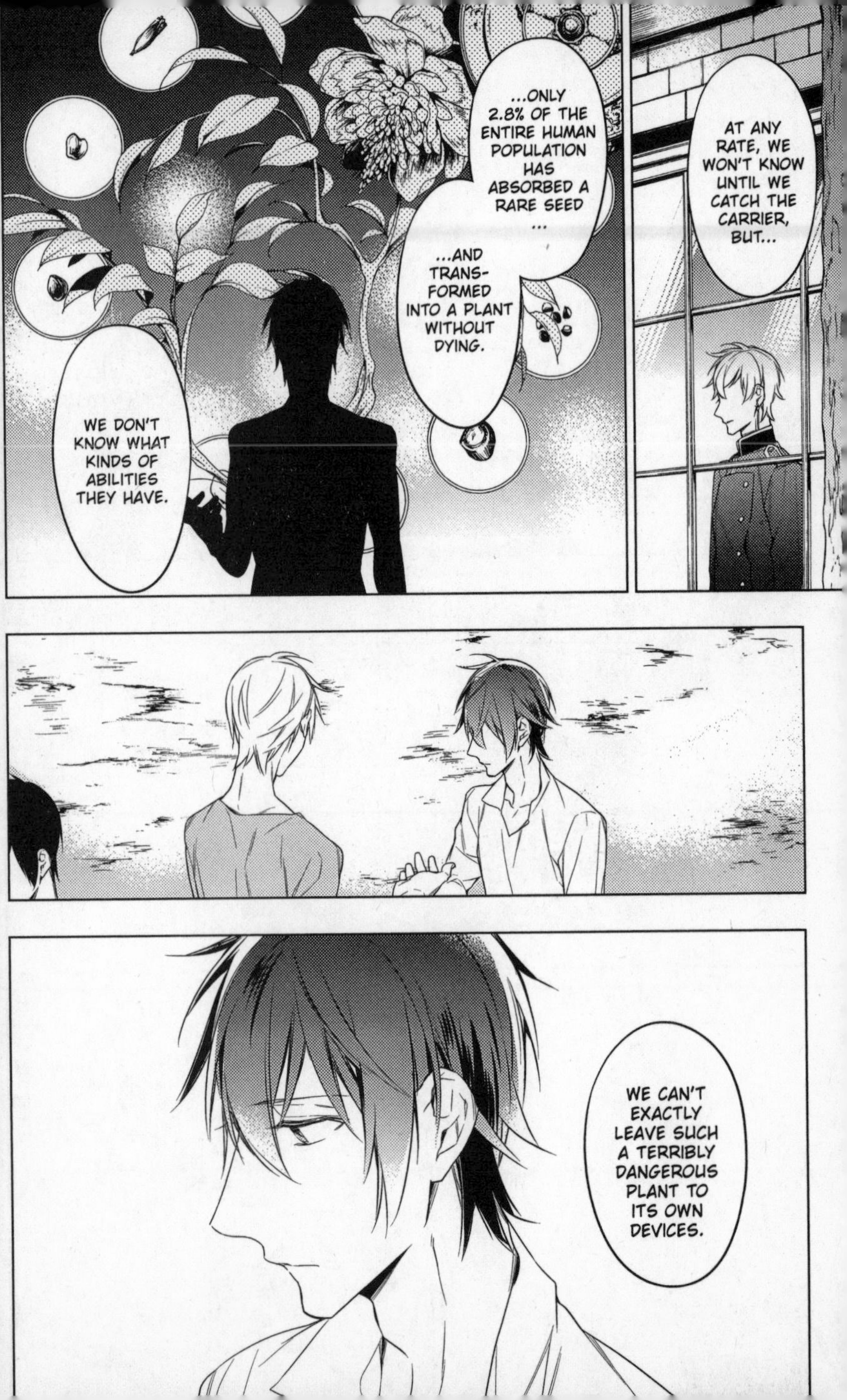
AT ANY RATE, WE WON'T KNOW UNTIL WE CATCH THE CARRIER, BUT...
...ONLY 2.8% OF THE ENTIRE HUMAN POPULATION HAS ABSORBED A RARE SEED ...
...AND TRANSFORMED INTO A PLANT WITHOUT DYING.
WE DON'T KNOW WHAT KINDS OF ABILITIES THEY HAVE.
WE CAN'T EXACTLY LEAVE SUCH A TERRIBLY DANGEROUS PLANT TO ITS OWN DEVICES.

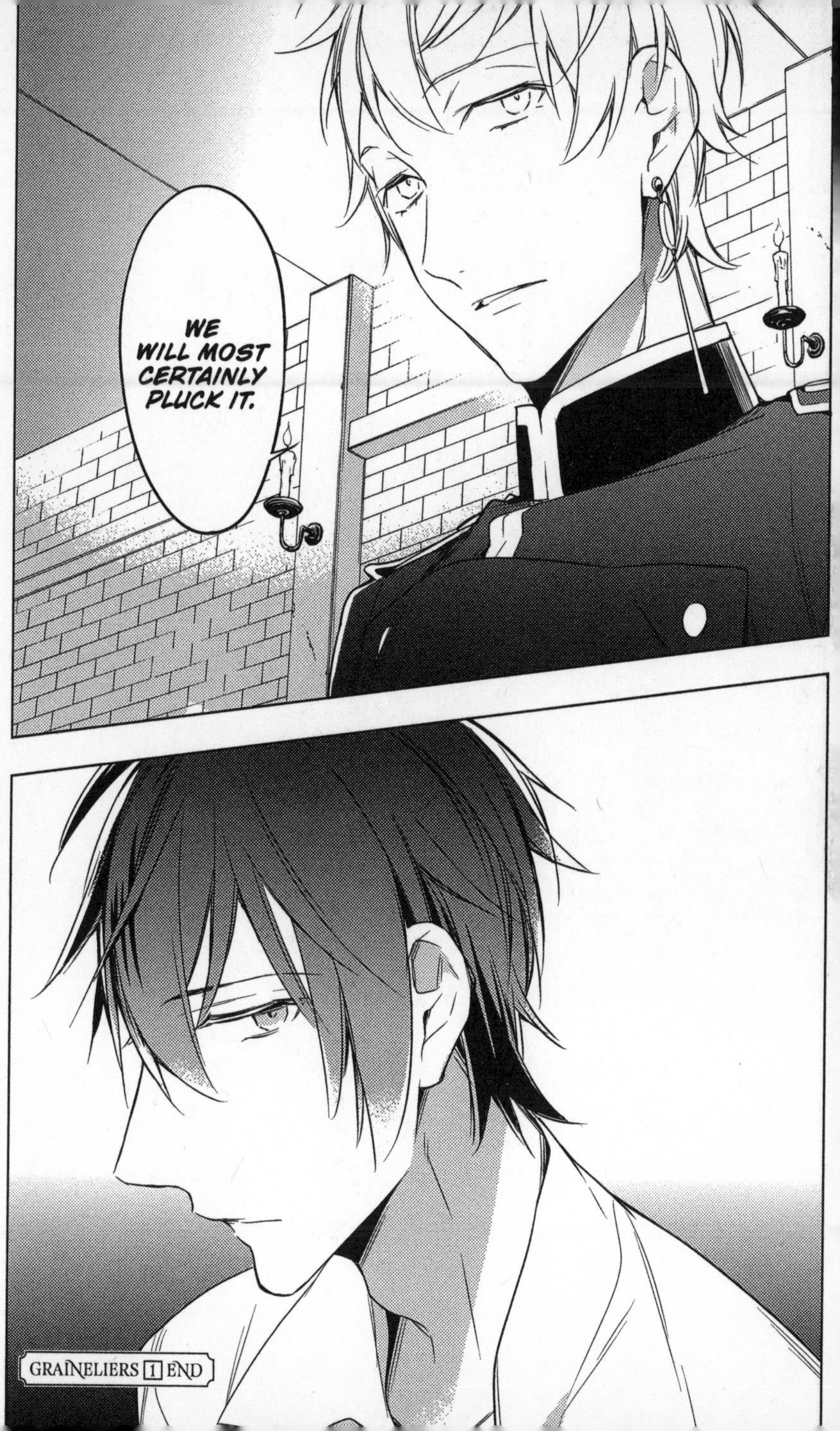
WE WILL MOST CERTAINLY PLUCK IT.
GRAINELIERS 1 END

Thanks a lot!

Thank you so much for reading!
I'd be delighted if we were to meet again.

Rihito Takarai

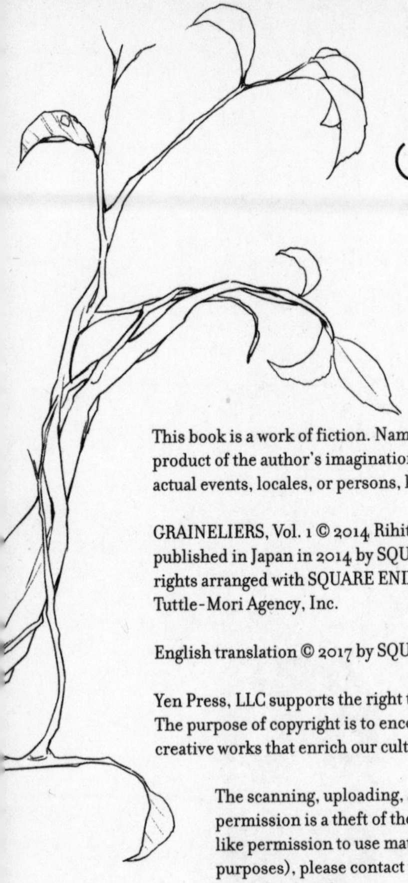

GRAINELIERS

1

Rihito Takarai

Translation: **JOCELYNE ALLEN**
Lettering: **ALEXIS ACKERMAN**

GRAINELIERS, Vol. 1 © 2014 Rihito Takarai / SQUARE ENIX CO., LTD. First published in Japan in 2014 by SQUARE ENIX CO., LTD. English translation rights arranged with SQUARE ENIX CO., LTD. and Yen Press, LLC through Tuttle-Mori Agency, Inc.

English translation © 2017 by SQUARE ENIX CO., LTD.

Yen Press
1290 Avenue of the Americas
New York, NY 10104

Visit us at yenpress.com
facebook.com/yenpress
twitter.com/yenpress
yenpress.tumblr.com
instagram.com/yenpress

First Yen Press Edition: December 2017

Yen Press is an imprint of Yen Press, LLC.
The Yen Press name and logo are
trademarks of Yen Press, LLC.

The publisher is not responsible for
websites (or their content) that are not
owned by the publisher.

Library of Congress Control Number:
2017949554

ISBNs: 978-0-316-41291-9 (paperback)
978-0-316-44838-3 (ebook)

10 9 8 7 6 5 4 3 2 1

BVG

Printed in the United States of America